World Power and World Money

For Holly

World Power and World Money

The Role of Hegemony and International Monetary Order

Andrew Walter

Revised edition

HARVESTER WHEATSHEAF

New York London Toronto Sydney Tokyo Singapore

First published 1993 by
Harvester Wheatsheaf
Campus 400, Maylands Avenue
Hemel Hempstead
Hertfordshire, HP2 7EZ
A division of
Simon & Schuster International Group

© Andrew Walter 1993

All rights reserved. No part of this publication may be reproduced, stored in a retrieval system, or transmitted, in any form, or by any means, electronic, mechanical, photocopying, recording or otherwise, without prior permission, in writing, from the publisher.

Typeset in 10/12pt Times
by Photoprint, Torquay, Devon

Printed and bound in Great Britain
by BPCC Wheatons Ltd, Exter

British Library Cataloguing in Publication Data

A catalogue record for this book is available from the British Library

ISBN 0 7450 1441 0 (pbk)

1 2 3 4 5   97 96 95 94 93

Contents

List of Tables and Figures	ix
List of Abbreviations	xi
Preface to the First Edition	xiii
Preface to the Second Edition	xvi
Introduction: Hegemony and international monetary order	1

Part I   The Theory of Hegemonic Stability and Monetary Order — 7

1 Political foundations of international economic order — 9
  1.1 Introduction: Economics and politics — 9
  1.2 The rebirth of economic interdependence — 11
  1.3 Economic interdependence and international relations — 13
  1.4 The balance of power and the international economy — 16
  1.5 The role of hegemony in the world political economy — 18
  1.6 Conclusion — 22

2 Domestic financial structures and monetary order — 27
  2.1 Introduction — 27
  2.2 Money, finance and politics — 28
  2.3 The rise of London as a financial centre — 31
  2.4 The Bank of England as central bank — 34

Contents

2.5 Financial hierarchy and monetary stability	36
2.6 Conclusion	44
3 Hegemony and international monetary order	**50**
3.1 Introduction	50
3.2 The critics of internationally managed money	51
3.3 A world central bank: The case for centralisation	63
3.4 Key currencies and international monetary order	66
3.5 Conclusion	78

Part II Hegemony and The Evolution of The International Monetary System since 1870 — 83

4 British hegemony and the international gold standard — 85
- 4.1 Introduction — 85
- 4.2 Britain's international position, 1870–1914 — 86
- 4.3 Britain and the emergence of the gold standard — 90
- 4.4 Britain and the operation of the pre-1914 gold standard — 93
- 4.5 Conclusion — 111

5 International monetary disorder in the interwar period — 116
- 5.1 Introduction — 116
- 5.2 The aftermath of World War I and the world economy — 117
- 5.3 Hegemonic power and the restoration of the international gold standard — 123
- 5.4 The operation and demise of the international monetary system 1925–31 — 126
- 5.5 Structural imbalances in the interwar world economy — 140
- 5.6 Conclusion — 144

6 American hegemony and the evolution of the international monetary system after 1945 — 150
- 6.1 Introduction — 150
- 6.2 American dominance and wartime planning — 151
- 6.3 The aftermath of the war and the failure of Bretton Woods — 157
- 6.4 The emergence of disequilibria and the problem of adjustment — 165

Contents vii

6.5 Solutions to the systemic disequilibrium? 171
6.6 Conclusion 188

7 The global financial revolution: Causes and consequences 195
7.1 Introduction 195
7.2 The nature of the international financial revolution 196
7.3 The causes of the international financial revolution 201
7.4 The economic consequences of financial integration 210
7.5 The political consequences of financial integration 219
7.6 Conclusion 240

Conclusion: Hegemony and international monetary order 249
Bibliography 258
Index 279

List of Tables and Figures

Tables

4.1 Discount rates and open market rates in the major economies, 1876–1914 and 1925–38	89
4.2 Growth characteristics of different periods in the world economy, 1820–1979	94
4.3 Cyclical characteristics of different periods for the world economy, 1820–1979	94
4.4 Shares of gold reserves of major countries	106
4.5 Growth of foreign investments of leading capital exporting countries, 1870–1914	108
5.1 British bilateral trade balances, 1913 and 1924	117
5.2 British current account, selected years	118
5.3 Economic and financial comparisons of major Western economies, 1870–1938	120
5.4 Government expenditures as a percentage of GDP, selected years	122
5.5 Net international capital inflows and outflows, 1924–31	141
6.1 Labour productivity, major countries, 1870–1984	152
6.2 Economic and financial comparisons of major industrial economies, 1950–85	153
6.3 General government expenditures as a percentage of GDP, selected years	156
6.4 Size and geographical distribution of US trade balances, 1938 and 1946	158
6.5 Growth of Eurocurrency market, 1964–79	182

x List of Tables and Figures

6.6	Currency composition of foreign exchange reserves, percentages, all countries, 1964–82	187
7.1	Estimated net international lending, 1975–91	198
7.2	Currency distributions: New international bank loans and bond issues	199
7.3	Shares of national currencies in foreign exchange reserves, 1978–90	200
7.4	Financing the US current account deficit, 1980–91	204
7.5	Net capital outflows, 1980–91, Japan and Germany	207
7.6	Trade patterns of OECD countries	215
7.7	Peak to trough amplitudes in recessions, industrial output, major groupings, 1960–82	217
7.8	Import and export penetration, major economies, 1960–87	232

Figures

4.1	British net capital outflow vs. growth in real GDP, 1870–1913	101
6.1	Gold composition of reserves, selected countries, 1950–72	166
6.2	US gold reserves and short-term liabilities to foreigners, 1950–72	167
6.3	Real GDP growth, Japan and Europe, vs. change in US external liabilities, 1958–91	183
6.4	Change in US external liabilities vs. economic activity in Europe, by quarter (selected periods)	185
6.5	Net US long-term capital outflows vs. real GDP growth, 1950–91	186
7.1	Current accounts and real exchange rates, US, Germany and Japan, 1975–89	212
7.2	Current account balances, major countries, 1970–91	220
7.3	Balances on official settlements, major countries, 1970–91	222
7.4	Mark/dollar and Yen/dollar exchange rates, 1971–92	223
7.5	General government deficits as a percentage of GDP, major countries, 1977–92	224

List of Abbreviations

BIS	– Bank for International Settlements
CD	– certificates of deposit
CRU	– composite reserve unit
ECA	– Economic Cooperation Administration
EMS	– European Monetary System
EMU	– European Monetary Union
EPU	– European Payments Union
FEER	– fundamental equilibrium exchange rate
FRBNY	– Federal Reserve Bank of New York
GDP	– gross domestic product
GES	– gold exchange rate
GS	– gold standard
IBF	– international banking facility
IBRD	– International Bank for Reconstruction and Development
IMF	– International Monetary Fund
IMS	– international monetary system
KCS	– key currency standard
MCS	– multi-currency system
MNC	– multinational corporation
NAC	– National Advisory Council on International Monetary and Financial Problems
OECD	– Organisation for Economic Cooperation and Development
OEEC	– Organisation for European Economic Cooperation
PPP	– purchasing power parity
SDR	– special drawing right
SII	– structural impediments initiative

xii *List of Abbreviations*

UNRAA – United Nations Relief and Rehabilitation Administration
WCB   – world central bank

Preface to the First Edition

This book grew out of a doctoral thesis submitted to Oxford University in the Summer of 1988 on the relationship between great powers and international monetary order, itself the product of a long interest in the field of international political economy. For two years after this highly theoretical introduction to the politics of international money and finance, I worked for J.P. Morgan, a major international bank with a long record of actively bridging the gap between international politics and finance. The opportunity of working in an organisation undergoing a radical (and partly self-imposed) restructuring, parallel to changes occurring in international financial markets in general, proved both enjoyable and invaluable. It also enabled me to gain much knowledge about the practical side of banking and finance, knowledge which would have been difficult if not impossible to glean from textbooks. I hope that some bankers may find the broad issues which the book raises of relevance and interest.

I have now returned to academic research and the graduate programme in international relations at Oxford University and this book is also aimed at an academic audience. To a considerable extent, it is concerned with a theme that will be familiar both to those with specific knowledge of international relations literature as well as to those with a general interest in contemporary international affairs. It is the idea, increasingly popular as the century draws to a close, that international monetary order is strongly associated with the presence of a dominant country or hegemony in the world economy. Hardly a day goes by without a newspaper columnist referring to the disorder in monetary or trade affairs and relating it to the decline of America relative to its wealthy allies in Europe and East Asia.

The issue of the impact of American decline is of obvious contemporary relevance, though I found the pre-1945 period to be of considerable interest and not without its lessons for international economic organisation. The attempt to place the history of international money from 1870 to World War II within the context of a changing balance of international power owes much to the existing work of economic historians, especially those who have recognised the link between politics and economics, often long before political scientists. The work of Charles Kindleberger in this respect is, of course, especially important. If I have ended up disagreeing with some of his interpretations, the importance of his work in this field is indisputable. The same can be said of some work by American scholars in international relations, most notably by Robert Keohane and Robert Gilpin, whose vigour in pursuing new ideas in international political economy provides its own refutation of the thesis of American decline.

The nature of the topic is such that I have concentrated upon relations between the major economic powers since the 1870s; consequently, the role of developing countries and the countries of what used to be called the Soviet bloc in the international monetary system is largely ignored. Money and finance is especially hierarchical, as many of these countries have found, and the structure of international finance tends to be determined by the great powers of the day. This is not to deny the importance of this structure for smaller powers, but that is another subject.

In attempting to bridge the usually separate disciplines of economics, international politics, and history, there is the usual danger that specialists in each of these fields may feel that insufficient attention is paid to their particular concerns. This is unavoidable, but I feel strongly that an interdisciplinary approach is the most fruitful path to political economy proper. Finding the correct balance of economic theory has been the most difficult task; much has been cut from earlier drafts. Virtually no attention has been paid to mathematical and game-theoretical literature, partly in the interests of general readability and partly out of a conviction that it is of limited value for discussions of this kind. Parts of Chapters 2 and 3 may still be difficult for non-economists, but I have tried to avoid technical discussions, jargon and formulae with these readers in mind.

Particular individuals have given general comments and advice for which I am grateful: Loukas Tsoukalis, Patrick O'Brien, Susan Strange and an anonymous referee. Others have given useful comments upon particular chapters: Massimo Fuggetta, Detlef Junker, and Sir Alec Cairncross. I would also like to thank Peter Johns of Simon & Schuster, who gave encouragement and comments on the overall structure. What follows is, of course, my own responsibility.

Andrew Walter,
St Antony's College,
Oxford,
September 1990.

Preface to the Second Edition

In coming back to this book to carry out revisions for the second edition, I have been struck by the pace of change in international money and finance since 1990. Events in Europe, at least from the perspective of Britain, have moved particularly fast. At the beginning of the decade, it appeared that the EMS was proving increasingly robust despite continued financial liberalisation throughout the Community, and that EMU was a real possibility by the end of the decade. Yet from the perspective of late 1992, on the eve of the completion of the Single Market, things have changed dramatically and we may be headed for another long phase of Euro-pessimism. In Japan and the US, meanwhile, the negative consequences of the financial excesses of the 1980s have come home to roost and have taken some of the shine off the Japanese model in particular. For some time, academic interest in international monetary and financial issues declined significantly as interest in trade issues boomed, and as everyone became accustomed to exchange rate and other forms of financial instability. However, the importance of money and finance has received powerful support from recent events.

I would like to say something here about the use of this book, particularly for students of international political economy. I believe that the basic analysis has held up reasonably well over the past few years, which is gratifying in a field in which much has become rapidly outmoded. This is perhaps particularly true of the recent experience of the EMS, where the argument that monetary systems in which constraints upon the key country are weak tend to instability over time, has proved relevant. The German model, heavily criticised at the beginning of the 1980s, and lauded by the end of that decade, is now looking in difficulty again as the financial and social impact of reunification has found the corporatist system wanting. This has placed unprecedented strain upon the EMS. For other countries, the early 1990s have also been traumatic. Indeed, the 1990s may be seen as a decade of the demise of economic models. The Scandinavian states and particularly Sweden and Finland, long thought of as having achieved a judicious blend of social welfare state and economic flexibility, are seeing their economies transformed very rapidly as increasing capital mobility has threatened the very basis of this compromise. This revised edition links these developments to the international financial revolution which is described at the end.

If there is an area in which the book perhaps ought to be significantly expanded, it is the interaction between the rise and fall and rise again of international financial integration over the past century and the *domestic* political economy of major states. In international relations, it is always tempting to overgeneralise or make unjustified assumptions about shifting domestic political coalitions, and to use convenient but sometimes misleading terms like 'US' or 'British' interests. What became clear by the 1980s, however, was that financial deregulation increasingly became a matter of domestic politics and distribution. Although this has long been clear in the realm of trade, international money and finance have for too long been seen as arcane subjects with only limited domestic political implications. The final chapter makes some effort in this direction, and interesting work is beginning to be done on the subject by other authors such as Jeffry Frieden. I hope that others who read this book will be tempted to pursue some of the issues which are raised here.

While those who are interested in contemporary money and finance might be tempted to skip to the final chapters, earlier theoretical chapters provide an important background to the nature and causes of monetary order on the domestic and international levels. Students of political economy need to have a basic understanding of the kinds of questions that have been posed by political scientists, economists and economic historians in attempting to address these issues. Although the organisational theme of the book is the relationship between hegemony and international monetary order, my criticisms of the existing literature suggest other approaches to these important questions. In particular, the idea that international economic order is more often the product of shifting relationships at the level of the domestic economy and the state rather than the hegemony of one country is a theme running throughout the book. Chapters 4 and 5 on the pre-1914 and interwar periods trace the way in which such shifts affected international economic relations. Finally, Chapter 6 on the Bretton Woods system and its breakdown provides some interesting parallels with the contemporary problems of the European Monetary System.

I would like to thank my colleagues in international relations at Oxford University and St Antony's College for their support over the past few years. I have particularly enjoyed having the freedom to design and teach a course in international political economy, and I am gratified in the interest that students have shown in it. Finally, I would like to thank Mark Allin and his colleagues at Harvester Wheatsheaf for their assistance in bringing about this revised edition. Any remaining errors are the fault of the author.

Andrew Walter,
St Antony's College,
Oxford,
November 1992.

Introduction

Hegemony and international monetary order

It has become commonplace to argue that over the last century or so hegemony has provided the foundation of order in the world economy. In a period when many have expressed concern about the prospects for international economic order in the face of American decline, there has been a strong tendency to look back to the 1950s and 1960s as an era when US dominance and international economic stability went hand in hand. American policy-makers and political commentators have often expressed the view that in a more pluralistic world, fostering economic cooperation between the major countries has proven more and more difficult. Academics in the international relations discipline have, by and large, accepted these basic premises. As Robert Gilpin has written: 'historical experience suggests that, in the absence of a dominant liberal power, international economic cooperation has been extremely difficult to attain or sustain and conflict has been the norm.'[1]

The 'theory of hegemonic stability', as it has become known, suggests that hegemony provides the preconditions (or 'regimes') for the operation of an open or 'liberal' world economic system. Such regimes, as Ruggie has argued:

> restrain self-seeking states in a competitive international political system from meddling directly in domestic and international economic affairs in the name of their national interests. And the strength of these regimes ... is backed by the capabilities of the hegemon. If and as such a concentration of economic capabilities erodes, the liberal order is expected to unravel and its regimes to become weaker, ultimately being replaced by mercantilist arrangements ... .[2]

The appeal of this theory is clear. It suggests a basic congruence in the relationship between two dominant powers, Britain and the US, and the international economic orders in which they played a key role, as well as a plausible explanation as to why international economic order is a transitory phenomenon. In particular, at a time when America's undoubted difficulties inspire almost daily comparison with Britain's fall from pre-eminence earlier this century, and when the world's economic and monetary problems frequently invoke memories of the troubled interwar period, its allure is hardly surprising.

Although this theory has been applied to a wide range of issues in international economic relations, that which will concern us here is its relevance to the area of international monetary relations.[3] On a general level, academic discussion of this issue has been dominated by the assertion of a prominent economic historian, Charles Kindleberger, that:

> for the world economy to be stable, it needs a stabiliser, some country that would undertake to provide a market for distress goods, a steady if not countercyclical flow of capital, and a rediscount mechanism for providing liquidity when the monetary system is frozen in panic.[4]

It is immediately apparent that Kindleberger's view differs considerably from that of the international relations writers quoted above. While the former have tended to stress the role of hegemony in maintaining the rules or regimes of a liberal world economy, Kindleberger holds that international monetary stability more particularly derives from an activist, managerial role on the part of the hegemon. Put differently, while political scientists have seen the main source of disorder as stemming from the anarchical nature of the international society of states, many economists like Kindleberger have seen the economic system itself as inherently unstable and therefore as requiring management. This distinction will constitute a basic theme of this book, since it is crucial for the way in which one might conceive the role of hegemony in fostering international monetary order.

Part I develops the consequences of the distinction between economic and political sources of disorder for the theory of hegemonic stability. In particular, Chapter 1 will consider the foundations of the theory and its relationship to traditional and contemporary approaches to the subject of international economic organisation and political economy. The ambiguity of the term hegemony, and the difficulty of defining it in quantitative terms, means that it is more fruitful to concentrate upon the various *functions* which a hegemon might play in the international monetary system.

Chapter 2 considers the relationship between political and monetary structures, focusing on the tendency for hierarchy to develop in financial systems. By briefly tracing the development of financial markets in Europe, we identify strong forces (some of which are political) towards centralisation and hierarchy in money and finance. The relationship between financial hierarchy and monetary order is easiest to understand by focusing upon one classic historical case in particular, that of the rise of the Bank of England to become a central bank for the English banking system and government. This leads us to consider the broad issue of the justification for a central bank in monetary theory and to the role it ought to play, using recent developments in the UK and US as illustrations.

Having considered the issue of the public management of money, Chapter 3 extends the implications of this for our discussion of international monetary order. We outline three main functions of hegemony in the international monetary system which correspond to different potential sources of disorder. First, what we term the function of 'rule establishment and enforcement' consists in the provision of the minimal political foundations for the operation of the world economy and monetary system, such as freedom of navigation, international property rights, relatively open markets, specific rules relating to international monetary transactions, and so on. Realists have focused on this function, as they see the basic cause of monetary and economic disorder as international political anarchy. Hegemony can overcome this anarchy to some extent by establishing and enforcing ground rules for international economic intercourse.

Second, hegemony might conceivably foster policy consistency between states in a complex monetary system. Liberal theorists have concentrated upon this function, stressing the 'leadership' hegemons provide by promoting 'regimes' which facilitate cooperation between states. In the absence of such regimes, it is held, the coordination of macroeconomic policies becomes difficult.

The final function which we distinguish allows for the possibility of instability endogenous to the monetary or financial realm, and includes the need for macroeconomic management, lender of last resort facilities to deal with financial crises, and provision of a structure of regulation and prudential supervision of the world's financial markets. Charles Kindleberger has been most prominently associated with this function of hegemony in the international monetary system.

Having established a firmer analytical basis for the theory, we turn in Part II to a consideration of the extent to which, in the two most celebrated cases of hegemony, this has accorded with reality. Chapters 4 to 6 consider in turn Britain's role in the international gold standard from the 1870s to World War I, the relationship of the economic disorder of the interwar period to the 'hegemonic interregnum' of that time, and the role of the US in the so-called Bretton Woods system after World War II. A final chapter is devoted to the evolution of the world's monetary and financial system in recent years and a consideration of the extent to which it is related to the decline of America relative to its major allies, Japan and Germany. It also considers the extent to which a more pluralistic international monetary system would be likely to be a more unstable or disordered one.

While such a broad overview leaves comparatively little space for historical detail, it has the advantage of enabling a general assessment of the theory and a comparison of the different periods. The conclusion reached is that the theory provides a very poor account of the historical evolution of the international monetary system over the last century and in particular of the roles played by Britain and America. None of the functions which we specified in Part I were carried out in any consistent manner by these two powers, in particular the roles of regime enforcement and maintenance, though also the function of monetary management. Leadership of a kind in international monetary affairs was sometimes exercised by Britain in its heyday, though not in a manner consistent with some of the more sweeping claims of the literature. In the American case, leadership was more visibly exercised in the 1950s and 1960s, but sometimes to the detriment of international monetary order.

International relations theory seems to have placed too great an explanatory burden upon the rise and fall of great powers as a determining influence of international monetary order. Certainly the presence of a dominant power is not a sufficient condition for international monetary order; it will be argued that it has not been adequately demonstrated that it is even a necessary condition.

The difficulties with the theory are perhaps most apparent in the contemporary era. Contrary to much recent literature, the US remains by far the most dominant actor in the world political economy, occupying a position that Britain probably never enjoyed even at the peak of its power. Rather than American decline, international monetary disorder can be attributed more fundamentally to the ongoing process of domestic and international financial liberalisation, a process in which the US has played a crucial role. As Richard Cooper noted in the late 1960s, rising interdependence would come into increasing conflict with the system of policy-making based upon the separate state; the revolution in global financial markets in recent years has raised the acuteness of this conflict to levels which have increasingly threatened the achievements of the postwar period. Whether in such circumstances the dominance of one country over the world's monetary affairs is indeed desirable is more doubtful than recent thinking would have us believe.

Notes

1. Gilpin, 1987, p.88.
2. Ruggie, 1982, p.381.
3. In particular, the international trade system will not be considered here in any detail, except in so far as it impinges upon the discussion of more general issues.
4. Kindleberger, 1981, p.247.

Part I
The Theory of Hegemonic Stability and Monetary Order

Part I

Chapter 1
Political foundations of international economic order

1.1 Introduction: Economics and politics

The relationship between economics and politics has reappeared as a key issue in international relations in recent years. The major developments of recent times, the supposed decline of America, the rise of Japan, the unification of Germany and Europe and the end of the Cold War and the Communist bloc all have important economic as well as security implications. In contrast to the early 1980s, when East–West conflict reached a new height, trade, investment and finance could dominate the international agenda in the 1990s.

The recent political revolutions in Central and Eastern Europe have drawn many to compare the present period with the upheavals of 1848. Writing on the eve of those revolutions, Marx and Engels expressed a common sentiment of the time that the prime mover of world affairs was economics: 'The bourgeoisie, by the rapid improvement of all instruments of production, by the immensely facilitated means of communication, draws all, even the most barbarian, nations into civilisation'.[1]

From this vantage point, economics appeared to be largely a force for peace. The idea of free trade and the benefits it could bring to all countries was an extension of Adam Smith's harmony of interests doctrine to the international level. As Cobden argued, the 'intercourse between communities is nothing more than the intercourse of individuals in the aggregate'.[2] Politics ought not to interfere with economics. At the domestic level, Smith accepted that the state must provide the minimal political foundations of order, following Hobbes and Locke:

10   The theory of hegemonic stability and monetary order

> [T]he sovereign has only three duties to attend to; . . . first, the duty of protecting the society from the violence and invasion of other independent societies; secondly, the duty of protecting, as far as possible, every member of society from the injustice or oppression of every other member of it, or the duty of an exact administration of justice; and, thirdly, the duty of erecting and maintaining certain public works and certain public institutions which it can never be in the interest of any individual, or small number of individuals, to erect and maintain. . .[3]

The state had to provide for the safety of its citizens; on this basis, Smith even supported the Navigation Acts, the bane of later English liberals.[4] This brings out a fundamental tension which pervades all liberal thought in international relations. The idea that there is a natural harmony of interests between men as men (rather than simply as citizens of a given state), has meant that the division of mankind into separate political associations is problematic. The spread of democracy might eventually eradicate domestic political repression, but on the international level at least, politics was the realm of violence, in marked contrast to the voluntary character of economic interaction. Some resolved this dilemma as Mill did, also writing in 1848:

> It is commerce which is rapidly rendering war obsolete, by strengthening and multiplying the personal interests which act in natural opposition to it. And it may be said without exaggeration that the great extent and rapid increase of international trade, in being the principal guarantee of the peace of the world, is the great permanent security for the uninterrupted progress of the ideas, the institutions, and the character of the human race.[5]

Though World War I shattered the substantial economic interdependence which had emerged over the course of the nineteenth century, liberal internationalism retained a strong grip upon the Western imagination in the interwar period. This was apparent in the widespread assertion of the principle of national self-determination and popular democracy as the road to a more peaceful world. It was also a vital element in Woodrow Wilson's idea of collective security and the conception of international organisation which underlay it.[6]
The collapse of the international economic order in the Great Depression, the rise of aggressive nationalist regimes in the 1930s and the failure of the League of Nations discredited internationalist liberalism in the years to follow. Few could ignore the fact that industrialism had brought with it not progress but two of the most destructive wars in the history of mankind. Mercantilism, the view that economics is merely the pursuit of politics by other means, came to dominate the practice of international relations from the 1930s. Economics was no longer seen as the means by which the political

Political foundations of international economic order 11

division of mankind would be overcome but as a source of national power, much as Thomas Mun had seen it in 1630:

> many well-governed states highly countenance the profession, and carefully cherish the action [of foreign trade] not only with Policy to encrease it, but also with power to protect it from all foreign injuries: because they know it is a Principal in reason of state to maintain and defend that which doth support them.[7]

Such a development was consistent with the revolution in economic thinking associated in the Anglo-Saxon countries with Keynesianism, which held that the state should intervene in the national economy to a much greater extent than envisaged by the classical economists. National economic stability became the overriding priority for both victor and vanquished after 1945, inevitably conflicting with the classical ideal of freedom of trade and capital movement.

1.2 The rebirth of economic interdependence

The intensity of the Cold War meant that deliverance from the realm of power-politics was seen as unlikely in the immediate postwar years. The extraordinary growth of the world economy, however, ultimately provided relief in this direction. The two decades which preceded the early 1970s represent what is perhaps the closest thing western capitalism has had to a Golden Age. Many of those who wrote in this era believed, at least tentatively, that the Mixed Economy constituted a solution to the grave shortcomings that the interwar years had exposed in 'competitive capitalism'.[8] Keynesian policy techniques gradually acquired a status of orthodoxy in academic and policy-making circles, at least in part due to the success which they enjoyed. Over the period 1955–73, the major industrial countries experienced an average growth in real gross domestic product (GDP) of 4.5 per cent per annum.[9]

Experience of the interwar and war years led mainstream liberalism to take on board Keynesian ideas, but what also impressed itself upon the minds of many was the link between the rising prosperity in the West and the increasing interconnectedness of the national economies which made up the 'core' of this economy. Rising economic interdependence could be witnessed in the growing level of trade as a proportion of GDP in the major industrial countries; over the 1955–68 period, growth in trade between the Organisation for Economic Cooperation and Development (OECD) countries averaged an annual 8 per cent, well outstripping the high rate of growth in output.[10] The rapid internationalisation of production represented by the rise of the 'transnational' corporation, followed by the internationalisation of finance with the growth of the Euromarkets, testified further to higher levels of economic interdependence amongst the western countries in particular. For many writers in this period, this dynamic process seemed to be bringing about the 'one world' which Marx and Engels had predicted in 1848 as the result of the spread of global commerce.

The multinational corporation (MNC) in particular was seen as rendering political boundaries irrelevant and fostering capital mobility and technology transferral on an unprecedented scale. In a famous if premature remark, Charles Kindleberger argued that 'the nation-state is just about through as an economic unit'.[11] The globalisation of the market economy was once again about to overwhelm the unnatural political division of mankind into separate states.

Doubtless many liberal economists were less optimistic than Kindleberger regarding the immanent demise of the nation-state due to the rise of transnational forces. The rise of the national welfare state had strengthened the role of the state in the domestic economy, a factor which was soon seen to be in contradiction with rising interdependence. One of the first books to address this was Richard Cooper's *The Economics of Interdependence* (1968). Cooper's central theme was that by the 1960s, the growth of economic interdependence had eroded the autonomy that states had once enjoyed to pursue domestic economic objectives. Specifically, domestic objectives such as the maintenance of a high level of employment and the stabilisation of the price level might conflict with external objectives such as the liberalisation of trade and capital flows. The dilemma which states found themselves in was 'how to keep the manifold benefits of extensive economic intercourse free of crippling restrictions while at the same time preserving a maximum degree of freedom for each nation to pursue its legitimate economic objectives'.[12]

The solution that Cooper himself preferred appealed to most liberal economists: the benefits of economic interdependence were so great that what should give way was not market integration, but the formal policy sovereignty of states. Only an acceptance by states to coordinate much more fully than ever before their economic policies could preserve the level of interdependence already achieved, let alone allow it to grow. If states would only recognise that their long-term interests lay in the full integration of national economies, the benefits that would follow would greatly outweigh the costs of any formal loss of national sovereignty.[13]

Cooper fully recognised that the political will required for such a step would probably not materialise; politics would continue to place limits on the economic progress that was possible and the welfare benefits that could be obtained. He therefore argued for a cooperative approach towards reducing the levels of interdependence amongst states as a preferable alternative to increasing resort to 'beggar thy neighbour' policies.[14] A great deal of the subsequent literature on economic interdependence developed the basic themes that Cooper had set out. The expanding literature on international economic policy coordination of recent years has encountered the same basic difficulty of how to encourage states to sacrifice a measure of policy autonomy so as to make joint management of interdependence possible.[15]

The less encouraging performance of the world economy since the early 1970s has made the costs of interdependence all too apparent to governments and their electorates. In the boom times of the 1950s and 1960s, the economic and political costs which followed from trade liberalisation could be more or less easily absorbed, but in the circumstances of the 1970s and 1980s this has become much more difficult. It is now impossible for states to ignore the domestic economic policies of their economic partners. Precisely for this reason, many argue that the need to coordinate policies has become greater than ever.[16]

1.3 Economic interdependence and international relations

Traditionally, the subject matter of international relations was the grand questions of war, strategy and international order. The rise of the modern states-system with the fragmentation of Christendom in the late Middle Ages and the subsequent experience of European statecraft suggested that the pursuit of power by all means deemed necessary was the basic premise of foreign policy. Economic policy usually only entered into discussion of 'high politics' when the sources of state power required enumeration. Those who characterised international politics as the pursuit of power in an anarchical environment could easily accept the mercantilist equation of the pursuit of power with the pursuit of national wealth, but the latter could be safely left to the economists.[17]

This perspective was challenged in the early 1970s by the new school of interdependence and transnational relations. The central theme in the attack launched against realism was that the latter viewed world politics in overly 'states–centric' terms. While such a view may have been appropriate, it was argued, in the European states-system of the sixteenth to nineteenth centuries, it was becoming increasingly irrelevant in a world of transnational actors and linkages. Many of the most important new actors and linkages were economic in character, such as the MNC, intergovernmental organisations like the World Bank and International Monetary Fund (IMF), the growth of international trade, finance, communications and the diffusion of technology. To regard economic issues as secondary to the perennial questions of high politics was to misunderstand the fundamental transformation which was taking place in world politics.[18]

In the most influential work in this genre, Robert Keohane and Joseph Nye argued that world politics was in the process of transformation from being an arena dominated by concerns of state power and security towards one characterised by 'complex interdependence'.[19] In a world of complex interdependence, transnational actors of all kinds would rival the nation-state in importance, the 'hard-shell' boundaries of states and hence the distinction between domestic and foreign policy would wither, force as a major instrument of foreign policy would decline in utility, and issues of high politics would no longer dominate economic issues.

Although the model of complex interdependence, like that of realism, was an ideal type, Keohane and Nye claimed that the former was 'fairly well approximated on some global issues of economic and ecological interdependence and ... [it] comes close to characterizing the entire relationship between some countries'.[20] The rise of international economic interdependence did not only influence the thinking of international relations scholars. In 1973, US Secretary of State and supposed arch-realist Henry Kissinger endorsed the notion that interdependence had transformed the nature of international power: 'Military muscle does not guarantee political influence. Economic giants can be militarily weak, and military strength may not be able to obscure economic weakness. Countries can exert political influence even when they have neither military nor economic strength'.[21]

Sentiments such as these were connected with the self-doubt that afflicted America in the wake of Vietnam. Western Europe and Japan, due to their 'economic miracles', were given the title of 'civilian powers'. While these countries still depended upon the US for military protection, their economic position vis-à-vis the US appeared to be an increasingly symmetrical one. Just as importantly, détente reduced the ability of the US to effect 'linkage' between its military preponderance and other international issues, further enhancing the relative power-position of Europe and Japan.

In much of the first generation of literature on economic interdependence, there was a strong sense of the web of mutual interest and cooperation that interdependence was weaving between men of all nations.²² This notion of the displacement of power in international relations was not what Kissinger had in mind when he spoke of the growing *non-homogeneity* of power and its *diffusion* between states. In fact, the naked optimism of the early interdependence literature did not long survive the upheavals of the early 1970s. It was soon realised that rising levels of economic interdependence did not simply displace old forms of conflict (if indeed they even did this); they were just as likely to create new ones. The long and acrimonious disputes over international monetary affairs culminating in the breakdown of the Bretton Woods system, the beginning of the ongoing trade dispute between the major industrial countries, the first oil crisis and the inflationary recession of 1974–5, all seemed to indicate that interdependence had created new problems in the relations between the major industrial countries.

Keohane and Nye in their 1977 book returned to Cooper's earlier point that interdependence restricted the policy autonomy of states, which was a cost in terms of domestic politics and policy-making. A 'politicisation' of international economic issues occurred as they came to impinge upon domestic political debate over distributional matters.²³ They also claimed that rising interdependence did not *displace* state power in international relations, but that on the contrary 'asymmetrical interdependence' constituted a potential source of power for states.

This apparent concession to the realist position was not as substantial as it first appeared, since the implication was that in circumstances of fully symmetrical interdependence, power would be displaced. The issue boiled down to whether relations between states, especially in the economic area, were in fact becoming more symmetrical; Keohane and Nye certainly thought so. If power was not being displaced, it was becoming increasingly 'non-homogeneous'. These authors talked of power as being constituted by an ability to influence 'outcomes' in particular 'issue-areas'.

In a manner reminiscent of the pluralist theories of power in American society during the 1950s, it was suggested that power was constituted by an ability to prevail over opponents in particular and explicit bargaining situations. As Kissinger had argued, states which were militarily strong could not expect to dominate, for example, international trade and monetary relations except on the basis of power resources specific to these areas. On the 'process' or bargaining level of international relations (in which economic matters were increasingly prominent), 'structural' power resources (military power and national wealth) were of increasingly limited value because of the difficulty of linkage.²⁴ An important theme of much of the subsequent literature was that 'structural power' was of crucial importance in determining the institutional and normative framework within which international economic activity operated.

1.4 The balance of power and the international economy

One of the earliest works to set out clearly the theme of the relationship between the shape of the international economic order and the balance of power between states was an article by Robert Gilpin entitled 'The politics of transnational economic relations' (1972). Gilpin's argument was that in the domestic realm, political structures of power determine the basic framework of economic activity. This, he claimed, was equally true on the international level; the transnational economic relations that were receiving so much attention ought not to be seen in isolation from or autonomous of the pattern of political relations between states in the postwar era. The critique of the apoliticism of much liberal theory in international relations was not in itself novel.[25] What was novel was Gilpin's interpretation of the history of international economic relations over the nineteenth and twentieth centuries.

He argued that the establishment and maintenance of the late nineteenth century and post-1945 'liberal' international economic orders was the result of the dominance of one 'hegemonic' state in the international political economy. The *Pax Britannica* and *Pax Americana* were both the source of the stability of the international economic system which these hegemons played a central role in creating, as well as a basic means by which their dominance over other states in the system was maintained and reproduced. In circumstances of hegemonic decline, when the formerly dominant state could no longer uphold the system, the international economic system would be subject to erosion and, ultimately, collapse. The most vivid example was held to be that of the Great Depression. Gilpin held this to be the product of:

> the failure of the United States to assume leadership of the world economy, a role that Great Britain could no longer perform. Whereas before the war the City of London provided order and coordinated international economic activities, now London was unable and New York was unwilling to restructure the international economy disrupted by the First World War. The result was a leadership vacuum which contributed in part to the onset of the Great Depression and eventually the Second World War.[26]

This opinion was echoed in the final chapter of a subsequent book by a prominent international economic historian on the Great

Depression. The timely appearance in 1973 of Charles Kindleberger's *The World in Depression* encouraged international relations theorists to approach the contemporary world economic crisis in the way in which Gilpin had suggested. In common with a number of other economic historians, Kindleberger held that one of the main causes of the Depression of the 1930s was the international monetary disorder of these years, but he added a political twist that extended Gilpin's argument. The stability of the international monetary system, and hence the world economy, rested upon the assumption of 'leadership' by the dominant international power of the day: 'The world economic system was unstable unless some country stabilized it, as Britain had done in the nineteenth century and up to 1913. In 1929, the British couldn't and the United States wouldn't.'

The moral of the story was clear: 'for the world economy to be stabilized, there has to be a stabilizer, one stabilizer.'[27] The notion of 'leadership' was different to Gilpin's emphasis on hegemonic dominance as important in the establishment and enforcement of the rules of international economic relations, but this became obscured in subsequent literature. By resting the ultimate explanation of the length and depth of the Great Depression upon the international political level, Kindleberger and Gilpin set the terms of the debate which followed. Above all, it opened the door to an international political theory of order and disorder in the world economy.[28]

The analogy of the decline of the *Pax Britannica* and its consequences was an appealing one, and soon references to the demise of the *Pax Americana* and the end of the 'American Century' abounded in the literature. This was an idea whose time had come. The experiences of Vietnam and Watergate, growing insecurity about rising American dependency upon foreign resources, the dwindling of the country's technological and productivity lead, rising inflation, unemployment and the balance of trade deficit all served to encourage a feeling of national malaise and uncertainty about America's future. Books such as the one entitled *America as an Ordinary Country* underlined the growing impression that the era of dominance which the US had enjoyed since 1945 was all of a sudden at an end.[29] Kenneth Oye stated in 1979, with evident resignation, that the 'role of the US in international relations has simply become that of a more normal state, with interests to be protected by limited means.'[30] This raised the question of whether it was right to believe that the US ever enjoyed *unlimited* means. More importantly, it implied that US decline, like that of Britain before it, might have a severely negative impact upon world economic stability.[31] As Robert Ozaki and Walter Arnold wrote confidently in 1985:

18 *The theory of hegemonic stability and monetary order*

> History indicates that the viability of an international economic order presupposes the presence of a leader nation powerful enough to impose a common code of conduct upon other nations. In the absence of such a hegemon the system is destined to disintegrate as each nation attempts to practice its own rules, not necessarily consistent with those of others.[32]

In this way, the issue of the relation between the international balance of power and the stability of the world economy came to be at the forefront of new work in the discipline. A major research programme was undertaken with an aim to transcend the narrow conceptual boundaries of international politics, and to establish the basis of a new field, 'international political economy'.[33] The phrase 'decline of American hegemony' came to saturate this literature, the central issue being whether the successful international economic order established after 1945 could survive in a 'post-hegemonic' era.

1.5 The role of hegemony in the world political economy

From the academic debate emerged what might be termed a 'neo-realist' synthesis. Gone was the full-blown version of the idea that the rise of interdependence would displace power in international relations. The pursuit of power was restored to primacy of place, as was the state as the central actor in world politics. On the other hand, the realists accepted that the pursuit of power and the pursuit of national wealth were inseparable and that this had major implications for the organisation of the world political economy. There was also a common acceptance of the term 'hegemony' to describe the role of the US in the international system after 1945 and that of Britain before 1914. Hegemony, however, meant different things to different people.

The ambiguity in the term makes any assessment difficult. *The Concise Oxford Dictionary* is of little help in defining 'hegemonic' as 'ruling, supreme', whilst at the same time suggesting that 'hegemony' connotes 'leadership, especially by one State of a confederacy.' The idea of 'leadership' itself is highly ambiguous, though to hold that a 'hegemonic' power is one which is ruling or supreme would seem to suggest something much stronger and possibly lacking the moral authority that we often associate with leadership. Some writers tend to run together quite closely the terms leadership and hegemony, but it seems clear that 'hegemony' is of little theoretical or descriptive value if it *does not* imply something considerably stronger than

Political foundations of international economic order 19

leadership (which we will take to have a strong connotation of natural or moral authority and guiding by example).

A primarily economic definition of hegemony is often employed by neo-Marxist writers and by some historians with a structuralist bent such as Walt Rostow. They take hegemony to mean a state which enjoys a comparative advantage in the production of high value-added goods, a significant technological lead over other countries, and privileged access to raw materials and to markets for its produce.[34]

A second usage, sometimes but not always a sub-category of the first, is one emphasised by international monetary historians such as Kindleberger. Here, hegemony is extended to include a management and leadership role for the dominant state in the world economy. Kindleberger focuses in particular upon the ability and willingness of the dominant state to manage the international financial and trade systems. A high level of economic development and a considerable surplus of savings over domestic investment encourages it to allow the rest of the world access to its large and efficient capital markets. This financial function is usually connected with an international monetary reserve role for its currency, as in the cases of the pound sterling and US dollar in the late nineteenth century and post-1945 international monetary systems.[35]

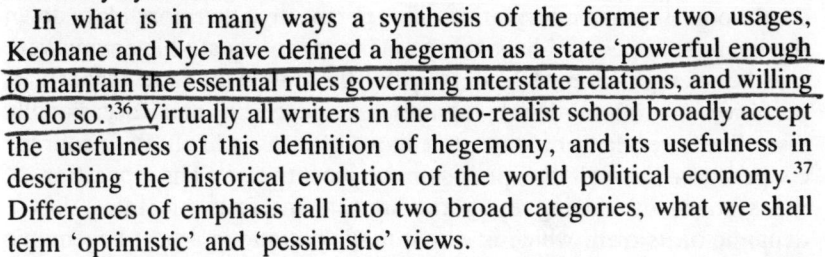

In what is in many ways a synthesis of the former two usages, Keohane and Nye have defined a hegemon as a state 'powerful enough to maintain the essential rules governing interstate relations, and willing to do so.'[36] Virtually all writers in the neo-realist school broadly accept the usefulness of this definition of hegemony, and its usefulness in describing the historical evolution of the world political economy.[37] Differences of emphasis fall into two broad categories, what we shall term 'optimistic' and 'pessimistic' views.

The optimistic view has as its distinctive characteristic the idea that whilst hegemonic decline is likely to lead to increasing disorder in the world economic system, there is no *a priori* reason why post-hegemonic cooperation should be impossible For example, American hegemonic power is seen as crucial in the establishment of the postwar international economic order, but not a necessary condition of its maintenance. This is because, as Keohane puts it:

> the common interests of the leading capitalist states, bolstered by the effects of existing international regimes (mostly created during a period of American hegemony), are strong enough to make sustained cooperation possible, though not inevitable . . . [H]egemony is less important for the continuation of cooperation, once begun, than for its creation.[38]

20 The theory of hegemonic stability and monetary order

The employment of the term 'regime' to designate the arrangements or institutions which embody sets of rules, procedures, norms and principles within an international issue-area[39] is also characteristic of this view. The emphasis is not so much upon coercion and the 'enforcement' of these rules, norms and principles by hegemonic power (though this is not ruled out), but on the way in which the establishment of regimes can encourage cooperation between states on the basis of common interests. As Keohane has written:

> regimes contribute to cooperation not by implementing rules that states must follow, but by changing the context within which states make decisions based on self-interests. International regimes are valuable to governments not because they enforce binding rules on others (they do not), but because they render it possible for governments to enter into mutually beneficial agreements with one another.[40]

Most importantly, regimes reduce the uncertainty which is responsible for the famous 'Prisoners' Dilemma' outcomes of game theory. By increasing the information which is available to the actors in bargaining situations, regimes supposedly facilitate the avoidance of mutually undesirable outcomes which derive from the mistrust that thrives in conditions of sparse information. This perspective therefore plays down the coercive aspects of hegemony and tends to equate hegemony with a rather benign form of leadership by the dominant state through its provision of international regimes. A hegemon may occasionally discipline a recalcitrant state, but more often it is likely to encourage cooperation through the provision of incentives.[41] The operation of the system, by relying upon the mutual interests of states, has a dynamic of its own, which is why it may continue in a post-hegemonic era.[42]

The optimistic view often uses the language of public goods to describe regimes. Kindleberger's model of a dominant state providing a public good of international financial intermediation is an oft-employed example, another being an open international trading system promoted by multilateral rules and institutions and the good example of the hegemon itself. To the extent that there are significant ongoing costs involved in the provision of international public goods, a 'free riding' problem may emerge. This is because other states in the system can benefit from the regimes at least as much as the hegemon, but may have little incentive to contribute to these costs. For this reason it is often held that hegemons typically pay an over-proportionate share of the costs of provision of these international public goods.[43] This contributes to the erosion of hegemonic power over time, and eventually a declining willingness and ability of the hegemon to provide the bulk of the resources for regime maintenance.

The second, 'pessimistic' perspective which it is possible to identify within the neo-realist synthesis places more emphasis upon the coercive side of hegemony and less upon the existence of mutual interests. Hegemony tends to be more forthrightly equated with the dominance and power of the leading state. Any 'cooperation' between states is held to be a product of inequality between states, or even of a dominant ideology which upholds this inequality, rather than due to the existence of substantial common interests. Many so-called 'neo-mercantilist' writers and a number of neo-Marxists as well are representative of this view.

Lacking the strong presumption of the existence of common interests between states that characterises the liberal tradition, these writers tend to refrain from speaking of hegemony as providing international public goods. Although they allow for the possibility that other states may benefit from the order instituted by the hegemon, they emphasise, as has traditional realism, the inequality and exploitation inherent in hegemonic systems. Gilpin is representative in arguing that:

> Since the Industrial Revolution, the two successive hegemonic powers in the global system (Great Britain and the United States) have sought to organise the political, territorial and especially economic relations in terms of their respective security and economic interests. They have succeeded in this hegemonic role partly because they have imposed their will on lesser states and partially because other states have benefited from and accepted their leadership.[44]

Since hegemony is more obviously connected with an international structure of dominance and dependence, it follows that as hegemony erodes, rising states which occupy a disadvantageous position in the system inevitably challenge both the hegemon and the order with which it is associated. Much more than in the former view, 'cooperation' is held to depend heavily on the continued presence of hegemonic power. For Calleo and Rowland, for example, the relative decline of American power means that: 'Europe is growing too powerful for the hegemonic relationship to persist . . . Unless . . . the institutions of the postwar economic system can adapt to a pluralist rather than a hegemonic order, that system will break down.'[45]

The pessimistic perspective is also distinguished by its 'long-view determinism'. Writers like Modelski and Rostow see the chronological and spatial clustering of technological innovation as playing a guiding role in the rise and decline of nations. Economically and technologically ascendant states, it is argued, have an interest in promoting a liberal international economic order in which they will be most able to benefit. Technological ascendancy is also likely to go hand in hand with military supremacy, which in turn facilitates their ability to protect their expanding overseas interests.[46]

Hegemonic decline is often less associated with the overprovision of regimes than with the 'law of uneven growth' which explained the hegemon's former rise to ascendancy. Imperial overstretch, however, can play a major role in the erosion of hegemonic power. Marxists often link the phenomenon of overstretch with the process of uneven growth inherent in the capitalist system, which in Lenin's view produced heightened competition between capitalist states for foreign markets and ultimately war.[47] Gilpin is not far removed from this position in arguing that 'the market produces profound shifts in the location of economic activities and . . . transforms the political framework itself, undermines the hegemonic power and creates a new political environment to which the world must eventually adjust.' He also accepts an argument common to neo-Marxist writing, that the hegemon gains the right of seignorage through the international use of its currency.[48]

1.6 Conclusion

The differences of emphasis within the debate over the role of hegemonic powers in the world economic order should not obscure the key elements common to liberals, neo-mercantilists and neo-Marxists alike. Most important is the agreement which exists on the *historical* role of hegemony in producing 'liberal' international economic orders or regimes, and the instability which is likely to arise with hegemonic decline. The disorder of the interwar period, for example, tends almost universally to be seen as an example of the consequences of an absence of hegemony.

As we saw, classical liberals such as Adam Smith saw a need for the state to provide the minimal political foundations of a market economy in order that its inherent dynamism could have full effect. What the neo-realist school of international political economy was suggesting was the application of this insight to the global level. The idea that a world liberal market economy could be self-sustaining was a delusion which only tended to arise in periods in which an established hegemony obscured the global political foundation of the economic system. States at the national level had a strong tendency to indulge in anti-liberal practices, and this was particularly the case when international public goods or hegemonic coercion were scarce. Hegemony was therefore the means by which the minimal political preconditions of an open world economic order could be established and maintained.⁴⁹

In 1980, Keohane formulated a 'basic force' model as a conscious caricature of the deterministic strain of writing on this topic, which serves as a good summary. He termed it the 'theory of hegemonic stability'.⁵⁰ This theory, which has since then become the focus of debate, rested upon two propositions: 'that order in international relations is typically created by a single dominant power ... [and] that the maintenance of order requires continued hegemony.'⁵¹ (NB. Words in square brackets within quotations are added by the author for clarification.)

As has been pointed out, Keohane's major concern was to criticise the theory of hegemonic stability on its second proposition; he largely accepted that the postwar international economic order was the product of US power, although he tended to disagree with the realists as to the way in which regimes facilitated cooperation. When it came to explaining the increased disorder in the world economy in the 1970s, Keohane saw the decline of US hegemony as a necessary cause, if an insufficient explanation, of this increased disorder. The theory of hegemonic stability was therefore a basic starting-point of analysis.⁵²

The key idea of neo-realism is that order in the world economy requires cooperation between sovereign states and that historically at least, hegemony has been a necessary condition for such cooperation. As in the interwar period, the problem of recent years has been seen as how cooperation might be fostered between the major states in the absence of hegemony. As Fred Bergsten, one of the less pessimistic writers on this topic, argued in 1974:

> The only successful international economic orders in history have been hierarchical indeed hegemonial, under the British in the nineteenth century and the Americans after the second world war ... There is no possibility of reconstituting the postwar economic order, even if it were desirable to do so, because the American domination which was its structural foundation has eroded too far.⁵³

Predictably perhaps, by the late 1980s there was a reaction to years of such 'declinist' thinking in American international relations literature. Sparked by Paul Kennedy's *The Rise and Decline of the Great Powers*, a new 'revivalist' school rejected the idea of substantial US decline, arguing that there was no challenger in sight to America's hegemonic status.⁵⁴ In common with neo-realism, however, the revivalist school has not overtly challenged the idea that hegemony is conducive of international economic stability and that US decline would (in principle at least) be likely to lead to greater economic disorder.

24 The theory of hegemonic stability and monetary order

The specific interest of this book is in the relationship between hegemony and international monetary order, though the general issues raised by the debate over America's position in the world are of relevance and will be dealt with in later chapters. The following two chapters are concerned with the general relationship between political structures and order in monetary systems. Before moving on to questions of hegemony and international monetary order in Chapter 3, the next chapter is concerned with how monetary order is produced in a 'closed' economy. Rather than reproduce the work of economists on basic monetary theory, however, it will focus upon the relationship between financial and political structures on the one hand and monetary stability on the other. We shall see that this has considerable relevance for our discussion of international monetary relations.

Notes

1. Marx and Engels, 1978, p.477.
2. James Shotwell drew the political implications of this view in suggesting that '[t]he political doctrine of international peace is a parallel to the economic doctrine of Adam Smith, for it rests similarly upon a recognition of common and reciprocal material interests, which extend beyond national frontiers.' Both quotes are from Waltz, 1959, p.98.
3. Smith, 1910, vol.II, pp.180–1.
4. *ibid.*, vol.I, p.408.
5. Quoted in Howard, 1981, p.37.
6. See *ibid.*, ch.4,5, and Waltz, 1959, ch.4.
7. Quoted in Shennan, 1974, p.90.
8. For example, Shonfield, 1965.
9. International Monetary Fund (IMF), *International Financial Statistics*, 1986 Yearbook.
10. Scammell, 1983, pp.126–7.
11. Kindleberger, 1969, p.207.
12. Cooper, 1968, p.5.
13. *ibid.*, pp.10,157–72,263–8.
14. *ibid.*, p.264.
15. For example, John Pinder has written that 'interdependence is a problem because it is both necessary to the development of the modern economy and eventually incompatible with the system of economic policy based on the nation-state. The solution is a joint policy system.' (Pinder, 1983, p.81.)
16. For example, Marris, 1984, and the citations therein.
17. See for example, Bull, 1977, and the introduction by Bull and C. Holbraad to Wight, 1979, pp.15–17.
18. Important works were Keohane and Nye, 1972; Mansbach *et al.*, 1976; Morse, 1976.
19. Keohane and Nye, 1977.
20. *ibid.*, p.25.

21. Quoted in Waltz, 1979, p.130.
22. For example, Mansbach *et al.*, 1976, pp.296–9.
23. Keohane and Nye, 1977, pp.9–19. See also Hirsch and Doyle, 1977.
24. Keohane and Nye, 1973, p.117. On the process level of analysis, what is termed 'sensitivity interdependence' is most important, whilst on the structure level, in which the underlying shape of rules and constraints is determined, 'vulnerability interdependence' is seen to dominate.
25. See Carr, 1951, p.117.
26. Gilpin, 1972, p.57. For a more recent elaboration, see Gilpin, 1987, ch.3.
27. Kindleberger, 1973, pp.292,305.
28. Kindleberger himself did not shrink from elaborating the consequences of his theory for the interpretation of the world economic crisis of the 1970s (see his 1976 article).
29. Rosecrance, 1976. See also Thurow, 1980.
30. Oye *et al.*, 1979, p.11.
31. See the discussion in Bergsten, Keohane and Nye, 1975.
32. Ozaki and Arnold, 1985, p.6.
33. Strange, 1970; Spero, 1977; Gilpin, 1975, 1987; Calleo and Rowland, 1973; Keohane, 1984.
34. See Amin, Arrighi, Frank and Wallerstein, 1982; Mandel, 1975, ch.4, and 1980, pp.30–6; Rostow, 1985; Modelski, 1983; Maddison, 1982, pp.29–42, 124.
35. Kindleberger, 1976, and 1986; Cohen, 1977, ch.7; Block, 1977; Brett, 1983.
36. Keohane and Nye, 1977, p.44. See also Keohane, 1984, pp.34–5; Gilpin, 1981, pp.144–5, and 1987, pp.72–4; Krasner, 1976, pp.322–3.
37. A notable exception to this broad generalisation is Susan Strange. See her 1982, 1986, pp.66–70, and 1987. Strange's argument is that the US remains the dominant state in the world political economy, but that its policies are the major cause of the international monetary instability of recent years. In fact, as we shall see, authors such as Keohane make some concessions to this point. Nevertheless, Strange would seem to agree with the basic argument that the fundamental requirement of international economic stability is responsible policies on the part of the hegemon. A similar position is taken by Russett, 1985.
38. Keohane, 1984, pp.43,12.
39. *ibid.*, pp.57–9.
40. *ibid.*, p.14.
41. On this point, see the article by Snidal, 1985.
42. Similar assumptions underlay much of the literature on macroeconomic policy coordination and Economic Summits since the 1970s, often with explicit reference to the need to foster a basis for 'post-hegemonic cooperation'. See Merlini, 1984; de Menil and Solomon, 1983; Putnam and Bayne, 1984.
43. Kindleberger, 1986, pp.7–11; Gilpin, 1987, p.76.
44. Gilpin, 1981, p.144. See also Katzenstein, 1978, pp.9–11. For some neo-Marxist writings which present a not altogether different perspective, Gunder Frank, 1983, p.13; Wallerstein, 'Crisis as Transition', in Amin, Arrighi, Frank and Wallerstein, 1982, pp.22–4.
45. Calleo and Rowland, 1973, pp.7,6.
46. Modelski, 1983, pp.116–21,128–35; Rostow, 1985; Maddison, 1982,

pp.29–42,124; Gilpin, 1981, pp.175–85, and 1987, pp.93–117.
47. Mandel, 1975, ch.4, and 1980, pp.30–6; Arrighi, 1982, pp.72–6.
48. Gilpin, 1987, p.77. Kennedy, 1988, concentrates on the overextension thesis.
49. Gilpin, 1981, p.138; Keohane, 1984, pp.88–9; Modelski, 1978, pp.216–18; Calleo and Rowland, 1973, pp.29–32.
50. Keohane, 1980.
51. Keohane, 1984, p.31.
52. See Keohane, 1984, pp.14,16,245–6.
53. Bergsten, 1975, p.342.
54. See Kennedy, 1990, and the books cited therein.

Chapter 2
Domestic financial structures and monetary order

2.1 Introduction

The previous chapter briefly outlined two views of the relationship between hegemony and international monetary order. The first view, generally held by political scientists, focused on the provision and maintenance of regimes by the hegemon, which promote consistency between national economic policies that would otherwise tend to be incompatible. The second view, espoused by Charles Kindleberger, was that the hegemon's dominance in the international financial system enabled it to provide stability by actively managing the world's monetary and financial system.

This raises a number of important questions. First, what has been the relationship between political authority and the development of money and finance? Second, how do patterns of asymmetry and dominance arise in financial structures? Third, in what ways can such patterns allow dominant actors to play a management role, and in what does this management role consist?

These questions may equally be asked of domestic or 'closed' economies as of the international economy. In fact, literature concerned with the theory of hegemonic stability has largely ignored these issues as they relate to either domestic or international economic organisation, which is a major shortcoming. There are good reasons why they are relevant to our present concerns. Economic theory in this area is highly developed and can provide important insights into questions of international monetary organisation. The way in which monetary stability is related to the domestic financial structure is highly analogous to the issue raised by hegemonic stability theory. It is also very difficult in practice to separate domestic from international money and finance. In particular, the financial structures of important economies such as Britain and the US are very relevant to any discussion of the international monetary role of these countries.

For these reasons, this chapter will discuss the questions raised above, largely in the context of a closed economy, leaving a fuller consideration of the international level to Chapter 3. To the extent that particular countries are discussed, we will focus upon Britain and the US because of their historical importance and direct relevance to our concerns.

2.2 Money, finance and politics

Money has its origin in the process of economic exchange, which is itself as old as human history. Economists have often assumed that barter, the process of economic exchange without the intermediation of money, chronologically and logically preceded the relatively recent monetisation of economic life. As the economic historian Michael Postan has argued, if a 'barter economy' ever existed, it 'must have disappeared earlier than the earliest point at which European history can be said to begin.'[1] Coinage was used in England long before the invasion of the Romans, and flourished in ancient Greece as far back as the sixth or seventh century before Christ. Whenever trade occurred between human communities, which it did from the earliest times, so-called 'primitive money' often came into usage. Trade between Europeans and African kingdoms in medieval times involved the use of all kinds of commodities as money, such as cowrie shells, salt, cotton cloth, horses, chickens, copper bracelets and gold dust. Furs and dried fish in northern America and Europe at various times served as money.[2]

What makes all of these money is their acceptability in the settlement of debts. Such acceptability as they enjoyed depended upon a social convention that they represented value in the abstract: they were demanded not only for their particular 'use value' but especially because they could be used to purchase other commodities. It is also important to recognise that paper money is as conventional as commodity money. Although states may act to make paper money legal tender for the settlement of debts, this is neither a sufficient nor necessary foundation of its broad acceptability in most modern economies. In a number of countries today, dollars or other 'hard'

Domestic financial structures and monetary order 29

currencies circulate where the domestic legal tender has lost its social acceptability and therefore value.

What has often been termed the 'state theory of money', the idea that money derives its value and hence usage from political authority, is misleading because it sees money as a political rather than a social phenomenon.[3] States may successfully meet debts to citizens by effectively forcing them to accept devalued money as payment, but this does not apply to the use of money *per se* nor to the origin of money. Periodic attempts by princes to debase the local currency generally led to its depreciation on the exchanges, discouraged traders from presenting coin for reminting to the mint, and encouraged the use of more reliable currencies and state mints by merchants and financiers.[4]

Barter, money and credit as forms of exchange have historically appeared together, and even in the advanced industrial economies it is only in comparatively recent times that the disappearance of widespread barter has become virtually complete.[5] Fairly sophisticated techniques of credit were very important in medieval commercial activity. As Braudel points out, though many feudal exchanges and relationships were characterised by payments in kind, credit as a form of social life had always been central to agricultural communities. When the Lord of the manor advanced grain to peasants because of the time lag between initial 'investment' and distribution of the final product, he was in effect extending credit on the basis of an expectation of repayment at harvest time.[6] In practice, it is often difficult to distinguish between barter, money and credit. For example, some early coins acted as a common standard of value and as a store of value, without actually being used as a medium of exchange. Many payments to the Church of an in kind form were often enforced by means of monetary fines.[7]

The role of money and credit in the process of economic exchange was most advanced when it came to long-distance trade. The trade routes and fairs of late medieval Europe had been long-established when the rulers of the rising states attempted to extend their limited authority over greater tracts of territory. While the perspective of the merchants and financiers of Europe was altogether more vast than the narrow concerns of the early statesmen of the West, it was not long before politics came to have a dramatic impact upon the development of money and finance.

The constant process of war gave states a natural interest in the further monetisation of the economy, since they needed access to resources requiring payment in coin, most notably human resources in the form of mercenary armies.[8] The long-term solution was to encourage the development of trade and finance and at the same time to promote a deeper and more stable base for taxation. Steps taken towards this were often slow and misdirected, periodically resulting in political unrest. In some states such as England and Holland, however, this process was considerably more rapid than in others.[9]

In the short term, money was the prerequisite of institutionalised, state-directed violence and therefore, to some degree, of political authority itself. Colbert, minister to Louis XIV of France, spoke from experience in arguing that 'everyone agrees that the might and greatness of a state are measured entirely by the quantity of silver it possesses.'[10] In all states for a considerable period, the pressures to obtain funds to finance excess state spending requirements led to a variety of responses.

Ministers took an increasing interest in the 'specie-flows' which accompanied long-distance trade. Given the constant drain of specie to the Far East and India to pay for the import of silks, spices and other luxury goods, the maintenance of a surplus 'Balance of Trade' became a central preoccupation of the mercantilist state. Restrictions on the export of bullion, however, were hardly ever very successful. Desperation could lead princes to debase the currency, but this would only tend to drive specie out of the kingdom.[11] In the end, monarchs were sooner or later driven to the houses of the money-lenders to supplement their financial resources. To quote Tawney:

> [T]he City interest was one of the great Powers of Europe . . . [B]ehind Prince and Pope alike . . . stood in the last resort a little German banker, with branches in every capital of Europe, who played in the world of finance the part of the *condottieri* in war, and represented in the economic sphere the morality typified in that of politics by Machiavelli's Prince.[12]

The history of private banking is to some extent a history of wealthy financiers who played a crucial role in the consolidation of state power, from the Bardi and Perruzzi in the fourteenth century to the Medici and Fuggers of the Renaissance to the Rothschilds, Bleichröders and J.P. Morgan in the nineteenth century. From the point of view of these bankers, the high risks involved in sovereign lending were offset by the benefits of maintaining intimate connections with political power. The bankers usually demanded security, often in the form of crown lands and mines, which they periodically had occasion to confiscate. A number of banking houses were nevertheless brought down by monarchs who defaulted on interest payments and often principal as well.[13] Through these financiers, states were able to tap into the resources of the transnational monetary circuit.

Another source of finance were capital markets, primitive forms of which were already in existence in thirteenth-century Italy and France, but which reached a fairly sophisticated stage in seventeenth-century Holland. Here, a series of costly wars and a relatively high level of economic development and savings led to the development of a broad market for government annuities in which thousands of investors participated.[14] Amsterdam had risen to be the dominant financial centre of the period, with flourishing markets in currency, bills of exchange and capital issues supporting the high level of mercantile activity in the United Provinces. Dutch financial practices as well as capital eventually found their way abroad and assisted the rise of similar markets in London in particular.

2.3 The rise of London as a financial centre

Financial developments in England from the end of the seventeenth century were of such historical significance that they have often been described in terms of a 'financial revolution'.[15] A major landmark was the creation of the Bank of England in 1694, on the basis of a deal between a number of London and foreign financiers and the Revolutionary Government. In return for providing the government with access to finance and rationalising its hitherto chaotic borrowing, the financiers hoped to obtain a monopoly of its financial business. In a remarkably short period, liquid markets for long term and short term (Exchequer bills) debt developed, supplanting the outstanding forms of government debt.[16] The ease with which the English were to finance subsequent wars has often been seen as an important factor in the rise of English state power. The centralisation of the taxation system and the creditworthiness that followed from Parliament's ability to guarantee these borrowings were also crucial, as was the commercial revolution. Over the course of the eighteenth century, interest on government stock fell from a peak of 10 per cent to around 3 per cent as its marketability improved, to the extent of attracting funds from abroad, especially from the Dutch.[17]

London's development into a financial centre for England as a whole was considerably enhanced by its position as the national capital and seat of government. The major companies of the day, the East India Company, the South Sea Company and the Bank of England itself all had important links with the government and competed for its business. The Bank of England was especially privileged in the financial sphere. After some initial uncertainty, the Bank was given a monopoly of the government's financial business, while other private banks were limited to a maximum of six partners, restricting their size. In its early phase of operation, it issued notes with a denomination of £10 or more, which circulated in London alongside the notes of the private banks and which were also issued to merchants and the large trading companies as credit. Despite periodic difficulties, the Bank's close relationship with the government helped. In 1742, it obtained a monopoly of joint-stock bank note issue and by the 1770s it had a virtual monopoly of notes and coins in circulation in London.[18] The private banks tended to settle balances with each other in Bank of England notes, eventually leading to the creation of a 'clearing house' in Lombard Street in 1773.

From the mid-eighteenth century, a great number of country banks were established in response to the growing commercial activity in provincial areas. These banks issued their own notes and would exchange them in the settlement of net balances. Despite their reluctance to cede power to the financial establishment in London, the country banks gradually came to settle balances with Bank notes (and later cheques), facilitated by the spread of Bank of England branches after 1826.[19] Country clearing gradually disappeared over the course of the nineteenth century as the country banks centralised their own operations in London, despite considerable initial reluctance in some cases.

The forces of attraction to London were strong. From the point of view of the large country banks (Lloyds, the Midland and the National Provincial), the extension of their branch network made desirable a centralised means of recycling surplus funds from certain branches (usually in the South) to others servicing the industrial areas in the North or, as the century wore on, to other countries. As funds became concentrated in London, the liquidity of the money and capital markets was further enhanced, adding to its attractions. The capital's communications and transport links, with the rest of the country and overseas, further facilitated this process.[20]

Relocation to London often involved some cost. When joint-stock banking was adopted in 1826, the Bank was given a monopoly on note issue within a 65-mile radius of London. The 1833 renewal of the Bank's charter allowed joint-stock banks of deposit to conduct business within 65 miles of London, but not joint-stock banks of note issue. The formation in that year of the London and Westminster Bank challenged the Bank's monopoly of joint-stock banking in its home territory, while others sometimes merged with a London bank (as did Lloyds and the Midland), or began a national branch network centred in London (Barclays). Besides the efficiency gains of centralising business in the nation's financial centre, these moves had the advantage of removing the necessity of paying correspondent banks in London for their services.[21]

City of London banks specialised in dealing in government bonds, shares of the major companies and undertook business for country and foreign clients. West End bankers catered mainly for the aristocracy, accepting deposits and engaging in mortgage and overdraft lending. The growing role of London in international trade finance created new business. With bills drawn on London financing a large proportion of world trade by the mid-nineteenth century, bill-brokers became increasingly important players in the money market. As will be seen in more detail in Chapter 4, foreign companies and governments increasingly held liquid sterling balances to effect payments and offset fluctuations in business. London's capital and equity markets came to dwarf those of other country centres such as Liverpool and Manchester, as well as other major foreign centres, attracting investment funds from home and abroad. By 1870, London was both a national and international financial centre, attracting funds from a wide range of sources and recycling them to domestic and foreign borrowers.

To what extent does London's rise as a financial centre demonstrate that there are general forces at work which lead to centralisation in financial systems? The competitive process itself is undoubtedly the major economic factor, since it pushes market participants to minimise transactions and information costs. These costs are likely to be significantly reduced when there is one vehicle currency for financial transactions and one financial centre in which funds are pooled and managed. Specialisation of financial function into trading, market-making, funds management and the various intermediary functions associated with the capital and equity markets becomes considerably more advanced in a large financial centre. Interbank markets are established and market participants can have personal contact. The increased liquidity and transparency that results from specialisation and transaction volume makes the markets in a financial centre attractive to investors.[22]

The transfer of surplus capital from savers to borrowers usually has a geographical dimension, as in the case of London and in other centres such as Paris and New York. Such transfers are more easily managed from one centre, as are functions such as matching seasonal imbalances in savings and investment (New York, for example, did this from an early stage).[23] Financial centres are usually favoured with good transport and communications links, part of the reason why they usually emerge in cities that are also commercial centres (London, Lyons, Frankfurt, Milan, Amsterdam and New York are all examples).

That London was England's political capital was an important factor in the rise of a financial hierarchy in which the Bank of England and London were placed at the top, as was legislation which directly favoured the Bank and its geographical location. French administrative centralisation was possibly even more important in the rise of Paris as the French financial centre, but New York succeeded despite various legislative attempts at decentralising financial power.[24] Additional examples of Frankfurt and Zurich in the twentieth century suggest that geographical proximity to government may not be decisive in the rise of financial centres, though government *business* is usually central.

London's rise to *international* prominence raises similar questions. It seems inconceivable that London could have become the major centre for capital exports to the Dominions, the Americas and other important countries without its trade links with these regions and without the accumulation of wealth in Britain due to its industrial revolution. Similar factors favoured Amsterdam before it and New York (over other rival centres such as St. Louis and Chicago) after it. The desire to reduce transactions costs by centralising clearing and funds management is also of importance on the international level, although the much greater degree of uncertainty that exists in international finance will limit these tendencies. As we shall see in Part II, the role of sterling and the dollar as international currencies owes much to the general tendency in financial markets to use one vehicle currency for transactions. Openness to international banks and an absence of excessive restrictions upon international financial business have also been important in the rise of international financial centres, as London's rise and that of other 'offshore' centres since the 1960s demonstrates. These issues will be returned to in later chapters.

2.4 The Bank of England as central bank

As a private company, the Bank of England conducted its business for profit. It was not averse to attempting to undermine rivals in financial difficulty, as when it refused to help the Sword Blade Bank, which collapsed in 1720. Similarly, as late as 1866, it allowed the collapse of its major rival in the bill market, Overend Gurney.[25] With its notes increasingly dominating the circulating media of the national economy, however, the Bank over time gradually acquired a public role which was in tension with its private business perspective.

The Bank's position in the financial system was, as we saw, considerably enhanced by its close relationship with the government and its monopoly on joint stock bank note issue. This position was also consolidated, as in the Sword Blade and Overend Gurney cases, by the periodic occurrence of financial crises. The panic of 1745 was probably a turning-point in this respect, when a run on the Bank's gold reserves was halted by the issuance of a declaration of faith in its notes by leading London merchants.[26] Over the following century, in many subsequent crises, other banks often found the Bank's notes to be acceptable as a substitute for hard currency, which in turn encouraged them to hold a greater proportion of their own gold reserves at the Bank. This growing centralisation of gold reserves in the English financial system led in fits and starts to the emergence of the Bank of England as a 'lender of last resort' to other banks. That is, the Bank's liabilities gradually came to be accepted as the base money of the banking system, so that access to these liabilities ultimately determined the solvency of particular banks.[27]

This process was accelerated by the suspension of the gold convertibility of the Bank's notes from 1797 to 1821, in response to the pressures emanating from the Continental turmoil due to the French revolutionary wars. During this period, the notes of other English banks were only acceptable on the basis of their convertibility into Bank of England notes, so that effectively the monetary base of the financial system was determined by the issue of inconvertible Bank notes. This situation was of course deeply worrying to the supporters of a fixed metallic monetary standard, the so-called Currency School, who asserted that the inflation which occurred in this period was the result of the over-issuance of notes by a profit oriented Bank of England.[28] The triumph of this orthodox view was to crystallise into the Bullion Report of 1810 and, after the restoration of gold convertibility in 1821, the Bank Act of 1844.

The Bank Act of 1844 separated the Bank into an Issue Department and a Banking Department, corresponding to its 'public' and 'private' roles. The Issue Department was allowed a fixed fiduciary note issue of £14 million, beyond which any additional note issuance had to be backed by gold. This institutionalised a mixed gold–paper monetary standard, recognising the transformation of the financial system brought about by the pre-eminent role of the Bank in that system.[29] On the other hand, the Act also reflected a fear that in the absence of a fixed fiduciary issue, the Bank's private interests might lead it to over-issue its notes and undermine monetary stability. Legislation was therefore required to ensure that the mixed monetary standard worked in practice like a purely metallic monetary standard.[30]

This was an illusion. In the financial crises of 1847, 1857 and 1866, the Bank Act had to be suspended so that the Bank could act as lender of last resort to the banking system and exceed its statutory fiduciary limit.[31] The everyday operation of the banking system had itself been dramatically transformed by the evolving hierarchical structure of the financial system. Banks had come to operate on a fractional reserve system, making loans to customers far in excess of their reserves of Bank of England notes, coin, and gold. Bank deposits had also become transferable, by the increasing use of cheques or by a bank issuing a note against itself which could circulate in the economy at large. This meant that the banking system could create money, by enabling a borrower to cancel debts by paying with a cheque or notes drawn against his bank.[32] The creation of bank credit over the course of the nineteenth century led to an enormous increase in the effective supply of money. Around 1800, bank notes and demand deposits accounted for less than one half of the amount of total monetary gold and silver in Europe; by 1913, notes and deposits were almost nine times the amount of metallic money in use.[33]

The shift from a banking system based upon metallic money to one based upon credit money not only increased the power of the Bank of England. The government could also borrow from the banks not simply in their capacity as intermediaries between government and savers, but as agents able to create money in their own right. The state's financial power had increased considerably, since in the end it could force the banking system to create the money it required, or what amounted to the same thing, force the central bank to take government debt onto its own books by issuing currency. The hope of champions of orthodox finance was that such inflationary financing would be constrained by the *external* obligation of the Bank to maintain a fixed parity between sterling and gold.

The Bank's task had become the *management* of the financial system, in terms of its lender of last resort role, and the custodian of sound money through its discount rate policy, raising its discount rate when there was a gold drain from the country to overseas. Using this policy instrument, the Bank of England has often been seen as having successfully managed the gold standard and thereby contributed to the reasonable degree of stability in the British monetary system after 1866.[34]

2.5 Financial hierarchy and monetary stability

The idea that an economy increasingly based upon credit money needs to be *managed* by a public monetary authority is central to our concerns. It is important to note, however, that economists have differed as to the sources of instability in credit-based economies, since this is important for the form that monetary management should take.

Domestic financial structures and monetary order

For most modern economists, money is a major exception to the broad rule of thumb that monopoly should be avoided as economically inefficient. A basic theme of modern monetary theory is that an economy in which there was no central bank money but only credit money issued by individual banks would be inherently unstable, as individual banks would have no incentive to limit credit creation and prices would tend to infinity. Monetary stability is seen to derive from the central bank's ability to control the overall level of credit creation by the banking system, by determining banks' reserve ratios (the ratio of required holdings of central bank money to deposits).[35] In this orthodox view, financial hierarchy and in particular the central bank's monopoly on the issue of base money are prerequisites for monetary stability.

Some have taken quite the opposite standpoint. Most notably, von Hayek has argued that the central bank's monopoly on the issue of base money is the source of monetary and financial instability in modern economies, a view with which Monetarists have tended to sympathise. As he has written:

> the chief blemish of the market order which has been the cause of well-justified reproaches, its susceptibility to recurrent periods of depression and unemployment, is a consequence of the age-old government monopoly of the issue of money . . . [Its] abolition . . . would provide an opportunity to extricate ourselves from the impasse into which this development has led. It would create the conditions in which responsibility for the control of the quantity of the currency is placed on agencies whose self-interest would make them control it in such a manner as to make it most acceptable to the users . . . Money is the one thing competition would not make cheap, because its attractiveness rests on its preserving its dearness.[36]

State interventionism in monetary affairs, above all 'the lender of last resort' role of central banks, prevents the price mechanism from redistributing profits over time and inducing a shift of resources into activities corresponding to changes in consumer demand. The basic assumption behind the von Hayek view is that the private market economy is inherently stable and that this principle should be extended to monetary organisation. Competition rather than financial hierarchy is the route to monetary stability.

Keynes disputed this theory in arguing that all market economies are subject to instability and that government intervention could assist in economic stabilisation. Central to the Keynesian view is the role of uncertainty about the future in producing economic fluctuations. Economic agents' demand for money as a store of value represents a desire for a reservoir of potential purchasing power and is therefore intimately connected with the general state of expectations about the future:

> [O]ur desire to hold money as a store of wealth is a barometer of our distrust of our own calculations and conventions concerning the future . . . The possession of actual money lulls our disquietude; and the premium which we require to make us part with money [the interest rate] is the measure of the degree of our disquietude.[37]

The concern which pervades Keynesian theory is that expectations of falling commodity prices may become self-fulfilling by leading agents to scramble for liquidity by generalised selling of commodities for money. As commodity prices fall, firms face greater than expected declines in sales revenues, causing them to reduce their current investment and production expenditures. A vicious cycle of declining incomes and prices may set in, and depressed business confidence or 'animal spirits' may attempt to find a refuge in money itself. The essential problem is that money is a non-reproducible asset, unlike many others, so that an increased demand for money is a demand for a 'commodity' which is not part of current output. This simple model suggested to Keynes that the deflationary consequences of a generalised liquidity crisis could be alleviated only by satisfying the desire of agents for liquidity, preventing widespread selling of commodities and consequent bankruptcies.

Expansionary monetary policy on the part of the central bank was seen as important, but fiscal policy could be used more directly to increase aggregate demand in the economy and improve business expectations. Although the emphasis of Keynesian economics was upon fiscal policy, the ability of the government to undertake emergency borrowing from the banking system was seen as fundamental. Financial hierarchy and the privileged position of the central bank and government were seen as factors which could be made to work for stability.

Keynes' analysis of the role of economic uncertainty helps to clarify why financial markets may be particularly subject to instability. Expectations about the future, upon which decisions to invest or to hold money are based, are in this view inherently incapable of being assigned probabilistic value. Long-term expectations are highly volatile because observed frequencies of past outcomes are not a reliable guide to the future:

> The sense in which I am using the term [uncertainty] is that in which the prospect of a European war is uncertain, or the price of copper and the rate of interest twenty years hence, or the obsolescence of a new invention . . . About these matters there is no scientific basis on which to form any calculable probability.[38]

The distinction between *uncertainty*, due to a lack of information about the future, and (insurable) *risk*, as the observable probability of particular outcomes, is crucial to the argument about equilibrium in a monetary economy.[39] If expectations are ineradicably subjective, then there is considerable potential for wide swings of sentiment. This is the point which Keynes makes in his analysis of the stock market.

The stock market plays a role in valuing the assets of firms, financial and non-financial. If there is no firm basis for the calculation of future returns, each stock market participant must be at least as concerned with the actions of others or the 'mood of the market'.[40] This means that expectations obtain a very conventional nature and may be particularly subject to periodic bouts of 'herd behaviour' and rapid revision in the event of shocks to previously established world-views. If investment decisions and appropriate levels of corporate indebtedness are correspondingly based upon expectations which are conventional, then market economies may be subject to periodic bouts of euphoria, followed by panics and widespread distress as commodities are devalued.

Economic history suggests that financial markets have been subject to considerable instability and that real economic instability has often been the result, which undermines the view of von Hayek that market economies are stable if only they are left alone.[41] It would also seem to be true that monetary management by central banks has been important in alleviating some of these tendencies to instability, or at least their consequences. The severe financial and economic instability experienced by the US economy compared to the British economy from the 1870s until World War II was probably due in part to the virtual absence in the US of a central bank along the lines of the Bank of England.[42]

The history of central banking has shown, however, that the ability of the central bank to manage the monetary system is much more difficult than many have assumed. The major debates between economists have centred around the question of whether the central bank has control over the total supply of money and credit in the economy. This is particularly crucial for the Monetarist view that monetary stability will follow from the central bank's adoption of a fixed growth-rate rule for the aggregate money supply.[43] The rationale for this policy prescription has rested upon their assertion that the aggregate demand for money is a stable function of a few major variables and that it has been fluctuations in the money *supply* rather than in money demand which account for changes in output and nominal incomes.[44]

This contention, among others, has been subject to growing criticism.

40 The theory of hegemonic stability and monetary order

In recent years, there is increasing evidence that previously observed long run stability in the aggregate demand for money function for major economies such as the US and UK has broken down. This coincided with a burst of financial innovation on the part of financial intermediaries as well as changes in policy on the part of the monetary authorities.[45]

The breakdown of the demand for money function defined as sterling M_3 (which includes all bank deposits, including CDs [Certificates of Deposit] and time deposits, held by UK residents and companies) is illustrative. Previous econometric studies had indicated a clear negative relationship between the demand for money (of all forms) and the general level of interest rates. These studies prompted the Bank of England in the early 1970s to adopt a policy of targeting M_3, rather than relying on a previous policy of discount rate manipulation and direct controls upon bank credit which was seen to have failed.[46] A strong demand for credit would in theory place pressure upon bank reserves, which should encourage banks to increase the (normally) positive differential of lending over deposit rates. This should reduce the demand for bank advances whilst at the same time the rising general level of interest rates should re-establish banks' portfolio equilibrium by attracting additional funds in wholesale deposit markets. In the context of monetary targeting, increased reliance upon the price mechanism would, it was thought, allow the market to establish its own equilibrium.[47]

What the Bank did not bargain upon was that aggressive competition amongst banks for loan business would push lending rates close to and sometimes below yields on wholesale deposits. The demand for bank advances showed evidence of being highly interest inelastic, leading commercial banks to maintain high interest rates on CDs in order to attract funds to satisfy reserve requirements. At times the differential between lending and deposit rates became negative, so that companies could make an arbitrage profit by borrowing from banks and re-lending to them in the CD market at a slightly higher rate. In such circumstances, the demand for loans became potentially infinite. The Bank experienced a serious loss of control over 1973 as the banks' prime lending rate rose from $8\frac{1}{2}$ per cent in January to 14 per cent in November, without any decline in the growth of bank lending. This eventually forced the adoption of direct credit controls in the form of the 'corset'.

The breakdown which occurred in the broader demand for money functions did not occur to the same extent in the narrower monetary aggregates such as M_1 (consisting of currency in circulation and demand deposits). This led some economists to argue that the greater stability of the demand for narrow 'transactions money' balances implied that

M_1 rather than M_3 would be a better target for policy. Most economists were sceptical of the value of controlling a monetary aggregate which had little relation to the expansion of credit in modern economies and limited real economic significance.[48] The increasing ease of shifting funds between demand and time deposits suggested that controlling M_1 would in any case hardly be a simple matter. The general lesson of monetary targeting in the UK in the 1970s is that when the authorities attempted to exploit an 'established' empirical relationship for policy purposes, the growing ability of banks and their customers to engage in asset and liability management in a deregulated financial system led to the breakdown of the empirical relationship. Attempts to control the growth of one particular kind of monetary asset leads to changes in the behaviour of private agents which either undermines the usefulness of the monetary target or renders the empirical relation upon which the target was based redundant. This tendency has become known in the literature as 'Goodhart's Law', which implies, contrary to the Monetarist position, that there are no empirical laws which are reducible to fixed policy rules in a financial system in which actors have a substantial freedom to innovate.[49]

American experience in the 1970s supports this interpretation. The Federal Reserve under Chairman Arthur Burns shifted toward a policy of targeting monetary aggregates in early 1970, though sluggish growth over 1970–1 also made the authorities reluctant to increase interest rates.[50] At the same time as the shift in policy-thinking, there were a series of innovations in financial markets which, as in the UK, tended to render the demand for credit increasingly interest-inelastic. The banks' move to floating-rate loan contracts in response to rising inflation and interest rate volatility was thought to shift the interest risk onto borrowers, but may also have led borrowers to continue to borrow at high levels when interest rates rose above 'normal' levels, on the expectation that they would be likely to fall in the future. The rise of financial futures also helped major borrowers to reduce the interest rate risk attached to borrowing by shifting the risk to others more willing to bear it. Inflation and changing postwar attitudes to indebtedness may have also played their part in reducing the interest-sensitivity of the demand for credit.

Continuing high demand for credit at higher interest rates led American banks like their British counterparts to meet their reserve requirements by borrowing in the interbank or CD markets. The existence of interest rate ceilings in many of these markets, however, periodically jeopardised their ability to raise sufficient funds to match their growing loan business. In 1973, rising interest rates on other deposits threatened to cripple the regulated CD market upon which commercial banks were increasingly reliant. The authorities reacted by lifting interest ceilings on CDs, enabling banks to compete aggressively for wholesale funds. As in the UK, perverse shifts occurred in the relationship between broad money aggregates and the general level of interest rates: the banks' prime lending rate increased from 6 per cent to $9\frac{1}{2}$ per cent from April to August, whilst credit expansion accelerated.[51]

Such acts of deregulation could not be insulated from the rest of the financial system. Retaining limits on interest rates for the deposits of non-bank financial institutions would only threaten them with wholesale disintermediation when the general level of interest rates rose sufficiently high, as happened over 1978–80. Again, the response of the authorities was to enable these institutions to compete with banks in the wholesale funds markets, by allowing them to issue six-month Money Market Certificates. Despite significant increases in interest rates, credit expansion reached an annual rate of around 20 per cent in 1979 and inflation rose, leading the Federal Reserve under its new chairman Paul Volcker to announce the adoption of a policy of 'strict' control of monetary growth regardless of the required increase in interest rates. The expansion of credit remained strong into early 1980 and inflation continued to accelerate, eventually forcing the Fed to impose direct controls on bank lending, leading to an immediate credit squeeze.[52]

In both the UK and US, the ultimate resort to direct credit controls was due to a dynamic relationship between financial innovation and deregulation. This significantly undermined the control over credit creation which the monetary authorities had traditionally possessed due to their ability to determine the general level of interest rates. As Wojnilower noted:

> No doubt there exist interest rate levels high enough to curb private credit demand, but the experience of the [1970s and] 1980s to date, featuring good times and bad, and intervals of double-digit as well as zero inflation, suggest that they lie well above the range of recent observation.[53]

Recent experience of monetary targeting in the major economies has led some Monetarists to retreat to a more basic position: that the central bank can in the last resort control the aggregate amount of its outstanding liabilities to the financial system, the monetary base (M_b).

There are a number of problems with this position. Not only is the relationship between M_b and the money supply (M_s) potentially unstable, but the central bank is also unlikely to be able to manipulate the monetary base as it pleases. There are several factors in the determination of M_b that lie beyond the control of the central bank. When the government is financing a deficit through the sale of Treasury bonds, any policy of refusal by the central bank to 'accommodate' credit expansion by its own open market operations does not prevent banks from asking the Treasury to reimburse maturing bond issues. This may allow banks in general (some will borrow via the interbank market) to obtain the required reserves on loans that they will have already made, whilst the Treasury's credit position at the Federal Reserve or the Bank of England will be reduced.[54] Also, under fixed exchange rates and currency convertibility, a restrictive monetary policy may be offset by foreign exchange inflows. Even under a regime of floating exchange rates, foreign exchange inflows may still constitute a source of change in the monetary base if the central bank intervenes to prevent excessive appreciation of the exchange rate and fails to fully 'sterilise' purchases of foreign exchange by financing them through the issue of a debt instrument not included in the monetary base.[55]

The lagged accounting basis upon which required reserves are calculated also means that banks tend first to make loans and then go about finding the funds with which to meet reserve requirements. They do this either by attracting sufficient deposits, borrowing in the interbank market, selling Treasury bonds, or in the last resort borrowing directly from the central bank's 'discount window'. This process is the reverse of that implied by the money multiplier approach, which sees banks as passively accepting deposits which they then loan out to others, and ignores the importance of liability management for banks and other financial institutions. The direction of causation is therefore likely to run from bank deposits to reserves (M_s to M_b) rather than vice versa.

Most importantly, the central bank will be unlikely to refuse to provide the financial system with the base money necessary for its continued solvency. To refuse to do so would seriously disrupt the whole financial system.[56] Of course, it may attempt to influence the lending policy of banks in the first place by less formal means (the 'nods and winks' for which the Bank of England is renowned), but this is something else altogether. In situations of imperfect information, there is unlikely to be any wholly objective means by which appropriate levels of indebtedness can be decided. Expectations regarding future business prospects will have a major impact upon the willingness of firms to go into debt and the desire of banks to lend to them and find the means of financing it.[57] Bank lending and levels of indebtedness, as historical experience has shown, can be subject to waves of euphoria followed by sharp curtailment.

2.6 Conclusion

If the central bank is unlikely to wish to force the banks and the government into default, what constitutes its power? As long as it retains a monopoly on the issue of base money within the financial system, the necessity for banks to maintain the convertibility of their own money into central bank money enables it to determine the price at which it supplies reserves to the banking system. This in turn enables it to influence the *general* level of interest rates throughout the economy.

The cost of funds to non-government borrowers is determined by an appropriate spread over the basic cost of funds, approximated in most economies by the yield on government debt of different maturities (the government being the privileged borrower in the financial system). Spreads over Treasuries (to use the US term) for borrowers in capital markets (from the 'triple-A' rated to less creditworthy firms and banks) will be determined by general investor confidence in the quality of their earnings, the investors' own desire to hold 'cash' and an allowance for transactions costs. For bank-intermediated lending, banks will lend to clients on a spread over their own cost of funds. Other financial intermediaries will specialise so as to reduce informational costs, such as building societies or thrifts which pool depositors' savings (for which they compete with banks) and use them for mortgage lending. Similarly, the cost of funds for borrowers will be determined by spreads over financial intermediaries' own borrowing costs, the spreads being a function of creditworthiness and liquidity considerations as well as transactions costs.[58]

As the central bank pushes up the cost of reserves, the whole spectrum of interest rates in the financial system also move up, depending on spreads, which will be significantly influenced by the general level of expectations. Banks with reserve:deposit ratios lower than that required by the authorities will normally be able to borrow funds from the interbank market at the going rate, as long as they are seen as 'solvent'. The ease with which solvent banks are able to obtain funds by this process of redistribution within the banking system and above all the price at which they do so is largely determined by the policy of the central bank.

Particular banks may at times lose access to the interbank market, such as the Franklin National Bank did in the US in 1974. Difficulties experienced by large banks can have significant externalities, such as resulting in runs on other banks in the system, leading to difficulties for borrowers in general, often forcing the central bank to intervene. In the case of Franklin National, the Fed was forced to lend directly to the bank through its discount window.[59]

Crises may also develop in which there is a large shift of funds away from particular kinds of institutions, such as the UK fringe banking crisis and the problems of the US real estate investment trusts in 1974, and the present widespread insolvency of US thrift institutions. In order to prevent liquidity problems spreading to the rest of the financial system, central banks, large banks and sometimes governments have often been required to step in to refinance the institutions or to protect depositors' funds.

Finally, a major shock to the general level of confidence in the economy might lead the central bank to act to prevent a general liquidity crisis in the financial system. The response of the Federal Reserve and other major central banks to inject liquidity into national banking systems in the wake of the global stock market crash of October 1987 is a good example of such a systemic operation. The absence of such lender of last resort intervention, especially in the US, was striking in the aftermath of the 1929 stock market crash, and was probably a major cause of the length and depth of the Great Depression which followed.[60]

While central banks (and governments) may be able to prevent full-blown financial crises of this kind, their role as lender of last resort is not without its drawbacks. The first has usually been described as the problem of 'moral hazard'. In providing the public good of preventing important financial actors from collapse, central banks may encourage free-riding behaviour from institutions which increases the fragility of the financial system as a whole. Banks which have avoided risky strategies and accepted lower returns may be unfairly penalised if others which realised higher returns by pursuing excessively risky strategies end up having their asset values underwritten by the central bank.

If large banks who are market leaders pursue aggressive lending strategies, smaller banks may be dragged along behind them, either due to a fear of losing market share or because of the costliness of information on the relative riskiness of different lending strategies. Small banks may also calculate that in the event that their solvency comes into question, the best protection against being left to fail by a central bank is to minimise the extent to which they deviate from the norm. These factors may encourage the development of patterns of herd behaviour in financial markets, exacerbating the problem of moral hazard and greatly reducing the central bank's ability to control the rate of credit creation.

A related consequence of the lender of last resort role of central banks is that by preventing financial crisis and cumulative bankruptcies, they tend to increase the inflation-proneness of the economy as a whole. This is compounded by the role of the government in its tendency to run deficits in economic downturns and act as a 'borrower of last resort'.[61] The central bank can force up interest rates to restrain credit creation, but it cannot squeeze too tightly for fear of precipitating widespread bankruptcies. Economic agents increasingly rule out debt-deflation of the 1930s kind as a likely outcome and adjust their behaviour accordingly.

The dilemmas of monetary policy create the need for a vital additional tool: the ability to supervise and regulate financial markets and intermediaries.[62] Because lender of last resort intervention is costly, authorities need to try to develop rules and guidelines which, without being onerous or excessively inequitable, discourage actions on the part of financial actors that are incompatible with their level of reserves or with the prudent management of their capital. Although this is a demanding task, it is nevertheless crucial to financial and monetary stability. 'Supervision' includes guidance of the 'nods and winks' variety and cannot be reducible to the mere enforcement of rules. This underlines the point that central banking is an art analogous to diplomacy, rather than a rule-based science. Regulators also need to be flexible in the face of change. New rules must be rapidly devised when old ones are made redundant by innovation or past deregulation.

The 1970s and 1980s have shown that financial deregulation and innovation can combine to produce destabilising situations in which central bank control over the financial system is severely reduced. Inadequate regulations for international commercial bank lending to developing countries in the late 1970s and early 1980s and governing the activities of thrifts in the US led to situations in which whole categories of financial intermediaries became either insolvent or dangerously exposed. History shows that competitive financial markets do not ensure stability; such stability can be encouraged by a combination of prudent monetary policy and regulation.

We have seen that there are strong forces which tend to create hierarchy in financial systems, both in geographic terms and in terms of their organisational structure. The development of financial hierarchy is often highly influenced by political authorities, as in the classic case of the rise of the Bank of England to a pre-eminent role in the English financial system, though this may not always be the case. What does seem clear is that any monetary management role which a central bank might play is intimately connected with its position at the top of the financial hierarchy. We also argued that monetary and financial stability is not likely to be either the outcome of a free interplay of market forces or due to the mere existence of a central bank attempting to follow a steady growth-rate rule for the money supply. Discretionary monetary management, which includes prudential supervision and regulation of financial markets, is a complex task but an important ingredient for stability in modern economies.

This is important for our understanding of the relationship between hegemony and the stability of the international monetary system. To the extent that the hegemon provides stability by managing the international monetary system, it presumably would do so by intervening on an international level in a manner similar to that of the central bank in a domestic monetary system. The argument also presumes that the hegemon has an ability to do so because of its dominant position in the world financial hierarchy. It follows that international monetary disorder is the product of the erosion of this dominant position and consequently in its ability and willingness to provide the public good of monetary management. This is implicit in Benjamin Cohen's argument that:

> the world monetary order has gone through two complete life cycles over the course of the last century . . . In each of the two cycles the monetary order was effectively organised around a single hegemonic country . . . Likewise, in each of the two cycles the managerial role of the dominant power was eventually undermined by the emergence of economic and political rivals; in each case, the fate of the monetary order was sealed when the hegemony underlying it became an anachronism.[63]

The problem with much international relations writing in this area is that it is very vague as to the role hegemony is meant to play in the establishment and management of the international monetary system. In the following chapter, we turn to consider how a hegemon might actively manage the international monetary and financial system, and in what such management would consist.

Notes

1. Postan, 1964a, p.3.
2. *ibid.*, Hicks, 1969, p.66; Braudel, 1981a, pp.436–8.
3. See Ernest Mandel, introduction to Marx, 1976, p.79. Mandel denies that Marx (and therefore himself) had a state theory of money, but in this passage he comes close enough to asserting one, as does Strange, 1982, p.80. For a discussion, see von Hayek, 1976, pp.21–32.
4. Hicks, 1969, pp.88–92.
5. Postan, 1964b. Barter as a form of economic exchange did not generally recede as time marched on; rather, barter transactions have fluctuated dramatically in their prominence over the centuries, never being entirely eliminated, and often springing into action in periods of wartime or when a currency shortage forced an economisation on cash transactions.

6. Braudel, 1981a, p.470.
7. Postan, 1964a, p.4.
8. Kennedy, 1988, p.76
9. Tawney, 1977, p.87.
10. Quoted in Braudel, 1981b, p.545.
11. An example of Gresham's Law, that 'bad money drives out good into hoarding or export'.
12. Tawney, 1977, pp.87–8.
13. Hicks, 1969, pp.85–7; Braudel, 1981a, p.393.
14. Kindleberger, 1984, p.159; Kennedy, 1988, p.78.
15. Dickson, 1967; Kindleberger, 1984, ch.9; Kennedy, 1988, pp.76–86.
16. Mathias, 1969, pp.165–6.
17. Kennedy, 1988, pp.80–2.
18. Mathias, 1969, pp.167–71.
19. *ibid.*, p.169; Kindleberger, 1984, p.78.
20. Kindleberger, 1974, pp.14–17.
21. Kindleberger, 1984, pp.84–5.
22. See the general discussion in Kindleberger, 1974.
23. *ibid.*, pp.52–5.
24. *ibid.*
25. de Cecco, 1974, pp.79–83.
26. Kindleberger, 1984, p.77.
27. See Hawtrey, 1962, ch.4.
28. See Thornton, 1962 [1802], pp.40ff, and p.236; Ricardo, 1951 [1811], pp.94–9.
29. The Bank's notes had in fact become legal tender under the terms of the 1833 Bank Act, but this merely recognised what was already practical reality.
30. Hicks, 1967, p.169.
31. Mathias, 1969, pp.356–7; Kindleberger, 1984, pp.91–2.
32. Hicks, 1969, pp.95–6.
33. Triffin, 1968, p.20.
34. For a classic statement, see Hawtrey, 1938, p.92. See also Kindleberger, 1984, pp.68–70. The Bank's discount rate policy and its role in monetary stabilisation will be examined in more detail in Chapter 4.
35. See Friedman, 1960, p.7. In Patinkin's famous exposition (1965, pp.302, 591–4), only the existence of 'outside' or central bank money ensures the existence of a real balance effect and the existence of monetary equilibrium. For an exposition of the money multiplier analysis, see Niehans, 1978, pp.272–7.
36. von Hayek, 1976, pp.13,73–4.
37. Keynes, *CW*, vol.XIV, p.116.
38. Keynes, *CW*, vol.XIV, pp.112–13. See also 1936, p.148, and his *Treatise on Probability: CW*, vol.VIII, ch.6. For a discussion, see Shackle, 1967, ch.11; Vicarelli, 1985.
39. Frank Knight made very similar points about the distinction between probabilistic risk and the fundamental uncertainty involved in business decisions in his *Risk, Uncertainty and Profit* (1921). Hence the widespread use of the term 'Knight-Keynes' uncertainty.
40. Keynes, 1936, pp.156–7. See also Grandmont and Malgrange, 1986, p.8; Hahn, 1984, pp.123–4.

41. See Kindleberger, 1978a, pp.47–60.
42. See de Cecco, 1984, pp.19–23.
43. See Goodhart, 1984, pp.186–7.
44. Friedman and Schwartz, 1963; Laidler, 1982, ch.1.
45. See in general, Goodhart, 1984; Lamfalussy, 1985; Wojnilower, 1980, and 1985.
46. Goodhart, 1984, pp.150–81.
47. *ibid.*, pp.82–4.
48. On this point see Thomas, 1981, pp.118–22; Wojnilower, 1980, p.324; Lamfalussy, 1981, pp.45–50.
49. Goodhart, 1984, p.110; Lamfalussy, 1985.
50. Wojnilower, 1980, pp.292–4.
51. *ibid.*, p.297; Minsky, 1986, ch.4.
52. Wojnilower, 1980, p.306; Aglietta and Orléan, 1984, pp.300–1.
53. Wojnilower, 1985, p.352.
54. Thomas, 1981, pp.128–33. Portfolio adjustments leading to changes in the public's holding of non-marketable debt in the form of savings bonds and certificates can also result in uncontrollable movements in the monetary base. See Goodhart, 1984, ch.6.
55. Interest rate effects will probably mean that there are in any case limits to the extent to which sterilisation can be utilised, especially if they lead to increases in interest rates on the instruments used to purchase the foreign exchange, which serve in turn to attract further capital inflows.
56. Goodhart, 1984, p.211.
57. Stiglitz and Weiss, 1981; Blinder and Stiglitz, 1983.
58. This is also true in theory for the cost of equity to firms, since equity prices should be inversely related to a discount rate representing a basic borrowing rate plus a significant spread for the greater illiquidity of equities.
59. Carron, 1982, p.399. See also Goodhart, 1986a; Minsky, 1982, introduction.
60. Bernanke, 1983.
61. Minsky, 1982, pp.xix–xx.
62. See Marquardt, 1987; BIS, 1986.
63. Cohen, 1977, p.105.

Chapter 3
Hegemony and international monetary order

3.1 Introduction

Having established that central banks can play a decisive management role in domestic economies, we turn to consider how hegemony might play a similar role in the international monetary system. In order to do so, we need to decide whether in fact the international monetary system requires management in the same way as the domestic one, and if so, what form this should take.

Conceivably, the management required on the international level might be minimal if *domestic* economies were managed and an appropriate 'linking mechanism' between national monetary systems were established (such as a system of flexible exchange rates). Stability on the international level could then be the product of stability at the domestic level. Hegemony might play a useful role by ensuring the smooth operation of the linking mechanism (the international monetary system), but it would not necessarily need to engage in the same sort of activities as do central banks on the domestic level. The fulfilment of such a role would approximate to what political scientists have termed regime establishment and maintenance.

Alternatively, managed parts may not add up to a stabilised whole, either because of an inadequacy in the linking mechanism or because a high level of interdependence between national economies may make policy formulation at the domestic level exceedingly difficult. Monetary stability would then be more of a top-down rather than a bottom-up phenomenon, and the role of hegemony would conceivably be much greater. Potentially disparate national policies may need to be coordinated and in a highly centralised international monetary system, a hegemon may have to engage in discretionary monetary management of a kind similar to that on the domestic level.

As can be seen, much will depend on the nature of the linking mechanism itself and whether it is appropriate to the degree of interdependence between national economies. This chapter will accordingly approach the question of the role of hegemony by considering different kinds of monetary system, from the least to the most centralised possible. In this way, it is possible to discuss the manner in which monetary and financial instability manifests itself in each type of system and how hegemony might play a stabilising role. Focusing on the adjustment mechanisms at work will also assist our discussion of actual monetary systems in Part II.

We shall begin by considering the argument which rejects even a minimal role for hegemony. The most radical form of this view is von Hayek's notion of a completely 'denationalised' world monetary order, though the Gold Standard and a floating exchange rate system also obtain much of their appeal because they deny a role for international monetary management. Whether it is possible to envisage a more extensive hegemonic role in the international monetary system depends considerably upon the shortcomings of these proposals for world monetary order.

3.2 The critics of internationally managed money

The 'denationalisation' of money

As we have seen, von Hayek strenuously rejected any role for public authority in monetary affairs, and this extends to the international level. Doing away with the central bank monopoly on the issue of currency would take the world back to a system to some extent similar to that which operated in Europe prior to the development of central banks. In such a world, private monies issued by individual banks would compete alongside each other, circulating irrespective of national borders amongst individual agents who had confidence in their underlying worth. While individual banks may overissue notes and become insolvent, transnational competition between banks will be sufficient to produce world monetary order.[1]

Vaubel has put forward a similar proposal for 'competing currencies', which would allow economic agents to open bank accounts, denominate contracts and conduct everyday business in whichever currency they would care to choose. Governments should only be permitted to borrow from private capital markets on an equal basis with other borrowers, while central banks should refrain from lender of last resort intervention and allow exchange rates to freely fluctuate. The basic idea is that by removing the central bank monopoly upon note issue in national economies, inflation would be eradicated by placing pressure upon issuers of currency to maintain its scarcity.[2]

The basic problem with such proposals is that they recommend a radical transformation in the financial structure of most modern economies. They aim quite explicitly at the dissolution of the financial hierarchy in which the central bank and the government (as the privileged borrower from the banking system) occupy pre-eminent positions. Of course, states will be highly unlikely to give up their monopoly over the issue of base money and their ability to borrow from the banking system, because it constitutes the basis of their financial power. Lurking behind the superficial optimism of von Hayek and his followers that abolishing financial hierarchy would solve the problem of global monetary order is a more fundamental pessimism that disorder will persist because of the unwillingness of states to relinquish their financial dominance. Ironically, this view ends up concluding with the Marxists that the instability of modern capitalism is ineradicable, though for different reasons.

There is also good reason to believe that this pessimism is misplaced. History, as has already been pointed out, does not demonstrate the validity of the view that competitive currencies ensure stability. Speculative excess followed by panics and crashes has marked financial history from long before the relatively recent acquisition of a monopoly on the issue of paper money by central banks. The Dutch tulip mania of 1636–7 and the subsequent crash is but one of many examples.[3] Such fluctuations were not simply the result of a miscalculation on the part of individual banks or investors, but the most serious of them were due to a generalised tendency for expectations to undergo marked shifts from euphoria to panic.

The problem for the Hayekian view is that not only will individual banks periodically be tempted to indulge in excessively risky lending practices, but that there is no guarantee that banks in general will not do so from time to time, with potentially disastrous consequences. Bullish expectations can lead to aggressive competition for market share between banks which can result in the financial system as a whole taking risks which in more sober periods are seen as excessive. In other words, there is 'an expectations coordination problem that cannot be solved efficiently by the market's invisible hand'.[4]

Von Hayek overlooks this problem in asserting that under a system of global free banking, a generalised panic and commodity price deflation would be impossible because issuing banks would have an interest in maintaining the profitability of their assets by making emergency loans to solvent borrowers.[5] This ignores the possibility that a major shock to expectations may dramatically change the very definition of solvency. In a highly developed international interbank market of the kind that exists today, 'solvency' problems in one segment of the market could easily raise doubts about the solvency of other actors. As other agents scrambled to possess monies of the highest quality, unless those banks whose liabilities were in greatest demand provided sufficient liquidity to all agents seeking it, it seems unlikely that a general deflation could be avoided.

Would the operation of the price mechanism ensure that such high quality monies would always be in sufficient supply? This may not be the case if these banks perceive an interest in allowing their monies to appreciate in value or (as may be more likely) if they have difficulty in finding enough creditworthy borrowers. The further likelihood that in the event of a major shock to expectations financial markets will be subject to herd behaviour leads one to be sceptical of the claim that sufficient liquidity would be available in all circumstances. As happened with the Bank of England and the Bank of France in the nineteenth century, some issuing banks may have an interest in allowing competitors which run into difficulties to go bankrupt, which could have negative consequences for the stability of the system as a whole.[6] As with public goods in general, there may not be sufficient incentive for the market to undertake a lender of last resort role itself.

Although the case for the denationalisation of money is flawed, it does not follow that some kind of management role is required on the international level. Domestic central banks may in principle be capable of acting as a lender of last resort in financial markets which fall under their own jurisdiction and managing their domestic monetary systems adequately. International monetary order may simply follow from the adherence on the part of domestic central banks to a strong external constraint which lies beyond political manipulation. This is the argument for the international Gold Standard.

The international Gold Standard

The international monetary system which arose in the three or so decades prior to the World War I and which is commonly referred to as the international Gold Standard (GS) continues to exercise a powerful grip upon the imagination of those who take an interest in world monetary reform. The idea that a system based upon gold is both impartial between countries and contains some internal ordering mechanism remains strong today, even if many would argue that it is inappropriate to present circumstances.[7]

The classical advocates of the GS usually made two major arguments in its favour. They asserted that the international adjustment mechanism under the GS is essentially automatic in that international payments imbalances will tend to be eliminated fairly rapidly by gold flows which are their counterpart. A second and connected claim is that the existence of a fixed gold price for domestic currency ensures that central banks which abuse their privileged position by indulging in or permitting inflationary financing will suffer a loss of reserves. The system therefore ensures that the rates of credit creation in the various countries cannot differ significantly over time, and that in the long run world prices will be determined by the quantity of gold in the reserves of central banks.

This argument is often extended to the well-known claim, most associated with de Gaulle, that the GS is politically neutral between states. Countries which have made this argument in the past tend not surprisingly to have been those which have enjoyed a very favourable gold reserve position, such as France and the US in the 1920s and France again in the 1960s.

The claim made for the GS adjustment mechanism is somewhat confusing because there is not one but many different models describing its operation. In the most widely known version, Hume's 'specie-flow mechanism', there are significant problems and inconsistencies.[8] The fundamentals of each model are, however, usually the same: an emphasis on the automaticity of the international adjustment mechanism (possibly supplemented by central bank policy) and an application of the Quantity Theory of money to the world economy. In modern terms, the GS adjustment mechanism is one version of the 'Monetary Theory of the Balance of Payments', where each country fixes its currency in terms of gold and remains willing to buy and sell gold for currency on demand.[9] Gold then represents international money, with fixed exchange rates and full currency convertibility ensuring an approximation to what Kindleberger refers to as the international public good of one global standard of monetary value.[10]

Hume's account concentrated upon the balance of trade, with an exogenous increase in the supply of gold in one country 'A' creating an excess demand for consumption goods as A's residents try to reduce their real money balances. This bids up prices (including wages) in A relative to those in country B, inducing residents of A to import more consumer goods from B. This leads to a trade imbalance (A's deficit to B) equal to the corresponding gold outflow to B, which will work automatically to eliminate the disequilibria in the goods and gold markets. Relative prices will adjust to their former levels as the redistribution of gold causes inflation in B and deflation in A. On the global level, nominal world prices increase in proportion to the change in the total supply of monetary gold.

Hume thereby hoped to demonstrate that the pursuit of a surplus balance of trade was nonsensical; all trade imbalances would be eliminated over time by gold flows which distribute gold reserves in a 'natural' relation to productivities and resource endowments of different countries.[11] However, if the goods produced in A are subject to competition (either as exports or as domestically consumed goods) from those produced in B, why should they not be priced out of the market when domestic prices rise in response to the increase in the money supply? The central problem with Hume's analysis is that it is in tension with another tenet of classical international trade theory, the 'law of one price'. This holds that allowing for such imperfections as tariffs and transport costs, international arbitrage will ensure that the prices of goods and gold will be equalised in different countries.

As theorists of the Monetary Approach have stressed, the assumption of perfect arbitrage in international markets must mean that relative prices are determined on world markets and the nominal price level by the world supply of gold. In that case, prices are exogenous to any one country (assuming it is 'small') and the GS adjustment mechanism cannot operate through any movement of relative national price levels. It has often been argued that the initial upward movement of consumer good prices in A could rest on the assumption that there are a significant number of goods which are 'non-tradeable' at present exchange rates, such that an increase in the money supply can lead to relative price movements of the kind Hume wrote about.[12] If an increase in the relative prices of non-tradeables *vis-à-vis* tradeable goods leads to a shift of domestic resources towards production of the former category of commodities, A's trade deficit with B will be correspondingly reduced and the international adjustment process will be slower than it would otherwise be.

Relative price movements are not even required for a specie-flow mechanism to operate, given the usual Quantity Theory assumptions. Increasing the gold supply in A will lead residents to undertake consumption expenditure in excess of their incomes from production, which will create a trade deficit with B and an outflow of gold. Long run equilibrium will be restored when nominal cash balances reach their desired level, but all along international arbitrage assures that the law of one price holds.[13]

The model can easily be extended to include capital account transactions. An excess supply of money implies excess demand for goods, financial assets and gold, leading to an overall balance of payments deficit. For those who adopt the Monetary Approach, an excess supply of money in one country is not likely to be absorbed by an increase in the general level of domestic prices or even an adjustment on current account, but rather by an outflow of short-term capital and hence monetary reserves towards those countries in which there is an excess demand for money. With free capital movements, the national money supply would become completely endogenous, with the result that the central bank could not affect domestic prices, interest rates or even incomes, but merely the composition of its own asset portfolio.[14]

In this extreme case, the central bank possesses no influence with respect to the real economy, and real economic equilibrium is determined by forces outside of the monetary sector. The international GS, as an external economic constraint upon national political authority, could prevent inflationary credit creation by the banking system which was accommodated by the central bank. For classical economists, the disappearance of gold as a circulating medium within states was not seen as disastrous for monetary order as long as it remained the basis of the international monetary standard.

This assumed that states would be willing to submit themselves to the 'rule of gold'. This was well-recognised in the interwar period with the spread of the notion of the 'rules of the game', which states ought to observe if the adjustment mechanism was to operate. Bloomfield has argued that there were two aspects to the notion of rules of the game, which arose due to increasing international capital mobility. The first was a negative one, that central banks should allow gold flows to have a full effect on the money supply (i.e. avoid sterilisation). There was also a second, positive sense of the idea, that central banks should reinforce the automatic effects of gold flows on relative prices by appropriate changes in discount rates, affecting international capital flows and the domestic rate of credit expansion by the banking system.[15]

The notion of rules of the game was a belated recognition of the fact that the operation of the international GS could not be viewed in a framework devoid of political assumptions, though it somewhat diminishes the claim for an 'automatic' equilibrating mechanism. If the operation of the GS depends upon the willingness of states to abide by the rules, then the stability or instability of the international monetary system associated with it must derive ultimately from the political rather than the economic realm. Here it is possible to see how hegemony, which could play no stabilising role under the strong form of the GS theory, might play an indirect role by enforcing the rules of the game. This 'enforcement' function of hegemony could serve to foster behaviour consistent with the operation of the international adjustment mechanism.

Proponents of the Monetary Approach have challenged the view that adherence to the rules of the game is important. They argue that if there is a high degree of international capital mobility, sterilisation of capital flows will not work in any case.[16] If the central bank is unable to affect domestic prices, interest rates or incomes, then it can hardly affect the operation of the equilibrating mechanism. It should be apparent that the Monetary Approach relies for its decisive results upon highly restrictive assumptions. Primary among these is the law of one price, a microeconomic assumption which depends upon the extent of international arbitrage in goods, gold and financial markets. As market imperfections such as tariffs, non-tariff barriers, transactions costs, imperfect information, market 'inertia' and so on are introduced, it becomes less likely to be satisfied. This means in turn that the specie-flow mechanism is itself likely to break down at least to some extent, and that payments imbalances will persist over time.

Further assumptions that are at odds with historical evidence are full employment of resources in the economy and a stable demand for money function. These mean that the supply of and demand for money are equated via the balance of payments and not by changes in the level of national income, so that money is completely neutral with respect to the real economy.[17] The final assumption of interest is that each country is assumed to be sufficiently small so that its monetary authorities have no influence upon world and therefore domestic prices and interest rates. Although it is usually argued that even large countries will suffer capital outflows if they undertake monetary expansion aimed at increasing domestic demand,[18] it does weaken the result that no central bank can influence domestic prices.

Even if we were to accept these assumptions, the result still depends upon the state abiding by the principles of freedom of trade and capital movements and the maintenance of full gold convertibility at the going rate. Clearly, it would be incorrect to argue that the state must accept no constraints upon its actions for the GS adjustment mechanism to operate. The political unreality of the argument for the GS is also apparent in the view that states in the international system will be indifferent to flows of gold. As Keynes pointed out after the collapse of the international GS in the early 1930s, the political and economic uncertainty which pervaded the contemporary international environment led to a natural desire on the part of states to accumulate gold reserves by running an external surplus. The domestic interest rate tended to be directed to the state of the external balance rather than that of the domestic economy, so that the international GS encouraged the adoption of mutually destructive competitive deflationary policies.[19]

In these circumstances, it is difficult to see how a hegemon could play a stabilising role, unless it were willing to run down its own gold reserves in favour of other states during a crisis.[20] The main potential role for hegemony under a pure international GS, therefore, is one largely restricted to establishing and enforcing the rules of the game, enabling the adjustment mechanism to operate. In the event that there is an international scramble for gold, there may be little that a hegemon could do to prevent competitive deflation. At least from an economic perspective, it would appear that hegemony is not likely to be able to offset the potentially dangerous instability at the heart of an international monetary system based upon gold.

Flexible exchange rates

The theories of flexible exchange rates that were developed prior to the 1970s assumed that in a world of low capital market integration, the demand for and supply of currencies would be determined by current trade flows. This meant that exchange rates would adjust automatically to ensure that the monetary value of exports and imports were always equated, or in other words that floating exchange rates would ensure that all countries would remain in current account balance. The 'relative Purchasing Power Parity (PPP) condition would hold, since an increase in the domestic rate of price inflation would encourage imports whilst discouraging exports, leading to an excess supply of the currency in exchange markets and a compensating depreciation of the exchange rate which would restore current balance.[21]

A further assumption was that exchange rates would adjust quickly and smoothly towards their equilibrium value, so that current account imbalances under a flexible exchange rate system would be short-lived. This meant in turn that the holding of foreign exchange reserves by central banks would become largely unnecessary. Intervention in exchange markets to prop up an exchange rate inconsistent with market equilibrium (as tended to happen under a pegged exchange rate system) would ultimately be self-defeating and give private speculators a sure bet.

Domestic economies would be 'insulated' from monetary shocks emanating from abroad, since nominal exchange rates would adjust to leave real exchange rates unchanged. Flexible exchange rates would give a country an extra degree of freedom in choosing its domestic macroeconomic policy mix and its own inflation-unemployment trade-off. Applying the principles of free market economics to the inter-

Hegemony and international monetary order 59

national monetary system would ensure that the pursuit of private (national) interest would be consistent with the (international) public good. As Harry Johnson wrote in 1969:

> The fundamental argument for flexible exchange rates is that they would allow countries autonomy with respect to their use of monetary, fiscal and other policy instruments, consistent with the maintenance of whatever degree of freedom in international transactions they choose to allow their citizens, by automatically ensuring the preservation of external equilibrium.[22]

The model of flexible exchange rates upon which such predictions were based was subject to substantial shortcomings. The assumption that exchange rates will move quickly to remove current account imbalances was hardly justified. Even if it could be assumed that exchange rates would move to maintain PPP in the long run,[23] there is no reason to expect that trade volumes would react quickly to changes in the terms of trade. Much would depend upon the price elasticities of demand for exports and imports; as people were to realise in the 1970s, there might be a perverse effect for a substantial period of time if these elasticities were low (the 'J-curve effect').[24]

Once allowance is made for capital account as well as current account flows, the possibility arises that current account surpluses or deficits can be sustained over time rather than necessarily being eliminated by exchange rate adjustments. The 'equilibrium' current account position for a country will then depend upon its propensity to trade off present and future consumption. The model which emerged and upon which subsequent developments in exchange rate theory and open-economy macroeconomics have been largely based was the Mundell–Fleming model. The main implications of this model were for the appropriate policy mix: in contrast to a fixed exchange rate regime, it was argued that under a regime of flexible exchange rates, monetary policy would gain in power whilst fiscal policy would be completely 'crowded out'. Concerning the stability of a floating exchange rate system there was little doubt.[25]

Experience in the 1970s with considerable volatility in exchange markets led to a modification of the Mundell–Fleming model which has come to dominate the literature in recent years. This was the 'asset market approach', which along with much contemporary macroeconomic theory introduced rational expectations into its framework.[26] The key element is a familiar one in monetary theory: the determination of the conditions for equilibrium in individuals' asset portfolios. If these portfolios consist of assets denominated in different currencies, expectations of exchange rate movements will lead to portfolio

60 The theory of hegemonic stability and monetary order

adjustment. It is assumed that the domestic interest rate must equal the foreign interest rate (assumed exogenous) plus a premium which equals the expected future depreciation of the domestic currency (the so-called interest rate parity condition).

Under the further assumption that adjustment in goods markets is slow while that in financial markets is instantaneous, this model has been used to explain the phenomenon of 'overshooting' of the exchange rate from its long run equilibrium value. An unexpected loosening of monetary policy will create additional stocks of assets denominated in a particular currency. For these to be held willingly, there must be an expectation on the part of individuals that they will be compensated in the future by a capital gain due to an appreciation of the exchange rate. The currency must therefore depreciate by an amount greater than the change in the nominal equilibrium exchange rate so as to create the expectation of a future appreciation. Due to the interest rate parity condition (equivalent to rational expectations), the domestic interest rate must fall, though will gradually converge to the world level as the domestic price of non-tradeable goods rises and the real exchange rate returns to its original value. How much the exchange rate depreciates will depend upon whether the monetary expansion is seen to be a one-off phenomenon (in which case the overshooting will be small and reversed in the next period) or whether it is expected to continue or even accelerate.

It is not clear what role if any the asset market approach allows for the current account or for PPP. Current account imbalances may create expectations of a changing distribution of global wealth in the long run, leading to portfolio adjustment and exchange rate changes. Some authors have seen current account balance as the only plausible long run equilibrium position.[27] This is important because it bears on the question of what is the long run equilibrium exchange rate for any particular currency. If current account balance represents external equilibrium, the equilibrium exchange rate will be that which produces it over the long run. Others such as Williamson argue that the long run or 'fundamental equilibrium exchange rate' (FEER) is that rate:

> which is expected to generate a current account surplus or deficit equal to the underlying capital flow over the cycle, given that the country is pursuing 'internal balance' as best it can and not restricting trade for balance of payments reasons.[28]

The essential problem is that not even economists, let alone market participants, know the correct model of the world economy, so that there is significant uncertainty about the value of the long run equilibrium exchange rate for any country. As Dornbusch has argued:

[there is a] possibility that exchange rates, in part, are determined by irrelevant information. Market participants may have the wrong model of fundamentals, and their expectations, based on the wrong model, will affect the actual exchange rate . . . This point is important because market participants may be impressed by a plausible fundamental variable, attribute explanatory power to it, and, consequently, make their expectations actually come true . . . It is important to recognise this, because in the past economists may have given excessive weight to the notion that the market knows 'the model' and, at the same time, is rational.[29]

As was argued in Chapter 2, even if agents are assumed to be rational, the conventionality of expectations may mean that exchange rates along with other asset prices are subject to considerable instability. This may be exacerbated by the fact that private banks and firms often hedge exchange rate risk and in trading are focused on very short term movements. Long-term 'fundamentals' are therefore of limited importance for market participants. In contrast to Friedman's famous contention that exchange rate speculation will be stabilising on average, there is likely to be a shortage of stabilising speculators in the market at any one time.[30] Speculative bubbles and herd behaviour in exchange markets may result in persistent misalignment of exchange rates from fundamentals. While the existence of forward, swaps, options and futures markets may help offset to some extent the risk involved in transactions involving floating exchange rates, this is only likely to be the case for discrete transactions rather than for flows of expenditure and sales. Many of these markets are in any case likely to be incomplete and/or costly, which means that private and public actors in open economies will still face considerable costs if exchange rates do exhibit instability and a tendency to misalignment.[31]

Empirical studies of the post-1973 period have shown that exchange rate movements have been largely unanticipated by the market, nor reflected in interest rate differentials or forward rates, contrary to the predictions of the asset market approach.[32] The evidence is also inconsistent with the model's predictions of virtually instantaneous jumps of exchange rates in response to unanticipated policy news, followed by a steady return to equilibrium levels. The continued rise of the dollar from 1981 to 1985 suggests both considerable inertia in expectations and the possibility that a speculative bubble built up by 1984, when it was clear to market participants that the dollar was already beyond sustainable levels. The 'anchor' of the model, the hypothesised real equilibrium exchange rate, seems to have itself been constantly revised as the actual exchange rate changed.[33]

If the market cannot be relied upon to provide its own stable anchor

62 The theory of hegemonic stability and monetary order

for expectations, there is an *a priori* case for either controls upon capital flows, or for concerted intervention in exchange markets by central banks and an unambiguous line on appropriate exchange rate patterns from monetary authorities and governments.[34] The former is in conflict with the strong presumption in economic theory that freedom of capital movements is desirable on efficiency grounds, as well as the difficulty of implementing capital controls in practice. The second, by providing an external anchor for expectations, may help stabilise market expectations and prevent the build-up of large current account imbalances due to persistent misalignments of exchange rates. As many have pointed out in recent years, any such policies on the part of authorities must be credible and will require both domestic and international economic policies consistent with desired exchange rate patterns.

There are considerable doubts as to whether a system of pegged exchange rates is compatible with national economic policy-making in conjunction with high levels of international financial integration. If market sentiment sees a contradiction between the configuration of national policies and a particular matrix of fixed exchange rates, the ability of central banks to maintain the existing pattern of exchange rates without compromising other policy goals will be very limited. This has led many to suggest that the most that can be attained in a context of high levels of financial integration is a commitment on the part of monetary authorities to 'target zones' for exchange rates with a band of perhaps 20 per cent around agreed central rates.[35] These zones would be used in conjunction with a system of multilateral policy surveillance to prompt changes in policy when exchange rates threatened to move outside the target bands. What must be debatable is whether bands of even ±10 per cent are sufficient to prevent the emergence of unsustainable policies and exchange rates.

The fundamental contradiction, in other words, is between a high degree of international financial integration and national currencies and economic policy-making, which can render *both* a fixed and a flexible system of exchange rates subject to periodic difficulties. A regime of 'fixed' exchange rates requires *de facto* coordination of economic policies in order to make credible a commitment to a particular pattern of cross-rates. A regime of flexible exchange rates is likely to require a more explicit form of policy coordination so as to stabilise market expectations and prevent major misalignments of currencies.

Not surprisingly, many authors have argued that one of the key functions of hegemony, especially under a regime of flexible exchange rates, is to foster such policy coordination. This would involve encouraging other states to adopt policies consistent with the maintenance of exchange rate stability, either through the provision of cooperative regimes or through outright coercion. Given today's levels of financial integration, the required policy coordination and the speed of its implementation is very high indeed, raising the question whether it could ever be adequate. Policy coordination between separate states will always be a slow and inefficient process, no matter how tight the regimes or how dominant the hegemon. The contradiction between high levels of financial integration and monetary decentralisation in the form of national currencies (which makes national economic policy possible), has led some to argue that the only alternative to reducing financial interdependence is to effectively abolish national currencies. This is the argument for a world central bank.

3.3 A world central bank: The case for centralisation

The idea of a world central bank (WCB) as a hypothetical solution to the problem of international monetary organisation has been a reasonably common one in the twentieth century. It is connected with the general tendency since World War I to see supranational institutions as the basis for order in international relations. Since it implicitly places most importance upon the *political* obstacle to international order, as an ideal type it has a considerable importance for discussions of hegemony and monetary stability. This is especially the case for international relations theorists, who tend to adopt a Hobbesian view of order in human relations, whilst economists often see more virtue in decentralisation. Behind much of the literature on the hegemonic stability thesis lies an assumption that a WCB would be a 'first-best' solution to the problem of international monetary order, but that in its absence hegemony is second-best. The case for a WCB is usually founded upon the notion that as in domestic monetary systems, there is some kind of inexorable historical tendency towards increasing levels of centralisation in international monetary organisation. The emergence of a hierarchy in national monetary systems, as in the British case, is seen as logical and necessary of extension to the global level.[36]

Similarly, most objections to the case for a WCB rest upon the argument made against all supranational solutions in world politics, that the 'domestic analogy' is inappropriate because there is no chance that individual states will cede national sovereignty to a supranational organisation.[37] This political objection to the case for a WCB should not obscure the substantial measure of agreement amongst economists and political scientists that a global monetary authority would constitute an *ideal* solution.

As mentioned above, a WCB would eradicate the problem of reconciling financial integration with international monetary decentralisation by effectively eliminating national currencies and central banks, enabling the centralised management of a world fiduciary standard.[38] This may not actually entail the outright abolition of national currencies; national currencies could be convertible into the world fiduciary currency at a fixed rate, which would be almost the same thing. National central banks would then create national credit, on a base of world fiduciary currency, in much the same way that banks do in domestic financial systems today.

As with the case for a central bank in a domestic economy, there are different views about what such management would entail. International Monetarists such as McKinnon argue that increasing levels of international financial integration render domestic Monetarist prescriptions invalid. The possibility of 'currency substitution' means that the demand for domestic currency is potentially unstable, while the global demand for money remains stable. McKinnon therefore argues for exchange rate and coordinated monetary targeting on the part of the major countries, the ideal behind his proposal being one in which a WCB would maintain a fixed rate of growth of the global money supply.[39]

For McKinnon, the source of international monetary disorder derives largely from the unwillingness of sovereign states to subordinate their domestic monetary policy to a consistent global rule. Like domestic Monetarism, it assumes that a fixed rate of growth of the money supply consistent with real economic growth would be sufficient to ensure monetary order. There is no reason, however, why such arguments should be any less problematic when transferred to the global level than they are on the domestic level. There is no good reason to assume that a WCB would be able to control the global rate of credit creation any more than can a domestic central bank, for all the reasons we have already outlined. Others have gone further than McKinnon to argue that a WCB should pursue discretionary monetary policies as well as act as a lender of last resort to the international financial system. As Cohen has written:

> Like a national central bank, the world central bank would perform two essential functions. In the short-term it would be a lender of last resort, providing an elastic supply of reserves ('crisis' liquidity) to governments to finance payments imbalances when and if circumstances warrant. In the long-term it would be a money creator, providing a steady growth of ultimate reserves ('trend' liquidity) to accommodate the needs of the

world economy as a whole. At all times the total stock of international reserves would be determined exclusively by the world central bank.[40]

Cohen's account raises a problem dealt with in the previous chapter but which is often ignored in discussions of world monetary reform. If central banking in general is subject to inherent tensions in its role as guardian of the currency and lender of last resort to the system, the idea that there exists an ultimate solution to the problem of monetary organisation either in domestic or international affairs loses its appeal. There is little recognition of this tension in Cohen's argument that a WCB could simultaneously provide both 'short run' and 'long run' liquidity, thereby producing international monetary order. A connected difficulty with his argument is the idea that the WCB would be able to determine what would in effect constitute the monetary base of the system.

The pressures are likely to be great for the WCB to provide national financial systems with the base money necessary for their continued operation, so that short run and long run liquidity becomes indistinguishable. Even if it could control the world's monetary base, it is unlikely that this would allow it to control global credit creation. This task would be made especially difficult if international banks were permitted to deal in the world fiduciary currency. In addition, a WCB's lender of last resort task would probably be even more difficult than that of a national monetary authority. On what basis should a WCB decide whether to provide crisis liquidity to a particular central or commercial bank which is experiencing financing difficulties? Central banking has an irreducibly subjective aspect, in part because the systemic importance of financial actors must play a part in such decisions. Such issues would be much more contentious on the global level than on the domestic, as the controversy over IMF 'conditionality' indicates.

The tendency to see a WCB as a technocratic solution to the problem of international monetary order overlooks the difficult issue of control over policies. Would these policies be 'democratically' formulated by obtaining a consensus from all countries involved, and if so, would they be at all coherent or sufficiently restrictive? If, on the other hand, policies were determined by the most powerful states in the international system, which would not after all be surprising in view of the history of international organisation, would they be in the interests of the weaker states? Formulating and implementing a *coherent* world monetary policy in the presence of such cultural, political and economic diversity may in fact require some degree of dominance on the part of particular groups or countries. In the end, then, a WCB may in fact be close to hegemony or dominance by a few powers over the international financial system. The likelihood that the dominant state or states within the international system would formulate policy with respect to their own interests rather than those of the whole, means that while this may result in policy coherence, the kind of 'order' provided may not be one in which all states or groups share equally.

3.4 Key currencies and international monetary order

The hegemon is often seen as obtaining the most flexibility in terms of playing a stabilising role in the international monetary system when its currency comes to attain the status of a 'key' currency. In a way analogous to the development of the Bank of England as a central bank in the English monetary system, a dominant role for the key currency country enables it to play a major role in world monetary affairs. It is often argued, for example, that the stability of the Bretton Woods system until the mid-1960s was due to an anti-inflationary monetary standard provided by American monetary policies.[41] Through the role of its currency in the international financial system, Kindleberger has argued that a dominant power ought to provide at least three major international public goods: relatively open markets in a glut, a countercyclical flow of long-term capital and lender-of-last-resort facilities in a financial crisis.[42] Since lender-of-last-resort facilities will raise the problem of moral hazard, an additional hegemonic role consistent with the Keynesian perspective would be the establishment of a regulatory framework for global financial transactions.[43]

Though emphasis has always been upon a key currency's role as a major reserve asset and intervention currency for central banks, more than likely it will also be a major 'vehicle' currency in international trade, in the international interbank market and in the denomination of international debt instruments. This leads to a demand for liquid assets denominated in a key currency above and beyond the direct involvement of the key currency country itself in international trade and capital flows. The state of the exchange markets for key currencies will become dissociated to some extent from the overall payments positions of the key currency countries; it is conceivable that there will be excess demand for a key currency even when the key country's balance of payments is in 'overall deficit'.[44] Portfolio shifts between assets denominated in different key currencies will play a crucial role in determining exchange rate movements as well as changes in central bank reserves.

This dissociation will be all the more prominent if the international banking system is able to grant loans or float bonds in the key currency 'offshore' and if the proceeds are convertible into other key currencies. In such circumstances, international liquidity will become in part *endogenous*: other states in the system may finance payments deficits by borrowing from the international (or transnational) banking system. The extent to which countries are able to gain access to private sources of international liquidity will depend upon their 'creditworthiness', whether international banks are finding it easy to refinance their positions, and finally upon the state of key countries' balance of payments. The latter will affect banks' liquidity as well as that of international investors who may subscribe to international bond issues by sovereign borrowers, and the related factor of the relative ease of credit conditions in key country financial markets will also play an important role.[45]

Historically, as we shall see in following chapters, key currencies have been connected initially with the gold-exchange standard, where the international role of gold is supplemented by one or more national currencies. The importance of the WCB model is clearest in the idea of a 'key currency standard', whose proponents argue that the role of a dominant state in the international financial system is to act as a prototypical central bank for the rest of the world. Finally, we will consider the implications of a 'multi-currency system' (in which a number of key currencies may co-exist) for international monetary stability.

The gold exchange standard

The gold exchange standard (GES) occupies a central place in international monetary history because of its connection with the key currency roles of the pound sterling and US dollar. Arthur Bloomfield defined a GES as a system 'under which the international reserves of a country with fixed (or periodically adjustable) exchange rates are held not only in gold but also in relatively substantial part in short-term claims on foreigners'.[46] This is analogous to the situation which prevailed in England until the late nineteenth century, when commercial banks had come to hold, in addition to gold and silver reserves, liquid claims on the Bank of England.

This analogy should not be pushed too far, since there is a major political obstacle to a transition towards a full gold bullion standard (in which only one central bank holds gold and the rest hold foreign exchange reserves) on the international level. Although metallic money is unwieldy as an international transactions and intervention currency, it is likely to retain a high attraction as a monetary reserve for national central banks *because it can be physically held*. In a politically uncertain world, gold is valued because it expresses sovereign control over monetary reserves, in contrast to short-term claims on foreign authorities, which can be repudiated, frozen or devalued.

National monetary reserves are desired by states for two main reasons analogous to the demand for liquidity by individuals.[47] First, they constitute a store of potential purchasing power and hence a buffer stock against adverse developments in a country's external payments position (a *precautionary* demand). This may include a role as collateral for borrowing in international capital markets. Second, reserves may be used in intervention on the foreign exchange market (a *transactions* demand). Countries will prefer steadily to accumulate foreign exchange reserves rather than suffer their gradual reduction, which means that they will wish in general to run an overall surplus on 'official' payments settlements.[48] Traditional 'mercantilism' is little more than common sense in a world of politically independent states.

The demand for net reserve growth means that there is a deflationary tendency in the international monetary system if there is no external source of liquidity to satisfy it. Under a GES, if the supply of new monetary gold is insufficient, net accumulations of key currency reserve assets can potentially fill the gap. The holding of liabilities of other central banks as national monetary reserves loosens the external constraint of gold convertibility for most countries and allows greater flexibility in balance of payments financing, especially for those states which allow their currencies to play key currency roles. For the latter, as long as their currencies remain valuable abroad, they can finance asset expansion through the issue of short-term liabilities to foreigners without a tightening of credit conditions at home.[49]

The operation of the GES has been a subject of considerable controversy, dominated by Triffin's assertion that it is 'inherently unstable'. The most controversial element centres upon the nature and degree of asymmetry in a system which accords a role to a particular national currency or currencies. On the face of it, the nature of the asymmetry is reasonably simple: the 'key' country fixes its currency in terms of gold, while the monetary authorities of the rest of the world peg their exchange rates to the key currency. This leads to an asymmetry in intervention responsibility: the key country intervenes in the gold market to stabilise the key currency price of gold, while central banks in the rest of the world intervene in currency markets to maintain the convertibility of their currencies and the key currency at the going exchange rates.

It follows from this that there are in principle two markets in which disequilibria could arise over the longer term, the gold market and currency markets, both of which are nonetheless linked by the unique

Hegemony and international monetary order 69

position of the key currency. The Triffin Dilemma holds that the GES is inherently unstable because equilibrium in one of these markets will result in disequilibrium in the other, so that no overall monetary equilibrium is possible. The demand for net reserve increases by central banks as international transactions expand means that, in the absence of a steady inflow of new gold, equilibrium in exchange markets requires continuing external deficits on the part of the key country. This creates a disequilibrium in the gold market as the short-term liabilities of the key country rise in proportion to its stock of gold. As Triffin himself expressed it:

> Barring a drastic revaluation of gold prices, the maintenance of adequate reserve levels will thus continue to depend on the growth of foreign exchange reserves as a supplement to gold itself. This, however, cannot fail to increase further and further the vulnerability of the world monetary system to shifts of confidence – justified or unjustified – in the national currencies actually used as reserve media.[50]

The first horn of the Triffin Dilemma was that if the need for growth in international liquidity was satisfied by accumulation of currency reserves, this would ultimately put into jeopardy the continued convertibility of the key currency into gold at the given price. The other horn of the dilemma was that if the key currency country took measures to restrain the growth of its liabilities to foreigners so as to maintain the existing price of gold, there would arise a shortage of international liquidity which would risk a contraction of world trade.

Triffin's analysis sparked off a debate in the 1960s which focused upon the gold-key currency relationship and the role of the latter in the international financial system. An important contribution was made by Kindleberger, Salant and Despres, who suggested that under the GES the key currency country acts as a bank to the rest of the world, providing a service of international financial intermediation by borrowing short (issuing short-term liabilities) and lending long (permitting foreign bond issues in its domestic financial markets).[51] This made it incorrect to view the net accumulation of its liabilities by foreign central banks (the 'official settlements' deficit) or by foreign official and private actors (the 'liquidity' deficit) as a deficit in the traditional sense, since some net accumulation of short-term key currency liabilities by foreigners constitutes an equilibrium condition of the system.

It was not clear, however, how this fitted in with the structure of the GES. Proponents of the financial intermediation hypothesis seemed to suggest that since the increase in liabilities of the key currency to foreigners is matched by an increase in assets, all 'deficits' run by the key country would be by definition demand-determined. This seems implicit in the argument that a key currency country ought to adopt an attitude of 'benign neglect' with respect to its balance of payments, in particular refraining from restrictions upon capital outflows, and also in the idea that gold plays no important role in the system.[52]

This is an excessively optimistic view. The logic of the financial intermediation hypothesis would suggest that the key country like any bank could succumb to the temptation of excessive balance sheet growth through the acquisition of relatively risky or less profitable assets. What is required is some kind of test of the 'profitability' of the service of international financial intermediation it provides, since the flow of income it can generate will be crucial in terms of maintaining international confidence in the value of its liabilities.

A positive flow of trade and investment income (a surplus on current account) would be a crude measure of this profitability. This will mean that the key country will accumulate assets abroad in excess of the increase in its liquid liabilities plus any diminution of gold reserves. If it does not have a positive current account flow, the value of its assets (both at home and abroad) will be called into question, which will in turn decrease confidence in its short-term liabilities at the same time as they are issued in increasing quantity. Unless there are corrective mechanisms which can quickly restore a positive flow of income from the rest of the world, there is a danger that there will be a flight from the key currency into other assets, financial or real, fuelling inflation. This first criterion of the successful operation of a GES in effect justifies a certain degree of 'mercantilism' in the name of international monetary order.

The traditional test of the policy stance of a key country and its profitability as a financial intermediary has been whether foreign central banks and private actors begin to speculate in the gold market against the key currency.[53] The maintenance of the convertibility of the key currency into gold would seem to be a condition of the accumulation of short-term key currency reserves abroad remaining 'demand-determined', since unwanted currency reserves can be exchanged by foreign central banks for gold, either through private sales or through their presentation to the key country for conversion. Such convertibility is also a major constraint upon the ability of the key country to export inflation to the rest of the world.

There is a problem with this second test of policy responsibility, since a shortage of monetary gold could arise even when the key country is running a positive current balance.[54] Gold is a commodity with private uses (including private industrial, ornamental and speculative demands) as well as that of a monetary reserve, and the amount of new gold available for reserve purposes will be that which is left over after private demands have been satisfied. In a system in which there is generalised commodity price inflation, the maintenance of a fixed official price of gold over time may become untenable as the profitability of gold extraction declines. The very existence of a shortage will be likely to induce speculation in favour of gold against the key currency, irrespective of the health of the external position of the issuing country. The Triffin Dilemma can come into play without the underlying profitability of the key country's current activities having been brought into question.

This problem ultimately derives from the natural instability of a monetary system based upon two monies, described in Gresham's Law that 'bad money drives out good'.[55] Gilbert has argued that this problem can be alleviated by adjusting the price relationship between gold and the key currency. If the role of gold is undermined by inflation and a relative abundance of key currency reserves, this would constitute what he termed a 'fundamental disequilibrium of the system', necessitating an increase in the price of gold.[56] This would enable other countries to maintain their desired gold ratios and the key country to buy new gold reserves from the private market so as to maintain confidence in the convertibility of its liabilities into gold. Unless the price of gold is 'fixed but adjustable' in the long run, a GES in circumstances of inflation would suffer the erosion of the gold convertibility of the key currency and break down. This would result in the loss of the basic test of the policy responsibility of the key country over the medium term: its ability to maintain the free convertibility of its currency into gold.

The claim is sometimes made that a gold price increase would be inflationary.[57] This is misleading since in effect it would rather represent an adjustment or accommodation to *past* commodity price inflation measured in terms of the key currency. With an appropriate gold price, the state of the key country's current account provides some criterion of exchange rate relationships. If, for example, the current account position of the key country is undermined due to relatively poor productivity or inflation performance, then there would need to be selective revaluations of currencies of major surplus countries against the key currency. This issue is in principle separate from that of the price of gold in terms of the key currency, though large revaluations of important currencies may help induce a gold shortage, which would require compensatory key currency devaluation against gold.

What then are the roles which a hegemonic state should play under a GES? First, as Kindleberger has stressed, a dominant state should maintain open goods and financial markets, recycling short-term and long-term capital abroad as necessary. As usual, however, financial hierarchy brings with it some potential dangers and this requires responsible policies on the part of a key country. A stable macroeconomic environment with low inflation would appear to be a necessary condition for the maintenance of the key country's international competitive position and its current surplus on its international activities. This also prevents it from exporting inflation abroad through the fixed exchange rate system. An additional constraint and an important measure of the responsibility of its policies is the maintenance of the gold convertibility of its currency, though from time to time the key country may also need to take responsibility for discretionary changes in the gold price.

The key currency standard

A key currency standard (KCS) is one clearly associated with the dominance of a particular currency and country in the international monetary system. In its purest form it would mean that all other countries fixed their currencies in terms of the key currency and transferred their monetary sovereignty to its central bank. It therefore involves a much greater degree of hierarchy than even the GES. As is usually pointed out, it would solve the 'consistency problem' in international monetary relations, whereby $n-1$ countries would set payments targets consistent with their exchange rate with the key currency, while the key country as the *nth* actor in the system would adopt a passive attitude towards its balance of payments.[58] It ought to do so because its overall payments position has little meaning beyond that of a residual of the rest of the world's payments positions.

Under a pegged exchange rate system with full capital market integration, the monetary authorities of the key country would be in the position of a central bank within a domestic monetary system, with its liabilities constituting the base money of the international monetary system. Though these liabilities may not have status as legal tender throughout the world economy, they would approximate a truly 'international money' because other monies would bear a stable price relation to it and ultimately derive their acceptability by being convertible into the key currency. It is only a short step to the assertion that in such circumstances, the key country ought also to accept the responsibilities of a world *central* bank along with its role as 'banker' to the rest of the world, providing a countercyclical flow of long-term capital and emergency liquidity in financial crises.[59] Again, this ought to be extended to include responsibility for the regulation and prudential supervision of international financial markets.

A good many of the criticisms of the KCS proposal, like that for a WCB, centre on the difficulty of effecting a transition from an international monetary system which is relatively decentralised to one in which power and responsibility is highly centralised. The 'dollar standard' school in the 1960s argued that the very logic of the contemporary dollar-based system meant that all countries would benefit by moving to a full dollar-standard, discarding gold entirely. Countries should therefore have been willing to accumulate only key currency reserves and to allow the proportion of their reserves held in the form of gold to erode over time. The key country should discontinue intervening in the gold market to support the official price of gold, with the aim of 'demonetising' this relic of a bygone era.

The reasons why such a development did not take place were not simply reducible to the irrationality of politicians. The central problem with the KCS proposal is its presumption that there is no contradiction between the 'private' role of the key country's financial system as banker to the world and the 'public' responsibilities of management that the proponents urge upon its monetary authorities. Kindleberger recognises this problem by arguing that such a centralised international monetary system would require full political integration at the multilateral level, institutionalising the management of the KCS.[60]

The potential for conflict between public and private roles was shown in the history of the Bank of England and need not be retold. How much more contentious would be a system giving discretion for lender of last resort intervention to a highly dominant central bank of one particular country? Would it ever be possible to distinguish on purely technical grounds whether the key country ought to provide financial assistance to a national central bank (or a foreign private bank) or whether it should refuse it in the interests of 'sound money'? The problem of assessing risk involved in bank or capital market lending to sovereign borrowers would make any regulation of such activities highly contentious.[61] As with the WCB proposal, the political difficulties involved can only be minimised if an overly technocratic conception of central banking is employed.

The potential contradiction between a key country's private and public roles can also be seen in the suggestion of Kindleberger and others that it adopt an attitude of benign neglect towards its balance of payments and above all the capital account. To interfere with the flow of capital would be incompatible with the banking role the key country performs for the rest of the world.[62] On the other hand, adopting an attitude of complete *laissez-faire* assumes that the operation of the global financial markets will not only be efficient but also stable over time. If it is accepted that some regulation would be necessary, should this be on a voluntary or compulsory basis? This raises the difficult issue of national jurisdictions, as well as the possibility that regulation, if onerous, could serve to encourage markets to deal in other currencies or to operate in foreign centres.

Whether the 'private' interests of the key currency country (the profits or seignorage it gains from its international banking services, the overseas activities and asset acquisition it can finance due to the role of its currency) will tend to have precedence over its international public responsibilities in a conflict is difficult to decide in principle. The crucial problem with a KCS is that there is little guarantee that the key country will be able to manage the system in a way that will suit all the diverse groups and countries involved. In contrast to a GES, in an inflationary situation there would be no means of placing pressure on the key country (through conversion of key currency balances into gold). The option of currency revaluation for other countries might jeopardise the competitiveness of domestic exporters and would mean implicit acceptance of the adjustment costs made necessary by the key country's policies. On the other hand, while constraints upon the key country would seem both necessary and desirable, it is unlikely that the key country would accept some kind of convertibility constraint under a system in which the international banking sector could create international currency reserves, since then it would be liable to reimburse such liabilities on demand.

In the event of inflation, then, a KCS may be very vulnerable to disintegration into a flexible exchange rate system and/or a 'multi-currency system', if private and foreign official actors diversified their portfolios to include assets denominated in other currencies.[63] A KCS with floating exchange rates may be especially prone to instability, since if foreign borrowers expect the key currency to depreciate in value in the future, an excess demand for key currency loans may develop, which if satisfied could set up an inflationary spiral with the key currency depreciating further and an unstable process developing.

Contrary to much recent international relations literature, the excessive dominance of one country may therefore be a mixed blessing in international monetary organisation. There seems little reason to presume that a KCS would be any less 'inherently unstable' as the much maligned GES. The obvious advantage that the latter has over the KCS is that a role for gold provides both some link with commodity prices as well as a constraint upon and a criterion for policy in the centre country. On the other hand, a significant role for gold goes against the general view amongst economists (following Keynes) that it is a 'barbarous relic' and the fact that it is a poor proxy for commodity prices.[64] It might be argued that the success of the European Monetary

System (EMS) has been due in part to formation of a 'key currency bloc' with the German Bundesbank at its centre.[65] This experience suggests that in circumstances of high levels of economic interdependence, the pressures towards key currency bloc formation are strong, especially when there is a low-inflation core country. Whether such an experience would be translatable to the global level is quite another matter, however, and even within the EMS there is considerable pressure from the non-German countries to 'multilateralise' the Bundesbank by creating a European central bank. Such a development would run against the grain of much contemporary international relations thinking, which would argue that international monetary organisation must adjust to political reality rather than vice versa.

On the global level, democratising a KCS would only lead back to the idea of a world central bank, with monetary policy being set by some kind of international monetary board. Just as the argument for a global central bank tended to converge upon that for hegemony on the part of one or a few countries, so too the argument for a KCS converges on that for a WCB. Neither may necessarily provide a fully satisfactory solution to the problem of international monetary order.

The multi-currency system

A multi-currency system (MCS) is one in which two or more currencies obtain key currency status and perhaps also come to play an important role in international financial markets. Central banks and private agents might come to hold asset portfolios denominated in a number of different currencies, for transactions, intervention, precautionary or speculative purposes. It is often argued that the international monetary system has in recent years come to take on such a form, due to the rising importance of the yen, mark and other currencies in private and central bank portfolios.[66] Correspondingly, the MCS has also been associated with multipolarity rather than hegemony in the international system.

Smaller countries may peg their exchange rates to those of the key currency country with which they conduct most of their international trade. Thus an MCS involves some degree of regionalisation or oligopolisation in the structure of international trade and payments, and accordingly stability will tend to be focused within rather than between currency blocs. As noted above, pressures for the development of currency blocs will be strong in circumstances of high economic interdependence. If there is considerable interdependence between blocs, pressures for stabilisation agreements between key countries may in turn be strong.

With the GES, the MCS has a reputation for inherent instability.[67] This is because of the potential for destabilising portfolio shifts between different key currencies, which may produce severe exchange rate misalignments and rapid changes in international reserves (and perhaps domestic liquidity) if central banks feel forced to intervene. The oligopolistic structure of an MCS is seen as the root cause of the inherent instability, which accords with the prediction of the theory of hegemonic stability that a pluralistic system is likely to be a disordered one. This view is particularly strong amongst radical authors, who tend to treat the existence of a number of competing key currencies as indicative of a more generalised crisis of hegemony in the international capitalist system. Relationships between these key currencies are seen as mirroring the relative strengths of national capitalisms.[68]

While an MCS implies some degree of inefficiency because of a decentralised international monetary structure, it may have one advantage that a KCS lacks: some form of constraint upon the centre countries. If key currencies are interconvertible in exchange markets, then a loss of market confidence in a key country's policies could threaten a destabilising depreciation of its currency. This will have an inflationary impact in the depreciating country and a deflationary impact in the appreciating countries, which depending upon relative policy preferences may lead to adjustments by national authorities. Of course, such policy adjustments are not certain, and as with a competitive currency system, there may be no guarantee against a *generalised* inflation or deflation.

In many ways it is fruitless to discuss in abstract the differences between key and multi-currency systems, since in practice it is likely that there will always be more than one key currency. What seems crucial is the *degree of asymmetry* in the respective positions of the key currencies which make up an MCS. If one currency plays a much more dominant role as an international reserve, transactions and intervention currency, while other international currencies serve mainly as a means for public and private actors to reduce capital risks by diversifying their portfolios, the international monetary system may remain too open to abuse by the major key country. If a dominant key country were able to rely upon other central banks to support its currency in exchange markets out of their own interests, it might be tempted to ignore in part the international consequences of its domestic policies. If credit conditions in the domestic economy of the primary key country are very important for those in international financial markets in general, an MCS may suffer from similar problems to the 'pure' KCS. A more symmetrical international monetary structure may place greater constraints upon each key country.

This leads to the issue of policy coordination between key countries and what sort of collective target they might pursue. Ronald McKinnon has persistently argued that under an MCS, the possibility of currency substitution between liquid assets denominated in different key currencies requires that central banks forsake national monetary growth targets and instead target exchange rates.[69] Unsterilised intervention on the part of key country monetary authorities to fix exchange rates would, it is suggested, neutralise shifts in key currency portfolio preferences on the part of private (and official) actors. McKinnon argues that the key countries should also coordinate their national monetary policies so as to pursue a *world* monetary target aimed at stabilising the PPP prices of internationally traded goods.

There are a number of problems with the McKinnon approach. The suggestion that a 'World M_1' should be defined and targeted by key countries assumes that currency substitution is most likely to occur with capital movements between liquid assets (bank deposits). Capital movements will more likely involve shifts between credit instruments denominated in different currencies rather than liquid bank accounts, so that M_1 would then be an inappropriate target both on a domestic and an international level.[70]

Even the global targeting of more broadly defined 'money' aggregates might not escape the difficulty encountered with domestic Monetarism: the breakdown of money demand functions once monetary aggregates were employed as policy targets. The sensitivity of capital markets to international interest rate differentials in a system with a high degree of capital integration implies that exchange rate targeting would have to rely more upon discretionary changes in interest rates. This reinforces a previous point that the main policy weapon available to central banks will be their control over the domestic level of short-term interest rates, since the endogeneity of the money supply will be heightened as international capital mobility increases.[71]

Unless there is substantial coordination of fiscal as well as monetary policies, the possibility of pursuing credible exchange rate (or target zone) objectives is minimal. This produces a major conflict between the desire of states (especially the most important states) to retain some degree of national policy independence and the requirements for stability under an MCS. Heavy reliance upon intervention in exchange markets may be insufficient to prevent large currency movements and will in any case undermine independent monetary policies and even domestic monetary stability. As noted above, whether the attempted international coordination of policies will be sufficient to produce stability in circumstances of high financial integration is debatable. This leads some to argue that controls upon international capital flows are a necessary condition for stability.[72] However, given the likelihood that financial markets will gravitate to the point of least regulation, in the long run there is likely to be no alternative to regulatory agreements between major countries.

3.5 Conclusion

We have outlined the various roles that hegemony might play in different kinds of international monetary system, noting that the scope for hegemonic intervention will be significantly enlarged the greater the hierarchy in the international financial structure. It may be useful to summarise at this stage the kinds of roles which hegemony might play in stabilising the international monetary system.

The first role is one referred to in the literature as regime establishment and maintenance. There may be important ground rules which facilitate the operation of a particular kind of monetary adjustment mechanism, as we noted was the case with the international gold standard. More generally, enforcement of the ground rules has often been extended to the encouragement of generalised adherence to principles of relative freedom of international trade and capital movements. A second role which may also involve the provision of regimes is the encouragement of policy coordination between states. As we saw, this is likely to become more important the higher are levels of interdependence between states, particularly financial interdependence.

A final role which can be distinguished is one of actively managing the international monetary system. We saw the possibility of management is likely to follow from the existence of key currencies, though there was no necessary reason to expect that such management would be forthcoming. Included within such a concept of management is a responsibility for the regulation and supervision of international financial markets to the extent that this is possible.

In general, we found that were these different roles to be performed by a hegemon, there was no necessary reason to believe that they might be sufficient to solve the problem of international monetary order. Enforcing the ground rules of the gold standard may not produce stability, while it must be doubtful whether policy coordination of a high degree is ever possible or whether it could be sufficient to produce order in circumstances of high financial integration. To a significant extent, it depends on where the main source of potential instability is seen. Political scientists tend to see instability as deriving from political anarchy, and therefore concentrate upon the functions of regime provision and maintenance. Economists are more often aware of the potential for financial markets to create their own instability, leading to a need for them to be managed and regulated.

Despite the arguments in favour of internationally managed money, we found that a high degree of centralisation in international monetary organisation is not necessarily consistent with international monetary stability. In particular, much will depend upon the policies that a dominant state in the system would follow and in very centralised structures the constraints upon key countries may be very weak indeed. Hegemony is certainly not a sufficient condition for international monetary stability and there seem to be no strong *a priori* arguments that it is even a necessary condition. The idea that the above functions can in principle be provided only by a single dominant state is a political or behavioural hypothesis which can only be tested against reality.

The problem is of course that the lack of historical cases is very restricting. Certainly it is conceivable that in the strongest form of a hegemonic system, the KCS, the dominance of one state could easily become an *obstacle* to rather than a necessary condition of stability. Once the extremely problematic nature of central banking is emphasised, the idea that lies behind much hegemonic stability theory, that a WCB constitutes an ideal solution to international monetary problems, is difficult to support fully. Economic theory certainly provides no clear-cut answer to the question as to whether hegemony is a necessary condition for international monetary order, and certainly no means of deciding whether (for example) an 'oligopolistic' MCS will be less stable than a 'hegemonic' KCS. The following part will consider some empirical cases, beginning with the international GS of the late nineteenth century, in order to extend the framework developed here and to throw light upon this central issue.

Notes

1. von Hayek, 1976, p.52.
2. Vaubel, 1977. Proposals for a European parallel currency, the latest version of which is the recent UK idea of a 'hard ecu' which would circulate alongside and compete with existing national currencies in the European Monetary System, spring from similar assumptions.
3. Kindleberger's *Manias, Panics and Crashes* (1978a) is the best account of the turbulent history of financial fluctuations.
4. Grandmont and Malgrange, 1986, p.8.
5. von Hayek, 1976, p.77.
6. As noted in Chapter 2, the Bank of England on more than one occasion in the past allowed a major competitor to collapse, while the Bank of

80 *The theory of hegemonic stability and monetary order*

France refused to assist the Pereires in 1868 (Kindleberger, 1984, p.280).
7. We will consider here the theories of the GS adjustment mechanism, leaving to the following chapter discussion of the actual working of the system.
8. See Eichengreen, 1985, pp.7–12, and Samuelson, 1980.
9. See Frenkel and Johnson, 1976b.
10. Kindleberger, 1981, ch.1.
11. Frenkel and Johnson, 1976b, p.35.
12. See McCloskey and Zecher, 1976, p.364.
13. Samuelson, 1980, pp.148–51.
14. Hawtrey, 1962, p.144; Frenkel and Johnson, 1976b, pp.37–41; Mundell, 1976, pp.107–8.
15. Bloomfield, 1959, p.47 and 1963, p.75. See also Triffin, 1968, p.4.
16. McCloskey and Zecher, 1976, p.361; Floyd, 1985, ch.4; Yeager, 1975, pp.302–3.
17. Frenkel and Johnson, 1976b, p.25.
18. McCloskey and Zecher, 1976, pp.359–61.
19. See Keynes, 1936, pp.348–9. Marxists have also tended to stress the mercantilist struggle for gold between states as problematic for the GS, but emphasise more deep-seated contradictions in international capitalism. See Mandel, 1980, pp.31–2.
20. It could undertake an international lender of last resort role if its own currency were acceptable to other states as a substitute for gold, but this would imply a much different kind of IMS to the gold standard, as we shall see shortly.
21. For example, Friedman, 1953. The relative version of PPP merely states that differential inflation between countries will be reflected in changes in spot exchange rates. The stronger 'absolute' version of PPP is derived from the law of one price, holding that if there exists a standard basket of goods in countries A and B, an amount x of currency A should buy just enough of currency B to be able to buy exactly the same basket of goods in B. The absolute version implies the relative PPP condition, but not vice versa. See McKinnon, 1979, ch.6.
22. Quoted in McKinnon, 1984, p.16.
23. As most economists point out, the lack of price arbitrage on similar goods within countries makes the absolute PPP criterion a highly implausible concept between countries.
24. Furthermore, non-price factors such as product quality, delivery times and after-sales service play an important role in manufacturing trade in particular, so that trade volumes may be increasingly insensitive to price. This is especially likely to be the case when a growing proportion of international trade is conducted between different branches of multinational corporations. See Kindleberger, 1981, p.190.
25. See Mundell, 1968, ch.18.
26. See Dornbusch, 1976, 1983.
27. For a discussion, see Bliss, 1986, pp.9–12, and Dornbusch, 1987, pp.6–14.
28. Williamson, 1983, p.14.
29. Quoted in Williamson, 1983, p.52.
30. See McKinnon, 1979, ch.7.
31. See Kindleberger, 1981, p.17; de Lattre, 1985, pp.85–100; McKinnon, 1988, pp.88–91.

32. Frenkel and Mussa, 1980; McKinnon, 1988, pp.84–6.
33. Goodhart, 1987, p.21; Koromzay, Llewellyn and Potter, 1987, pp.23–31.
34. Dornbusch, 1987, pp.15–17; Koromzay, Llewellyn and Potter, 1987, pp.37–40; Allsopp, 1987, pp.44–8.
35. See Williamson, 1983, pp.62–78; Williamson and Miller, 1987; Scammell, 1987, ch.5.
36. The name most associated with this view is Robert Triffin (see his 1968, part II). Cooper, 1987, ch.13, presents a similar view.
37. Some West European nations at present appear willing to contemplate relinquishing their monetary sovereignty to a supranational institution so as to achieve European monetary union, but until this happens history is on the side of the sceptics.
38. Cohen, 1977, pp.198–202, 219–20; Kindleberger, 1981, p.178; Helding, 1979, pp.60–3.
39. McKinnon, 1984, pp.67–9.
40. Cohen, 1977, pp.198–9. See also Helding, 1979, pp.60–3.
41. McKinnon, 1984, pp.5–9; Keohane, 1982, pp.7–12; Schwartz, 1983, pp.16–20.
42. Kindleberger, 1986, p.8.
43. See, for example, Strange, 1986, pp.175–81.
44. Brender, Gaye and Kessler, 1986, pp.44–9.
45. See Aglietta, 1985; Guth, 1985; Swoboda, 1980; International Monetary Fund (IMF), *Annual Report*, 1985, pp.48–62; Carli, 1985, and the comment by Goodhart. The issue as to whether the international banking system constitutes an independent source of liquidity creation is a controversial one. In practice, offshore activities of banks seem highly dependent upon their ability to refinance themselves in domestic money markets.
46. Bloomfield, 1963, p.19.
47. Cohen, 1977, pp.34–5.
48. See Meier, 1980, ch.5, for a discussion of this and other accounting definitions.
49. This has often been compared to the 'seignorage' or profit that states traditionally made on the minting of coins.
50. Triffin, 1961, p.87.
51. See Kindleberger, 1981, pp.43–7,101–9; Salant, 1972. These authors became associated with the so-called 'dollar standard' school, which argued that the world should accept the logic of financial intermediation, discard gold and move towards an IMS centred purely upon the dollar.
52. See Despres, Kindleberger and Salant, 1966, pp.526–9.
53. Kindleberger, 1981, p.135.
54. Gilbert, 1980, pp.35–41.
55. Kindleberger, 1984, p.6.
56. *ibid.*, pp.xii–xv. This was to be distinguished from a fundamental disequilibrium of any given currency, which would arise if the maintenance of a particular exchange rate became incompatible with domestic economic equilibrium over the course of the business cycle.
57. For example, Kindleberger, 1981, p.82.
58. Cohen, 1977, pp.224–5.
59. Kindleberger, 1976, 1985.
60. Kindleberger, 1981, pp.29,107.
61. See Eaton, Gersovitz and Stiglitz, 1986; Sachs, 1984.

62. Kindleberger, 1981, pp.44–7,102–3.
63. A system in which there is a dominant key currency but in which exchange rates are flexible is often termed a 'weak' KCS, since no one currency can approximate an international standard of value or unit of account.
64. Cooper, 1987, ch.2.
65. See Tsoukalis, 1987.
66. See Thygesen, 1985; Brender, Gaye and Kessler, 1986.
67. *ibid.*, pp.137–9.
68. For example, Sandretto, 1983, pp.148–53.
69. McKinnon, 1984, 1988.
70. Thygesen, 1985, pp.147–9; Dornbusch, 1988, pp.110–11.
71. See Goodhart, 1986b, pp.96–100.
72. For example, Tobin, 1982b, p.116.

Part II
Hegemony and The Evolution of The International Monetary System since 1870

Part II

Chapter 4
British hegemony and the international gold standard

4.1 Introduction

This chapter will consider in what way, if any, the operation of the international monetary system of the period 1880–1914 was due to the hegemonic role that Britain is often held to have played. As argued above, there are various ways in which a British hegemon might conceivably have helped stabilise the system, dependent in part upon how one sees the gold standard adjustment mechanism as having operated in practice. Many authors have emphasised the way in which the '*Pax Britannica* . . . determined the general structure of international relations until the collapse of the system under the impact of World War I.'[1] Gilpin elaborates on what we have termed the basic rule-provision and enforcement function of hegemony:

> [A] primary objective of British foreign policy became the creation of a world market economy based on free trade, freedom of capital movements, and a unified international monetary system. The achievement of this objective required primarily the creation and enforcement of a set of international rules protecting private property rights rather than the more costly and less beneficial task of conquering an empire. [Great Britain therefore] assumed the responsibility of organising and defending the world market economy; [it] promoted free trade, provided investment capital, and supplied the international currency. In effect, [it] provided the public goods necessary for the functioning of efficient world markets because it was profitable for [it] to do so.[2]

Similarly, Britain is often held to have promoted policy consistency and facilitated the gold standard adjustment mechanism by establishing and maintaining the 'rules of the game' outlined in the previous chapter.³ Many have gone further to argue that the structure of the pre-1914 international financial system was such that the so-called gold standard was in fact a gold exchange standard or even a key currency standard centred upon sterling. This supposedly allowed Britain to act as a world monetary manager. As Cohen argues:

> [T]he classical gold standard was a sterling standard – a hegemonic regime – in the sense that Britain not only dominated the international monetary order, establishing and maintaining the prevailing rules of the game, but also gave monetary relations whatever degree of inherent stability they possessed . . . It did not regard itself as responsible for global monetary stabilisation or as money manager of the world. Yet this is precisely the responsibility that was thrust upon it in practice . . . The widespread international use of sterling and the close links between the larger financial markets in London and smaller national financial markets elsewhere inevitably endowed Britain with the power to guide the world's monetary policy.⁴

The notion that Britain was able to manage and stabilise the international monetary system of the decades before 1914 because of its dominant role in the world's commercial and financial markets is one which recurs in much of the recent literature. Kindleberger argues in similar fashion that the stability of this system was due to the international public goods that Britain provided: international banking services, an international currency, an open market for the rest of the world's exports and in the event of a global liquidity crisis, lender of last resort assistance.⁵ Even some radical authors have suggested that financial instability in the pre-1914 world capitalist economy was alleviated by British hegemony, although they refrain from using the language of international public goods.⁶

The growing consensus that Britain played a crucial management role in the pre-1914 international monetary system necessitates that this chapter focus largely upon this idea, though we shall also deal briefly with the claim that British dominance assisted the establishment of the operating rules of the system. Before going on to discuss these monetary questions, we need to consider the basis of British 'hegemony' in this period.

4.2 Britain's international position, 1870–1914

Even at the height of its relative international preponderance in 1870, the aggregate size of the British economy was probably smaller than that of the US and Russia, although its head-start had made it by far the largest industrial power of the time (table 5.3 – page 120).[7] Britain's share of global industrial production has been estimated at 32 per cent in 1870, with 23 per cent for the US, 13 per cent for Germany and 10 per cent for France. By 1913 Britain's share seems to have declined dramatically to around 14 per cent, with the US share having increased to more than double Britain's, Germany's about 16 per cent and France's only 6 per cent. Additional evidence suggests that the rates of growth of output per head in the four decades after 1873 were faster in the US and Germany than in Britain.[8]

Such estimates, while suggesting caution in the attribution of 'hegemonic' status to Britain in the three or four decades before 1914, understate that country's unique role in the world economy in these years. Around 1860, Britain had an unrivalled lead in modern industries, producing around half of the world's iron, coal and lignite and consuming just under half of its raw cotton output.[9] This was reflected in its dominant position in world trade. British trade in the decade 1860–70 represented perhaps a quarter of world trade, more than double the share of the nearest rival, France. With the spread of industrialism in Europe and the rest of the world, this share gradually declined to around 16 per cent by 1900–13, though was probably still larger than that of Germany, France and the US.[10]

Britain's share of world trade in manufactures seems to have shown less erosion over the period. In 1899, this share was estimated at 33 per cent, her nearest rivals being Germany and France with 22 per cent and 14 per cent respectively. By 1913, the same source has the British share falling to 30 per cent, Germany's growing significantly to 27 per cent, the US's share 13 per cent and France's 12 per cent.[11] We can tentatively conclude that during the period of the international gold standard, Britain was the world's most important importer and exporter of manufactured goods, and the largest importer of raw materials, but that over time its lead eroded to the extent that on the eve of World War I, the assumption of this mantle by Germany was within sight. This view is reinforced by evidence which suggests that Germany and the US were probably ahead of Britain in the development of 'leading edge' industries such as chemicals and electricals at the end of the nineteenth century.[12]

British industrial pre-eminence was not, as Kennedy has pointed out, entirely reflected in military terms.[13] Britain was a naval power rather than a land power, with a tenuous commitment to intervention in the European balance of power. The other major economic powers were certainly not dependent upon Britain for their security in the way that they were upon the US after 1945. Britain's naval and imperial dominance was in part due to its lack of entanglement with great powers in Europe and abroad, and the consequent absence of a large army. By the turn of the century, this situation had dramatically changed and probably contributed to the rapid erosion of Britain's lead.

In addition to its naval and commercial pre-eminence, one of the most telling measures of Britain's international position was its international financial role. Here Britain's relative dominance did not decline as dramatically over the 1870–1913 period as did its relative economic size and trading position. During these decades London remained the world's premier gold, money and financial market, acting as a financial centre in which foreign actors held significant liquid assets (convertible into gold) and which channelled long-term capital abroad. Over this period, sterling bills and short-term credits financed perhaps 60 per cent of world trade.

London was also an international clearing centre, due to Britain's pivotal position in the structure of international trade and payments. British trade deficits with Europe and North America and surpluses with the Dominions and Colonies assisted the rise of clearing in sterling, effected through the London banking system. London's role as the world's major insurer, carrier and commodity market was also due in part to its central position in the Empire's international trade, which contributed to growing invisible earnings and an important vehicle and denomination role for sterling.[14]

The patterns of international trade and finance were such that foreigners with large international commitments came to hold sterling assets in order to be able to deal with fluctuations in their external position. This process was assisted by the decline of the bill of exchange from the late nineteenth century and the increasing use of short-term sterling deposits to finance international trade. This included central banks, initially those of the British Empire, which held claims on overseas London banks.[15] There are few reliable figures on Britain's liquid liabilities before World War I, though Lindert guesses that in 1913 sterling balances held by foreign monetary authorities were more than two and a half times Britain's gold reserves of $170 million. Including privately held sterling balances would give an external liquid liability to gold reserve ratio close to the 4.67:1 that the Macmillan Committee estimated for the end of 1928. Lindert also estimated (for 1913) that compared with world official gold reserves of $4,900 million, foreign exchange reserves totalled about $1,125 million, though it is doubtful that even a majority of this was held in sterling balances, with German marks and French francs making up a considerable proportion. German marks may have been used by more countries as a reserve currency than was sterling, though it was mainly on the

Table 4.1 Discount rates and open market rates in the major economies, 1876–1914 and 1925–38.

	Before 1914		1925–38	
	Open market rate	Central bank discount	Open market rate	Central bank discount
	Arithmetic Mean			
New York[a]	4.85		2.69	2.76
New York[b]	3.73		2.79	
London	2.64	3.36	2.43	3.39
Paris	2.45	2.92	3.09	3.68
Berlin	3.16	4.17	4.81	5.53
	Coefficient of variation			
New York[a]	0.23		0.68	0.47
New York[b]	0.67	0.80		
London	0.43	0.29	0.76	0.41
Paris	0.27	0.19	0.48	0.41
Berlin	0.33	0.21	0.36	0.35

[a] Commercial paper.
[b] Call money.
Source: Morgenstern, 1959, table 85, p. 377.

Continent that they were important as an international reserve currency.[16] This implies that at least by the end of the period, there had been some evolution of the international gold standard towards a gold-exchange standard.

In terms of the structure of international finance, there is additional evidence that other financial centres provided some competition for London. Short-term interest rates in Paris were consistently below those of London or any other centre in the pre-1914 era (see table 4.1). This indicates that Paris was a more 'liquid' market than London, supported by France's much more plentiful gold reserves and the Bank of France's lesser dependence than its British counterpart on discount rate changes in monetary management.[17] On the other hand, London's long-term interest rates were consistently lower than those in other financial centres, an indication of both the efficiency and the attractiveness of London as a source of long-term capital. At contemporary exchange rates, the book value of UK foreign investments has been estimated at $19,500 million in 1914, and that of the next largest investing countries, France and Germany, estimated at $8,600 and $6,700 millions respectively (tables 4.1 and 4.5).

The bulk of Britain's foreign investment was in the Americas, the

Dominions and the Indian subcontinent, while on the European continent and in Russia, German and French finance dominated.[18] This led to steadily growing investment income which in Britain's case was sufficient to offset a deteriorating trade balance and to produce a positive current account balance over the century before 1914 (table 5.2 – see page 118). These trends were connected with the increasing share of services in the British economy and the possibility that high rates of foreign investment contributed to lower rates of capital formation at home than in the US and Germany.[19] In terms of the broad picture suggested by raw data, Britain's international financial dominance, while indisputable, needs to be qualified. Before turning to the operation of the gold standard, we will discuss the role which Britain played in its establishment.

4.3 Britain and the emergence of the gold standard

Was British hegemonic power instrumental in the establishment of the ground rules for international trade and capital accumulation in the second half of the nineteenth century? Its naval power undoubtedly did help maintain freedom of navigation, but Britain's lack of military presence except on the periphery of the European continent meant that its ability to link economic and military issues was very limited when it came to relations with the other great powers. Britain could hardly hope to have much influence over the domestic economic policies of these other major countries, nor is there any convincing evidence that it attempted to exercise such influence.

It has been argued that 'Britain used its influence to usher in the age of free trade'.[20] Whether this had much effect, however, is debatable. Britain's adoption of a programme of free trade, whilst a great boon to primary producing and some newly industrialising countries, did not lead immediately to a marked shift to similar practices abroad, though it certainly provided an incentive for foreign manufacturers to export to this large market. Industrialisation in the other major countries and increasing levels of world trade had the effect of creating lobbies representing domestic agricultural and manufacturing interests, but these were by no means always in favour of free trade.

The shift to freer trade in the major European countries that occurred in the middle of the century came about because of the existence of strong state structures which often overrode the demands of protectionist lobbies. In Germany and France, the most important continental trading nations, the level of dependence on external trade in the first case and a strong state committed to free trade in the latter prevented the adoption of the extreme protectionism of Russia and the US.[21] Kindleberger claims that British influence was greatest at the doctrinal level:

> [T]he countries of Europe in this period should not be considered as independent economies whose reactions to various phenomena can properly be compared, but rather as a single entity that moved to free trade for ideological or perhaps better doctrinal reasons. Manchester and the English political economists persuaded Britain, which persuaded Europe – by precept and example.[22]

If hegemonic 'power' in this case amounted largely to the ideological importance of the British model, it was of a fairly flimsy kind. Britain was unable to arrest the general tendency towards a resurgence of protectionism from the time of the generalised economic downturn of the early 1870s. It is sometimes argued that part of the reason why British influence was not great was because it refrained from employing the weapon of retaliatory protectionism until the development of Imperial Preference in 1932. Whether such retaliatory action could have provided much benefit to the British economy is very difficult to say, though the admirable doctrinal attachment to the principle of free trade was probably beneficial to the stability of the world economy. Most other countries had a pragmatic attitude and found no difficulty in discarding the ideological baggage when they felt that British exports threatened their domestic industries.

The relatively uninhibited flow of capital established in this period was also due to a natural self-interest on the part of other countries to develop their industry and extend their economic presence in their particular sphere of influence. The bulk of Britain's overseas investment in the second half of the nineteenth century were in the major projects of railways and other public utilities in the Americas and the Dominions, while German and French financiers organised similar loans to Russia and the Ottoman Empire.[23]

It is often claimed that orthodox economic ideas were most important when it came to monetary issues. These took a long while to catch on elsewhere: Britain restored the link with gold in 1819 after a highly charged debate, but the other major countries of Europe did not move to the gold standard until the 1870s. Even from this time, bimetallism (the use of a gold and silver monetary standard) continued to have its supporters in Germany and especially the United States. The practice of bimetallism was becoming increasingly difficult, however, and it seems likely that the basic reason for the shift to the gold standard in the 1870s, beginning with Germany in 1871, was the rapid increase in the supply of silver and its consequent depreciation in value from the 1860s.[24] In this sense, British power had little to do with the emergence of the international gold standard in the 1870s. As Nurkse observed in 1944:

> The nineteenth-century gold standard system did not emerge as the result of an international convention or agreement imposing a set of formal obligations on the member countries. It sprang up spontaneously through the recognition by various individual nations of certain common objectives, chief among them being exchange stability.[25]

Perhaps the model of industrial and financial success which Britain represented played some role in encouraging other states to move to the adoption of the gold standard. There was also the argument for Paris and Berlin that going onto gold was necessary in order to capture some of the lucrative international financial business from London. For those countries who wished to attract capital from the major financial centres, considerations of creditworthiness may have played an important role in the decision to adopt gold as the standard. The older British colonies (except South Africa) had been linked to gold following Britain, though the remainder were on an effective silver standard until the depreciation of silver led them to link their currencies to sterling in the later nineteenth century.[26]

For the Austro-Hungarians, Russians and Italians, arguably the most important factor in their decision was one of prestige. In the gold standard debate of 1892, a deputy of the Austrian parliament claimed that: 'We cannot have a separate, an insular, currency continue: if we want to take part in the competition of civilized nations, we too must accept the international means of payment, and the international measure of value is just nowadays gold.'[27]

It is difficult to argue that British power played a very direct role in the emergence of the international gold standard in the last quarter of the nineteenth century, though it may have served as a model which other states saw as desirable to emulate. Metallic monetary standards were seen in most countries as the only viable long-term solution to the problem of monetary organisation, whilst, ironically enough, the countries of the British Empire tended to be amongst those most willing to adopt hybrid systems with a large fiduciary element.[28] Having discussed the role of hegemonic power in the establishment of the international gold standard before 1914, we may now turn to consider its role in the operation of this system.

4.4 Britain and the operation of the pre-1914 gold standard

The stability of the world economy 1870–1913

The idea that the few decades before World War I represented a Golden Age for the international economy is widespread. Despite the enormous structural changes going on in the major countries during this period, the growth in trade interdependence between the principal economies of Europe was considerable. Over the period 1870–1913, Maddison has estimated that world real GDP grew by an average of 2.5 per cent per annum, while world exports grew at an average rate of 3.9 per cent.[29] The absence of devaluations or even major currency crises for the most important of the international currencies during these years also testifies to considerable stability in the international monetary system. Relative stability compared with the interwar period is also apparent in evidence relating to the levels and volatility of interest rates in both periods. In his historical study of international financial relations since the late nineteenth century, Morgenstern found that central bank discount rates were generally lower in the pre-war period than after 1918, particularly for the Reichsbank. The variability of discount rates and short-term market rates was also less before 1914 (table 4.1 – see page 89). The picture for the US is somewhat muddied because of the creation of the Federal Reserve in 1913, though even here there is greater variability in short-term market rates in the later period, albeit at a lower average level.

Even before 1914, there were occasions on which the degree of strain in the international financial and monetary system was severe. Morgenstern found that all major currencies violated a generally accepted principle of the gold standard, that the maximum range of fluctuation of currencies should be within the so-called 'gold points'. That such violations were not only frequent but often also persistent (especially for Berlin and New York) indicated both periodic international financial stress and deviation of practice from gold standard theory.[30]

The fact that devaluations were largely resisted was not due to an *absence* of instability, but a willingness on the part of monetary authorities to tolerate (or an inability to prevent) substantial real economic fluctuations. Examining tables 4.2 and 4.3 (taken from Maddison's study of growth and fluctuations in the world economy), it is apparent that the general performance and stability of the world economy in this period is superior compared with the interwar years. The evidence also suggests, on the other hand, that in terms of both

Table 4.2 Growth characteristics of different periods in the world economy,* 1820–1979.

	(Annual average compound growth rates)			
	Real GDP	Real GDP per head of population	Tangible reproducible fixed capital stock**	Volume of exports
1820–70	2.2[a]	1.0[a]	(n.a.)	4.0[b]
1870–1913	2.5	1.4	2.9	3.9
1913–50	1.9	1.2	1.7	1.0
1950–73	4.9	3.8	5.5	8.6
1973–9	2.5	2.0	4.4[c]	4.8

Notes: * Arithmetic averages of figures for the 16 major economies.
** Excludes residential capital stock.
[a] Average for 13 countries.
[b] Average for 10 countries.
[c] 1973–8.

Source: Maddison, 1982, table 4.9, p. 91.

Table 4.3 Cyclical characteristics of different periods in the world economy,* 1820–1979.

	Maximum peak-to-trough fall in real GDP (or smallest rise)**	Maximum peak-to-trough fall in export volume	Average unemployment rate (% of labour force)	Average annual rise in consumer prices
1820–70	−6.7[a]	−21.7	(n.a.)	0.2[b]
1870–1913	−6.1	−18.2	4.5[c]	0.4
1920–38	−11.9	−36.5	7.3	−0.7[d]
1950–73	+0.4	−7.0	3.0	4.1
1973–9	−1.3	−6.4	4.1	9.5

Notes: *Arithmetic averages of figures for the 16 major economies, annual data.
[a] Denmark, France and UK only.
[b] France, Germany, Sweden, UK and US only.
[c] UK and US 1900–13.
[d] 1924–38 for Austria and Germany, 1921–38 for Belgium.

Source: Maddison, 1982, table 4.10, p. 91.

real economic performance and stability, the world economy under the classical gold standard was considerably worse off than in 1950–73 and even as compared to the 1973–9 period.

It would be dubious to attribute this difference in real performance solely to changes in the international monetary regime as there are a host of other important factors involved, such as the considerably heightened role of the state in the domestic economy after World War II. Despite the difficulties of comparison, it should be emphasised that the 'stability' often associated with the classical gold standard was of a very limited kind, and that in terms of modern experience, the real fluctuations which the world economy underwent in this period demonstrate considerable instability.

Considering the rapid rate of structural change in the domestic and world economies of this era, what stability there was might be seen as remarkable. This may have been due more to the relative openness of the major export markets during this period than to the gold standard itself. Open and expanding markets facilitated long-term adjustment to changes which might otherwise have resulted in unmanageable disturbances to the structure of international payments.[31] The contrast with the interwar period is this respect is great.

Even Britain experienced cyclical fluctuations in real national output which (by more recent standards) could be seen as exhibiting considerable instability, and the British economy was more stable than the average of the major countries. Such stability as there was probably accrued mainly to the large, industrialising countries of Europe, rather than to the 'peripheral countries' in the international economy.[32] Currency instability was most apparent in South America and those countries highly dependent upon external supplies of capital and prone to great surges of development, such as Australia, Canada and the US.[33] The dependence of many peripheral economies upon commodity exports to the centre countries, the demand and (short run) supply of which tended to be price-inelastic, meant that their balances of trade were very sensitive to fluctuations in demand emanating from the centre.[34]

Not only were their export receipts likely to fluctuate in a more volatile fashion, but the amplitude of recessions in real output and in the *volume* of exports was also greater in the peripheral countries. Of the sixteen economies studied by Maddison, the largest peak-to-trough falls of export volume during this period were recorded by Australia, Italy, Denmark and Japan, while the smallest were in Norway, Sweden, the UK and France (in that order). The average maximum peak-to-trough falls in real GDP for Australia, Canada, the US and Japan was 12.7 per cent (by any measure a large figure), while for the Low

Countries, Scandinavia, Germany, France and Britain the figure was a comparatively low 3.0 per cent.[35] It is difficult to reach strong conclusions from this data because the higher growth rates experienced in countries like Australia, Canada, South Africa and the US, as well as the stage of development of their economies, would lead one to expect greater instability of their economies than those of the 'core' countries. During this period, the white British Dominions and some countries such as Argentina became some of the richest in the world on an income per capita basis, which precludes too rigid an interpretation of the 'structural asymmetries' in the international gold standard.

The case is often made that because the direction of long-term capital flows was from centre to periphery, the major creditor states determined the stringency of financial conditions in the rest of the world. Britain, it is argued, could raise the discount rate in order to slow the rate of capital export, thereby improving its own balance of payments at relatively minimal cost to itself in the short run, whereas the peripheral countries were more or less at the mercy of monetary management in the creditor countries.[36] In many cases, the bulk of net capital imports were very concentrated in a few years, such as for Australia in the 1880s, Canada in the decade before World War I, Argentina in the second half of the 1880s and South Africa in 1902–5, only to fall dramatically when fears of creditworthiness began to take hold in the capital exporting countries. Although it may be wrong to see foreign capital imports as having played an overwhelmingly dominant role in these countries' capital formation, in peak periods the ratio of net capital imports to gross domestic capital formation probably approached 50–60 per cent in the cases of Australia, New Zealand and Canada, though this ratio was subject to considerable instability.[37]

Triffin also argued that London's role in the financing of peripheral countries' exports meant that Bank Rate increases had a favourable effect on Britain's terms of trade in a downturn. By forcing a quicker liquidation of commodity stocks, this would exert downward pressure on the prices of Britain's major imports, to the detriment of commodity exporters in the periphery.[38] The empirical evidence for this hypothesis is scanty. Studies of factors affecting terms of trade have shown that there was a broad inverse relationship between British terms of trade and the business cycle, or that British export prices fell more rapidly in recessions than did import prices, but this is not the effect Triffin suggested. Much more important than interest rate changes were the fluctuations in demand which bore no simple relation to British discount rates. More competitive British export prices may have been a factor leading to the subsequent recovery of the cycle, since Britain was generally led into the boom phase by rapid export growth. The UK trade balance tended to improve with the business cycle, with exports being further promoted by generalised growth and British capital exports.[39]

The greater instability of the capital-importing economies does nonetheless imply that the benefits of the pre-1914 international monetary system were to some extent concentrated in the core economies. This challenges not only the classical theory of the operation of the gold standard system, but also the idea that the international gold standard constituted an international public good, the benefits of which were equally available to all. It may not be inconsistent with the coercive view of hegemonic power, that the hegemon will use its power to construct and maintain an international economic order in its own particular interest. As Cohen has written, 'the stability insured by British monetary management was confined largely to the core of advanced nations in Europe and the regions of recent settlement'.[40]

The adjustment mechanism and the rules of the game

Most of those who have examined the operation of the international gold standard have concluded that there is a major discrepancy between the predictions of classical theory and the empirical evidence. For example, contrary to the predictions of the price-specie flow mechanism, price changes in different countries were positively rather than negatively correlated in the short run, suggesting that the relative price mechanism was weak or even inoperative between countries.[41] Parallelism can also be witnessed in international business cycles and in the growth of international trade, with exports and imports growing together for a good deal of the period rather than moving in opposite directions.[42] In general, the classical view that adjustment proceeded through equilibrating changes in countries' balances of trade has been seriously disputed; a number of countries were able to finance persistent current account deficits (North America, the Dominions) or sustain surpluses (Britain, France and Germany). This attests to the growth of trade and financial interdependence in the pre-1914 years.

The inadequacy of actual flows of gold to explain the balance of payments adjustments that did take place led Friedman and Schwartz to argue that it was the money supply which determined domestic prices and incomes in the short run, with gold reserves being part of the monetary base. A loss of gold reserves, given the concentration by central banks upon reserve to liability ratios, would signal a shift in monetary policy which would create domestic price and income effects sufficient to restore balance between countries.[43] This argument assumes that the rules of the game of the gold standard were by and large observed by central banks, in the positive sense that reserve losses would signal a tightening of monetary policy sufficient to effect the adjustment without a further running down of gold reserves.

Problems arise with this explanation because it appears that in practice, interest rates between countries moved in parallel rather than in opposite directions.[44] There is also little evidence to suggest that central banks *did* observe the rules of the game during the pre-1914 period in the sense of reinforcing changes in gold reserves with monetary policy adjustments. As Bloomfield found in his study of this question, central banks consistently violated the rules of the game in this positive sense, both before and after 1914.[45] By and large, Bloomfield felt that in the purely passive sense of allowing changes in gold reserves to have their effect upon commercial bank reserves, central banks did observe the rules, and that this was a major reason for the rough stability of the international monetary system during these years. This, he believed, was largely due to a consensus between major states on the usefulness of maintaining the gold parity and a related willingness in the end to accept the consequences for domestic economic activity.[46] Goodhart's conclusion to an empirical study of the British banking system of the period goes even further to argue that in periods of domestic expansion, the Bank of England:

> did not reinforce the liquidity pressures on the banking system ... by deflationary open-market operations. Instead the Bank seems to have generally followed the practice of passively granting the discount market the accommodation required, at that level of Bank rate chosen by itself.[47]

The flexibility provided by the lender of last resort role of the Bank of England *vis-à-vis* the British banking system was, Goodhart argued, a major reason for the absence of major financial and economic crises in Britain during the period. Strict observance of the rules of the game, allowing the monetary base to reflect gold flows, would have led to considerable financial and real economic instability, both in Britain and abroad. By downplaying the importance of the rules of the game in the operation of the British and international monetary systems, these findings conflict with the common claim in the literature that the British hegemon played an important rule-establishment and enforcement role. Ironically, that Britain provided a bad example by *not* observing the rules may have been an important explanation of the relative stability of the British economy (and to some extent the world economy).

An alternative explanation could be provided by the Monetary

Approach, which denies the relevance of adherence to the rules of the game to the operation of the gold standard adjustment mechanism. Its supporters argue that the parallelism of international price and interest rate movements is explained by arbitrage in international goods and financial markets.[48] The related idea that central banks had no influence over domestic interest rates, however, would appear to be incorrect. It is generally accepted that the Bank of England at least had considerable influence over domestic interest rates through manipulation of its discount rate.

Morgenstern and others found significant imperfections in the international financial markets of the period, with large differentials in interest rates on similar assets across countries persisting over time. There is also much evidence of imperfection in the currency markets of the period.[49] In addition, while the monetary approach assumes that income effects of changing credit conditions will be negligible due to a permanent state of full employment equilibrium in the real economy, the evidence suggests that changes in credit conditions did affect real income both in Britain and abroad.[50] In general, the monetary approach exaggerates the level of financial integration which existed in the pre-1914 period and underestimates the financial asymmetries which favoured the most important countries.

The 'management' of the international gold standard

If it is doubtful that hegemonic rule enforcement was of importance in the operation of the international gold standard, did the Bank of England, at the centre of the British and international banking systems, manage the gold standard for itself and the world as a whole? At least in the British case, there is evidence that discretionary central bank policy helped stabilise the British monetary system. Did it consciously or by default stabilise the world monetary system as well? Kindleberger suggests that this explanation best accounts for the operation of the system:

> [T]he Bank of England set the level of world interest rates, which accounts for the fact that national interest rates moved up and down together, while other countries had power only over a narrow differential between the domestic level and the world rate. With sterling bills traded worldwide, serving as a close substitute for money in foreign countries, and their interest rate manipulated in London, the gold standard was a sterling system.[51]

This highly asymmetrical system, with London at the apex and with the Bank of England able to determine domestic and world interest rates through its discount rate policy, stabilised the world's financial structure and prevented major upheavals in the system of fixed exchange rates.[52]

This view raises a number of issues about the operation and stability of the international financial system in this era. Most of the time, international financial markets operated within limits that were to some extent self-imposed. One of the most important of these limits may have been psychological: the acceptance by most central banks and financial markets of gold as the ultimate international measure of value. Sterling as private and official international credit money was acceptable because of the generally held assumption that it was convertible upon demand into gold on the London market. That the Bank of England's ratio of gold reserves to total short-term liabilities to foreigners could be as great as 1:4.5 or more without confidence problems arising implies that the market believed that convertibility would in the end be assured. This seems to be supported by the general presence of 'stabilising' short-term capital movements during this period.[53]

It is important to note that while this certainly reflected confidence in Britain's ability and willingness to maintain the external gold convertibility of sterling, this must also have been the case for other important countries like France and Germany and in fact most gold standard countries. As Bloomfield found, 'only a trifling number of countries were forced off the gold standard, once adopted, and devaluations of gold currencies were highly exceptional.'[54] The major countries were on the whole willing to accept the costs of domestic economic adjustment so as to maintain the gold convertibility of their currencies, though there were a number of instances in which countries had to undertake emergency borrowing from abroad. As a result:

> relatively excessive (from an international point of view) internal expansions tended to have effects similar to balance of payments pressures, as far as the managing Authorities were concerned, and to result in situations where rates of domestic expansion were moderated in the short run. The obverse was true in periods of recession.'[55]

The acceptance of a fairly strong external constraint upon domestic economic expansion was sufficient to produce a reasonable degree of stability in the international monetary system.

The persistently strong current account position of Britain during the gold standard era meant that the main avenue through which an external imbalance could emerge for that country was through the capital account. The financing of foreign companies, institutions and governments was necessarily constrained to some extent by the availability of credit for particular industries and countries in the major

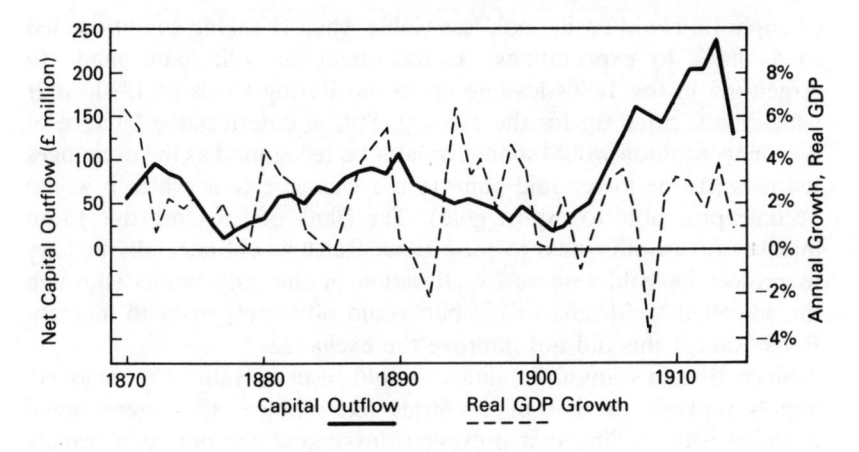

Source: Feinstein, 1972, tables 6 and 15, appendix.
Figure 4.1 British net capital outflow vs. growth in real GDP, 1870–1913.

international financial centres. If a foreign borrower ran up against the limits of its existing borrowing capability, or if there were changes in its perceived creditworthiness, market reactions would be fairly rapid. Access to the wholesale debt markets for such borrowers or for the London branches of their domestic banks to credit in the discount market would be increasingly difficult.[56]

Although such self-regulating factors may have been important most of the time, overlending or overborrowing periodically occurred, creating international imbalances which required policy adjustments, often in the wake of crises. For example, the international cyclical upturn from 1910 led not only to a rapid growth in British trade, but also pushed vast funds from Britain (half national savings) to countries like America in particular (see figure 4.1). The financial panic which broke out on Wall Street and on the bourses of Europe when the likelihood of war in Europe became clear in July 1914 engendered a run on the City of London, America's and the world's largest creditor with a considerable stake in the New York market.[57] As Kindleberger has written: 'The 1914 British [lending] bubble would have shortly burst had the outbreak of war not halted its expansion and deflated it prematurely'. The result was that the Bank had to launch 'the most pervasive lender-of-last-resort operation of the time'.[58]

Part of the problem was that in the case of overlending, the deterioration in the lending country's payments position would not appear immediately, since foreigners might take some time to draw down bank balances held in London or Paris. Loans made in periods of euphoria could easily look less viable when changing conditions led to a shock to expectations, as was the case with loans made to Argentina in the 1880s leading up to the Baring Crisis of 1890, after which loans dried up for the country. Still, a deteriorating balance of payments position would sooner or later be recognised as the exchanges fell towards the lower gold point (the exchange rate at which it would become profitable to export gold). The Bank of England, due to an inability or unwillingness to raise Bank Rate, would normally first try to protect its gold reserve by alteration of the gold points (through the so-called 'gold devices'),[59] but would ultimately need to increase Bank Rate if this did not improve the exchanges.

Since Britain's liquid liabilities to gold reserves ratio was relatively high compared to that of countries like France, the international confidence in sterling that prevailed throughout the period is usually attributed to the potential 'pulling power' of the Bank Rate. For example, Cohen argues that 'virtually any amount of money could be drawn into London, whenever it was necessary to maintain external liquidity, by raising interest rates.'[60] An increase in Bank Rate, made effective in the market through open market operations, would work to improve the capital account balance in a number of ways. The various mechanisms which operated also serve to illustrate most vividly the degree of asymmetry and hierarchy between different countries under the international gold standard.

First, higher interest rates in London would attract short-term capital from abroad, since the probability of exchange gains was high, whilst it would induce investors or banks to delay the transfer of funds abroad. Here, we encounter a problem, since if the Bank of England raised domestic interest rates, would this not force rates up in other countries (as Kindleberger seemed to be suggesting above), leading to a potentially destabilising deflationary process? Part of the reason why deflation was not widespread was that some major countries, France in particular, relied to a much lesser extent than Britain on discount rate changes in their monetary management. France's gold reserves were more than three times those of Britain's and gave it much more room to adopt an approach of waiting until the storm was over.

Peter Lindert argued that even in the absence of changes in international interest rate differentials, London had superior 'pulling power' not only over the shallower financial centres in Europe, but also over the other major centres of Paris and Berlin. When discount rates rose together, the tendency of the banking system to increase the liquidity of their portfolios would inevitably lead to a movement of short-term funds towards the largest financial centres. The operation of this international adjustment mechanism depended upon a hierarchy of financial centres: London occupied the first tier, Berlin and Paris the second, while Amsterdam, Vienna, Zurich, Milan, Brussels and others occupied a third.[61] Britain did not simply export deflation to Berlin and Paris, because these two centres, especially Berlin, could in turn attract funds from the third tier of countries in central Europe, most of whom consistently ran payments surpluses in the years before 1914. Lindert concluded that the 'ability of the system to tap surplus-country funds in support of key currencies seems to have contributed to the stability of, and confidence in, the key currency system before 1914.'[62]

Another element in the adjustment response set in train by an increase in Bank Rate in London was the sensitivity of finance bills to variations in interest rates. Given the dominance of British finance bills in international trade, this would add to the Bank of England's ability to improve the exchanges in the short run. An increase in interest rates may have delayed the issuance of new long-term foreign bonds as well, temporarily reducing the rate at which long-term capital left the country.[63] Contrary to Triffin's argument about the terms of trade effects of discount rate changes, what evidence there is suggests that the most important factor in the adjustment mechanism was short-term capital movements rather than current account adjustment. This is not to argue that changes in discount rates did not have any real effects, but these are difficult to quantify.[64]

In summary, higher interest rates in Britain were an important factor in the international adjustment mechanism which was intimately connected with the hierarchical structure of the world financial system. Net capital inflows from Paris and Berlin were not necessarily deflationary for the rest of the world if surplus funds were transferred from the third tier of countries in Europe to the major financial centres. The ability of Paris in particular to resist discount rate rises in times of crisis may have been especially important in preventing a deflationary process spreading to other countries. In other words, although Britain may have been at the top of this financial structure, this does not support the view that the Bank of England could manage the system alone or that it was necessarily conscious of the international dimensions of its actions.

Two particular aspects of the claim made for Britain's active role as world monetary manager require additional attention. First, the idea that Britain provided lender of last resort finance to the rest of the world in periods of financial distress is crucial to the concept of management. Second, there is the oft-made claim that Britain also (presumably unconsciously) stabilised the world economy by engaging in long-term countercyclical lending.

Turning to the issue of the provision of short-term finance, it is necessary to point out from the beginning that the evidence pertaining to the question is very sparse. One thing that can be said with relative certainty is that the slenderness of the Bank of England's gold reserves and capital meant that often it could not hope to play any direct role in offering short-term credits abroad in periods of distress. In fact, the very limited reserves of the Bank of England tended to necessitate that it did the opposite (by raising discount rates and attracting gold in times of difficulty), which would hardly indicate stabilising behaviour.[65] Most economists have therefore concentrated upon Britain's position as the world's largest gross short-term creditor before 1914 in trying to demonstrate that its net creditor position fluctuated in a stabilising manner. The idea that Britain managed the international gold standard amounts to the proposition that its liquidity position *vis-à-vis* the rest of the world fluctuated in a way conducive to the stability of the system.

Given the almost complete lack of statistical evidence regarding the relationship between Britain's net liquidity position and the international business cycle, it is impossible to decide whether Britain expanded her short-term credits abroad in times of domestic recession and contracted them in times of ease. As Jacob Viner noted in 1945:

> It is a commonplace that England was during the nineteenth century the efficient manager of the international gold standard, and that the Bank of England was the agency through which this management was applied. It is extraordinary, however, how little systematic study of the workings of the pre-1914 gold standard has ever been engaged in, and how little concrete evidence has been available as to the extent or the quality of its management.[66]

The state of the empirical evidence, unfortunately, has little improved since then, though the view Viner referred to has continued to play a prominent role in the post-1945 literature. For example, E.S. Shaw believed that: 'Great Britain was the pre-1914 International Monetary Fund. Her loans to countries having temporary difficulties with their balances of payments saved the borrowers from gold exports, exchange depreciation, or internal deflation.'[67]

Although the period 1880–1914 experienced no severe, prolonged, depression comparable to that of 1929–33, there was considerable economic instability, some examples of exchange depreciation and exchange controls in both centre and periphery in these years. The pre-1914 era was by no means the trouble-free golden age that some suggest. More specifically, there is little evidence that Britain acted as a lender of last resort on the Continent of Europe or in North America.

Even within the Empire itself, local financial crises in the nineteenth century were more often dealt with by local institutions and local funds, though such action was often insufficient to prevent considerable distress. There seem to be isolated instances in which colonial governments in the 1890s in Australia and India gained some aid in crises from the Bank of England and the British money market, though the evidence points more in the direction of a severely underdeveloped lender-of-last-resort facility even in the heart of the Empire.[68] Kindleberger himself has taken a fairly qualified view in recent years, arguing that 'the existence of an international lender of last resort made the financial crises of 1825, 1836, 1847, 1866 and 1907 more or less ephemeral, like summer storms, whereas its absence in 1873, 1890, and 1929 produced deep depressions'.[69]

Bloomfield, who examined extensively the role of short-term capital flows in the pre-1914 system, felt that while Britain managed its own gold standard, he was sceptical of the claim that Britain played a management role in the international system as a whole, especially of the idea that it did so consciously. The City of London was concerned with its own liquidity position and the profitability of its operations, but there was no firm evidence to suggest that it expanded its net foreign credits unless it was seen as profitable to do so.[70] The paradox here is that if the City of London had not operated on the basis of profitability, then the international confidence in sterling, upon which the internationalisation of the British banking system depended, might have been impaired. It seems likely that the London financial community sometimes acted to reduce its overseas commitments in times of difficulty, as was probably the case in the period following the world downturn of 1873 and after the severe crisis of 1890. Put differently, if we ought to regard the stability in the value of sterling as an international public good (something Kindleberger for one has often suggested), then there may have been a trade-off between a stable pound and the British financial system's ability or willingness to act in a manner conducive to anti-cyclical short-term capital flows.

In the absence of statistical evidence, the claim that Britain managed the international gold standard amounts to the belief which Hayek and others exhibited that banks' decisions based upon considerations of profitability would not conflict with the conditions for systemic stability. Acting as a 'bank' for the rest of the world, which Britain to some extent did, is not necessarily the same thing as acting as its proxy *central* bank. The doubtfulness of the claim that Britain performed the latter role in addition to the former means that international relations writers may simply be repeating an old claim of economists which has little basis in fact.

Table 4.4 Shares (per cent) of gold reserves of major countries.

Country	1889	1899	1910
UK	6	5	4
France	17	14	15
Germany	6	5	4
Austria-Hungary	2	8	6
Russia	4	7	1
United States	29	26	33
Other	36	35	37
Total	100	100	100

Source: de Cecco, 1974, table 13, p. 244.

The suspicion that this is so is heightened by the prominence in the literature of the idea that only hegemonic powers like Britain have provided international lender-of-last-resort facilities.[71] Historical practice was considerably more complex. There is little evidence to suggest, as we have seen, that the practice of granting emergency credits to foreigners was widespread in the period. When central banks did grant emergency loans to foreigners, it was by no means always a case of Britain lending to other countries. In fact, while the Bank of England lent money or gold on such a basis to the Bank of France in 1846 and 1860, in the classical era of the international gold standard, Britain tended to be on the receiving end because of its low level of reserves. In the Baring crisis of 1890 the Bank of England borrowed £3.8 million in gold from the French and Russian central banks, and during the 1907 crisis the Bank of France again came to the aid of the British with a shipment of 80 million francs in gold.[72]

As the international competition for gold reserves increased in the later years of the gold standard era, of which the 1907 crisis was a manifestation, Britain's slender gold reserve, coupled with the growing reserve role of sterling, made her potentially more dependent upon emergency assistance (or at the least, cooperation) from the strong gold centres like France and the US (see table 4.4).[73] As to the net short-term creditor positions of countries like Germany and France and their relationship to the international business cycle, again the almost complete lack of information allows no categorical answer, though what evidence there is (relating to France) suggests that there was no clear trend to a stabilising or destabilising pattern.[74]

This leads to a general point which deserves emphasis: it is unlikely that Britain provided the necessary conditions for the maintenance of the pre-1914 system alone, since at least in times of strain it relied upon cooperation from the central banks of other great powers, especially the Bank of France. When it is recalled that on the Continent, Berlin and Paris were the most important financial centres, and that the mark and franc were used as reserve currencies along with sterling, the picture of the pre-1914 international monetary system appears more pluralistic than the term hegemony conveys. The broad policy consistency which operated under the international gold standard was more the product of similar domestic monetary institutions and a commitment to the general observance of an external monetary constraint, rather than the 'policy cooperation' which was to become such an important issue in the twentieth century. The Bank of England was arguably foremost in its selfish management of Britain's gold standard. Viner's judgement was harsh in this respect:

> the Bank of England never showed any interest in developing connections with other central banks and in systematically planning in advance for collaboration in case of need . . . [It] was completely unenterprising and unimaginative. It contented itself with looking after convertibility of its notes, and left it to other countries to keep their monetary affairs in order in the same narrow sense . . . [Hence] as far as the international aspect of the gold standard was concerned, there is nothing . . . which gives any support to the claim that the Bank 'managed' the gold standard.[75]

It is easy to exaggerate the influence of the Bank of England or any other central bank in the international financial system of the time. The size of the capital flows that passed through London and the other financial centres dwarfed Bank of England reserves. The Bank also had increasing difficulties in making its discount rate effective in the market from the 1880s. The rise of the large joint-stock banks and their increasing dominance of the money market resulted in an erosion of Bank of England power because the former were not compelled to hold cash reserves or deposits with the central bank. Although in practice some such reserves were held by the banks, the absence of legal reserve requirements meant that the Bank of England lacked a key element of monetary policy. In the years before 1914, this loss of control over the domestic money market accelerated.[76]

What of the related claim that the flow of British long-term investment was countercyclical, increasing in times of domestic recession and decreasing during domestic booms? In the last quarter of the nineteenth century, foreign investment over the 'long swing' and domestic activity were in general negatively correlated, though in the shorter run, this was not always the case.[77] From what it is possible to tell from the statistical evidence, the first half of the 1870s, the end

Table 4.5 Growth of foreign investments of leading capital exporting countries, 1870–1914 ($ million).

Country	1870	1885	1900	1914
United Kingdom	4,900	7,800	12,100	19,500
France	2,500	3,300	5,200	8,600
Germany	n.a.	1,900	4,800	6,700
United States	n	n	500	2,500

n.a. = not available.
n = negligible.
Source: Woodruff, 1966, p. 150.

of the 1880s, and turning points in the domestic cycle are possible exceptions to the long swing pattern, when domestic boom coincided with large capital exports (see figure 4.1). From around 1905, with British foreign investment rising to new heights, there was a considerable period of pro-cyclical movement in net capital exports.[78] Britain may not have been the consistent countercyclical capital exporter that some believe it to have been.

Other countries such as Germany and France were important exporters of long-term capital before 1914 (see table 4.5). Both France and Germany were active investors on the Continent, and France in Africa and Latin America. There is evidence to suggest that French foreign investment and domestic activity were positively correlated at least some of the time. In addition, the gross flow of long-term investment capital from the major countries to the capital importing countries was subject to considerable instability.[79]

The pro-cyclical flow of international lending in many of the years 1870–1914 is understandable if the dependence of the British economy upon growth in international trade is taken into account. If developing countries were to maintain credit-worthiness and grow at the same time, then they had to export more goods to the centre countries (Britain included). The latter would join in the process of importing and exporting more goods, as well as making new investments in the periphery. This kind of sustainable, positive relationship between international trade and investment flows was made easier as the flow of savings from the advanced countries was going to finance investment in infrastructure and similar basic development in the periphery.[80] In conjunction with the rapid advances in sea transport over the nineteenth century, this dramatically increased the supply and made cheaper the food and raw materials which the advanced countries wished to import. Eventually, however, industrialisation outside Europe, above all in

North America, would have more ambiguous consequences for Europe's position because it led to the rise of import and ultimately export competitive industries in these countries.

Britain's rising trade deficits with Europe and North America in the decades before 1914 made it increasingly reliant upon less competitive export markets in the Empire. The Empire's trade surpluses with Europe and North America and its willingness to conduct its financing largely through the British banking system allowed Britain to clear its deficits with the other advanced countries and to pursue the global economic and political role to which it had become accustomed. As a result, the strength of the major creditor economy during this period derived in part from its commanding position within Empire trade and finance, but it would be an exaggeration to speak of its 'hegemony' over other large economies. As Saul points out, '[h]ad not British exports ... found a wide-open market in India ... it would have been impossible for her to have indulged so heavily in investment on the American continent and elsewhere.'[81]

Foreign investment and the financial services offered by the City of London were to provide the key to Britain's current surpluses over the period as the role of manufacturing in the economy declined. How long this could last was debatable, since the export of around 40 per cent of domestic savings in this period was possibly aggravating the problem of slower capital accumulation at home than in other major countries. The last years of the nineteenth century also saw the emergence of rival financial centres in Berlin, Paris and even New York, providing competition in the field of financial services and resulting in some degree of change in the international financial hierarchy in which Britain was at the top. Such trends would detract from Britain's ability in the long term to maintain such a strong current account position and at the same time preserve its pre-eminent role in much of the periphery and on the oceans. The growing dependence upon invisible trade if anything tied Britain to dependence upon the maintenance of international peace even more than the free-trade doctrines of the mid-nineteenth century.[82]

The breakdown of the Concert of Europe exposed this weakness, compelling Britain to allocate more of its limited resources to the defence of the homeland. As many have pointed out, the fact that it was able to operate and defend a global Empire on the cheap was largely due to its industrial lead and 'the fact that outside Europe Britain largely operated in a power-political vacuum.'[83] With a host of rival powers challenging Britain's industrial and imperial position by the late nineteenth century, in retrospect the rapidity of Britain's relative decline seems less surprising than it might otherwise.

This inevitably led to some erosion of Britain's financial pre-eminence, while on the domestic front, the Bank of England was having difficulty in managing the domestic money market, especially given the growing role of short-term capital movements. These problems came to a head by 1907, when a financial crisis in New York spread to London, forcing the Bank to resort to a large loan from the Bank of France. Bank Rate, due to both internal and external developments, was becoming less powerful as a means of managing Britain's own gold standard, let alone that of the world. By 1914, the position of the Bank of England had so deteriorated *vis-à-vis* the joint stock banks that in the financial crisis of July–August 1914, the government had to intermediate between the two parties, suspending the Bank Act and monetising the bill market.[84]

At the same time, pressures to focus more attention on the domestic economy were growing in all states. The beginnings of a fundamental shift in the domestic balance of power between state and market economy was under way, with reformist moves in Bismarck's Germany, in Britain and elsewhere resulting in a growing share of state expenditure in GDP.[85] This growing state role, soon to be dramatically enhanced as a result of World War I, was ultimately to clash with the demands of the external constraint represented by the international gold standard. While the dominant attitude in Britain remained one of *laissez-faire*, financial crises in 1890, 1907 and 1914 highlighted the growing vulnerability of the British economy to developments abroad.[86] The increasing importance of short-term capital movements and the growing competition for gold in the years after 1900 (the political implications of which were highlighted by Germany's creation of a 'war-reserve' of gold in Spandau in Berlin) left Britain particularly vulnerable.

For those who wished to retain the multilateral system of the pre-1914 world, there was, even as early as 1907–8, increasing recognition of the growing volatility of international financial movements, connected with calls for higher gold reserves to enable the maintenance of more stable interest rates and/or to create a war-chest. Less important but nevertheless telling was a 'growing sentiment in certain quarters in favour of some kind of systematic international monetary cooperation, the absence of which was a conspicuous feature of the pre-1914 arrangements.'[87] As we shall see, while the process of 'national economic integration' progressed during and after World War I, the failure to foster any new basis for international monetary cooperation eventually led to a complete breakdown of the old order.

4.5 Conclusion

In summary, the theory of hegemonic stability does not provide a satisfactory account of the relationship between the international balance of power in the pre-1914 era and operation of the international gold standard. Britain played a very limited role in the establishment of the gold standard in the 1870s; economic and political factors very indirectly connected with British power and influence provided a more important impetus. The idea of Britain fostering order by upholding the ground rules of the international economy and monetary system was also found to have little basis in reality. Even if it is useful to describe the international gold standard as a regime, given the lack of strong rules, it was a regime which owed its establishment more to perceived national interest than hegemonic power.

The stability of the exchange rate structure during this period was to some extent achieved at the expense of macroeconomic stability, both in Britain and the other major countries and more so in the periphery. In Britain's own case, stability relative to what was to come after the war was due in no small part to the Bank of England's growing role as a central bank which managed the British financial system given the constraint of a very slender gold reserve. Relative stability in Britain was probably important for stability in the rest of the world, given that country's pivotal international position. That Britain's own success was not usually at the expense of other countries appears to have owed less to any world monetary management role than to the ability of other major countries to maintain monetary stability when London was absorbing gold. In times of severe crisis, the strong financial position of Paris was especially useful in maintaining international stability.

It might be more true to argue that the pre-1914 structure rested less upon British hegemony than the general dominance of the European great powers over their own spheres of influence. This was reflected in their financial dominance over smaller states in the European area and abroad. Britain's own strong current account position and ability to invest abroad at a remarkable rate was very dependent upon its position within the trading and financial structure of the Empire. The collapse of the Concert of Europe in 1914 was as destabilising for Britain as it was for the rest of the world.

Also important for the operation of the international gold standard was the assumption that there was little alternative but for the monetary authorities to maintain their par-values in terms of gold. The reigning assumption of the pre-1914 period was that gold was an immutable standard, above all for sterling itself, and this probably played an important role in stabilising financial markets. Once the experience of the Great War was to shatter this assumption along with many others, stability would be much more difficult to attain. Most countries were willing to accept before 1914 that a strong external constraint upon domestic economic expansion was unavoidable. To some extent this may have been due to the development of domestic and international banking, which allowed a degree of flexibility which could not otherwise have been provided by the inelastic supply of gold. The relative openness of the major countries' markets also helped facilitate adjustment to the rapid structural change which was occurring, preventing the emergence of imbalances which might have disrupted the international monetary system. British attachment to freedom of trade and capital flows was important and to that extent Britain exercised 'leadership'. When it came to international monetary affairs, however, British interests were limited to managing its own gold standard with little thought of promoting cooperation between the major countries, despite the difficulties posed by growing short-term capital movements.

Private financial markets, while innovative, exhibited considerable tendencies towards instability, and the ability of governments or central banks to offset this was not great (nor was this seen as surprising). Ultimately, the limited role of the state in the economy was inseparable from the domestic social structure of the major countries. To put it differently, relative stability was not only enjoyed by the dominant states of Europe to a much greater degree than those in the periphery, but also by some domestic social classes more than others. A consensus existed on the possibilities of state intervention which may in part have been related to an ability of the ruling elites to pass on the costs of economic instability to other groups in society. The breakdown of this domestic political 'consensus' was, it will be argued, a key factor in the international monetary instability of the interwar period. Any theory which attempts to provide an account of international monetary relations before 1914 largely in terms of the structure of the international states-system risks overlooking a number of important domestic and attitudinal factors unique to the pre-war world. 'Hegemony', as applied to Britain's position in the international system from 1870–1914, cannot bear the weight of explanatory power that some have tried to thrust upon it.

Notes

1. Gilpin, 1981, p.135.
2. *ibid.*, pp.138–9.
3. Gilpin, 1987, p.126.
4. Cohen, 1977, pp.81–2. Gilpin's latest position is also consistent with a Keynesian interpretation (1987, p.124).
5. Kindleberger, 1973, p.292, 1984, p.70. See also Minsky, 1979, pp.110–11.
6. Brett, 1983, pp.19, 29–30; Sandretto, 1983, pp.104–5; Mandel, 1980, pp. 30–6.
7. Many of the figures contained in table 5.3, and much of what follows on the relative size and importance of national economies should be treated with caution. Much of the literature in this area places excessive weight on what can only be described as very inadequate estimates of the relative international positions of major economies. Although the quality of the data for the post-1945 period is more reliable, as we shall see, such comparisons have been complicated enormously by large movements in exchange rates over the past two decades. With this caveat in mind, such estimates can be of use in giving an *indication* of relative economic weights of major countries.
8. Floud and McCloskey, 1981, pp.7–8.
9. Kennedy, 1988, p.151.
10. Rostow, 1978, pp.70–2.
11. Maizels, 1963, table 8.1, p.189.
12. *ibid.*, pp.191–4, and Rostow, 1978, pp.178–85.
13. Kennedy, 1988, pp.152–8.
14. Williams, 1968, p.268; Triffin, 1968, pp.10–11; de Cecco, 1974, pp.104–6.
15. Williams, 1968, pp.286–7.
16. Lindert, 1969, pp.17–25,37–40; Bloomfield, 1963, pp.13–14.
17. Kindleberger, 1984, pp.265–8.
18. Woodruff, 1966, pp.150–4.
19. Floud and McCloskey, 1981, ch.1; Maddison, 1982, p.38.
20. Gilpin, 1987, p.73.
21. See Kindleberger, 1978b, pp.39–65; Mathias, 1969, p.316; Checkland, 1964, p.67; Stein, 1984, pp.367–74.
22. Kindleberger, 1978b, p.65.
23. Stern, 1987, ch.8,15; Kindleberger, 1984, ch.12,14.
24. de Cecco, 1974, ch.3; Kindleberger, 1984, pp.64–7.
25. League of Nations, 1944, p.231.
26. Williams, 1968, pp.272–4.
27. For a discussion and the above quotations, see Yeager, 1984, pp.657–9.
28. Williams, 1968, pp.272–4.
29. Maddison, 1982, p.91. See also Maizels, 1963, pp.80,98.
30. Morgenstern, 1959, ch.5.
31. I am indebted to Sir Alec Cairncross for this point.
32. Triffin, 1968, pp.8–14; Lindert, 1969, pp.47–57; Moggridge, 1972, pp.6–7.
33. Bloomfield, 1963, pp.83–4; Williams, 1968, p.272.
34. Moggridge, 1972, p.6.
35. Calculated from Maddison, 1982, table 4.1, p.67. See also p.61.
36. Triffin, 1968, p.8.

37. For evidence, see Bloomfield, 1968a, charts 1 and 2, pp.8–9, and Appendix 3.
38. Triffin, 1968, p.9. Others have also emphasised this effect, e.g. Cohen, 1971, pp.62–3.
39. Rostow, 1978, pp.94,329; Kindleberger, 1956, ch.7; Cairncross, 1953, pp.189–92.
40. Cohen, 1977, p.82.
41. Triffin, 1968, pp.5–6. This makes Gilpin's assertion that 'Hume's price-specie flow mechanism continued to characterise international monetary relations into the twentieth century' (1987, p.121) difficult to support.
42. Between 1890 and 1913 'the value of exports and imports in Belgium, France, Germany, Britain and the US moved in the same direction in 72.9 and 73.9 per cent of the years observed. The trade balances of these countries moved in the same direction 68.7 per cent of the time.' (Moggridge, 1972, p.5.) Morgenstern (1959, pp.44–8) found that over 1878–1914, the three major European economies were in the same 'reference' phase of the business cycle 83 per cent of the time, though the US was the odd man out, being in the same phase only 53 per cent of the time. See also Maizels, 1963, table 4.4, p.89.
43. Friedman and Schwartz, 1982, pp.28ff.
44. Triffin, 1968, p.12; Bloomfield, 1959, pp.35–7.
45. Bloomfield, 1959, pp.48–51.
46. Ruggie, 1982, p.386, and van Buren Cleveland, 1976, p.57, make similar points.
47. Goodhart, 1972, pp.218–19. There is even some more recent evidence which suggests that some (probably limited) degree of sterilisation of the impact of gold flows upon bank reserves may have occurred in the short run, though it is doubtful whether this was due to any conscious anti-cyclical policy on the part of the Bank of England. See Dutton, 1984, and Dornbusch and Frenkel, 1984, pp.244–8.
48. McCloskey and Zecher, 1976, pp.371–9; Pippenger, 1984.
49. Morgenstern, 1959, pp.160–5,276; Bloomfield, 1963, p.45.
50. See Williams, 1968, p.276; Goodhart's comments on Pippenger, 1984, especially pp.229–30.
51. Kindleberger, 1984, p.70.
52. Cohen, 1977, p.82.
53. Bloomfield, 1963, pp.43–4; League of Nations, 1944, pp.15–16. Bloomfield notes, however, that destabilising movements of short-term capital were greater than has sometimes been assumed, and that in at least two important cases (the US and Russia) such movements led to the adoption of temporary exchange controls (1963, ch.5).
54. Bloomfield, 1968b, p.27, note 2.
55. Moggridge, 1972, p.6.
56. Williams, 1968, pp.276–7.
57. See de Cecco, 1974, ch.7, and 1984, p.18.
58. Kindleberger, 1984, pp.259,291.
59. Moggridge, 1972, p.8, note 4.
60. Cohen, 1971, p.59.
61. Lindert, 1969, pp.47–57.
62. *ibid.*, p.57.
63. Moggridge, 1972, p.9; Bloomfield, 1963, ch.3.

64. See the discussion in Moggridge, 1972, pp.10–13; Lindert, 1969, pp.44–6.
65. Viner, 1945, p.63.
66. *ibid.*
67. Quoted in Bloomfield, 1963, p.77.
68. See Pressnell, 1982, and comments by Bloomfield and Fischer, especially pp.151–60.
69. Kindleberger, 1986, p.9.
70. Bloomfield, 1963, p.77.
71. For example Cohen, 1977, pp.81–2; Krasner, 1976, p.336; Gilpin, 1987, p.309.
72. Kindleberger, 1984, p.281.
73. See Bloomfield, 1963, pp.30–3; Pressnell, 1968, especially pp.219–28; de Cecco, 1974, pp.115–26.
74. *ibid.*, pp.65–70.
75. Viner, 1945, p.64.
76. See de Cecco, 1974, pp.86–102.
77. Cairncross, 1953, ch.7.
78. Kindleberger, 1984, pp.256–9, and 1985, p.9; Bloomfield, 1968a, pp.22–4; Cairncross, 1953, pp.187ff.
79. Bloomfield, 1968a, pp.32–3, and Kindleberger, 1984, p.258.
80. Williams, 1968, pp.281–2.
81. Saul, 1960, p.88. See also pp.62–3, and de Cecco, 1974, pp.26–38.
82. See the good general discussion in Kennedy, 1981, pp.17–73.
83. *ibid.*, pp.32–3.
84. de Cecco, 1974, ch.7.
85. See Stone, 1983, part II.
86. Bloomfield, 1963, pp.88–9; Pressnell, 1968, pp.220–27.
87. Bloomfield, 1963, p.91.

Chapter 5
International monetary disorder in the interwar period

5.1 Introduction

This chapter will consider the hypothesis that the instability of the international monetary and financial system of the interwar years was due to the absence of a hegemonic power. Since this period of 'interregnum' between British and American hegemonies is often compared with the contemporary era, it is crucial to an analysis of the theory that hegemony is a necessary condition of international monetary stability.

Depending upon the emphasis, different commentators allow varying degrees of 'autonomy' for economic and monetary factors in explaining the instability and breakdown of the system in the Great Depression. Those who stress the function of hegemonic rule-enforcement place least emphasis upon autonomous economic or monetary factors and much more upon the political causes of instability. Keohane's claim can be interpreted along these lines:

> [W]hat prevented American leadership of a cooperative world political economy in these years was less lack of economic resources than an absence of political willingness to make and enforce rules for the system. Britain, despite its efforts, was too weak to do so effectively.[1]

Rather than concentrating upon the absence of effective regimes, others emphasise the absence of global monetary management on the part of a dominant power as the crucial factor which distinguishes the interwar period from the pre-war international gold standard. Kindleberger has stated this case most vividly in arguing that the length and depth of the Great Depression and the collapse of the international

International monetary disorder in the interwar period   117

Table 5.1   British bilateral trade balances, 1913 and 1924 (£ million).

Area	Balance	Balance	Change
W. Europe	−16.9	−29.0	−12.1
Cent. & S.E. Europe	−21.2	+22.1	+43.3
S. Europe & N. Africa	+6.1	+0.6	−5.5
Turkey & Middle East	−8.5	−22.6	−13.5
Rest of Africa	+19.8	+7.8	−12.0
Asia	+35.7	+31.5	−4.2
USA	−82.2	−162.6	−80.4
British N. America	−3.2	−35.2	−32.2
West Indies	+0.2	−12.4	−12.6
Cent. & S. America	−17.2	−61.2	−44.0
Australasia	−8.7	−18.7	−10.0

Source: Moggridge, 1972, p. 34.

monetary system was due to the absence of a 'stabiliser': 'In 1929 the British couldn't and the United States wouldn't.'[2] Some radical writers like Mandel have integrated this view into their accounts of the period. Mandel speaks of the 'procrastination' of the imperialist powers during and after 1929–33, even quoting Kindleberger on the lack of leadership in the crisis by either Britain or America.[3]

Most commentators rightly see World War I as a fundamental turning-point in the evolution of the world political economy, and it is important initially to consider the general economic impact of that war upon the relative power-position of the major countries. In a number of important respects, the war had the effect of accelerating tendencies which were already apparent well before 1914. We turn now to a broad overview of these developments.

5.2   The aftermath of World War I and the world economy

The most important effect of the war for our purposes was the way in which it accelerated the decline of British power relative to that of the US. This can be seen in a number of aspects. For example, Britain's international trading position deteriorated most dramatically in trade with the 'dollar area'. This can be seen by comparing estimates of Britain's bilateral trade balances in two reasonably representative years, 1913 and 1924 (table 5.1). The only improvement in Britain's bilateral trade balances between these years was with Central and South-Eastern Europe, to a large degree the result of the temporary

Table 5.2 British current account, selected years (£ millions).

Year	Merchandise trade	Invisible trade	Net investment earnings	Current A/c balance	Current A/c as % of GDP
1870	−33	53	35	55	4.9
1880	−88	63	58	33	2.5
1890	−53	66	94	107	7.3
1900	−129	59	104	34	1.7
1907	−84	102	144	162	7.5
1913	−82	117	200	235	9.3
1920	−176	239	254	317	5.1
1924	−214	96	196	78	1.8
1925	−265	85	232	52	1.1
1926	−346	91	237	−18	−0.4
1927	−270	129	239	98	2.1
1928	−237	121	240	124	2.7
1929	−263	116	243	96	2.0
1930	−283	104	215	36	0.8
1931	−322	56	163	−103	−2.4
1932	−216	38	127	−51	−1.2
1933	−192	30	154	−8	−0.2

Note: Figures before 1907 are from a different primary source.
Source: Feinstein, 1972, tables 3 & 15, appendix.

weakness of German exports in its traditional markets in the first half of the 1920s. Because trade deficits with the bulk of Europe and the dollar area rose at the same time as its traditional surplus with the Empire deteriorated, Britain's ability to clear its deficits with the other major industrial countries had clearly declined. This situation was aggravated by the fact that although the surplus on invisibles rose in nominal terms from 1913 to 1924, in real terms it actually fell by more than 25 per cent (the visible trade deficit had deteriorated by more than 100 per cent in real terms). This reflected the sale of assets and official borrowing (largely from the US) during the war, as well as a general loss of financial business due to the rise of New York as a rival financial centre to London.[4]

As can be seen from table 5.2, the marked deterioration in Britain's trade position over the period 1913–24 represented an acceleration of a trend which had been evident for the previous half a century. With the postwar erosion of London's position in international finance *vis-à-vis* New York (and later Paris) and the loss of its pre-eminent role in international shipping and ship-building, Britain would be unable to rebuild its international financial position unless it could effect a massive turn-around of its trade balance. Table 5.3 (column 5) gives some indication of how New York managed to overtake Britain in the interwar period as the major source of international capital funds. Morgenstern found that from 1876 to 1914, long-term interest rates in New York were always higher than those in London, while from 1925 to 1931, they were higher just more than half the time.[5]

Perhaps the most important consequence of the deterioration in Britain's current account position was that it gave the British economy and British policy-makers much less room for manoeuvre. Above all, given the size of the merchandise trade deficits with the dollar area and Britain's growing inability to cover these through invisible earnings, Britain's dependence upon the management of the US economy and fluctuations emanating from the dollar area in general was considerably increased.

Not only Britain was increasingly dependent upon the American economy. The economic dislocation in Germany, Europe's traditional capital goods exporter along with Britain, meant that Europe as a whole was dependent not only upon US merchandise exports in the early years after the war but also upon US capital exports in order to finance large bilateral trade deficits with the dollar area. Though France sustained a current account surplus for the ten years after 1920, in real terms this was substantially reduced from pre-1914 years. Germany, like all the major European countries, ran a large bilateral trade deficit with the US over the 1920s, but largely due to outflows of reparation payments, it also ran current account deficits for most years even though by the second half of the decade it was running substantial bilateral trade surpluses with its European trading partners.[6] That the major economy in Continental Europe required a net capital inflow to sustain its level of imports and domestic growth was to prove a central structural weakness in the interwar world economy.

As table 5.3 indicates, the relative weight of the US economy in the world economy was considerably enhanced as a result of the war and that of Europe as a whole reduced. The 1920s saw the US economy producing on average well over 40 per cent of world manufacturing output, with Britain producing less than a quarter of this figure. The aggregate size of the US economy was probably greater than that of Britain, Germany and France together, a position which Britain had never enjoyed. The large primary producing sector in the US constituted an additional strength which Britain lacked, though the latter's service industries and some manufacturing sectors were probably still second to none. It is clearly arguable that at least on the raw figures, 'hegemony' in terms of economic preponderance had passed from Britain to America, though the latter's relationship to the world economy was strikingly different to Britain's before 1914.

Table 5.3 Economic and financial comparisons of major Western economies, 1870–1938.

Year	Country	1. Ratio of real national product to British RNP	2. Share of global industrial output (%)	3. Share of world exports (%)	4. Share of world industrial exports (%)	5. Share of world stock/ flow of foreign investment (%)[i]	6. Share of world stock of monetary gold (%)
1870	UK	1	32	25		58	
	US	[a]1.20[a]	23	8		net debtor	
	Germany	n.a.	13	10		12	
	France	0.61	10	10		30	
1913	UK	1	14	16	30	57	3.4
	US	[b]2.24[b]	36	11	13	net debtor	26.6
	Germany	1.03	16	12	27	16	5.8
	France	0.50	6	7	12	26	14.0
1920	UK	1					9.4
	US	3.05					36.1
	Germany	n.a.					3.2
	France	0.66					11.9
1928	UK	1	9[c]	14	22[e]	28[g]	7.2
	US	3.66	42	14	20	43	39.6
	Germany	0.97	12	9	20	net debtor	6.2
	France	0.74	7	6	11	22	12.1
1938	UK	1	9[d]	14	21[f]	14[h]	10.6
	US	3.22	32	10	19	78	57.0
	Germany	1.35	11	9	22	net debtor	0.1
	France	0.56	5	4	6	1	9.6

Notes: [a]1869–78. [b]1904–13. [c]1926–9. [d]1936–8. [e]1929. [f]1937. [g]1921–9. [h]1930–8. [i]Share of stock of foreign capital of three major creditor countries to beginning 1914, % share of flows of foreign capital from creditor countries after World War I.

Sources: Column 1: Clark, 1957, tables 21–3, 40; Column 2: Rostow, 1978, table II-2, p. 52; Column 3: Rostow, 1978, table II-8, pp. 70–3; Column 4: Maizels, 1963, table 8.1, p. 189; Column 5: Kuznets, 1966, pp. 322–3; Column 6: Lindert, 1969, p. 10, Hawtrey, 1947, appendix, pp. 254–5, and *Federal Reserve Bulletin*, February 1940, p. 164.

For example, by the late 1920s the US share of world exports was similar to that of Britain and Germany, but the proportion of manufacturing exports to total manufacturing production (about 8 per cent in 1929 compared to 27 per cent in Germany and 37 per cent in Britain)[7] suggests that the US was still a relatively autarkic economy. The way in which America had built its leading international position through the expansion of an 'internal frontier' was in marked contrast to Britain's dependence on the world economy. There was also an imbalance between the relative autonomy of the US economy and the increasing financial integration of New York into the world economy during the postwar period. The rest of the world's difficulty in financing its current deficits with America led to the problem of how to 'recycle' American surpluses, which averaged $1.4 billion[8] per annum 1920–30. Total US net capital outflows over 1919–23 were $5.1 billion, but this was well under its cumulative current surplus over the same period of $12.4 billion. As a result, US gold reserves, having represented close to 40 per cent of world reserves at the end of the war, increased further to 44 per cent of the world total by 1923.[9]

The term 'dollar shortage' is not an inappropriate characterisation of the situation in the post-World War I years. From March 1919, the Bank of England ceased providing official support for sterling, which fell to what was then an all-time low against the dollar of $3.40 in February 1920. With other formerly important currencies like the mark and franc trading at fractions of their pre-war parities, the dollar was the only important currency on the gold standard and in which a considerable degree of confidence remained.

The most important cause of America's rise to net creditor status was due to US government credits to allies during the war, officially valued at more than $10 billion in 1919, though the real value of these assets was probably considerably less.[10] The bulk of these debts were owed by Britain, France and Italy, with France, Italy and Russia in turn owing Britain an amount not very much smaller. Two consequences of importance flowed from the American insistence that the allied war debts be paid back in full with interest. First, it perpetuated the *status quo* under which Britain was the creditor of less solvent countries (above all Russia), while the bulk of US loans had been to the British and French. Second, it virtually ensured that the allies would insist that Germany pay substantial reparations so as to be able to repay their creditors, which further hindered a solution to the Franco-German problem in Europe, and set up a pattern of international financial transfers that was to collapse in the Great Depression.[11]

Another important consequence of the war for international monetary relations was the growing role of the state in the domestic economy.

Table 5.4 Government expenditures as a percentage of GDP, selected years[12].

Year	France	Germany	Britain	US
1870		9[a]	9	
1880	21[b]	10[c]	10	
1890		13[d]	9	7
1900	20[e]	15[f]	14	
1910		16[g]	13	
1913		18	12	9
1920			26	
1925	31[h]	25	24	12[i]
1930	24[j]	29	25	
1938	39[k]	43	30	22[l]

Notes: [a] 1872. [b] 1875–84. [c] 1881. [d] 1891.
[e] 1885–1913. [f] 1901. [g] 1907. [h] 1920–4. [i] 1927.
[j] 1925–34. [k] 1935–8. [l] 1940.

Source: Rostow, 1978, table N-6, p. 730.

Table 5.4 gives a rough indication of the rise in government expenditure as a proportion of GDP in the major western economies. At least in the cases of Germany and Britain, there is a discernible trend towards a growing state role well before 1914, and in all cases the war seems to have marked a watershed, with the state contribution to GDP remaining well above pre-1914 levels after the war.

A number of factors were involved, such as the rise of revolutionary and workers' parties with the extension of suffrage, the 'radicalisation' of Liberalism, and increased social welfare transfers due to the displacement of individuals and social classes as a result of industrialisation and war. On the European continent, Charles Maier has pointed to a rise in 'corporatism' as an attempt to solve the problem of postwar social and economic stabilisation.[13] This involved a blurring of the old distinctions between state and society, politics and economics, and for a time gave increasing influence to organised labour and business groups. Though macroeconomic policy in the modern sense remained largely a matter for central banks, the growing demand for finance on the part of government served to constrain the financial autonomy of central banks at the same time as political pressures on monetary policy were increasing. The blurring of the distinction between state and economy implied (in Myrdal's classic elaboration) a contradiction between an international monetary system which imposed deflationary 'discipline' on countries with external deficits and the rise of the national (or nationalist) welfare state.[14] In the 1930s, one of these had to give way.

5.3 Hegemonic power and the restoration of the international gold standard

The argument that economic ideology played a role in the restoration of the international gold standard in the mid-1920s has been important since Keynes' writing on the subject. He felt that the dominance of the classical model of the gold standard in British thinking was a decisive factor in Britain's return to gold in 1925.[15] The Cunliffe Committee on Currency and Foreign Exchanges after the War, set up in January 1918 to examine the question of monetary reconstruction:

> *assumed* that Britain would return to the gold standard at the pre-war par [of £3 17s 10½d per ounce of gold], and members of the Committee and witnesses did not question this assumption by either considering alternative gold standard rates or alternative currency policies.[16]

In practical terms, the restoration of the pound sterling at par was intimately connected in the official and private mind with the restoration of Britain's pre-war international financial role and prestige, even at some cost to domestic manufacturing industry. Other countries in Europe and the Empire were rapidly moving towards restoration of the gold standard over 1924 and in Churchill's mind at least, Britain could not be seen to be left behind.[17]

On the European continent, where considerable economic and political instability reigned in the post-war years, considerations of domestic monetary stability were probably most crucial in leading to the eventual restoration of the gold standard in the major countries. Sweden and then Germany were the first of these to return to gold in 1924, the latter having recently emerged from extreme hyperinflation and complete currency breakdown. The experience of countries such as France, Germany, Belgium and Italy with floating exchange rates in the years after the war had not been a happy one either, with speculative capital movements often leading to violent swings in exchange rates. It was not surprising that in these circumstances, Britain was not alone in looking back with nostalgia to the Golden Age before 1914.

Though it is often asserted that the US in the interwar years failed to accept the mantle of 'hegemonic leadership' which had passed from Britain, it could plausibly be argued that the US did a considerable amount (or at least saw itself as doing so) in terms of establishing the ground rules for a restored liberal world economic order. The US assisted the restoration of the international gold standard by providing (through the indirect channels of New York bankers and Federal Reserve officials) financial support for many countries, including Britain, Germany and France, to return to gold parities. As the strongest economy in financial and trade terms and with the world's largest gold reserves, the US had a clear interest in encouraging other major economies to stabilise their currencies in terms of gold. Though Germany, Britain and the other European states saw their own interests as consisting in a return to the gold standard, American assistance was important.

The most obvious example of this was the Dawes loan to Germany in 1924, organised largely by a consortium of American banks in cooperation with central bankers, which allowed that crucial country to stabilise its currency against gold and lay the basis for the growth of the later 1920s. The Dawes loan marked the beginning of a period of substantial US capital outflows and set the stage for the return of Britain and other countries to the gold standard. The US Federal Reserve and private banks also offered funds to promote the stabilisation of sterling.[18]

Though the US government itself was unwilling to commit itself to Europe's recovery in a direct way, it was perfectly willing to see private American capital play a key role in this process. The Edge Act of 1919 recognised explicitly that the world economy required substantial outflows of American capital, though it was intended from the start that this be left to private business rather than government. In placing such an emphasis upon the role of business in promoting US foreign policy aims, the Americans were not very different from the British either before or after the war. The British had traditionally seen their interests as lying in the promotion of free trade and a climate suitable for the foreign investment associated with it.

Many important Americans, especially those in the Harding administration, were also quite clear about where their interests lay and what should be done to achieve them, though the relatively closed nature of the American economy had not created a wide basis of popular support for economic internationalism.[19] It was not so much that the US Republican administrations of the 1920s lacked 'vision' as to how the US should exercise leadership in the world economy, though they might be accused of lack of realism as to what was required for the achievement of their goal of peace and stability in Europe. The American vision of a reconstructed and peaceful world was reflected in a legalistic and technocratic approach to diplomatic issues such as the war debts and reparation problems. The Republican policy of non-recognition of the USSR has been partly attributed to the primacy which the US placed upon international property rights in its diplomacy, and the policy of the Open Door and the opposition to colonialism can also be seen in terms of establishing ground rules for international liberal capitalism.[20] American support for the disarmament cause, the treaty of Locarno and finally the Kellogg–Briand Pact of 1928 can all be interpreted as the application of a consistent vision. As Leffler has observed, this combination of economic and political aims in US diplomacy 'assumed that while they were laying the basis for Europe's recuperation and America's prosperity, they were also establishing the framework for a stable and peaceful world order along liberal capitalist lines.'[21] It almost goes without saying that before the adoption of the Hawley-Smoot tariff in mid-1930, the failure of these goals was already apparent.

In at least one respect, European and particularly British initiatives were as important as American ones in setting the stage for international monetary reconstruction. Britain dominated the international monetary conference at Genoa in Spring 1922, while the US under the Harding administration did not attend in an official capacity because of a concern not to give *de facto* recognition to the Soviet regime or to the European idea of linking war debts and reparation payments.[22] The proposals of the Conference were largely a product of British aims: 'economisation on gold' through the promotion of a domestic gold bullion standard and the explicit adoption of a gold exchange standard in countries that were not 'gold centres'. Britain believed that the achievement of monetary stability in Europe would foster the revival in international trade that she so badly needed, and that the proposals to economise on gold would help protect Britain's weakened financial position. In contrast to its prewar attitude, Britain now felt that central bank cooperation could ensure stable relations between the major currencies and coordinate the demand for gold.[23] At least in their intentions, the participants of the Genoa conference signalled a willingness to contemplate a considerable degree of international monetary reform.

Although it is debatable as to what effect the proposals had on the subsequent course of events, there was a broad shift over the 1920s in the direction of practical measures to economise on the monetary use of gold, and a series of monetary stabilisations at depreciated exchange rates, in line with another recommendation at Genoa. Nurkse argued that innovations in central bank statutes in the years immediately following the Genoa conference 'were strongly influenced by the Genoa resolutions', and more recently Eichengreen suggested that the Genoa proposals were a 'major accomplishment' for Britain in the face of US opposition and its own financial weakness.[24] It seems probable,

126 *Hegemony and the evolution of the international monetary system*

however, that these shifts would have taken place to some degree anyway for basic economic reasons, especially the much-heralded impending gold shortage and the process of centralisation and rationalisation in monetary systems, which was already well under way before the war.[25]

More importantly, the Genoa conference failed to provide any answers to the fundamental structural problems of European reconstruction and the war debts-reparation issue and was in this sense a very limited accomplishment. Perhaps limited accomplishments were as much as one could reasonably expect given the difficult circumstances. As we shall see, the interwar period was marked by a general failure on all sides to comprehend that new solutions were required in the much-changed circumstances of the postwar world.

5.4 The operation and demise of the international monetary system, 1925-31

World economic instability in the interwar years

It is unnecessary to go into much detail to establish that the world economy in the interwar period suffered from considerable instability; even less is it necessary to establish that the restored international gold standard collapsed. The most probable date for pinpointing the collapse of the gold standard is September 21, 1931, when the British suspended the gold convertibility of sterling, after the Bank of England had lost £200 million in gold and foreign exchange since July 13 of that year.[26] Not only did the collapse of sterling convertibility signal the end of the gold standard in a key part of the world (Germany and Central Europe had already departed from it), but the dramatic 30 per cent depreciation of that still crucially important currency over the remaining part of 1931 was a further blow to the world economy at a time when it was already very weak. The 1930s and 1940s were years in which an increasingly smaller number of countries maintained full currency convertibility, with direct controls on trade, exchange and capital flows becoming the norm.[27] The restoration of an international monetary system with generalised currency convertibility had to await the late 1950s.

The currency disorder which reigned until 1925 outside of the US and a few relatively unimportant countries has already been touched upon. This instability was evidenced in the destabilising short-term capital flows noted by contemporaries, which suggested a lack of market confidence in the exchange rates between the major currencies and the policies which supported them.[28] Even over the relatively prosperous years of 1925-8, the weakness of sterling in particular was strongly in evidence. Morgenstern found that sterling's violation of the gold points over the 1925-31 period was both persistent and of considerable magnitude, occurring to a much greater extent than in the pre-1914 period.[29] The stress to which the international monetary system was subject might also be seen in the higher level and volatility of central bank discount rates and short-term interest rates in the major centres over 1925-31, as compared to the pre-1914 period (table 4.1).

With respect to the real performance of the world economy in the interwar period, we saw how this was significantly worse as compared with the pre-1914 era, though especially so when compared to the post-1945 performance (tables 4.2 and 4.3). Possibly most important is that while world economic instability in the pre-1914 period was concentrated in the periphery, in the interwar period it was at least as acute in many of the core countries. The average maximum peak-to-trough fall in real GDP over 1920-38 for the US and the major European economies excluding Scandinavia was 13.1 per cent, while for the largest peripheral economies of Australia, Canada and Japan the figures were 8.2 per cent, 30.1 per cent and 7.2 per cent respectively.[30] The period 1920-38 was the only one for which Maddison found the average annual rise in consumer prices to be negative (table 4.3). Even the second half of the 1920s, a period of relatively good real performance and stability, saw a gradual decline in world wholesale prices.[31]

Rather than recount in detail the course of international economic and monetary relations in the interwar period, we will consider various explanations of the instability and breakdown of the international monetary system in the early 1930s. Such explanations range from those current at the time which focused upon the shortage or maldistribution of gold, to more contemporary arguments relying on the absence of a hegemon willing or powerful enough to act as an international lender of last resort in the crisis of 1931. The relative merits of these theories are crucial in terms of deciding the importance and nature of the link between the changing balance of international power and the stability of the international monetary system.

The gold problem

One common explanation for the difficulties and subsequent breakdown of the interwar international monetary system is that the short supply and/or the maldistribution of world gold reserves exerted a severely deflationary effect upon the world economy, eventually forcing important countries off the gold standard. From before the return of Britain and other countries to gold in the mid-1920s, the issue of the adequacy of the supply of new gold to meet world reserve demand was a central theme of contemporary discussions. The main argument was that wartime and postwar inflation eroded the real price of gold in major countries, inhibiting the supply of new gold and increasing the non-monetary demand for the metal. This meant in turn that countries would have to accept deflation of wages and commodity prices until equilibrium was restored, or return to the gold standard at depreciated par-values.

British officialdom believed returning to gold at a depreciated value would be inflationary and discourage monetary discipline. Hence the proposal at Genoa that there should be economisation on the use of gold rather than an increase in its average price. The Genoa Conference accepted that a number of European countries (and others highly dependent upon them) could do nothing to avoid returning to gold at par-values significantly depreciated from their prewar levels, though Britain and the US were determined not to devalue. Britain hoped instead that the role of foreign exchange reserves might be institutionalised according to a set of rules, though was prevented in this by the opposition of the US and other important actors to the gold exchange standard.[32] Sterling (and the dollar) did come to play an unprecedented reserve role in the 1920s, though Britain failed to institutionalise the gold exchange standard.

There are a number of problems with the view that the problems of the interwar period were due to a shortage of monetary gold. First, the global monetarist theory of international reserves and prices upon which it is based is not supported by the evidence. There was in practice no mechanical relation between the global supply of gold, the supply of credit, and prices, and hence no obvious conclusions to be drawn from declining gold production.[33] This makes it impossible to determine what would have constituted an 'adequate' level of world gold reserves, though many tried at the time. Cassel and others argued that in order to have stable prices, the supply of world monetary gold ought to grow in some sort of rough proportion to the trend rate of growth in global output, about 2.8 per cent per annum.[34] From 1915, world gold production fell below this figure, which would have implied a required increase in production of about £100 million in 1921. Between 1921 and 1929, new annual gold production was in the range of £68 to £84 million.[35] New gold production was not the only source of gold reserves. Triffin estimated that 31 per cent of the growth in world monetary reserves over the period 1914–28 was due to the withdrawal of gold coin from circulation, 30 per cent to increased holdings of reserve currencies, and 39 per cent due to new gold production in excess of that used for non-monetary purposes.[36] However, given the limits on the first (and arguably the second) source, the dwindling surplus of new gold production would eventually place the role of key currencies in some difficulty.

The collapse of the gold exchange standard over 1929–33, leading to a large increase in the gold price and a devaluation of commodities, might be seen as supportive of the gold shortage explanation. The revaluation of gold over this period accounted for 107 per cent of the total increase in the value of world monetary reserves. On the other hand, the liquidation of foreign exchange reserves reduced the value of world reserves by 28 per cent, with the virtual completion of the process of the removal of gold coin from circulation contributing only 6 per cent and new gold reserves 15 per cent to the total value of world reserves.[37] The collapse of confidence in key currencies over this period may have been due to an undervaluation of gold *vis-à-vis* currencies in general,[38] but this is complicated by the fact that sterling, still the most important key currency of the time, was probably undervalued relative to the dollar and the French franc.

To use terms prominent in the debates of the 1960s, there may have been two factors in operation, one a fundamental disequilibrium in the UK balance of payments, and the other a disequilibrium in the relationship between the price of gold and key currencies in general. Roosevelt's increase in the price of gold from $20.67 to $35 per ounce in early 1934 constituted a *de facto* recognition of the latter disequilibrium and served temporarily to remove it, but until then neither Britain nor the US saw an increase in the gold price as a solution.[39] International monetary 'leadership' in the 1920s consisted, in terms of the orthodoxy of the time, in resisting all attempts to undermine monetary discipline, which was how an increase in the gold price was viewed.

At the time, more attention was focused upon the maldistribution of gold reserves and particularly the accumulation of gold by France and the US.[40] In 1920, the US possessed 36 per cent of the world's gold reserves and this steadily increased over the next four years so that by the end of 1924, its holdings represented 47 per cent of the world total. From 1924 to mid-1928, the situation in the rest of the world improved considerably due to large US capital and gold outflows and the accumulation by the French monetary authorities of large foreign exchange reserves. From the time of the *de facto* stabilisation of the franc in December 1926 to its *de jure* stabilisation in June 1928, speculation in favour of the French currency had resulted in the accumulation of $1.2 billion in currency reserves at the Bank of France, most of which was in sterling.[41]

The situation dramatically deteriorated from 1928. The Bank of France shifted policy towards converting what it saw as its excessive foreign exchange reserves into gold. The Bank and its Governor, Moreau, believed that heavy intervention in the exchange markets had jeopardised domestic monetary control, and were explicit about using the Bank's sterling reserves as a form of leverage over Britain on a number of issues.[42] In addition, the New York stock market boom increasingly drew investible funds from America and the rest of the world, which reversed the trend of the previous four years of large US net capital outflows.

With the renewed influx of gold into the US and France, Britain alone lost $300 million in gold and foreign exchange reserves in the 16 months from July 1928, and monetary policy in Britain and Europe was gradually tightened.[43] This aggravated the steadily worsening economic climate in central Europe, which eventually led to a full-blown financial crisis beginning in May 1931. This spread to Germany and then Britain by July and led to speculation against the pound and gold losses of such proportions that Britain was forced off gold in September. By the end of 1931, France and the US between them possessed 63 per cent of the world's monetary gold reserves, up from 52 per cent at the end of 1928.

Both Nurkse and the Macmillan Committee in their assessments of the interwar currency experience argued that the accumulation of gold by France and the US over 1928–31 was especially destabilising because it was accompanied by a massive sterilisation of these inflows. If the monetary authorities of these countries had observed the rules of the game by allowing reserve increases to feed through into domestic credit creation, then expansion in France and the US would have improved the external positions of the other major countries and eventually led to a reversal of the gold flows.[44] Friedman and Schwartz estimated that if the US had refrained from sterilising net gold inflows over 1925–9, wholesale prices would have remained constant rather than falling 8 per cent, taking some of the pressure off the British economy.[45] The step from this argument to the claim that the essential problem with the interwar world economy was the absence of a hegemonic power willing and able to enforce the rules of the game is a short one.

Upon closer consideration, however, this argument is problematic for the following reasons. As argued in the previous chapter, it is very doubtful whether Britain was ever able to 'enforce' the rules of the game against recalcitrant states, so it would be wrong directly to connect British decline with the sterilisation of gold flows by other major states. The idea of the 'rules of the game' was a post-World War I invention, which suggests that other factors were at work here which may have had no necessary connection with British decline. The growing role of the state in the domestic economy and the growing expectation of many both inside and outside of policy-making institutions that monetary policy would have to take increasing account of its domestic impact inevitably meant that the attachment to the 'rules' waned considerably. This was a result of long-term changes accelerated by the war, such as spreading democratisation in many countries, conservative fear of revolutionary forces and the growing role of big business and labour in the economic system, rather than due to British decline.[46]

The image of British weakness in the face of mercantilist policies on the part of other states also underestimates the extent to which British policy itself was partly to blame. Other states, after all, had always been 'mercantilist' by British standards (non-adherence to free trade, excessive accumulation of gold, etc); to follow a policy which depended upon a high degree of cooperation from abroad was, in retrospect at least, a somewhat foolhardy enterprise. The return to gold convertibility at the old exchange rate with the dollar was made in full awareness that it would necessitate a considerable degree of deflation as well as dependence upon developments in the US, though it was hoped that American inflation would make this task easier.[47] As it turned out, US prices over the 1920s showed a deflationary trend, which made the British determination to hold the $4.86 parity even more deflationary. The poor performance of British exports in the 1920s (even relative to Continental Europe and to previous trends), comparisons of wholesale price-indices and other measures of competitiveness, continuing balance of payments problems and sterling weakness, and finally continuing high unemployment all point to a classic case of currency overvaluation.[48]

Not only did the British authorities largely brush away the problem of maintaining the prewar dollar exchange rate, but they gave insufficient consideration to the possible effects of exchange rate decisions on the European continent. The breakdown of the German monetary system in the early 1920s, the severe depreciation of the French franc over 1924–6 and a large degree of chance led to a resolution of this issue in a manner much different to that in Britain. Certainly Moreau, the Governor of the Bank of France, was alive to the deflationary effects of an overvalued exchange rate and to the need to avoid the 'British mistake' of 1925.[49] The massive inflow of capital into France over 1927–8, though encouraged by the open preference of some Bank of France officials for a return to the prewar parity, suggests that the rate chosen undervalued the franc relative to sterling. Additional evidence for this is the difference in real economic performances in the 1920s. The growth of real output for France over 1921–9 has been estimated at 6.3 per cent, compared to 4.5 per cent for the US, 2.7 per cent for Germany (1926–9), 2.7 per cent for Italy and 1.9 per cent for the UK.[50] France consistently ran current account surpluses over 1925–30, averaging $235 million per year and representing a higher proportion of national output than the average British and US current surpluses over these years (not including net transfers) of $296 and $1,090 million respectively.[51]

The German position is less clear. The German current account was in surplus only in one year (1926) over the 1925–9 period, and it was dependent upon heavy capital inflows. In this short space of time, Germany could not manage to overcome the structural burdens it had acquired due to the war: large reparation payments to the allies, loss of income on foreign investments, and loss of territory and industry due to the Versailles treaty. Even so, Britain's trade deficits with Europe led Keynes and the Macmillan Committee to argue that sterling was particularly overvalued with respect to the German, Belgian and French currencies, to the order of 30 per cent.[52]

Moggridge goes further to argue that given the dramatic deterioration in Britain's international financial position since 1914, 'an exchange rate which did not undervalue sterling *vis-à-vis* the dollar was probably too high.'[53] Unless Britain could restore its current account position to one approximating that of the pre-1914 years, the precondition of a relatively autonomous international monetary policy and financial role would not be met, leaving itself excessively dependent upon policies and conditions in the US. While it may be plausible to argue that there was something 'inevitable' about Britain's return to gold at the pre-war dollar parity, this does not negate the fact that there were important voices, such as Keynes and Reginald McKenna (chairman of the Midland Bank), who vigorously opposed the orthodox position and whom Churchill gave some hearing.[54] There was an undeniable element of choice in the government's policy, which implies that political decisions played a part in creating the economic weakness that Britain suffered in the 1920s.

British determination to adhere to the decision of 1925 led not only to excessive dependence upon the surplus countries of the US and France, but also upon the nebulous 'market'. In many ways it was the international financial markets, through their uneasy confidence in sterling throughout the 1920s, which constrained British monetary policy and thereby (due to London's still central role in the international financial system) had such a negative impact upon the world economy.

Though the policy of the Bank of France of systematically running down its large sterling reserves from 1928 played a role in weakening sterling, there is little evidence that central banks played a large role in withdrawals from London in the weeks before September 21. The origin of the crisis of sterling from mid-July 1931 seems to have been market fears that London would be particularly affected by the freezing of short-term assets in Germany and Austria.[55]

While the uncooperative behaviour of the US and France played an important role in the deflationary pressures that undermined international monetary stability in the late 1920s, the war seems to have broken, once and for all, the long run of confidence in sterling witnessed before 1914, and British policy did little to restore this. Hawtrey, a major critic of Bank of England policy in these years, argued that the Bank ought to have been prepared to 'let gold go' from the beginning if it wished to take the gold standard seriously. If Britain could remain on the gold standard only through continued deflation, then either the return to gold was premature or the restoration of the $4.86 parity was a mistake.[56]

The failure of policy coordination

Another explanation of the disorder of the interwar period is the view that the emergence of rival financial centres in New York and Paris undermined London's ability to manage the system through a manipulation of Bank rate. In an oligopolistic international financial system with more than one centre, no one central bank could 'call the tune' and so policy stalemates arose, encouraging destabilising short-term capital movements.[57] In the absence of hegemonic leadership, there was little policy coordination between these centres to replace the pre-1914 London-based system and so the interwar system inevitably collapsed.

The preliminary difficulty with this argument is that our examination of the pre-1914 era is at odds with the assumption underlying this view that Britain managed the international monetary system of that period. On the other hand, an important element of the classical international gold standard was the financial hierarchy, with London at the top and Berlin and Paris being able to attract short-term capital from smaller surplus states in Europe when necessary. It is in this sense that the above argument is appealing, since it suggests that the undermining of this hierarchy at least made it difficult for Britain to manage its *own* gold standard. With respect to the management of the international monetary system as a whole, the theory of hegemonic stability holds that in a pluralistic system without a dominant player, the development of a coordinated approach to policy formulation is virtually impossible.

This argument derives much of its initial appeal from its irrefutability. It is impossible to prove or disprove the counterfactual, whether if one dominant centre *had* existed such policy coordination would have been forthcoming. The difficulty is that the counterfactual hypothesis is crucial to the argument, because it raises the issue of whether there were other factors that contributed to the failure of policy coordination.

One key factor which had little to do with the absence of a hegemon was surely the widespread failure of policy thinking at the time. In the 1920s, the intellectual predominance of classical economics precluded 'fiscal policy' in the modern sense, so that the policy burden inevitably fell upon central banks. Cooperation between central banks in the interwar period was of a very *ad hoc* and infrequent kind, though calls for more far-reaching coordination of national policies occurred. This represented if anything an improvement on the situation which prevailed before 1914, when cooperation was extremely infrequent.

Not surprisingly, calls for more thoroughgoing cooperation came mostly from Britain, which had the greatest foreign obligations but which had suffered a considerable reduction in monetary autonomy. Governor Norman of the Bank of England, in giving evidence to the Macmillan Committee, argued for greater international cooperation 'to pursue a common monetary policy and do away with the struggle for gold.'[58] While this appeal came rather late in the day and, as in the years before 1914, little was to become of it and other such proposals, in fact the 1925 to 1928 period witnessed a degree of central bank cooperation, limited though it was, that would have been unthinkable in the decade before 1914.

Of course, states only agreed to coordinate policies when it was in their particular interest to do so, such as in 1927 when the US agreed to lower interest rates at home, ostensibly to take pressure off European currencies but also to stimulate growth at home. In the same year the central banks of France, Britain and the US agreed to cooperative measures in the currency and gold markets which assisted beleaguered sterling. It is difficult to find any substantial evidence that at any stage subsequent to that time, any other major country saw much to be gained by pushing sterling off gold, and the Bank of England clearly counted on this.[59] The shift in French policy in mid-1928 and the development of a domestic policy stalemate in the US at the same time showed that cooperative measures were a fair weather phenomenon; domestic considerations had come to be at least as important for policy formulation as the external rule of gold.

With the recovery of the US economy from the mild recession of 1927, the New York stock market entered into a bull phase and interest rates began to rise. New issues of foreign securities peaked in 1927 at $1,114 million and continued at a similar rate until mid-1928. Over 1924–8, new issues averaged $940 million per year, with US direct investment abroad averaging $340 million per year over the same period. The favourable effect these net capital outflows had on the European economy cannot be doubted, and prosperity began to return to Europe and conditions of relative normality prevailed. By mid-1928, however, long-term lending by the US began to fall dramatically, while foreign investors wishing to participate in the stock market boom switched funds from other financial centres to New York. Foreign holdings of liquid US assets rose by more than $1 billion over 1927–9.[60]

Both the Federal Reserve Board and the Reserve Bank of New York felt that the stock market boom had a potentially dangerous speculative element. The Board recommended a policy of direct pressure on banks to push them to discriminate against 'speculative loans', whilst taking the view that discount rate increases and/or open market sales might weaken the real economy when no signs of retail price inflation and some signs of economic slowdown existed. The New York Fed, on the other hand, represented by Governor Harrison, the successor to Benjamin Strong, became convinced that the speculative boom could only be broken by a short sharp rise in discount rates so as to pave the way for a return to lower interest rates over the longer term.[61]

Clarke has argued that the debate had an important international dimension as well. Norman of the Bank of England felt that high US interest rates and stock market speculation were threatening the position of the pound and the international gold standard in general by dragging up the level of world interest rates. Harrison came to accept Norman's analysis of the international effects of the US situation, also believing that an end to the stock market boom and a diversion of funds away from financial to real investment would be in the best interests of the US economy.

The stalemate in policy that emerged, with the Board disapproving of the New York Fed's decision to raise its discount rate to 6 per cent in February 1929, had the effect of prolonging the boom and the capital inflow until the stock market crashed by itself in October 1929.[62] This and the subsequent unwillingness of the Board to undertake decisive lender of last resort action to ensure liquidity in the wake of the crash has attracted criticism from all quarters. Most authors have echoed the criticism of Friedman and Schwartz of the 'ineptness' of monetary policy before and particularly after the crash, with consequences for both the US and world economies.[63] If we add this to the criticisms that may be levelled at the British authorities' handling of the UK economy, it would appear that a good many of the problems of the 1920s may be attributable to the difficulties of *domestic* monetary management in the major countries.

This was due in part to the manifest inadequacy not only of the policy thinking of the time, but also of policy tools and institutions. On both domestic and international levels, structural changes so rapid and far-reaching were occurring that they overwhelmed the ability of most policy-makers to understand them, let alone develop new tools and institutions to manage them. The general trend towards the much greater role of bank credit in the domestic economy was one which all major countries experienced, and which raised increasingly difficult problems for monetary management and theory of the time.

Compounded on top of this was the much greater volume of government borrowing, which made monetary policy more dependent upon the fiscal and debt management activities of government than ever before. The Bank of England had to struggle for three years after the end of the war to regain control of the money market, given heavy government refinancing demands and strong private sector liquidity. The decline of the commercial bill and the rise of the Treasury bill reduced the volume of funds held in London, because the Treasury bill, unlike the former, did not automatically attract foreign capital. In addition to this, the decline of the finance bill, which had traditionally been more sensitive to changes in Bank Rate, rendered London more dependent upon the attraction of funds from abroad than previously.[64] On the other hand, the Treasury bill and the tool of open market operations after the war gave the Bank increased leverage in the domestic market at least.

Compared to other central banks, the Bank of England was in a most enviable position. The reconstituted Reichsbank, for example, could hold no government debt, and in the period of massive capital inflows over 1926–8, it effectively lost control of the money market.[65] The Bank of France (like that of Switzerland) could not undertake open market operations, and had to cooperate closely with the Treasury to maintain monetary control.[66] The constitution of the gold standard in many states, especially the 'proportional' system on the Continent and in the US, was consistently criticised by the British for its inflexibility and tendency to encourage excessive gold accumulation.[67] The US and France maintained gold backing of central bank liabilities usually well in excess of the legal minimums of 30 to 40 per cent. While there is little doubt that this was excessive, flexibility was not an attribute particularly evident in the British case either. Their unwillingness to increase the fiduciary issue in the circumstances of the late 1920s and during the Depression years because of a fear as to its effects upon confidence in sterling suggests that British claims as to the flexibility of their own system may have been exaggerated.[68]

The difficulties of central banking in these years is perhaps nowhere more apparent than in the US. The Federal Reserve System, created only in 1913, had a federal, decentralised, structure. The more internationalist leanings of the New York Fed, situated in the country's international financial centre, were often out of place in a system where the sheer size and relative insularity of the domestic economy tended to dominate policy considerations. The Federal Reserve Board, situated in Washington and responsible for the overall stance of policy, was inevitably more influenced by such considerations.[69] The policy stalemate that developed, with the Board supposedly in charge of the overall direction of policy and the New York Fed by far the most powerful of the Reserve Banks, was highly destabilising. Maddison for one takes a different view to Friedman and Schwartz, insisting that the Great Depression which followed the crash 'was probably mainly attributable to the fact that the USA was trying to run a major capitalist economy with the financial institutions of a rural frontier society.'[70]

The years of foreign investment and growth in world trade had increased the importance of foreign transactions for some sectors of the American economy, but these were the exception rather than the rule. Though the absolute contribution of US foreign trade and investment in national output had risen, on some measures the openness of the US economy actually fell in the 1920s from prewar levels. Leffler estimates that the ratio of exports to total production fell from 12.8 per cent in 1899 to 9.8 per cent in 1929, while the percentage of farm income derived from exports fell from 16.5 per cent in 1914 to 15 per cent in 1929. The rapid expansion of the domestic market for manufactures in the 1920s provided the bulk of the growth in demand for manufacturing industry, with the ratio of machinery exports to total machinery production falling from 10.6 per cent in 1914 to 8.6 per cent in 1929.[71]

The relative autonomy, evolving institutional basis, domestic policy orientation and inexperience of the US authorities would have had few consequences for the outside world if the relative weight of the US in the world economy had not become so important as it was in the 1920s. The US was not only by far the largest economy, but also the world's major importer of commodities, and over 1925–9 was the third most important export market for Britain and Germany and the fifth most important for France.[72] The fluctuation of the US business cycle was therefore of considerable importance for the strength of international commodity prices and for the world economy as a whole. The US was also Europe's most important source of long-term capital during the 1920s. After the stock market crash, although new foreign issues in the US revived somewhat in 1930, they collapsed to new lows for the postwar period by 1931, with the worsening of the Depression at home and abroad.

Whether due to inept policy or inadequate institutions or both, most sides in the debate argue that as in the 1920-1 recession, the US led the rest of the world into depression from 1929.[73] Over the period 1929-33, US output fell by 30 per cent, Germany's by 16 per cent, France's 11 per cent and the UK's 6 per cent. In Central Europe, the falls were probably even greater than in Germany, though less than in the US and Canada.[74] The shock to global demand caused by the fall in US output, the accumulation of gold reserves by France and the US and the impetus this gave to deflationary policies already chosen in other countries, as well as the virtual cessation of international capital flows all contributed to the onset and depth of the global Depression.[75]

Is it plausible therefore to argue that the international monetary system would have been more stable had the US taken on the responsibility of 'global monetary manager'? American authorities were patently unable to stabilise the highly volatile US economy; it is difficult to believe that they could have done a better job on the international level. Though it may be true that greater international policy coordination between the US and other countries could have made a substantial contribution to world economic stability, the first requirement of such cooperation is an ability to manage domestic economies. In other words, the presence or not of a hegemonic power in the international system has little bearing upon whether policy thinking, tools and institutions are adequate at any given time for the purposes of monetary management.

The absence of an international lender of last resort

We arrive now at the argument that what was lacking in the 1920 and 1931 crises was an international lender of last resort.[76] Arguably there was some precedent for international lender of last resort action, and given the financial situation in Europe, such assistance could probably only have come from the US. The problem in assessing this claim is that again we are faced with a situation in which the outcomes are 'overdetermined', making it difficult to put a finger on any single factor. If the Bank of England *had* possessed adequate resources, for example, would it have offered sufficient assistance to other countries in a crisis?

In the 1920 crisis, there is not much evidence to suggest that Britain was willing to accept such responsibility but found itself too weak to do so. On the contrary, the Bank of England succeeded in convincing the Treasury in the winter of 1919–20 of the need for deflation, which was subsequently pursued with vigour.[77] Moggridge has also pointed out that since most of the European currencies at that time were more or less freely floating against one-another and the dollar, there was little rationale for supporting particular par-values with emergency credits. If lender of last resort action is seen as maintaining the convertibility of a narrow range of assets into central bank money or gold at a fixed price, then to suggest that the depth of the recession at the beginning of the 1920s was due to the absence of an international lender of last resort is rather ambiguous.[78]

The argument that emergency credits could have alleviated the distress which occurred in Europe over 1929–31 is more plausible, both because international credits were organised in 1931, and because (unlike in 1920) the signs of generalised financial crisis are unmistakable. The story of the emerging difficulties of the Austrian bank Kreditanstalt in April 1931, leading to the run on German banks and subsequently on British banks in July has been told in detail elsewhere.[79] It is probably true that the size of and delays in the granting of the loans to Austria and Germany exacerbated the collapse of confidence in central European banking systems. That this was so with regard to the international loans to Britain as well is not at all clear.

With the spread of the crisis to the UK, substantial loans of $125 million were forthcoming from both the Federal Reserve and the French banking system at the end of July 1931, sums that were to prove inadequate in the circumstances, but which in absolute terms were historically unprecedented.[80] Even after these loans, the Bank of England continued to lose foreign exchange and gold reserves, prompting it to approach the private markets in New York and Paris. After the formation of a National Government willing to carry out the fiscal economies that virtually all central and private banks involved believed to be necessary, New York and Paris each provided another $200 million in late August. All in all, about $1 billion in emergency credits had been raised by international markets and central banks since May.

The fact that the sums involved were completely without precedent suggests that the delays and the political manoeuvres which accompanied them should not be seen as entirely surprising. Despite their size, however, the credits were inadequate to halt the spreading crisis and the loss of confidence in sterling and the Reichsmark. This raises the possibility that virtually no amount of emergency assistance possible at the time would have sufficed to prevent the collapse of these currencies. The marked deterioration of the British invisible surplus over 1929–31 would in any case have faced British authorities with very difficult decisions. As Moggridge has written:

> Even without the liquidity crisis of 1931, Britain faced a serious balance-of-payments problem that entailed a substantial measure of additional deflation if the authorities were to avoid depreciation. Whether or not Britain or the international economy could have coped with such additional deflation is arguable. But in a world where devaluations of the sort that have characterised the Bretton-Woods system were almost unthinkable, it is likely that any additional assistance to meet Britain's underlying balance-of-payments problem would have carried such deflationary conditions, as, of course, did the second round of lending to Britain during the liquidity crisis.[81]

What some economists have found problematic with Kindleberger's position is that it ignores the possibility that the fundamental disequilibrium in the British balance of payments was so great that the time was past when emergency credits could be of much use.[82] A similar point could be made about the weakness of the German payments and financial positions, as well as those of most of Central Europe. It is not clear that additional credits would have avoided further severe deflation; additional deflation would probably have been a condition of their being granted. The problem was not only one of the disruption of the *supply* of credit, but also the unwillingness of governments to act as borrowers of last resort (i.e. expansionary fiscal policy) within domestic economies. Short-term credits could not relieve the underlying structural weaknesses, and markets had rightly lost confidence in the ability and willingness of governments to tackle the structural problems.

These problems, rather than the absence of a hegemon, produced large contradictions between perceived national policy imperatives and international requirements. The emphasis often placed in the literature upon the absence of lender of last resort facilities or upon the failure of international policy cooperation seems to concentrate on the symptoms rather than the causes of the instability in the system.

5.5 Structural imbalances in the interwar world economy

One structural imbalance that was given little attention at the time and to which we referred above was the existence of a severe misalignment of exchange rates. In the face of a weakening current account and slow growth at home, the British continued to rule out

Table 5.5 Net international capital inflows (+) and outflows (−), 1924–31 ($ million).

	\multicolumn{7}{c}{Creditors}						
	1924	1925	1926	1927	1928	1929	1930	1931
USA								
long-term	−672	−543	−696	−991	−798	−240	−221	215
short-term	119	−106	419	585	−348	−4	−479	−637
France								
total	−535	−450	−483	−504	−236	20	257	791
UK								
total	−380	−261	126	−385	−569	−574	−112	313
	\multicolumn{8}{c}{Germany (major debtor)}							
long-term	238	289	346	424	426	157	266	43
short-term	227	549	−170	613	541	325	−137	−585

Source: United Nations, 1949, pp. 18–19.

devaluation as an option until it was too late, and then allowed sterling to depreciate precipitously.[83] Although a major realignment of exchange rates would have been virtually unthinkable at the time, it may have been the only way in the end to prevent the deflation which ensued.

Connected with the disequilibrium in the pattern of exchange rates is a more general issue, raised at an early stage by Keynes' *Economic Consequences of the Peace* (1919). This was whether the peace settlement in Europe laid adequate foundations for prosperity and stable growth. Keynes felt strongly that the political clauses of the peace treaties were completely in opposition to economic sense, above all with respect to their treatment of continental Europe's most important economy, Germany. The reparation obligations imposed by the allies upon Germany[84] were (he felt) beyond its capacity to pay and likely to impoverish a country on whose future Europe's own to some extent rested. Whether Keynes' arguments were valid or not, the peace settlement and the sharp criticism of it had as its legacy both German resentment and French isolation, as well as a peculiar pattern of international capital flows which was ultimately to prove unsustainable.

Table 5.5 shows the extent to which Germany was dependent upon substantial capital inflows in the second half of the 1920s, the bulk of which came from the US. Total German long-term capital inflows over 1924–30 amounted to over $2 billion, compared to the $2.5 billion which one source has estimated was made in reparation payments in the 1920s until their almost complete cessation in the crisis of 1931.[85] The American refusal to write off war debts or officially to recognise any connection between them and the reparation payments that the allies were demanding of Germany was one of the crucial factors in ensuring that country's uncharacteristic dependence upon external sources of capital. One of the underpinnings of the pre-1914 system was thus weakened, whereby Britain could attract capital from continental centres like Germany without creating a credit squeeze in Europe. After World War I, the state of Europe's financial relations was so parlous that a credit crisis in America and Austria brought down the whole house of cards.

The high proportion of short-term capital in Germany's total capital imports even in the good years of 1924–8 was also a problem (table 5.5). This made its net financial position very vulnerable to disruption as a result of shifts in investor confidence or in relative returns, as the post-1928 period showed. The short maturity of investments probably reflected investor unease about the political and economic fragility of postwar Europe, as well as the greater ease of transferring funds between countries due to improvements in technology.

The contrast of this situation with the post-1945 period, when the US claimed no war debts from its allies and ensured adequate net capital flows, is obvious. It has led more than one author to claim, following Keynes, that what was lacking after World War I was a programme for European recovery and reconstruction founded upon the interdependence of the individual economies.[86] Instead, the two major creditor countries, Britain and the US, saw no alternative but to promote reconstruction by encouraging the revival of private capital flows to Europe and the periphery. Yet if the flow of private investment capital from the major creditor countries did not always fluctuate in a stabilising fashion before 1914, even less so was this the case after the war. US long-term investment in the 1920s and 1930s was broadly pro-cyclical in nature, rising and falling with domestic investment, except at turning points of the cycle.[87] Not only US but also British and French lending abroad collapsed once the Depression gained momentum. In 1931, the year of the collapse of the international monetary system, more long-term capital flowed *into* the US, Britain and France than outwards.

It was apparent at the very beginning of the 1920s that US private foreign lending would be incapable of fully substituting for the virtual cessation of US Government credits a year after the war. The termination of US Government war and relief credit arrangements to foreign governments meant that net official capital outflows fell from $2.3 billion in 1919 to $175 million in 1920. With net private capital outflows increasing only from $169 million in 1919 to $554 million in 1920, it was not surprising that severe deflation ensued in war-torn Europe, especially given the shift to deflationary policies in Britain and the US.[88] Not until the renegotiated settlement on German reparation payments and the Dawes loan of 1924 could US private capital be persuaded to take up the slack, despite the explicit policy of the Republican administration in favour of foreign investment.

Even then, there was no guarantee that capital outflows would continue once begun; the domestic American frontier of investment opportunities was rapidly expanding with the exploitation of new technologies and automation in the 1920s, and capital imports in those years were often substantial. The high returns offered by these opportunities and the stock market boom in the second half of the decade raises considerable doubts as to whether the US had made a full transition to a consistent net exporter of capital on the British model.[89] If so, Europe's dependence upon American capital after 1918 was a structural weakness which proved to be disastrous from all points of view. It derived from the inability of the major powers to solve the intimately connected problems of French security, German power in Europe and the reconstruction and recovery of the European economy as a whole. With the British and Americans unwilling to give the French the security guarantee they wanted and with all major creditor countries preferring private market rather than governmental approaches to the problem of European economic reconstruction, the inadequacy of economic policy cooperation was only the tip of the iceberg.

The final structural problem which we might point to is a related one of differences in the volatility of particular national economies. The US economy in particular was subject to a greater degree of both financial and real instability than the economies of Western Europe. In contrast to the pre-1914 world, when the most volatile economies were concentrated in the periphery, the increasing international prominence of the US economy was arguably a destabilising factor for the world economy as a whole. This issue is difficult to separate from that relating to the shortcomings of monetary policy and financial organisation in the US. In the mid-1920s, however, Benjamin Strong expressed awareness to the British authorities of a particular vulnerability of the American economy to extreme booms and busts, and was concerned about the potential consequences of this for the other countries.[90]

Empirical work has provided some support for the hypothesis. The maximum peak-to-trough fall in output over the hundred years from 1870 was consistently greater in the US (by a factor of two or more) than the average maximum fall in Britain, France and Germany. Eric Lundberg, in his comparative study of economic instability, found that in the interwar period (as for the post-1945 era) 'the United States and Canada show instability far above the other countries.'[91] It has often been found that the most volatile economies in any given period have usually been small, highly open economies, exposed to the effects of fluctuations in international business cycles and trade. The US stands out as a relatively closed economy which consistently exhibited a degree of volatility usually confined to the small economies of Europe and the periphery. Reasons given for this range from the 'frontier mentality' thesis, which might lead to greater swings in expectations as new opportunities arise,[92] to the one already examined of inexperienced and decentralised policy institutions.

Another explanation which might be added to this, and one which is especially interesting in the present context, is the peculiarly fragmented nature of the American financial system, which might be especially prone to financial instability and the disruption of credit flows. In contrast to the more oligopolistic character of banking systems in most large European countries since the late nineteenth century, the US banking system is marked by the vast number of small banks which enjoy significant shares of local banking services. The institutional decentralisation of the Federal Reserve system parallels a quite radical decentralisation of power in the private banking system. The vulnerability of this system to massive dislocation seems confirmed by the experience of the Great Depression, when thousands of the country's banks failed.[93] This leads us back to the point that the inability of US policy-makers to cope with this vulnerability was a key factor in the global depression which ensued.[94]

5.6 Conclusion

When we add to the problems of US economic management the consistently protectionist stance of American trade policy in the 1920s, that contributed to the large US current surpluses with the rest of the world, America appears to be a major source of structural imbalance in the world economy. Should then the US government have exercised 'leadership' by providing massive official assistance to Europe and opening its markets so as to create the conditions for a return to economic stability? Phrased in such terms, and with the experience of the Marshall Plan behind us, such a conclusion would be tempting.

It would also be ahistorical, in that a programme of government-sponsored credits would have presumed a degree of governmental intervention which virtually no one expected could continue beyond the war itself. The doctrine of *laissez-faire* remained strong in most of the major countries in the 1920s, and it is by no means clear that if Britain was in the position of the US after 1918, it would have chosen a more radical solution. Britain's own role in most international monetary conferences of the period was usually to call for a return to 'sound finance' and for a reduction in the role of the state in the economy.[95] European governments in general did not have the commitment to sustaining the postwar boom that was arguably so important to the post-1945 recovery. On the contrary, the strength of the commitment on the part of authorities in the important European countries (above all in Britain, but also in France) to return to prewar exchange parities necessitated sharp and determined deflation in 1920 and again at the end of the decade.[96]

The problem with the theory of hegemonic stability as applied to the interwar period is not so much the economic arguments in themselves, but the weight placed upon their supposed causal connection with the decline of British hegemony. There are other factors which can account for the absence of real solutions to the problems of the 1920s besides a simple absence of dominance on the part of one country. For example, the sterilisation of gold inflows on the part of France and the US probably did exert deflationary pressure on the rest of the world, but this was part of a secular trend towards an increased state role in the domestic economy and not a decline in 'hegemonic enforcement' of the rules of the game. Ultimately, the rise of the interventionist state was in contradiction with the operation of an international monetary system based upon an immutable external convertibility constraint.

Second, an attachment to classical economic precepts resulted in a series of disastrous policy errors, especially the British return to the pre-war exchange rate in 1925 and the generalised deflation in the early stages of the Great Depression. Even if an able and willing hegemon *was* present, who can say whether the outcome would have been significantly different. Arguments that the monetary disorder was due to policy conflict and the inadequacy of lender of last resort facilities in the crises may overlook the fact that deeper structural factors lay underneath these failures. In the absence of a stable foundation for European economic reconstruction (especially that of Germany) and given the difficulty of managing a very unstable US economy, all the policy cooperation in the world may not have been enough to have stabilised the world economy at the end of the 1920s.

146   Hegemony and the evolution of the international monetary system

As Stephen Clarke concluded in his study of the period:

> it is difficult to conceive of any extension or modification of central bank cooperation – within the realm of what was then considered possible – that would have been sufficient to maintain exchange rate stability in the circumstances of political and economic disintegration that prevailed.
>
> Indeed, the conclusion seems inescapable that the failure of central bank cooperation in 1929–31 was only part of the larger failure of the Western democracies to deal successfully with the economic and political problems of the time.[97]

At the very least, attention to the international economic imbalances may have entailed a negotiated sterling devaluation in terms of the dollar and the franc, an increase in the gold price *vis-à-vis* all currencies, a lasting improvement in Germany's international financial position, and last but not least, expansionary fiscal policies on the part of governments. Conflict between the major countries was part of the reason why such an approach was out of the question. As has been emphasised, it was also due to mistaken decisions and policies, inadequate institutions and intellectual constraints in the face of complex economic and financial changes. The war had accelerated a process of fundamental social and economic change in all countries, above all in terms of blurring the old distinction between state and economy, but it was not until the 1930s that the consequences of this for economic theory were more fully elaborated.[98]

The outcome of the crisis of 1929–33 was the disintegration of the international monetary, financial and trading systems, but in a broader sense it ensured for a long time that externally imposed deflation would not be allowed, either by radical right, left, centrist or conservative regimes, to threaten the basis of the existing socio-economic order. From then on, as Myrdal argued, the problem of international economic organisation was how to combine the benefits of relative openness and economic interdependence with an acceptance of the national welfare or corporatist state. The complexity of this problem and the diversity of approaches and circumstances amongst the major powers suggests that one should be cautious in attributing the breakdown of the international monetary system in the interwar period to an absence of hegemonic power or leadership, unless by that phrase it is meant such a web of issues and hypotheses that the result follows simply by definition.

Notes

1. Keohane, 1984, p.34. See also Krasner, 1976, pp.338–40; Gilpin, 1987, pp.88,128–31.

2. Kindleberger, 1973, p.292. See also Cohen, 1977, p.88; Gilpin, 1987, p.130.
3. Mandel, 1980, pp.30–6, and 1985, p.135.
4. Moggridge, 1972, pp.31–3.
5. Morgenstern, 1959, p.470.
6. See Mitchell, 1975, pp.508–73,821ff.
7. Maizels, 1963, p.223; Leffler, 1984, p.258.
8. Throughout, 'billion' will mean one thousand million.
9. US Department of Commerce, 1964, table 1; League of Nations, 1944, pp.233,240.
10. National Industrial Conference Board, 1929, p.48.
11. Clarke, 1967, pp.20–1; Schuker, 1976, pp.6–14; Leffler, 1979, ch.1–3.
12. See also Peter Flora, 1983, pp.376–7,383–4,440–1, for sometimes varying figures to those above.
13. Maier, 1975.
14. Myrdal, 1960, pp.119–30.
15. See Keynes, 'The Economic Consequences of Mr. Churchill', in *CW*, vol.IX, pp.212–15.
16. Moggridge, 1972, p.18.
17. See Gilbert, 1976, p.100.
18. The Americans had in fact resisted British pressure to stabilise the mark on a sterling basis until the pound returned to gold convertibility, and this put additional pressure on the British to re-establish gold convertibility as soon as possible. See Clarke, 1967, pp.40–81; Leffler, 1979, p.99.
19. The 'internationalist' Republicans included Secretary of Commerce Hoover, Secretary of the Treasury Mellon, Secretary of State Hughes and Harding himself. See Leffler, 1984, and 1979, pp.40–81. For early recognition of the implications of US current surpluses, see US Federal Reserve Board, *Annual Report*, 1919, pp.23–5,55,518–21, and 1920, pp.20–6.
20. Leffler, 1984, p.235; Lipson, 1985, p.68.
21. Leffler, 1984, p.241.
22. Clarke, 1973, pp.8–11.
23. *ibid.*, pp.11–14. See also League of Nations, 1944, pp.27–8.
24. League of Nations, 1944, p.30; Eichengreen, 1987a, p.22.
25. See Triffin, 1968, pp.24–42.
26. Clarke, 1967, pp.216–18.
27. League of Nations, 1944, pp.162–89.
28. See League of Nations, 1944, pp.117–22.
29. Morgenstern, 1959, p.267.
30. Note that even if the US is excluded from the European group, the average figure is still a high 11.1 per cent, which compares to an average 3.5 per cent maximum fall in GDP for the European countries over 1870–1913. Figures are calculated from Maddison, 1982, table 4.1, p.67.
31. Friedman and Schwartz, 1963, pp.241–4.
32. Clarke, 1967, pp.34–44.
33. Lewis, 1978, pp.87–93; Kindleberger, 1984, pp.68–70,331,364–8, and 1985d, pp.262–70.
34. Cassel, 1921, pp.82–4. See also Joseph Kitchin, 'Gold Production', in Royal Institute of International Affairs (RIIA), 1931, pp.58–68, who believed that a growth rate of 3.1 per cent to 3.4 per cent p.a. was necessary to maintain stable prices.

35. Kitchin, 1931, p.58.
36. Triffin, 1968, p.42. See also Hawtrey, 1947, pp.112–15.
37. *ibid.*
38. Nurkse (League of Nations, 1944, p.132) appears to have accepted this explanation.
39. *ibid.*, p.22.
40. For example, Committee on Finance and Industry, 1931, paras. 158, 162–72.
41. Clarke, 1967, pp.111–37. Figures on gold reserves from Hawtrey, 1947, pp.254–5.
42. See Moreau, 1954, ch.15–18.
43. *ibid.*, pp.147–50; Hawtrey, 1938, pp.139–40.
44. League of Nations, 1944, pp.105–6; Committee on Finance and Industry, 1931, paras. 153,183–5,248.
45. Friedman and Schwartz, 1963, p.284.
46. Maier, 1975, pp.580–94. It should be noted that this did not only mean that policy-makers were willing to abandon the rules of the game only when their observance would have led to deflationary pressure. Indeed, in Britain, the overriding aim of maintaining sterling's gold convertibility in the 1920s tended to ensure that departures from the rules were often designed to ensure *additional* deflationary pressure (see Clarke, 1967, pp.97–105).
47. Keynes, *CW*, vol.IX, p.226; Moggridge, 1972, pp.18–24.
48. Moggridge, 1972, pp.100–27; Morgenstern, 1959, ch.5; Clarke, 1967, pp.104–7.
49. Kindleberger, 1984, ch.19; Clarke, 1967, pp.111–12.
50. US Bureau of the Census, 1975, part 1, series F 1–5, p.224; Mitchell, 1975, pp.785ff. British, US and Italian figures are for GNP, while those for France and Germany are for NNP.
51. Calculated from Mitchell, 1975, pp.821ff, and US Department of Commerce, 1964, table 1, using official exchange rates.
52. Keynes, *CW*, vol.IX, p.211; Committee on Finance and Industry, 1931, paras. 121–5.
53. Moggridge, 1972, p.105. See also Moggridge, 1969, ch.2.
54. See Gilbert, 1976, ch.5.
55. Clarke, 1967, pp.202–18; Kindleberger, 1984, pp.378–80.
56. Hawtrey, 1938, p.141, and 1962, pp.233–40.
57. This position was perhaps first elaborated by Brown, 1940, especially vol.II, pp.774–91. See also Dam, 1982, pp.68–9; Cohen, 1977, pp.88–9; League of Nations, 1944, p.191; Eichengreen, 1987a, p.39; Gilpin, 1987, pp.129–30,310.
58. Quoted in Hawtrey, 1938, p.142.
59. Clarke, 1967, pp.117–32; Kindleberger, 1984, pp.343–5.
60. All figures here are taken from US Department of Commerce, 1964, table 1.
61. Friedman and Schwartz, 1963, pp.254–5.
62. Clarke, 1967, pp.151–7; Kindleberger, 1985d, pp.267–9.
63. Friedman and Schwartz, 1963, pp.407–19.
64. Moggridge, 1972, pp.35–6.
65. Clarke, 1967, p.109.
66. Eichengreen, 1987b, p.11; RIIA, 1931, pp.158–9.

67. For example, see RIIA, 1931, pp.84ff.
68. See Friedman and Schwartz, 1963, p.249, and Hawtrey, 1962, p.236.
69. See Leffler, 1979, ch.7, and Clarke, 1973, p.34.
70. Maddison, 1977, pp.459–60. For a similar view, see de Cecco, 1984, pp.19–23.
71. Leffler, 1984, pp.258–9.
72. Mitchell, 1975, pp.545,548,600.
73. Friedman and Schwartz, 1963, pp.360–2; Maddison, 1977, pp.457–60; Bernanke, 1983, p.274; Hamilton, 1987, p.145. For a more qualified position, see Temin, 1976, pp.152–9.
74. Maddison, 1977, p.457.
75. The Friedman-Schwartz view (1963, pp.301–5) that the cause of the Great Depression in the US was the mistake of the Federal Reserve in allowing the money supply to fall so much has been subjected to considerable criticism. See Bernanke, 1983, and Temin, 1976, esp. ch.6.
76. Kindleberger, 1984, p.331, and 1985d, pp.271–2.
77. Moggridge, 1972, pp.23–5; Howson, 1975, pp.28–9.
78. Moggridge, 1982, p.176.
79. See Kindleberger, 1973, ch.7; Clarke, 1967, pp.182–218.
80. In what was probably the largest international lender of last resort operation before 1914, the Bank of France bought $15.4 million of sterling bills with gold in the 1907 crisis (Kindleberger, 1984, p.281).
81. Moggridge, 1982, p.183.
82. For example, Hirsch and Oppenheimer, 1977, pp.618–19. Clarke (1967, pp.204,221) is also sceptical on this point.
83. Clarke, 1967, pp.218–19.
84. Provisionally fixed in May 1921 at 132 billion gold marks plus 26 per cent in export taxes over 42 years (Kindleberger, 1984, p.298).
85. Zacchia, 1977, p.580.
86. For example, Milward, 1984, pp.463–6; Moggridge, 1982, pp.179,183.
87. See Kindleberger, 1985c, pp.141–4.
88. US Department of Commerce, 1964, table 1; Friedman and Schwartz, 1963, pp.231–44; National Industrial Conference Board, 1929, pp.159–60; Leffler, 1979, p.27.
89. As the National Industrial Conference Board pointed out in 1929 (p.118).
90. Clarke, 1967, p.106.
91. Lundberg, 1968, p.73. See also Maddison, 1982, table 4.1, p.67, and the more detailed discussion in Rostow, 1978, pp.329–43.
92. Kindleberger (1985c, p.142) presents an explanation of instability in US foreign lending based upon such a theory.
93. The similar scale of the failure of thrift institutions in the US in the late 1980s is but the latest episode in a history of periodic national financial disasters.
94. Bernanke, 1983; Fisher, 1933; de Cecco, 1984, pp.19–23; McClam, 1982, pp.258–65.
95. Ruggie, 1982, p.391.
96. Milward, 1984, pp.464–6; Lundberg, 1968, pp.71–2; Schuker, 1976, pp.34–56.
97. Clarke, 1967, p.221.
98. See Shackle, 1967, ch.9–18.

Chapter 6
American hegemony and the evolution of the international monetary system after 1945

6.1 Introduction

The indisputable dominance of the United States after 1945 and its role in the revival of economic interdependence and prosperity in the industrialised world provides the theory of hegemonic stability with its most enticing example. While the preceding chapters have argued that the theory encounters problems when applied to the pre-World War II era, it can be argued that 'American hegemony, rather than being one more instance of a general phenomenon, was essentially unique in the scope and efficacy of the instruments at the disposal of a hegemonic state and in the degree of success attained.'[1] This chapter attempts to give a broad analysis of the claims made for American hegemony after 1945 with respect to its role in the so-called 'Bretton Woods' system.

For some, the primary function of the US after the war was establishing and maintaining the rules and institutions of a 'liberal' world economy.[2] The view is commonly expressed that US dominance was crucial for the establishment and maintenance of the Bretton Woods regime, and that US decline was equally crucial in its subsequent downfall.[3] We will therefore need to examine the role which the US played in the establishment of the postwar international monetary system.

Most commentators would argue that the American role went well beyond one of rule-enforcement, to include that of the active management of the Bretton Woods international monetary system. As

American hegemony and the international monetary system

Calleo writes: '[It] is widely accepted that the United States has acted since World War II as a kind of world central bank, creating by its deficits the additional credit necessary to service an expanding world economy.'[4] Not surprisingly, with US hegemony seen as crucial in stabilising the international monetary system, the consequences of US decline for international monetary order have typically been seen as overwhelmingly negative. On the one hand this is meant to have led to increasing American unwillingness to bear the costs of the provision of these international public goods, and on the other a growing inability to do so as the forces of foreign economic nationalism steadily eroded relative US dominance.[5] By the mid-1980s, the notion that the relative decline of American economic power entailed growing conflict in the world economy was widespread in academic, journalistic and even policy-making circles. The Bretton Woods system, a product of US hegemony, was the first casualty of the end of the American Century.

6.2 American dominance and wartime planning

The international political, economic and financial consequences of World War II were in many ways similar to those of the 1914–18 war, but altogether more far-reaching. At the height of the conflict, in Paul Kennedy's words:

> Former Great Powers – France, Italy – were already eclipsed. The German bid for mastery in Europe was collapsing, as was Japan's bid in the Far East and Pacific. Britain, despite Churchill, was fading. The bipolar world, forecast so often in the nineteenth and early twentieth centuries, had at last arrived . . . and of the two [superpowers], the American . . . was vastly superior.[6]

The extraordinary superiority of the US in the depths of the global conflict could be demonstrated in virtually every variable of power one could think of. It had long possessed a marked advantage in labour productivity, underlining the organisational and technological basis of its dominance (table 6.1). In terms of sheer size, the US economy dwarfed the others in a way in which Britain's had never done (table 6.2). America had become the workshop of the Allied war effort and the demand for its food and capital goods would remain strong after the war. All in all, the US was the only major economy to have benefited from the war, its real output having doubled, its goods having captured important new overseas markets, its merchant fleet unrivalled, and its gold reserves having grown to two-thirds of the world total.

Planning of the shape of the postwar international monetary system

Table 6.1 Labour productivity (GDP per hour worked), major countries, 1870–1984 ($US at 1984 PPPs).

Year	France	Germany	Japan	Neth.	UK	US
1870	1.05	1.13	0.37	2.02	2.13	1.95
1890	1.42	1.63	0.53	n.a.	2.82	3.02
1913	2.21	2.50	0.81	3.35	3.59	4.58
1929	3.21	3.11	1.42	4.96	4.52	6.73
1938	4.14	3.85	1.77	4.91	4.91	7.12
1950	4.54	3.67	1.52	6.17	6.41	11.14
1960	6.95	7.13	2.70	8.62	8.04	14.44
1973	14.31	13.94	8.39	16.77	13.91	19.29
1984	20.78	19.28	11.85	20.72	17.17	21.12

Source: Maddison, 1987, table A-5, p. 683.

began during the War, and there is little doubt that US economic and financial power played a major role in the outcome. It would be wrong, however, to overlook the role of Britain, despite the large discrepancy in the relative strength of the two powers. What was unprecedented was the direct presence of the US in the negotiations and the fact that the other major industrial countries, which were either enemies of the US and Britain or under enemy occupation, played virtually no role.

An important factor in the outcome which was not reducible to relative power positions was the role of a relatively small number of internationally-minded experts (the most famous of these being Keynes and Harry Dexter White). In many ways these experts had more in common with each other than with powerful political currents in their own countries.[8] Keynes' overriding concern to banish the 'deflationary bias' of the international gold standard was largely shared by the US Treasury negotiating team under White, whose aim 'was not to restore a regime of private enterprise but to create a climate of world expansion consistent with the social and economic objectives of the New Deal.'[9] In principle, then, both were agreed that a key objective of international monetary reform would be to prevent external payments imbalances from precipitating a deflationary spiral of the kind witnessed in the Depression years. This was consistent with the fundamental shift in the balance between state and economy which had occurred since the late nineteenth century in most advanced countries and which was accelerated by the war.

Even so, there were major differences between the Keynes and White plans for international monetary reconstruction. In part, these inevitably reflected the national interests of the countries they

Table 6.2 Economic and financial comparisons of major industrial economies, 1950–85.

	Country	1950	1955	1960	1965	1970	1975	1980	1985
1. Ratio to US GDP[a]	US	1.00		1.00			1.00[d]		1.00[e]
	Germany	0.14		0.22			0.23		0.22
	Japan	0.10		0.16			0.33		0.40
	UK	0.22		0.21			0.19		0.17
	France	0.14		0.15			0.19		0.19
2. Shares world exports[f]	US	17	18	17	16	15	13		12
	Germany	3	7	10	11	12	11		10
	Japan	1	2	3	5	7	7		7
	UK	11	10	9	9	7	5		6
	France	5	6	6	6	6	6		6
3. Shares world imports[f]	US	16	14	13	13	14	13	13	19
	Germany	4	6	8	10	10	9	10	8
	Japan	2	3	4	5	6	7	7	7
	UK	12	12	10	9	6	6	6	6
	France	5	5	5	6	6	7	7	6
4. Shares world reserves (–gold)[b]	US	10	6	7	5	6	2	4	7
	Germany	1	11	18	10	17	14	12	10
	Japan	4	6	8	6	8	6	6	6
	UK	4	2	4	2	3	2	5	3
	France	1	6	3	6	2	4	7	6
5. Shares world gold[c] reserves	US	68	62	47	34	30	27	28	28
	Germany	—	3	8	11	11	12	10	10
	Japan	—	—	1	1	1	2	3	3
	UK	9	6	7	5	4	2	2	2
	France	2	3	4	11	10	10	9	9

Notes: [a] $US at 1984 PPP. [b] SDR millions. [c] Million oz. [d] 1973. [e] 1984. [f] IMF, 1988 (Current Exchange Rates).

Sources: 1. Maddison, 1987, table A-1, p. 682. 2, 4, and 5. IMF, *International Financial Statistics*. 3. IMF, 1982; United Nations, 1987, p. 22.

represented. The continued growth of US gold stocks during the war years encouraged American financial élites to continue to look with favour upon the idea of a full restoration of the international gold standard.[10] Such views carried sufficient weight with the economic nationalists in Congress to rule out the adoption of early versions of the Keynes and White plans, both of which envisaged a considerable degree of supranational control over international capital flows and liquidity, as well as exchange rates and national macroeconomic policies. The unacceptability of Keynes' supranational Clearing Union to the US Congress had much to do with the fact that the US would be the major creditor country after the war. This ensured that a much less radical American plan, based upon a Fund made up of member state contributions of gold and foreign exchange, became the basis of the Bretton Woods agreements.[11]

Both the American and British Treasury teams had sufficient political support to resist pressure from financial circles for a return to the gold standard. This enabled Britain to gain some important concessions which were to make Bretton Woods a compromise rather than a *Diktat*. This is most apparent on the question of adjustment responsibilities between countries. Britain feared that without adequate safeguards in terms of placing symmetrical pressure on both surplus and deficit states to adjust to imbalances, the prospect of postwar recession in the US might jeopardise Britain's ability to maintain full employment without resorting to direct trade and exchange controls. The Americans made three concessions to British fears.

The first of these was the famous 'scarce currency clause', which justified the Fund's rationing of a currency in short supply as well as restrictions by other countries of transactions in that currency. Whether this concession would prove significant or not was difficult to tell, since much would depend upon whether the Fund was allowed to undertake sufficient lending in a particular currency for a shortage to develop.[12] Second, the Americans agreed to increase the Fund's resources from the $5 billion initially envisaged to $8.8 billion, their own contribution constituting about 35 per cent of this figure. The US was unwilling, however, to accede to the British idea that quota contributions be unconditionally available for short-term financing needs. Keynes therefore pushed the Americans to give way on their firm opposition to the idea that exchange rate changes should be a matter of national policy sovereignty, rather than requiring permission from the Fund.[13]

In what was a major concession, the US accepted automatic Fund concurrence in exchange rate changes of less than 10 per cent and even in changes of more than 10 per cent if this was shown to be necessary for the correction of a 'fundamental disequilibrium' (a necessarily vague concept).[14] On the whole area of Fund control over members' domestic policies, the final agreements also removed original provisions which allowed the Fund to require changes in policies incompatible with external equilibrium. Without these concessions, the British could never have sold the agreement to Parliament and the country, in which case the US goal of re-establishing an international monetary and trading system based upon the principle of multilateralism would have been left in shreds.

The multilateral element of the agreement was apparent in its provisions for the elimination of quotas on imports and for the convertibility of currencies on current account, though even then only after a 'transition period' after the war of uncertain length (a factor which assisted the eventual adoption of the agreement by the British Parliament).[15] There was also a clear presumption on all sides that since the rationale of a well-functioning international monetary system was to facilitate the growth and liberalisation of trade, current account restrictions ought to be discouraged, though controls on capital flows were seen as acceptable and probably necessary both to facilitate exchange rate stability and to prevent disruption of domestic monetary order.

The tendency in international relations literature to equate the 'liberalism' of Bretton Woods (and indeed the GATT) with that of the classical era of British dominance, is, as Ruggie has argued, mistaken. The Bretton Woods agreements (and even more those which followed) were the product of a necessary compromise between the principles of multilateralism and domestic interventionism.[16] What Ruggie terms 'embedded liberalism' to describe this compromise might just as well be termed 'embedded mercantilism'; in practice, primacy of place would come to be accorded to national economic sovereignty.

For the British, and especially the Labour Party, the commitment to full employment after the war and to the establishment of the welfare state was non-negotiable. This shift in domestic political forces and attitudes occurred in most major countries after the war and was reflected in a significantly greater contribution of government expenditure to GDP in the following years (see table 6.3). As a result of this development, Bretton Woods hardly constituted a clear set of 'rules' defining various adjustment responsibilities in the way that is often implied. The lack of agreement between the US and the British over the provision of liquidity and the distribution of responsibilities for adjustment between surplus and deficit states resulted in a very ambiguous compromise. All that was ruled out (and only then after the end of the transition period) was exchange restrictions on current transactions. There was also a presumption against frequent use of

Table 6.3 General government expenditures as a percentage of GDP, selected years.

Year	France	Germany	UK	US
1938	29	37	29	22[a]
1950	38	n.a.	35	22
1960	39	32	35	28
1970	39	39	42	34
1975	43	49	51	35
1980	44	49	47	35
1985	50	49	46	38

Note: [a] 1940. The figures provide only a very rough guide, due to differences in definitions and difficulties of measurement.

Source: Flora, 1983, ch. 8; Nutter, 1978, pp. 49–50; IMF, various years.

exchange rate changes for adjustment to external disequilibria,[17] but much would depend upon the extent to which in practice states would choose to exercise their right to employ that option. It is not surprising that the historian of the monetary negotiations called the agreements 'a kind of do-it-yourself kit with rather defective instructions.'[18]

Not only were adjustment responsibilities left unclear, but in one crucial area, the role of reserve currencies in the system, the silence was deafening. Financial conservatives in the US were vociferous in their criticism of the negotiations on this very point. Professor John Williams, Vice-President of the Federal Reserve Bank of New York and a leading representative of the financial establishment, argued that the US should support the restoration of a dollar-centred gold exchange standard through a stabilisation agreement between the key currencies (an extension of the model of the 1936 Tripartite Agreement between Britain, France and the US). Though there is some evidence that White and Treasury Secretary Morgenthou had sympathy with this idea, both were suspicious of what the latter had termed the 'usurious money-lenders', and also could not be seen to accept the criticism of the bankers (among others) that the provisions for the transition period contained in the Bretton Woods agreements were completely inadequate.

Keynes himself had also objected to granting a special position for any currency in the IMF articles.[19] Although it was clear to everyone that the dollar would be for a considerable time the only currency that was fully gold-convertible (at $35 per ounce), there was little discussion as to the general position of reserve currencies, what exactly 'balance

American hegemony and the international monetary system

of payments equilibrium' entailed for a key currency country such as the US, and the extent to which reserve growth ought to be made up of dollars (or sterling) as well as new monetary gold. An obscure provision in the articles provided for

> the Fund by a majority of the total voting power [to] make uniform proportionate changes in the par values of the currencies of all members, provided each such change is approved by every member which has ten percent or more of the total of the quotas.[20]

This appeared to allow for a proportionate revaluation of all currencies in terms of gold (in which par-values were to be expressed), though the implications of this for the relative positions of key currencies and gold in the international monetary system were left unexplored.

The idea of Bretton Woods as a regime which, backed by American hegemony, governed international monetary relations in the postwar era also glosses over the fact that (as critics at the time charged) the agreements were completely inappropriate to the circumstances of the postwar world. Before long, the Bretton Woods framework was pushed aside to make way for new approaches. In many ways, as we shall presently see, the role of the US in the international monetary system was established *outside* the formal structure of the Bretton Woods agreements.

6.3 The aftermath of the war and the failure of Bretton Woods

By the end of the war, Britain had suffered a further dramatic weakening of its relative position. Churchill's determination to fight Nazi Germany regardless of the financial consequences had created a situation even more pressing than the aftermath of World War I. Despite Lend-Lease, Britain lost one quarter of its total national wealth in the war, had external debts in excess of £2 billion in mid-1945, and faced a massive reduction in income from shipping and foreign investments. With plans for reconstruction and recovery envisaging a high level of imports for a number of years after the war, without exports at least double the level of prewar years, it would be unable to finance the inevitable deficit with the dollar area.

This difficulty was made more acute by the fact that Britain's main trading partners in the East no longer ran a payments surplus with the dollar area (table 6.4). When the US abruptly terminated Lend-Lease in August 1945, the new Labour government had little alternative but to dispatch Keynes to Washington in September 1945 to negotiate a loan from the Americans.

Table 6.4 Size and geographical distribution of US trade balances, 1938 and 1946 ($ millions).

Region	1938	1946
Europe	+380	+1,653
Latin America	+39	+201
North America	+104	+273
Asia	−26	+218
Africa	+32	+91
Oceania	+39	−33

Source: Milward, 1977, p. 358.

The US loan to Britain of $3.75 billion, agreed in December 1945, is important for two reasons. First, the US administration saw the loan as a means of accelerating the adoption of the multilateral obligations contained in the Bretton Woods agreements. Attached to the loan were provisions for the full convertibility of current sterling-area receipts and for an end to quantitative discrimination against American goods, as well as an obligation to make sterling convertible for current transactions within one year of the effective date of agreement (July 1946). The transition period had been reduced at a stroke to eighteen months. In Britain, these conditions 'were variously seen as an encroachment on Britain's economic sovereignty, an attempt to break up the Commonwealth and Empire and a first step towards "enslaving" a socialist Britain to capitalist America.'[21] Yet the British cabinet felt that they had little choice but to accept the loan with its conditions, however reluctantly.

On the American side, the loan was sold to Congress on the grounds that Britain's key role in international trade and payments necessitated American financial assistance, though only with the conditions attached. Deteriorating relations with the Soviets eventually gave the US another reason to provide special assistance to Britain as a major ally. The loan agreement was therefore something of a concession to the key currency school's arguments for treating Britain as a special case, while at the same time an attempt to maintain the pretence that the Bretton Woods institutions were an adequate solution to Europe's postwar problems.[22]

Any such delusions were rapidly dispelled with the return to sterling convertibility on current account in July 1947. The run on the pound that ensued was so rapid that the loan threatened to be exhausted in a matter of months, with the result that Britain was forced to renounce convertibility after only seven weeks. The attempts of the US administration to apply the Bretton Woods formula to the postwar circumstances had ended in failure, and from then on Britain would resist American and IMF pressure to accept convertibility obligations until the British government itself believed that the time was ripe to do so.[23]

Britain's difficulties were part of a larger, general problem of how the acute structural disequilibrium in international trade and payments ought to be dealt with. The need for reconstruction in many countries necessitated high levels of imports from the dollar area for the foreseeable future, with little means of financing them out of current exports. Some indication of this is given in table 6.4, comparing US bilateral trade balances with other regions in 1938 and 1946.

The United Nations Relief and Rehabilitation Administration (UNRAA), with most of its resources contributed by the US, was to deal with immediate war-relief requirements, but provided no solution to the reconstruction problem. The US government, itself concerned about the need to finance exports after the war, had placed its hopes in the International Bank for Reconstruction and Development (IBRD), set up with the IMF in 1944. However, the IBRD's resources were restricted to those that it could obtain from the international capital markets, which were inactive. As in 1919 when American official aid dried up, the world was faced at the end of the war with an imminent collapse of the postwar boom.[24]

The European crisis of 1947 remains a controversial matter. Its overt form was a 'crisis of confidence' due to widespread shortages and the breakdown of centre-left coalitions on the Continent, although the shortages were in part a product of the investment boom which had begun at the end of the war. In 1947, gross and net capital formation for all of Western Europe (outside of Germany) was higher than in 1938, itself a year of high investment due to rearmament programmes.[25] As Milward has argued, in economic terms the crisis was in the *international framework* in which the national economies were operating, above all in the prospective inability of the international monetary arrangements to finance the large US current surplus at the end of the war.

Unlike in 1920, after 1945 the transformation of the domestic political situation ruled out deflation as an option for a number of countries, especially in Britain and France. The determination of these countries to pursue a policy of rapid growth and reconstruction of their economies necessitated vital strategic imports from the US, which with the termination of UNRRA aid and other US relief aid over 1947 (and again no prospect of private investment filling the gap), could not be financed. European leaders could see the crisis looming but could think of no way out; the hope could only have been that in contrast to the post-World War 1 circumstances, the US would act out of its own strategic interest to produce a major new initiative.[26]

Before Secretary of State Marshall made his famous Harvard speech in June 1947, the deteriorating relationship with the Soviet Union and the perception in the State Department that Western Europe was in the midst of an economic, political and moral crisis, was bringing about an important shift in US policy. Increasingly it was felt that only a massive programme of American economic assistance to Europe could avert the disaster which threatened. The objective of Marshall Aid was an ambitious one: the path to European economic 'viability' and containment of the emerging Soviet threat would be through the economic and even political integration of Western Europe.[27] This would provide a fundamental solution to the productivity gap with the US and the supposedly related dollar shortage. It would further allow Europe to do without dollar aid by 1952 and eventually to take on the multilateral obligations of Bretton Woods. For the foreseeable future, however, the US had to accept that Bretton Woods provided no solution to the structural problems of the international economy.

It is often argued that Marshall Aid gave the American hegemon the means to exercise its economic power to achieve a new and more appropriate international monetary regime. As Keohane has written, 'the United States could use the influence provided by European reliance on its aid to take the lead in creating and maintaining a new set of post-Bretton Woods rules for the world financial system.'[28] There are two issues at stake here: first, whether Marshall Aid gave the US leverage over specific important issues in the monetary area after 1947, and second, whether the new policies and institutions that evolved constituted a new regime or set of rules as Keohane suggests.

There was not one but at least two major factions in US foreign economic policy during these years, with conflicts being regularly aired in the meetings of the National Advisory Council on International Monetary and Financial Problems (NAC). One group, comprised of the IMF, Federal Reserve Board and Treasury representatives, were against European integration to the extent that it significantly retarded the adoption of the Bretton Woods articles. The other group, led by the Marshall planners in the Economic Cooperation Administration (ECA) and State Department, believed that Bretton Woods was an ultimate goal but that European integration was a necessary first step.

Neither of these two factions fully achieved its objectives, largely because what each was proposing was something upon which most European countries were united in opposing. Countries like Britain and France were resentful of American attempts to push them into adopting policies consistent with Bretton Woods that they saw as impossible in the circumstances. In most countries reconstruction necessitated conserving scarce dollars, which gave the US little choice but to tolerate continuing exchange controls. The 1940s and early 1950s saw an expansion of bilateral currency arrangements to a much greater extent than in the 1930s.[29] In practice, the emphasis upon investment and the step to 'viability' meant that the ECA criticised deflationary Italy and West Germany to a much greater extent than relatively inflationary France, though such criticism produced no major policy reversals.[30] If inflation *was* gradually brought under control in countries like France, there was also a clear incentive to do so from the national standpoint.

On the issue of exchange rates, it is true that the US attempted to use Marshall aid as a means of increasing surveillance over recipients' policies, arguing that any prospective changes in exchange rates ought first to be discussed with the IMF. Since this went beyond the requirement for mere notification in the IMF articles, Britain and France were strongly opposed, forcing the IMF and US Treasury to back down. The French were also criticised by the IMF for their adoption of a multiple exchange rate system, but the NAC was convinced by the ECA to drop the demand for a single French parvalue on the basis that it would be politically unacceptable in France.[31]

The further deterioration of the British payments position over 1949 suggested to the NAC that what was needed for a more rapid move to economic viability and convertibility was a devaluation of sterling and other European currencies against the dollar.[32] The reluctance of the French (who had devalued the franc in January 1948) and British to contemplate devaluation when they were both concerned to resist inflationary pressures has led to the suggestion that the US 'forced' the devaluations of sterling and other countries in September 1949.[33] Cripps (Britain's Chancellor of the Exchequer), like a number of British officials, was against devaluation *alone*, because of scepticism as to whether it could improve Britain's net dollar position. The steady loss of reserves, market expectation of devaluation and mounting evidence of uncompetitive export prices in dollar markets eventually brought the British cabinet in July 1949 to vote in favour of devaluation, though Cripps was able to delay action until September 18.[34] Market forces had made the devaluations inevitable.

The move to extra-European currency convertibility and a reduction in discrimination against American goods made little practical progress in the Marshall aid years. Nor could it be argued that ECA and State Department desire for rapid European economic and political integration was a complete success. Fostering mere *cooperation* on such issues as the sterling devaluation of 1949 and within the Organisation for European Economic Cooperation (OEEC) in general had proved all but impossible.[35] Here US policy ran up against the immovable barrier of the British refusal to accept full integration into a United States of Europe, as well as the unwillingness of other major countries like France to move any faster or further along the road towards European integration than they themselves saw as possible or desirable.

In the monetary area, the ECA proposal for a European Payments Union (EPU) at the end of 1949 brought out the difficulties with the American approach. This proposal was for a new system of net multilateral settlement of balances between members of the OEEC as well as the sterling area, for the substantial elimination of quantitative restrictions on trade within the OEEC, and for an EPU Board which would facilitate the coordination of national monetary and economic policies. The ECA's objective was an ambitious one: 'a common [European] monetary system, the equivalent of a single currency', as a first step towards the eventual adoption of multilateral trade and dollar convertibility for Europe as a whole. IMF and US Treasury fears that this would represent the fusion of West European countries into a 'soft currency' sterling bloc, which would continue to discriminate against American goods, led to their insistence that the IMF administer EPU, but the Europeans refused this.[36]

The Europeans would not be pushed into monetary integration either and refused to establish a Board with powers to harmonise national financial policies. Adjustment responsibilities within EPU provided for a sliding scale of settlement in dollars and credits that aimed at putting pressure on deficit countries to adjust and surplus countries to redirect exports towards the dollar area. This enabled a compromise between the European states.[37]

Just as crucial was the end of the US policy of opposition to the sterling area. The sterling depreciation probably made some contribution to the improvement in the British payments position in 1950, but this in itself could not alleviate the difficulties posed by the sterling balances accumulated during the war. Britain was unwilling to accept anything like sterling convertibility until the US agreed to support sterling's role in EPU settlements and to ensure sterling-area insulation against conversion of sterling balances by continental countries.[38] Though EPU was a major step in the liberalisation of trade and payments within Europe and beyond, it was neither a regime imposed by a US hegemon nor a new solution to the structure of *global* payments. The Europeans were able to resist US pressure on some fundamental issues (notably integration) and established a set of institutions more appropriate to European circumstances.[39] Their ability to do so was enhanced by the development of the Cold War, which prevented the US from pushing important countries like Britain and France too far because of the potential consequences for Western security.[40]

Ironically, the American perception of continued structural economic weakness in Europe was already in the process of being outmoded over 1949, first by the large devaluations against the dollar in September, and second by the beginnings of the postwar boom in Western Germany. The exceptional growth of the German economy provided a crucial market for European exports, as well as ultimately relieving the dependence of those economies upon imports of *American* capital goods for industrial restructuring. As a result, 'several of West Germany's neighbours moved into the pattern of export-led growth which dominated the boom of the 1950s.'[41]

In contrast to Britain and the sterling area, whose external position remained more dependent upon economic developments in the American economy, the improvement of the continent's trade balance with the US meant that the boom was increasingly Euro-centric. By mid-1952, continental Western Europe was in almost exact balance on all private transactions with the US, so that the net flow of US government expenditure and aid (maintained by the military expenditures following in the wake of the Korean War) was adding to those countries' reserves, especially those of West Germany. The West German current account swung into surplus in 1951, a pattern which would lead to strains within EPU and ultimately within the international monetary system in general.

Europe's improving current account balance with the US allowed growth in European trade and output to continue largely unaffected by the American recessions of 1953–4 and 1957–8, which suggests that it is an exaggeration to hold that the boom was largely a product of growth in America.[42] The US willingness to open its markets to foreign exports, in contrast to the protectionism of the interwar period, was certainly an important factor in Europe's ability to finance imports from America (and was even more important for Japanese recovery). Official and private capital flows further improved Europe's international finances. Outside of Britain, however, the major export market for most European countries was West Germany and this country in turn sent a great majority of its exports to other European countries. Contrary to American fears, Europe had in fact made an enormous step towards 'viability' by the end of Marshall aid.

From the American point of view, the movement of its overall payments position into deficit was seen as a result of the peculiar circumstances of the time and as unlikely to persist. Though US official settlements deficits over the period 1950–7 totalled $6.2 billion, the cumulative current account surplus was $5.5 billion in spite of considerable discrimination against American goods, leaving little doubt as to the strength of the competitive position of leading US industries. The par value of the dollar in terms of gold during these years seemed unchallengeable, and the loss of $1.7 billion in gold reserves over 1950–7 was seen as a healthy redistributive movement. The rest of the deficit was largely financed through the voluntary accumulation of dollar liabilities abroad, which established the dollar as the world's major reserve currency.

World reserves grew by over $8 billion over the period, with new monetary gold and foreign exchange reserves each accounting for 46 per cent of this increase, and new reserve positions at the IMF for only 8 per cent.[43] The compound growth of total world reserves was about 2.2 per cent per annum over 1950–7, while the volume of world trade in the 1950s expanded at over 6 per cent per annum (and real output at about 4 per cent), which suggests that the growth in international liquidity was not excessive in this period. The West European countries in particular experienced high rates and stability of growth (see tables 4.2 and 4.3), facilitating adjustment to growing trade interdependence.

Though gradual *de facto* moves towards currency convertibility had been made in Europe during the 1950s, especially in those countries with strengthening payments positions, controls on current and capital transactions were the rule. London's international commodity and gold markets were reopened in the mid-1950s, but much of the trade finance business in sterling had shifted to offshore centres like Zurich. The City of London was in favour of a return to full sterling convertibility, but the British authorities were unwilling to do so as long as they feared that convertibility would only lead to massive conversions of sterling balances into dollars. This fear prompted the British to obtain the European Monetary Agreement of 1955, which established that any return to multilateral convertibility in Europe would be a collective one.[44]

By the end of 1958, the overwhelming success of economic reconstruction and the stability of the domestic social contract in Europe gave the Europeans themselves a great incentive to liberalise markets (and hence exchange controls). In the context of a major improvement in the British balance of payments and a French devaluation, the West Europeans moved collectively to adopt convertibility on current account in December 1958.[45] To the extent that the multilateral obligations of the Bretton Woods agreement became operable, they did so after the establishment of the national welfare state in Europe.

Despite this possibly unprecedented stability and growth, some strains were beginning to emerge. Of the $6.5 billion increase in monetary reserves of OEEC countries over 1950–7, the accumulation of reserves by West Germany accounted for $5 billion.[46] In addition to the role of the dollar in the international monetary system, the pre-1958 period saw the establishment of a pattern of persistent US overall deficits (but large surpluses on current account) and German current and overall surpluses. The question would soon arise as to whether these payments 'disequilibria' were unsustainable and if so, what measures of adjustment ought to be taken and by whom.

6.4 The emergence of disequilibria and the problem of adjustment

After averaging $770 million per annum over 1950–7, American official settlements deficits took a sudden turn for the worse over 1958–9, averaging $3.2 billion in these two years. The question arose as to whether this represented a temporary setback or if it heralded a fundamental worsening of the US payments position. As the US economy moved out of recession in 1959, a significant deterioration of the trade balance suggests that by the end of the 1950s the US was facing for the first time since the war serious competition in international markets for exports, especially from West German manufactures.

Imports were also beginning to make inroads into US markets in traditional areas of local producer dominance, such as automobiles.[47] From averaging $5.4 billion over 1956–7, the trade surplus fell to $3.3 billion in 1958 and $1 billion in 1959. The competitiveness of American industry seems to have improved considerably over the next few years, however, in part due to the excellent US wage and price inflation record over the late 1950s and early 1960s (wholesale prices were unchanged 1958–64) and to reduced discrimination against US exports. Average yearly trade and current account surpluses over 1960–5 were $5.3 billion and $4.5 billion respectively, at a time when the domestic economy was booming.

Another source of deterioration in the US payments position was the increased net outflow of private long-term capital from 1956. American 'multinational' companies sustained their competitive advantage by relocating production facilities abroad in these years, especially

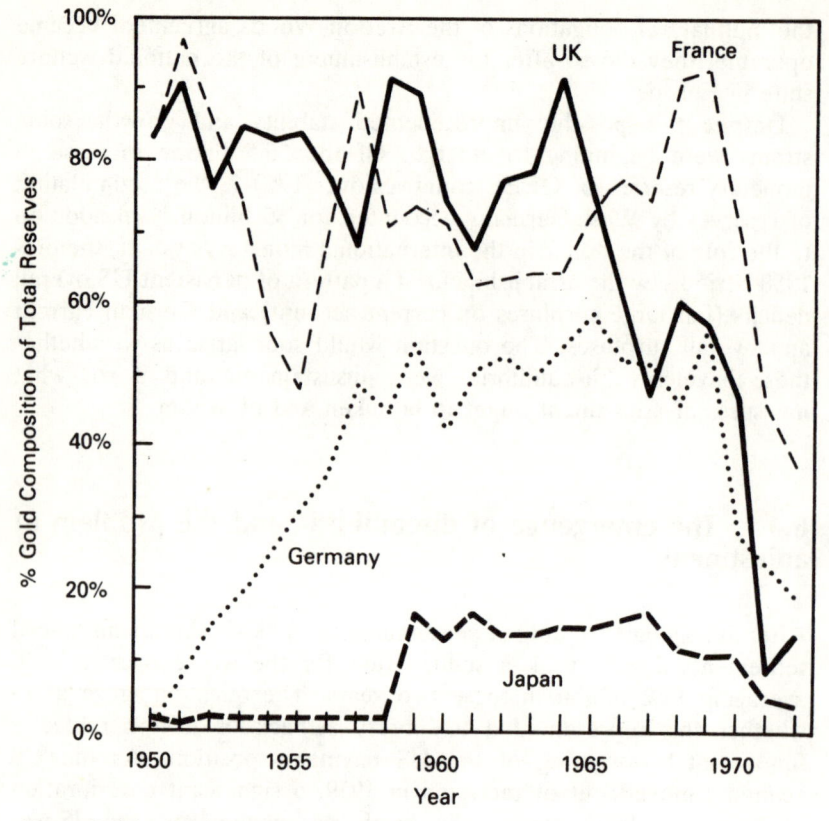

Figure 6.1 Gold composition of reserves, selected countries, 1950–72.

Note: Gold valued at SDR 35/ounce.
Source: IMF, *International Financial Statistics*.

in Europe, which was likely in the long run to erode the US trade surplus.

Perhaps most striking was the loss of US gold reserves: in 1958–9, it lost $3.4 billion in gold reserves, compared to only $1.7 billion in the previous eight years. It was not just that the US trade and overall payments position had deteriorated, but that in the late 1950s there was a shift in the reserve preference of central banks in favour of gold rather than dollars (see figures 6.1 and 6.2). Other industrialised countries had been able to accumulate monetary reserves over the 1950s because of a persistent tendency to current account surplus and net capital inflows, though there had been setbacks for France and Britain in and after the time of the Suez crisis. The US had seen the steadily strengthening reserve position of its allies as a positive sign of

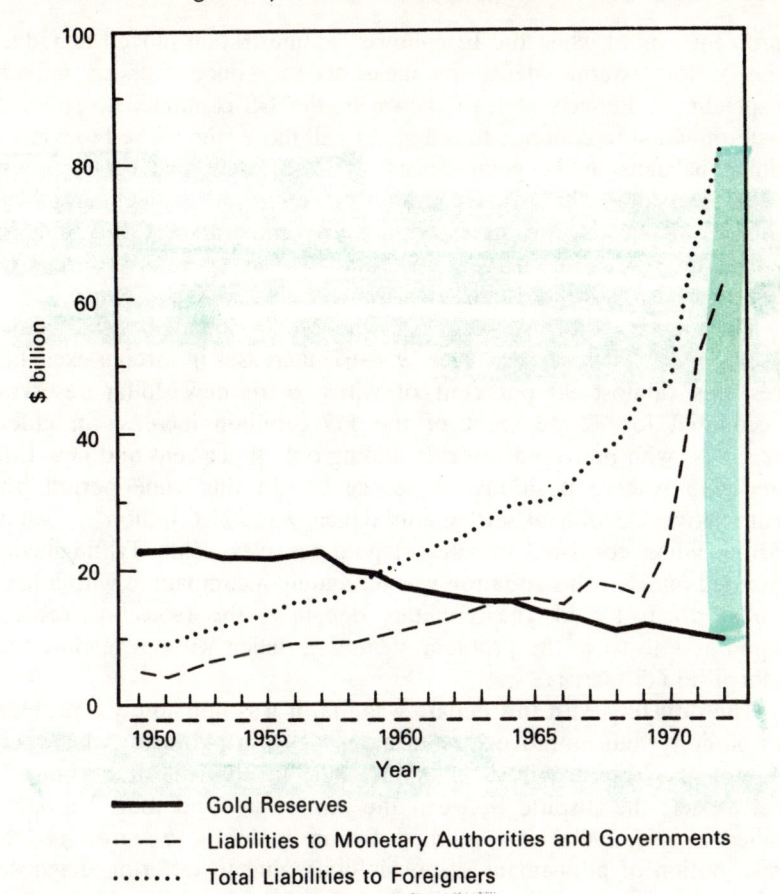

American hegemony and the international monetary system

Figure 6.2 US gold reserves and short-term liabilities to foreigners, 1950–72.

Note: Gold valued at SDR 35/ounce.
Source: IMF, *International Financial Statistics*.

Legend:
— Gold Reserves
--- Liabilities to Monetary Authorities and Governments
······ Total Liabilities to Foreigners

their growing economic and political stability, though this attitude was soon to change. As the international public and private role of the dollar steadily grew over the 1950s and 1960s, the desire of the rest of the world as a whole to accumulate reserves *and to maintain their gold composition* was gradually eroding the US gold stock and ultimately the gold convertibility of the dollar at $35 per ounce. This was what Robert Triffin had recognised at the end of the 1950s and became known as the Triffin dilemma, as discussed in Chapter 3.

Though Triffin's analysis was hardly popular with the US government and monetary authorities, by 1960 there was some recognition that a problem existed when the Eisenhower administration moved to reduce the overall external deficit by measures to reduce overseas military expenditure. Publicly at least, however, the US continued to stress its determination to continue to sell gold to all those who wished to convert dollar balances at the going price.[48] To the extent that central banks tried to maintain the gold composition of reserves by obtaining gold in the *private* market, this increased pressure on the market price of gold, which underwent a flurry in October 1960 as speculative pressures drove the London gold market price as high as $40 per ounce.

The growing shortage of gold in the 1960s coincided with a major growth in dollar reserves. Over 1958–67, increases in foreign exchange reserves (almost 90 per cent of which were new dollar reserves) accounted for 72 per cent of the $17.1 billion increase in global reserves, with new gold reserves adding only 9 per cent and new IMF and BIS reserve positions 19 per cent.[49] In this same period, the cumulative US official settlements deficit was $21.6 billion, of which $10.8 billion consisted in sales of gold reserves. With Triffin having pointed out that this situation was ultimately incompatible with a fixed dollar price of gold, the monetary debate of the 1960s was centred upon how to solve the problem of the US deficit without leading to a global liquidity crisis.

The difficulty with this debate was that it was not simply a problem of liquidity, but moreover one of *adjustment*, in particular who would accept the responsibility for adjustment to this disequilibrium. In retrospect, the dispute between the Americans and their European allies in the 1960s was marked by an inability to agree on the distribution of adjustment responsibilities, due to differing diagnoses of the nature of the disequilibrium in the international monetary system. The debate was conducted in international forums such as the Bank for International Settlements, and the Economic Policy Committee and Working Party 3 of the newly formed OECD.[50] Robert Solomon, an American representative in Working Party 3 for a number of years, observed that:

> European criticisms in Working Party 3 focused on US monetary policy, which was alleged to provide excess liquidity to the American economy and to keep interest rates too low, with the result that US investors had an incentive to place funds abroad. This in turn swelled both the overall US deficit and European surpluses. American officials, in turn, argued that European countries were relying too heavily on monetary policy and not enough on fiscal policy to restrain aggregate demand ... and repeatedly charged that Europeans tended to regard the US deficit, rather than the European surplus, as the aberration that needed correction.[51]

The Europeans argued that US dollar deficits were supply-determined and the Americans that they were demand-determined, with each side demanding that the other make the appropriate policy adjustments. In a sense, each side in the dispute was partly correct in its diagnosis of the disequilibrium. Each had focused upon two different asymmetries in the Bretton Woods system that had existed from the very beginning: the Americans upon that which favoured the running of payments surpluses and the Europeans upon that which allowed reserve currency countries to finance deficits through the issuance of short-term liabilities.

Ironically, during the war, the British had directed their efforts to removing the bias in favour of surplus countries, but American financial strength had militated against any correction of this imbalance. By the 1960s, with persistently large overall US deficits, the tables had turned, with the Americans criticising the Europeans for their seemingly insatiable desire to hold 'barren gold', their continuing restrictions on US exports, and their high interest rates.[52]

From the European perspective, an exchange rate consistent with the maintenance of a current account surplus favoured domestic exports, a high level of employment and productivity growth and reduced the adjustment costs flowing from higher levels of import-penetration. As a result, while there was a presumption on the part of most countries that resort to devaluation should be avoided (the Italian experience over 1963–4 being a good example), in the presence of persistent current account weakness they were generally willing to make large devaluations (such as Western Europe in general over 1948–9 and France in 1958). The other side of this coin was that countries with excessively strong current accounts proved very reluctant to revalue their currencies, and when they did (such as West Germany and Holland in 1960) it tended to be of small magnitude.[53]

Current surpluses also allowed the accumulation of foreign assets, foreign aid expenditure and the financing of exports without a rise in net external indebtedness. The steady accumulation of monetary reserves was an understandable objective in a growing world economy and arguably had become increasingly necessary in the 1960s, given rising trade interdependence and the growing importance of private short-term capital flows. In sum, current surpluses (or 'mercantilism') provided an important cushion for the national welfare state in an increasingly interdependent world economy.

For the Europeans, the problem was the asymmetry which allowed reserve currency countries, above all the US, to finance excessive deficits by flooding the world with dollars. The political attention given to the large US capital outflows in the 1960s revolved in part around the idea that the privilege conferred on the US by the key currency status of the dollar allowed it to exchange paper dollar assets for control over European resources. The French in particular, not altogether unreasonably, held that the periodic conversion of dollar reserves into gold at the US Treasury was the main means of placing an external constraint upon American policy. Any solution to the international payments disequilibrium should therefore come from the US, though whether tighter US monetary policy was in European interests is debatable. Certainly, the Europeans (let alone America's other trading partners) did not want to see a devaluation of the dollar relative to other currencies. Large US current account surpluses over 1960–7 (averaging $4 billion per annum) suggest that the dollar was not overvalued during these years; without large net outflows of long-term capital these current surpluses with the rest of the world would not have been sustainable. Most people recognised that any dollar devaluation *vis-à-vis* other currencies would probably be met with retaliatory devaluations.

Even if the US had been successful in reducing its outflow of long-term capital and official foreign expenditure, foreign governments would have been forced into adopting restrictive measures to deal with a dollar shortage. In the Kennedy and Johnson eras, various measures to reduce the long-term capital outflow (the Interest Equalisation Tax, voluntary and finally mandatory capital export restrictions) were attempted, along with other measures to reduce the costs of official foreign expenditure (such as the various 'offset agreements' with West Germany). The failure of these programmes significantly to reduce the deficit was in part due to the private and official demand for dollars as the major source of international liquidity, as well as domestic US financial regulations and the unwillingness of the US to place punitive restrictions upon corporate foreign investment or US banks' Euromarket activities.[54] More generally, the overall US deficit was consistent with the global role adopted by America after 1945. As David Calleo has written:

> In reality . . . the United States had no real intention of giving up its foreign 'burdens', including the tribulations of monetary hegemony. Overseas troops and investments were expressions of American ambition and power as well as idealism. The United States was not running deficits to provide liquidity to others, but as a by-product of pursuing its domestic and foreign ambitions.[55]

There was also a broad European desire for continued American engagement in Western Europe's affairs, which made Europe's position in the international monetary debates somewhat tenuous. The debate on international monetary reform was caught in an impasse, with neither side willing to accept responsibility for adjustment to the

American hegemony and the international monetary system 171

payments disequilibrium or to alter the basis of the postwar political–military structure. To many, this seemed to be the result of 'the redistribution of economic power between the reconstructed economies of Europe and Japan on the one hand, and of the United States on the other ... [preventing] the advanced countries from meeting the crisis in a coordinated fashion.'[56] In order to decide whether the crisis was due to a relative decline of American power, we need to consider the various proposals for the reform of the system.

6.5 Solutions to the systemic disequilibrium?

The main solutions urged upon the governments at the time by academics and officials were perhaps four: an increase in the gold price, a move to greater exchange rate flexibility or even floating exchange rates, a full dollar standard and centralised liquidity creation through an enhanced IMF.

Gold and reserve currency country adjustment

Until around 1967, the health of the US current account suggests that the disequilibrium which had arisen in the gold exchange standard was due to the shortage of gold rather than an overvaluation of the dollar in terms of other currencies. This suggested to some a need for an increase in the price of gold in terms of all currencies, so as to revalue US gold stocks and increase the flow of new monetary gold into the system.[57]

Opposition to this proposal was very strong. Triffin called it a 'false solution', while the official US attitude from the time of the gold market flurry in 1960 was that the $35 per ounce price of gold was the 'pillar of the postwar system'.[58] American policy, from the organisation of the Gold Pool in 1961 aimed at stabilising the market price of gold to the Two Tier Arrangement of 1968 which abandoned the long attempt to prevent the private market price of gold from rising above the official price, was set firmly against any change in the official dollar price of gold. As a result, over the 1960s the gold convertibility of the dollar was placed in increasing doubt and the international monetary system evolved from a gold exchange standard towards a dollar standard.

An initial argument made against the gold price proposal was that it would not be distributionally neutral. The main beneficiaries of such a rise, it was held, would be the gold market speculators and the world's major gold producing nations, the Soviet Union and South

Africa. Similarly, those allies who had willingly held dollars rather than consistently converting them into gold, Japan, West Germany and Canada (in marked contrast to the French from 1965), would allegedly suffer most. Although such arguments may well have carried some weight with the US government in the 1960s, it must be asked whether the US could have in any case ultimately prevented the gold price from rising.

The willingness of various US administrations after 1970 to allow and even encourage large dollar devaluations also suggests that in the final event, accounting losses by foreign central banks were of limited importance. This objection, moreover, did not meet the basic question at issue, which was whether an increase in the gold price would have been sufficient to remove the systemic disequilibrium, which would have benefited all countries, not least the US itself. The US was after all the world's largest holder of gold reserves, while the dollar's link with gold provided US authorities with a criterion of balance of payments discipline and exchange rate management.[59]

By far the most compelling argument for academic economists was that raising the gold price would have provided no 'permanent' solution to the problem of international monetary order. As we saw in Chapter 3, in a world of creeping inflation, the maintenance of a gold exchange standard would require a revaluation of gold from time to time.[60] John Williamson has put the academic case succinctly: '[w]hat most economists doubted was not the feasibility of such a strategy, but its desirability, as opposed to the alternative of developing a fiduciary reserve asset.'[61] The idea of a fundamental instability in the gold exchange standard meant that for many economists salvaging the system was irrational. It goes without saying that the gold exchange standard was not an ideal system by any means, but as shall be argued shortly, it is questionable whether economists of this bent had asked themselves whether a more ideal system was a *political* possibility.

One of the more likely reasons for official US opposition, at least from the mid-1960s, was that the main proponents of a gold price increase on the international level were the French, whose proclamations on the subject no doubt hardened American determination to resist anything that could be associated with the maintenance of the role of gold in the international monetary system. The French policy had long been aimed at reducing the role of reserve currencies and the 'exorbitant privilege' (or seignorage) which that role accorded to the major Anglo-Saxon countries.

This policy became more aggressive under de Gaulle, initially in the Composite Reserve Unit (CRU) proposal in 1963–4, intended to achieve a 'camouflaged' increase in the gold price by creating CRUs in uniform proportion to gold reserves and requiring settlement of deficits in a fixed proportion of gold and CRUs.[62] American inaction prompted de Gaulle (in his famous press conference of February 1965)[63] to give vocal support for an enhanced role for gold, which reinforced the impression that the French wanted to foster a return to a pure gold standard in which there would be no exorbitant privileges.

Though other French officials such as Giscard d'Estaing and even Michel Debré were at pains to stress that France was not asking for a return to the gold standard, they held that a higher gold price was still necessary to bolster the gold exchange standard. From the American point of view, the gold price proposal was consistently presented as implying a 'radical change' in the system and even a return to the gold standard.[64] This in turn prompted the French to take the offensive by seeking to impose gold discipline on the US by regularly presenting dollars for conversion at the American Treasury.

This confrontational policy had two effects. First, it became a question of American national pride to resist the French demands and strengthened the Johnson administration's determination to find a replacement for gold in the international monetary system. This was nothing but the logical extension of the refusal to raise the official gold price. The step from here to the Two Tier Agreement of March 1968 and ultimately to Nixon's *de jure* suspension of the gold convertibility of the dollar in August 1971 was not very far.

Second, French policy made it difficult for other European nations to present dollars for conversion without appearing to be conspiring with the French against American leadership. After 1968, with the official convertibility of the dollar into gold increasingly untenable due to a European fear that major conversions of dollars would prompt the closing of the US gold window, the world was on a *de facto* dollar standard.

To complicate matters, the inflationary impact of Johnson's economic policy during the Vietnam war years led to a rapid deterioration in the US balance of payments deficit and large accumulations of dollar reserves in the rest of the world (see figure 6.2). The massive deterioration of the US official settlements deficit from 1969 owed something to the erosion of the current account surplus, but even before this the gold exchange standard had effectively collapsed due to the growing inconvertibility of the dollar into gold at the official price. Only the US had the power to remove the gold shortage by a revaluation of gold, but it chose not to do so.

Whether this was a mistake remains a highly controversial question. Ultimately, the issue boils down to whether the gold exchange standard was worth restoring, if only in order to buy time for a more thoroughgoing reform of the international monetary system. As will be argued subsequently, the main difficulty with the argument for an increase in the gold price is whether a system based upon exchange rates pegged to gold was compatible with an international monetary system in which the role of private capital flows was increasingly important.

The world central bank option (SDR-STANDARD)

The fundamental reason why most economists opposed a restoration of gold exchange standard was because they believed that there was a much more rational and permanent alternative to a system based upon the vagaries of gold production and reserve country deficits. The ultimate aim of their proposals for an enhanced IMF with the power to create and manage global liquidity in the way that Keynes had envisaged during the war was to create a world central bank.[65] As argued in Chapter 3, the crucial difficulty was how to effect a transition from an international monetary system in which central banks had sovereign control over reserves (and at least in principle over monetary policy) to a system in which such monetary sovereignty would be abolished or at least severely constrained.

The role of the IMF in the international monetary system had remained a relatively marginal one. Its ability to affect the adjustment issue between the major countries was extremely limited, while there was little indication that the SDR would be allowed to grow into a major global reserve asset.[66] Above all, as the importance of the dollar in the international monetary and financial system steadily grew in the late 1960s and into the 1970s, the incentive for the US in particular to accept a collectively managed system correspondingly declined.

The American decision to promote the creation of an international fiduciary asset (which became the SDR) in mid-1965 was an attempt to head off French and other European proposals aimed at maintaining or enhancing the monetary role of gold. With the Two Tier agreement and the effective isolation of the French, the US had substantially achieved its aims. As Solomon noted, 'contrary to the French approach, the special drawing right (SDR) was being regarded as a substitute for gold.'[67] Whether SDRs could also replace reserve currencies and in particular the dollar was not at all clear, and seemed to depend upon the lingering hope of many that US dollar deficits would somehow disappear and thereby give SDRs a chance to come into their own.

The evolving structure of the international financial system and America's global commitments made the permanent disappearance of the US deficit an extremely unlikely event. With the *de jure* abolition of gold-dollar convertibility in August 1971 and the effective acceptance of the other countries of a dollar standard with the Smithsonian Agreement of December 1971, the Nixon administration removed the remnants of the main external constraint upon domestic policy under which it had increasingly chafed.[68] In such circumstances, would it have been surprising if the US proved reluctant to accept an even tighter external constraint upon its domestic and foreign policies than had existed in the days of the gold exchange standard?

The abortive monetary reform negotiations which followed the Smithsonian realignment over 1972–4 in many ways were a re-run of the long debate over adjustment responsibilities. The Europeans and Japanese were intent upon removing the asymmetry in the system about which they had always felt indignant, while the Americans complained of the need for constraints upon surplus states. The Europeans correspondingly insisted upon the adoption of an SDR-standard based upon the principle of compulsory 'primary reserve asset settlement', which would have removed the role of reserve currencies in the settlement of imbalances and placed considerable pressure upon any deficit country to adjust.[69]

For its part, the US presented an alternative proposal in September 1972 for a 'reserve indicator system' that defined certain 'objective' points beyond which if a country's reserves increased or fell, would oblige it to adopt adjustment measures, including exchange rate changes.[70] The Americans would only agree to the restoration of dollar-convertibility into primary reserve assets (which would be SDRs) as long as the upper 'primary asset holding limit' defined a point beyond which further accumulations of dollar balances would be inconvertible. In other words, the US appeared unwilling to agree to any 'tight' settlement system for reserve currency balances.

What the other countries overestimated was the US desire to compromise its demands in order to achieve an agreement. The dollar remained by far the most important reserve currency in the system, and with the complete breakdown of the fixed exchange rate system in March 1973, the situation had seemingly changed in the favour of the US. There, floating exchange rates were seen as a means of attaining complete autonomy for domestic economic policy as well as providing a means by which market pressure might be brought to bear upon persistent surplus states to accept either currency appreciation or domestic reflation.[71] By this time, even very trade-dependent countries like West Germany had come to see floating *vis-à-vis* the dollar as a preferable alternative to an inflationary dollar standard, but the continued commitment to exchange rate stability in continental Europe was demonstrated in the development of the 'snake' and later the European Monetary System.[72]

The oil crisis in autumn 1973 sounded a convenient death-knell to the reform negotiations during which neither side had been able to agree on the basics. Williamson argues that the final outcome was little short of total failure: 'There was no agreement on a set of rules for assigning adjustment responsibilities, no design of a viable adjustment mechanism, no introduction of an SDR-standard, no substitution and no curb on the asymmetries.'[73] Williamson's argument that the failure was ultimately due to a lack of political will and the general incompetence of the negotiators seems implausible. It exaggerates the extent to which the failure of the reform negotiations should be seen as a defeat for the Nixon administration's desire to prevent any circumscription of the autonomy of US domestic and foreign policy. The emerging *status quo* was probably seen by the American authorities as much more satisfactory than any formal agreement they might have got with the other countries and also more acceptable than a gold exchange standard restored through an increase in the gold price.[74]

Although Williamson argues that the Europeans made a mistake by failing to bow to the strength of the US negotiating position and accept the US reserve indicator system as a basis for negotiation, the extent to which the Europeans' hearts were set on a full SDR-standard must also be questioned.[75] After all, was it likely that surplus states would be entirely happy about accumulating international fiat money in the form of SDRs, when only months earlier they had been calling for a revaluation of gold? With gold denied any formal systemic role by the US, the European governments pushed without great conviction a system which, though intellectually appealing to economists, did not solve the basic *political* problem that these countries wanted a system based upon 'tight' settlement in assets that were not another country's or organisation's liability. To describe the continued attraction on the part of national central banks to gold as an 'irrational prejudice'[76] is a typical example of many economists' failure to comprehend the political foundation of the demand for gold as an asset which can be held.

It is therefore not entirely surprising that the major countries have since that time demonstrated a complete unwillingness to enhance the role of the SDR beyond its very limited present one.[77] The creation of the SDR has not represented an important exception to the general trend towards a much greater role for reserve currencies in the international monetary system, to the trend towards a system based more and more upon private exchange and capital markets rather than upon the principle of collective management. Similarly, the common idea that what emerged from the breakdown of the Bretton Woods system and the failure of the international monetary reform efforts was an international monetary 'non-system' exaggerates the extent to which there was ever any agreement on the fundamental issue of adjustment responsibility.[78]

The notion of a non-system (or absence of rules) has also encouraged the view that this outcome can be explained by an 'absence of hegemonic power' in the post-Bretton Woods era. This is misleading because it underestimates the role that American policies in particular have directly or indirectly played in fostering a system founded upon market principles. The idea of a non-system keeps open the hope that the long-term trend of the evolution of the international monetary system will be towards one founded upon collective monetary management. Whatever one's views regarding the likelihood of an 'ultimate solution' in international monetary affairs, it is difficult not to conclude that internationalist economists have underestimated the political difficulty of the world central bank proposal in a world of separate states.

Exchange rate flexibility

From the late 1960s, a number of economists and officials began pushing for the introduction of greater exchange rate flexibility in order to facilitate adjustment to payments disequilibria. There was undoubtedly a need to make it easier for governments to adjust exchange rates in the face of persistent disequilibria, such as in the case of Britain over 1964–7, as well as to encourage chronic surplus states to undertake adequate revaluations. There were moves within the IMF to promote the 'crawling peg' idea, which gained some support from the US, Germany and Italy, though the traditional supporters of a fixed rate system (France and Belgium) remained opposed.[79]

One of the most difficult issues in the debate was in deciding whether the disequilibrium would have been ameliorated by a devaluation of the US dollar. Over 1955–61, the US economy had been experiencing relatively slow growth of 2 per cent per annum, compared to between 5 per cent and 9 per cent for most of its major allies.[80] The Kennedy administration's determination to boost this sluggish growth by a series of tax cuts heralded a new era of Keynesian expansionism in American policy-thinking, though in practice fiscal expansionism was more a facet of the Johnson years and afterwards.[81] From 1962 onwards, the US economy experienced a much higher pressure of demand than for any time since the Korean war, with real GDP growth jumping to an average of 4.9 per cent per annum over 1962–8. In 1965, unemployment fell below 4 per cent, capacity utilisation hit record levels and consumer price inflation rose from 1.7 per cent in 1965 to 4.2 per cent in 1968.

The problem in retrospect appears to have been that just as the fiscal expansionism of the Vietnam war and Great Society years reached its peak, US productivity growth showed a marked tendency towards a long-term decline, reducing the scope for non-inflationary increases in real income.[82] Besides the marked decline in the US trade and current account surpluses in 1968–9 (to an average of $600 million and $500 million respectively) and the emergence of large surpluses in countries like West Germany, Japan and Canada, there is additional evidence that the US dollar by this stage had become overvalued relative to some (though not all) other foreign currencies. American export unit values rose by 6.5 per cent over 1965–8, while in France and West Germany they hardly rose at all and even slightly declined in the case of Italy.[83]

From 1968, then, but probably not earlier, there was a good case for selective revaluations of a few important currencies like the Deutschmark (DM), Swiss franc and Japanese Yen against the dollar. American pressure on the major surplus countries to revalue did increase around this time, though this was hampered by the American refusal to revalue gold.[84] It is difficult to see what contribution revaluations on the part of the other major countries could have made to the systemic disequilibrium between gold and the dollar, especially since it would have further eroded the real price of gold in the revaluing countries.

The US trade balance in 1971 was in deficit for the first time in the postwar period. With the Nixon administration increasingly concerned about the impact of a overvalued dollar on domestic employment, US policy became more aggressive in demanding revaluations against the dollar on the part of other industrial countries. Some have argued that US policy under Nixon was aimed from the beginning at forcing America's allies to revalue their currencies through a policy of 'benign neglect' of the US external position (that is, allowing the continued accumulation of inconvertible dollar balances by foreign countries). Charles Coombs of the New York Federal Reserve felt this view to be exaggerated, but argued that 'benign neglect ... provided an intellectual rationale for all the accumulated frustrations of the Nixon administration in the trade policy area.'[85]

Over 1970–1, the stance of monetary policy moved in the direction of expansion in the US, while in Europe (especially in Germany) it moved in the opposite direction as the Bundesbank sought to head off rising inflation. Interbank and other deposit rates in Germany hit their highest levels for years, prompting US banks to repay borrowings from the Euromarket made in the monetary squeeze of 1968–9. American official settlements deficits reached catastrophic proportions of $10.7 billion in 1970 and $30.5 billion in 1971. Foreign central banks bought $35 billion in 1970–1, with the Bundesbank alone buying over $11 billion in foreign exchange from January 1970 to May 1971, at which time it decided to float the DM. The Dutch Guilder was also floated at the same time and Austria and Switzerland revalued their currencies by 5 per cent and 7.1 per cent respectively.[86] If the US administration had indeed wished to force the surplus countries to choose between domestic monetary instability and revaluation it was not altogether unsuccessful. The increasing linkage of monetary conditions in the US and Europe due to the growing size of the Euromarkets was rendering a fixed exchange rate system unworkable.

Solomon relates that even in mid-1971, the US 'did not yet have a coherent plan for bringing about a broad and sufficiently large realignment of currencies.'[87] The reigning assumption in the US administration seemed to be that a negotiated realignment of currencies was impossible. Without trying to negotiate a settlement, the Nixon administration decided to apply shock tactics in the final run on the dollar by declaring on 15 August 1971 a suspension of gold convertibility and placing a 10 per cent surcharge on imports as a means of forcing Western Europe and Japan to revalue.

Connally, Nixon's Treasury Secretary, maintained the traditional line that as the US could not change the gold value of the dollar, other countries had to revalue against the dollar. The Americans also argued that they required an average current account surplus of about $9 billion per annum (calculated on a 'full employment basis') out of a total estimated OECD surplus of $11 billion, so as to finance America's international obligations. The adjustment, in other words, had to come from the surplus countries, and at the same time they were called upon to make greater contributions to Western defence and to liberalise their domestic markets.[88]

In denying any responsibility for adjustment, the US was effectively refusing to rehabilitate the gold exchange standard and demanding that other countries peg their currencies to an inconvertible dollar. Not surprisingly, the other countries were opposed to the idea that they ought to accept all the adjustment responsibility as well as a *de jure* dollar standard, with no assurance from the American side that it would accept any external constraints upon its policies. Nor could they agree that the US be granted a kind of natural right to over 80 per cent of the OECD current surplus.

In the end, the strength of the US bargaining position at Smithsonian led to an agreement on the part of the other countries to revalue their currencies in return for a minimal American concession to revalue gold to $38 per ounce.[89] In real terms, the gold price was hardly changed and the dollar remained inconvertible. As Solomon has written:

> In the end, it was the ability of France to hold out while other countries felt a more urgent need to end the crisis that led most of us, rightly or wrongly and with varying degrees of distaste, to capitulate on the gold price question. We comforted ourselves with the knowledge that the continued inconvertibility of the dollar would give the United States considerable leverage in future negotiations over reform of the system.[90]

For the other countries, above all the French, even the minimal US concession on the gold price was a basic precondition for the agreement reached at Smithsonian because it implied that the US accepted some responsibility for the international payments disequilibrium. Keohane seems to miss the point in arguing that the decline of American power was a necessary condition of the breakdown of the 'Bretton Woods system' in 1971: 'Had the US been so dominant in 1971 [as in the 1940s], it could have forced other countries to revalue their currencies . . . but by 1971 the US was no longer strong enough to do this, even after destroying the old Bretton Woods rules.'[91] There was simply no Golden Age in which the US could ever 'force' other countries to revalue; indeed, the reason why it *could* do so in 1971 without giving any real ground on the gold question was because of the weakness of the other countries' bargaining position. The international relations school has somehow overlooked the fact that in essence the rest of the world had tied itself to a dollar standard with no guarantees or constraints on US policy, and that the US refused to make the only concession that possibly could have restored the 'Bretton Woods system'.

If measurement of US balance of payments 'equilibrium' and hence 'discipline' was difficult before, it was to prove virtually impossible now. Without gold convertibility of the dollar, the US had few usable reserves and hence means of managing the exchange rate, and private currency markets lost an anchor for expectations. The breakdown of the fixed exchange rate system which occurred over 1972–3 in the face of continuing large official settlements deficits and a corresponding explosion in global liquidity was implicit in the Smithsonian agreement.

This shift to flexible exchange rates was welcomed by a number of economists, especially American ones, who believed that flexible exchange rates would remove the asymmetry favouring surplus states

American hegemony and the international monetary system   181

and that pegged exchange rates were inappropriate for a relatively closed economy like the US.[92] Smithsonian represented the Waterloo of the French policy to maintain a role for gold in a system with pegged exchange rates. West Germany, in contrast, by this stage longed to be free of the inflationary trap of a fixed exchange rate with the dollar.[93]

In George Shultz from May 1972 the US had a Treasury Secretary who was known to favour a system of floating exchange rates, and over 1975–6 the US would win a final battle against the French to legalise the floating which had continued since Spring 1973. The agreement reached at the November 1975 Rambouillet Summit was then enshrined at the January 1976 Jamaica Special Meeting of the IMF. The agreement sanctioned the adoption of exchange rates 'of a member's choice', gave the US a veto over any future proposal to return to a pegged rate system, and abolished the official price of gold.[94]

Though Treasury Secretary William Simon termed the Jamaica agreement 'the most significant development in the international monetary system since the Bretton Woods agreement',[95] it would soon become clear that the move to flexible exchange rates had in fact failed to remove the asymmetries which had always existed in the international monetary system. It will be argued in the next chapter that the extent to which the shift to flexible exchange rates in the early 1970s represented a fundamental caesura in international monetary organisation has been exaggerated.

The dollar standard: The US as world central bank?

In the absence of a desire to retain the gold exchange standard, of the political unlikelihood of an SDR standard and the inability of exchange rate flexibility to provide a full solution, was the only alternative the dollar standard? Proponents of the dollar standard had strongly criticised the series of attempts in the Kennedy and Johnson years to reduce the 'deficit' through restrictions on capital outflows: the 1963 interest equalisation tax, voluntary restrictions on bank lending to foreigners in 1965 and further mandatory restrictions on capital exports in 1968.[96] On the other hand, the encouragement of US multinationals to meet their financial requirements in the Eurodollar market, where US banks were permitted to operate without the regulations which applied to onshore banks, had in conjunction with US deficits further encouraged the growth of the offshore capital markets (see table 6.5). The Eurodollar market took over from US onshore markets as the major source of long term debt for governments and multinational

Table 6.5 Growth of Eurocurrency market, 1964–79.

Year	Size[a] ($US billion)	Annual growth (%)
1964	11.6	
1965	14.5	25.0
1966	17.4	20.0
1967	20.8	19.5
1968	29.7	42.8
1969	44.0	48.1
1970	57.0	29.5
1971	71.0	24.6
1972	92.0	29.6
1973	132.0	43.5
1974	177.0	34.1
1975	205.0	15.8
1976	247.0	20.5
1977	300.0	21.4
1978[b]	377.0	25.0
1979	475.0	26.0

Notes: [a] Eurocurrency assets or liabilities of banks in European centres at end of period, net of double counting. [b] First quarter.

Source: Meier, 1982, p. 176.

corporations. London regained its position as the centre for international financial business, but this business was centred on the dollar and the major players were American banks and their clients.

The logic behind the dollar standard idea consisted in the proposition that with the erosion of the gold exchange standard, little sense could be made of the concept of US balance of payments equilibrium. The payments 'deficit' was by definition an equilibrium position and benign neglect was the appropriate response. The fallacy upon which this idea rested was that the erosion of a criterion of US external discipline did not matter. Its proponents usually argued that the basic criterion for stability under such a system was 'stabilising' monetary policies on the part of the US, but this often begged more questions than it answered. McKinnon is more specific in arguing that 'America's principal international monetary obligation was not the *pro forma* link to gold but rather to maintain stable dollar prices of internationally tradable goods as well as an open capital market.'[97] Even this rule contained no criterion of US payments discipline or indeed of what constituted an equilibrium exchange rate for the dollar.

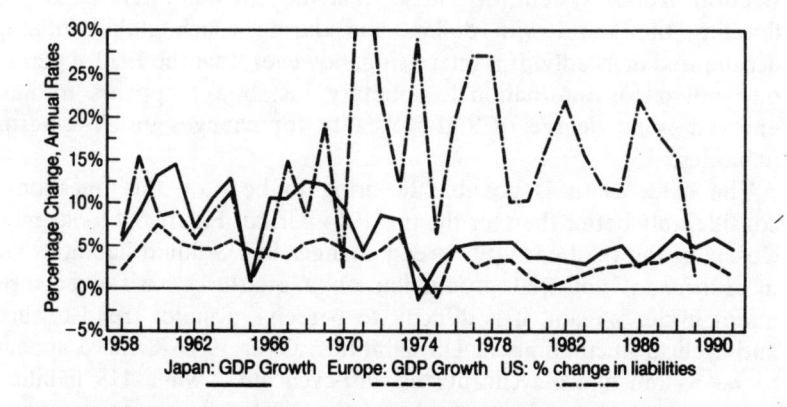

Note: Germany includes the former GDR from 1990.
Sources: IMF, *International Financial Statistics*; European Commission, *European Economy*.

Figure 6.3 Real GDP growth, Japan and Europe, vs. change in US external liabilities, 1958–91.

If the economists who supported the idea of a dollar standard had few answers to these questions, even less was it realistic to hope that private currency markets could provide their own anchor for the dollar exchange rate, or to expect that foreign central banks ought to remain willing to fix their currencies to the dollar in the event of a crisis of confidence in the private markets. Even less realistic was the expectation that the American authorities would adopt an attitude of benign neglect towards the balance of payments; the policy of the Nixon administration over 1971–3 was to restore the US external position and competitiveness by forcing appreciation on the part of the major surplus countries.

If it is accepted that the US provided the service of financial intermediation for the rest of the world (and especially Europe) that the dollar standard school claims, did it also act as a stabilising central bank? Figure 6.3 gives a rough indication of the fluctuation in US liquid liabilities to foreigners relative to growth in real output in Europe and Japan. It is difficult to find a clear trend towards an expansion (reduction) of US liquid liabilities to private and official foreigners during cyclical downturns (upturns) in the European and Japanese economies from 1958. In the 1958–64 period, US short-term liabilities grew at a fairly steady pace at a time when there was high growth in the other major industrial economies. From around 1968, it appears that there is a change in the situation, with much volatility and high growth in US liabilities. It was in these final years of the

Bretton Woods system, of course, that the US was often accused of flooding the world with dollars and during which global inflation accelerated markedly. It is interesting, however, that the 1970-4 period, one noted for international monetary instability, appears to have enjoyed some degree of anti-cyclicality for changes in US external liabilities.

The evidence it is possible to bring to bear on this question is considerably better than for the pre-1914 period. Figure 6.4 looks more closely at the relationship between changes in US liquid liabilities and in European industrial production on a quarterly basis over three major cycles. Again, it is difficult to perceive a major trend towards anti-cyclical fluctuations in US liabilities. Over 1965-8, there appears to be as much pro-cyclicality as anti-cyclicality, while US liabilities seem to have fallen in the midst of the 1974-5 downturn in Europe (and abroad). The 1980-3 experience is if anything worse, with fluctuations in US liabilities tending to be positively correlated with deviations in European industrial production from its trend rate of growth.

Some of the lender of last resort facilities established in the 1960s (most notably the Gold Pool and the sterling support facilities) were an attempt to live with disequilibria rather than adjust to them. In addition, though the US played an important role in organising the Basle swap network and increased IMF borrowing provisions over 1961-2, these were cooperative agreements based upon a mutual interest in preventing the growth of international capital mobility from undermining the pegged exchange rate system.[98] The $1 billion loan to Italy arranged by the US, Britain and Germany in March 1964 when there was much speculation on a lira devaluation was probably the most successful of these *ad hoc* measures. Although the US took the lead in arranging the credit, it is interesting that like other similar operations of the period, other important countries were involved, as before World War II.[99]

In terms of the relationship between US long-term capital outflows on the one hand and US domestic growth on the other, figure 6.5 shows that there is evidence of an inverse relationship in some years. As with Britain in the pre-1914 period, however, net US long-term capital outflows seem to be dominated by medium-term swings. In particular, net capital outflows grew considerably from 1962, at the same time that the domestic economy began to experience much higher growth than it had in the 1950s. Since the end of the 1970s, large net *inflows* of direct investment from abroad have made the US a major importer of long term capital. Kindleberger himself is therefore rather sceptical of the claim of counter-cyclicality for US lending abroad in the Bretton Woods

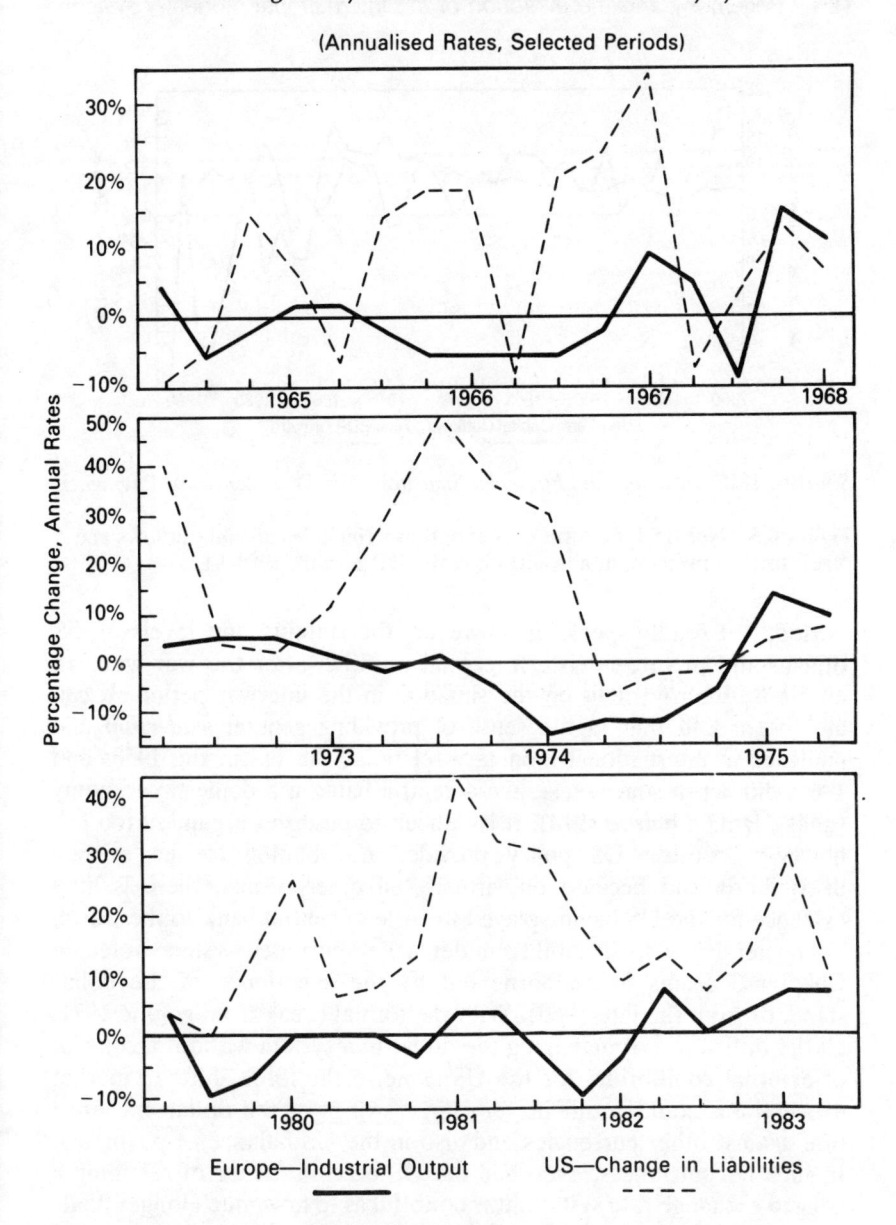

American hegemony and the international monetary system

(Annualised Rates, Selected Periods)

Figure 6.4 Change in US external liabilities vs. economic activity in Europe (industrial production, seasonally adjusted, deviation from trend), by quarter (selected periods).

Sources: IMF, *International Financial Statistics*; OECD, Main Economic Indicators.

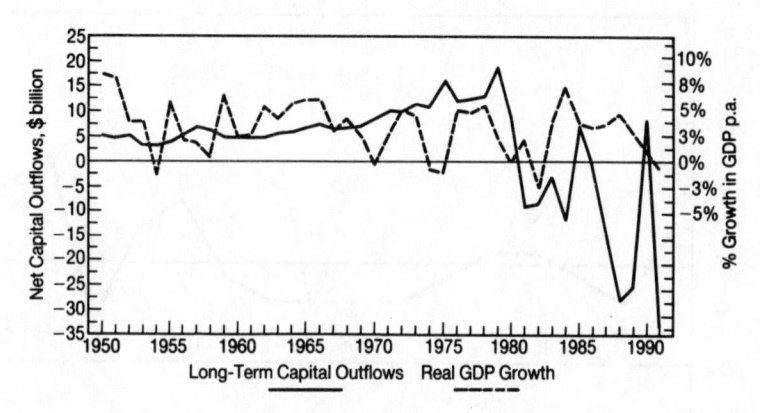

Sources: IMF, *International Financial Statistics*; OECD, *Balances of Payments*.

Figure 6.5 Net US long-term capital outflows (includes official outflows and direct foreign investment abroad) vs. real GDP growth, 1950–91.

period.[100] Broadly speaking, however, the stability and levels of US official and private long-term capital outflows after the war were an enormous improvement on the situation in the interwar period. It can also be argued that in the sense of providing general *leadership* and guidance in international monetary relations, the US in the 1950s and 1960s did act in some sense like a central bank in a domestic economy (unlike Britain before 1914). It is difficult to push this argument too far, however, because US policy provided no solution to the existing disequilibria and because on virtually all other counts, there is little evidence for the US having played the role of central bank to the world.

The tendency to instability under a key currency system noted in Chapter 3 seems to be borne out by the experience of the dollar standard from the late 1960s. With the formal break from gold in 1971, all the difficulties of managing the dollar in a system without a concept of external equilibrium for the US came to the fore. Shifts in market expectations could result in very large swings of the dollar exchange rate against other currencies and also in the US balance of payments. In such circumstances, even had the US been in favour of retaining a pegged exchange rate system, it is doubtful as to how much longer floating exchange rates could have been avoided. When they did come, this did not lead, at least immediately, to any diminution in the international reserve role of the dollar – on the contrary (see table 6.6).

Nixon had pledged in his 1968 campaign to remove all capital controls, and political pressure to do so built up after the abolition of the gold convertibility of the dollar.[101] That this was incompatible with

Table 6.6 Currency composition of foreign exchange reserves, percentages, all countries, 1964–82.

Year	US $	£ UK	FFR	SFR	DM	YEN	ECU
1964	67.6	21.5	1.5	0.2	0.1	–	–
1965	66.4	22.3	1.5	0.1	0.2	–	–
1966	67.8	21.8	1.7	0.2	0.2	–	–
1967	68.0	19.4	1.7	0.2	0.4	–	–
1968	60.9	21.3	1.3	0.3	0.5	–	–
1969	59.1	20.1	1.1	0.6	0.7	–	–
1970	77.2	10.4	1.1	0.7	1.9	–	–
1971	77.4	8.7	1.0	1.1	3.3	–	–
1972	78.6	7.1	0.9	1.0	4.6	0.1	–
1973	76.1	5.6	1.1	1.4	7.1	0.1	–
1974	77.8	6.5	0.7	1.5	6.1	0.1	–
1975	79.5	3.9	1.2	1.6	6.3	0.5	–
1976	79.7	2.0	0.9	1.4	7.0	0.8	–
1977	79.4	1.6	1.0	2.0	8.2	1.2	–
1978	76.9	1.5	0.9	1.4	9.9	2.5	–
1979	62.4	1.8	0.8	2.0	10.4	2.6	13.9
1980	56.2	2.5	1.0	2.6	11.9	3.0	17.0
1981	58.9	2.0	1.0	2.6	11.0	3.4	15.3
1982	59.9	2.0	1.0	2.4	10.4	3.5	14.4

Note: Changes in country coverage (especially in 1970) may affect the comparability of the data.

Source: IMF, 1983.

the apparent US commitment to maintain a fixed parity for the dollar was shown in the flight from the dollar that followed Secretary Shultz's February 1973 announcement of a further 10 per cent dollar devaluation and of the US intention to phase out all existing capital controls by the end of 1974.[102] Capital controls were in fact abolished at the beginning of 1974, linked with the official encouragement of American banks in the 'recycling' of OPEC oil surpluses and with the revival of New York as an international financial centre. This was entirely consistent with the American aim of fostering an international monetary system organised on the basis of market principles, as was the 1976 decision to eliminate from the presentation of US balance of payments statistics any measure of the overall 'deficit'.[103]

Even in the heyday of what has become known as the Bretton Woods system, there is little evidence to back up the often made claim that the US stabilised the system by playing the role of a discretionary monetary manager. The dominant financial position of the US gives some support to the notion of the key currency standard school that America provided a service of international financial intermediation, although most of this business was conducted in offshore markets by the end of the 1960s. As with Britain before the First World War, it is possible that acting as an international financial intermediary and acting as a discretionary manager were two tasks which were not necessarily compatible. The role of the dollar in the international financial system became so extensive that it undermined the monetary system based upon a fixed link with gold, but in so doing it removed a criterion for external balance for the US itself. Once this had happened, it was only a matter of time before the fixed exchange rate system fell apart.

6.6 Conclusion

If it is unlikely that the US played the role of discretionary monetary manager for the world after 1945, what was the cause of the stability in the international monetary system in the 1950s and 1960s? It would be wrong to argue that this had nothing to do with the leadership role that the US undoubtedly saw itself as playing in the West. The security structure and the (temporary) resolution of the German problem in Europe removed the fundamental problems that had undermined attempts to create a stable environment for economic growth and prosperity in the interwar period. American promotion of a much more open international trading system was of central importance in fostering a stable world economy, as was the size and stability of official and private long-term capital outflows.

There were many other important factors at work, however. The ability of the Europeans to find a much more satisfactory solution to problems posed by the interdependence of their economic and political security than after the First World War was of central importance, though again the American role was crucial in stimulating a European solution. The ability and willingness of governments to play a much greater role in domestic economic stabilisation in most of the major economies than in the 1920s helped promote an almost uninterrupted period of rapid growth. The compatibility of this with a fixed exchange rate system was assisted for a time by moves towards trade liberalisation and often quite wide-ranging controls on the movement of short-term capital in particular.

The period from late 1958 to the mid-1960s is often seen as the heyday of the Bretton Woods international monetary system. The principles laid down during the war are seen as finally having come into their own, with a period of monetary stability and growing economic interdependence being fostered by US hegemonic leadership.[104] The 'Bretton Woods system', in fact, is a very elusive entity. While the growth in prosperity and economic interdependence is indisputable, from the late 1950s, the international monetary system was evolving in a direction ultimately incompatible with the premises of pegged exchange rates, capital controls and collective management outlined at Bretton Woods. The shortage of gold was an immediate cause of disequilibrium in the system, and in the absence of a US willingness to increase the gold price, the gold exchange standard was bound to break down. That it limped along for another decade is not so much indicative of a decline of American power as of the ability of the US to implement a number of *ad hoc* policies to bolster the gold-dollar system. Other states, such as Germany, Japan and the UK, by and large supported the US in this (with the notable exception of France) because they too had an interest in the continuation of the system and in accepting the initiatives of their major ally.

Even a very dominant America could not, however, avoid the ultimate collapse of the gold exchange standard in the face of a gold shortage and an ever-expanding role of the dollar in international financial markets. From around the mid-1960s, US policies were aimed at removing the role of gold in the international monetary system. This, and the subsequent promotion of a system founded upon private capital markets and floating currencies was the most important policy factor in the so-called breakdown of the fixed exchange rate system over 1968–73. Of course, it would be wrong to argue that the growing role of private financial markets were entirely a product of American policies; in part it was also due to innovations in the private markets themselves as well as the adept manoeuvres on the part of other countries (above all the UK) to accept unregulated Eurodollar banking activities on their territory. It is still largely true, however, that by the mid-1970s, and contrary to the decline of hegemony thesis, the US had largely succeeded in reshaping the international monetary system in a way that was seen as advantageous for America, though not one which was necessarily stable.

As a result of much greater capital mobility than in the 1950s, strong currency countries like Germany found it virtually impossible to maintain a fixed exchange rate with the dollar and at the same time conduct an independent monetary policy oriented towards domestic price stability. These countries were able to find an alternative more attractive than the dollar standard through exchange rate appreciation, low inflation and high productivity growth. As always, it was the non-key currency, deficit countries with high inflation that had to bear the greatest costs under the new system. On another level, the breakdown of a system of fixed exchange rates reflected the tension between growing international financial integration and the continued primacy of the national interventionist state. The unwillingness of the major countries to give up national control over monetary policy meant that by the early 1970s, most welcomed the shift to a flexible exchange rate system. Ultimately, however, they would find that flexible exchange rates could provide no effective insulation from the ever-increasing levels of financial integration. The result has been growing calls for the coordination of national economic policies, yet even in the days of greatest American strength, such efforts have been conspicuously insufficient to prevent rising international monetary and financial instability.

For the US, not only was a return to any form of primary asset-based convertibility for the dollar impossible with central banks increasingly able to borrow dollars in the Euromarkets, but the attachment to the principle of pegged exchange rates rapidly faded in the early 1970s. This created an additional problem for private exchange markets, since without a strong commitment to an exchange rate target on the part of the US authorities, expectations and capital flows were increasingly subject to large swings.

Finally, the growing role of private financial markets did not remove a fundamental asymmetry in the structure of the system: the key role which the US financial system and its offshore adjuncts play in the system as a whole. In spite of the declining weight of the US in the world economy, in the early 1970s it still dwarfed other major industrial economies and it remained the most important trading country, though perhaps the least affected by rising economic interdependence. The role of the dollar reached a new height in the 1970s with the rapid growth of private and official international dollar balances (figure 6.3, table 6.6) and with the end of a formal role for gold. The following chapter will argue that financial integration has in many ways strengthened the transmission mechanisms from US policies to other states in the system, at a time when US authorities have had increasing difficulties in managing the domestic economy.

In conclusion, the image of the 'breakdown' of Bretton Woods due to the decline of American power is most misleading because it underestimates the *continuity* in the evolution of the international monetary system since the late 1950s. Since the early 1970s, private capital markets have grown rapidly, further displacing the elements of collective monetary management envisaged at Bretton Woods. The following chapter will argue that this, rather than hegemonic decline, provides the key to the growing instability of the global monetary system.

Notes

1. Keohane, 1984, p.37.
2. Gilpin, 1975, p.85.
3. For example, Kennedy, 1988, p.434.
4. Calleo, 1970, pp.86–7. See also Cohen, 1977, pp.96–7; Gilpin, 1987, pp.133–6; Silk, 1987.
5. Katzenstein, 1978, p.6. Although we will concentrate here upon international money rather than trade, the rise of protectionism and of the more aggressive US trade policy stance of 'reciprocity' since the 1970s is generally seen in similar terms.
6. Kennedy, 1988, p.357.
7. I have recalculated Maddison's US figures, using revised US GDP estimates. See Maddison, 1987, p.682.
8. For two complementary accounts of the negotiations, see Gardner, 1980, and Van Dormael, 1978.
9. Gardner, 1980, p.76.
10. Van Dormael, 1978, pp.97,129–49,247–9.
11. Gardner, 1980, p.112; Van Dormael, 1978, p.85.
12. Keynes' initial scepticism about the practical value of the scarce currency clause is clear from Harrod, 1951, p.550. This would turn out to be justified in the crisis of 1947, although by the 1960s the US would become a major deficit state and would find itself relatively powerless to require adjustment on the part of strong surplus states such as Germany.
13. Van Dormael, 1978, p.163.
14. *ibid.;* Gardner, 1980, p.115.
15. Van Dormael, 1978, pp.251–68.
16. Ruggie, 1982.
17. The administration sold the agreement to Congress by arguing that exchange rate changes would only be used as a 'last resort'. See Gardner, 1980, pp.135–6.
18. Gardner, 1985, p.16.
19. See Van Dormael, 1978, pp.165,200–49.
20. Article IV, section 7. For a discussion, see Gold, 1965, pp.30–43.
21. Bullock, 1983, pp.122–3. See also Gardner, 1980, pp.210–23.
22. Gardner, 1980, pp.236–54; Kindleberger, 1984, pp.429–32.
23. Gardner, 1980, ch.16.
24. Kindleberger, 1984, ch.23.
25. Milward, 1984, p.37.
26. *ibid.,* p.50; Bullock, 1983, ch.10.
27. For the most detailed account of the Marshall Plan and its origins, see Hogan, 1987. See also *Foreign Relations of the United States [FRUS],* 1947 (3), pp.230–2; Kennan, 1967, ch.13,15; Gaddis, 1982, ch.2,3.
28. Keohane, 1984, p.143; also Block, 1977, pp.89–102.
29. De Vries and Horsefield, 1969, ch.14.
30. Milward, 1984, p.197; Hogan, 1987, p.436. The 'counterpart funds', on which US Treasury hopes for leverage over European economic policies were pinned, were in practice used largely by the ECA to facilitate capital formation, to offset deflationary impacts in some economies and later to help underwrite the trade and payments agreements (Hogan, 1987, pp.152–6).

31. *FRUS*, 1948 (3), pp.597–613,1069–77.
32. *FRUS*, 1949 (4), pp.377–83,391–4,397–9,793–7. See also Cairncross, 1985, ch.7.
33. For example, Block, 1977, p.98.
34. See Cairncross, 1985, pp.165–85; Harris, 1982, pp.434–7. The sterling devaluation of 30.5 per cent, more than was generally expected, was followed by equivalent devaluations by the Scandinavian countries, and devaluations of 30.2 per cent, 21.8 per cent, 20.6 per cent, 12.3 per cent and 8 per cent by the Netherlands, France, West Germany, Belgium-Luxembourg and Italy respectively.
35. Bullock, 1983, pp.532–41,659–61,705–9,720–3.
36. *FRUS*, 1950 (1), pp.815–21.
37. Kindleberger, 1984, 437–42; Hogan, 1987, pp.321–3.
38. Hogan, 1987, pp.320–1; Milward, 1984, pp.326–32,472–4; Cairncross, 1985, pp.289–94.
39. See Milward, 1984, pp.501–2; Hogan, 1987, pp.438–45.
40. See Acheson's memorandum to Truman of February 16, 1950 (*FRUS*, 1950 (1), pp.834–41), expressing concern that ERP had achieved little in terms of dollar viability for Europe and that this would necessitate further measures to close the dollar gap after the end of Marshall aid in 1952. Acheson's main argument for this was the security angle, as it was for Kennan in a draft memorandum to Acheson only a day later (*ibid.*, pp.160–7).
41. Milward, 1984, p.488 (see also pp.349–59); United Nations, 1954, pp.353–60; Cairncross, 1985, pp.207–11.
42. As does Gilpin, 1987, p.133. For evidence, see United Nations, *Economic Survey of Europe*, 1954:I, pp.33–6 (especially chart 9), and 1959:I, pp.1–6; IMF, *Annual Report*, 1954, p.29; US Bureau of the Census, 1956, p.915.
43. Figures calculated from OECD, *Balances of Payments*, and IMF, *International Financial Statistics*, 1980 Yearbook.
44. Strange, 1976, p.36; Horsefield, 1969, pp.353–5,397–402.
45. See Deutsche Bundesbank, *Auszüge aus Presseartikeln*, January 3, 1959 [1].
46. Bank for International Settlements (BIS), *Annual Report*, 1971–2, p.14.
47. *ibid.*, pp.5–10.
48. Many have argued, including ex-officials of US monetary authorities, that from this time pressure was placed upon America's allies not to convert dollar reserves into gold (e.g. Coombs, 1976, p.8). From 1958 to 1964, the proportion of the official settlements deficit financed by gold sales did fall steadily from 99 per cent in 1958 to 8 per cent in 1964.
49. IMF, 1983, pp.10–22. For figures on the declining production and availability of new gold for monetary purposes, see BIS, *Annual Report*, 1971–2, p.8.
50. Strange, 1976, ch.3,4.
51. Solomon, 1982, p.54.
52. See Council of Economic Advisers, *Economic Report of the President* [hereafter *ERP*], 1959, pp.57–9, 1960, p.68, and 1961, pp.39–41.
53. See Gilbert, 1980, pp.84–8; Solomon, 1982, pp.58–60,86–113; Strange, 1976, pp.129–33,147.

54. In the crisis at the end of 1967, Johnson moved to impose mandatory controls on foreign direct investment by corporations and foreign lending by US banks. Yet the improvement in the balance of payments in 1968 was also due to tighter US monetary policy, leading banks to borrow from their Euromarket subsidiaries, which would sooner or later need to be repaid. Part of the difficulty, in other words, was due to the increasingly important relationship between the domestic and offshore banking systems. See Strange, 1976, ch.6; Solomon, 1982, ch.6.
55. Calleo, 1982, p.89.
56. Katzenstein, 1978, p.6.
57. See Gilbert, 1980, p.xiii.
58. For a detailed history of the US official attitude on this question, see Gilbert, 1980, especially pp.125–49, and Triffin, 1961, pp.79–82; Hinshaw, 1967. For a comprehensive statement from Johnson's Secretary of the Treasury, Henry Fowler, see his speech of September 24, 1968, in Bundesbank, *Auszüge*, October 9, 1968 [69].
59. Gilbert, 1980, p.xiv. Another less than compelling argument was that Congress might be unwilling to grant the authorisation required for an increase in the gold price, though in fact there were movements within Congress from a very early stage to double the gold price. The most adamant opposition always came from the US Treasury itself (see *The Times*, February 23, 1959).
60. There was also some suggestion that this would only lead to increased speculative demand for gold, though this would be unlikely if the rise in the official price were large enough to convince private and official agents that another increase would be long in the distant future (*ibid.*, pp.144–6).
61. Williamson, 1977, p.31. See also Triffin, 1961, pp.81ff; *Frankfurter Allgemeine Zeitung*, January 24, 1968; Hinshaw, 1967, ch.6.
62. Solomon, 1982, pp.76–7. See also Horsefield, 1969, pp.254–6,294–5.
63. See *Le Monde*, February 6, 1965.
64. See *New York Times*, March 29, 1968, and the earlier speech by the Chairman of the Federal Reserve Board, William McChesney Martin, in Bundesbank, *Auszüge*, February 23, 1968 [16].
65. See Triffin, 1961, part II, ch.2,4, and 1968, part II.
66. For an assessment, see Scammell, 1975, ch.5–7.
67. Solomon, 1982, pp.143–4.
68. For semi-official rationalisations of this strategy, see the US Council on International Policy, 1971, and the Commission on International Trade and Investment Policy, 1971. See also Gowa, 1983; Coombs, 1976, ch.12; Gilbert, 1980, pp.150–63.
69. See Williamson, 1977, pp.61–6.
70. The US negotiating document is reprinted in *ERP*, 1973, appendix A.5.
71. See Volcker, 1978–9, p.3.
72. See Emminger, 1979, p.4.
73. Williamson, 1977, p.73.
74. Alfred Hayes, then President of the New York Federal Reserve, remarked in 1974 that 'I was always of the view that, once the key element of the postwar system no longer existed, i.e., the link between the dollar and

gold, it would not prove possible to agree in advance to a complete new system.' (1974, p.290.)
75. Williamson, 1982, pp.304–5. See also Solomon, 1982, pp.244–65.
76. *ibid.*, p.33.
77. See US Treasury, 1985, and Group of Ten Deputies, 1985, especially ss.69–76.
78. Max Corden has been one of the most persistent proponents of the idea that the present international monetary system is one based upon market principles rather than a 'non-system' (see his 1985, ch.12). Where we part with Corden is on his assertion that the transition to this privatised system has removed the asymmetries associated with the gold exchange standard (e.g. pp.90–1).
79. Solomon, 1982, pp.166–75.
80. These and the following figures are taken from IMF, *International Financial Statistics*, various yearbooks.
81. Calleo, 1982, part I.
82. On this point, see Denison, 1985, ch.3; Maddison, 1987; OECD, 1987b.
83. For additional evidence, see BIS, *Annual Report*, 1971–2, p.8.
84. See Solomon, 1982, ch.10.
85. Coombs, 1976, pp.208–9.
86. Bundesbank, *Annual Report*, 1971, pp.21–3,30–3.
87. Solomon, 1982, p.179.
88. See Nixon's address in Bundesbank, *Auszüge*, August 17, 1971 [64], and Solomon, 1982, ch.12.
89. The Yen, DM, Swiss franc, Dutch Guilder (and Belgian franc) were revalued by 16.9 per cent, 13.6 per cent, 13.9 per cent and 11.6 per cent respectively against the dollar, and the other major currencies by lesser amounts.
90. Solomon, 1982, p.198.
91. Keohane, 1982, p.16. See also Gilpin, 1987, pp.135–40.
92. See Calleo, 1982, pp.70–3.
93. See Emminger, 1979.
94. Solomon, 1982, pp.271–80. Also agreed at Jamaica were the 'Guidelines for Floating' which were intended as a concession to French fears that legalisation of floating would reduce external discipline on countries. In practice, the role it gave to IMF 'surveillance' over member states' policies was minimal (see the retrospective judgements in Group of Ten Deputies, 1985, ch.3).
95. *US News and World Report*, January 26, 1976.
96. See Despres, Kindleberger and Salant, 1966.
97. McKinnon, 1979, p.261. See also his 1984, pp.8–9.
98. On these developments in the 1960s, see Strange, 1976, pp.84–9,136–50.
99. Solomon, 1982, pp.52–3.
100. Kindleberger, 1985a, p.10. Some degree of counter-cyclicality in long-term lending does seem to be in evidence in the 1968–76 period.
101. Solomon, 1982, p.197.
102. National Advisory Council on International Monetary and Financial Policies, *Annual Report*, 1972–3, pp.7–8.
103. For a discussion of this change, see Stern *et al.*, 1977, especially Triffin's contribution.
104. For example, Keohane, 1984, pp.149–50.

Chapter 7
The global financial revolution: Causes and consequences

7.1 Introduction

A common theme in much of the literature concerned with contemporary global economic problems is that their roots are held to lie in the erosion of US hegemonic power. As a more pluralistic international system emerges, continued deterioration in the 'liberal regimes' established after 1945 is seen as likely, if not inevitable. One of the aims of this chapter will be to consider the extent to which widely observed instability in the contemporary international monetary and financial system is the product of hegemonic decline.

As in earlier chapters, we can distinguish between different variants of this hypothesis. Some focus on the supposed erosion of the ground rules of the liberal world economy in recent years, in particular the rise of the 'new protectionism'. Robert Gilpin argues that '[p]rotectionism and economic nationalism are once again threatening the liberal international economic order with the relative decline of American power.'[1] Others focus more specifically upon the problem of achieving policy consistency or coordination in a pluralistic states-system. This perspective sees the emergence of an international monetary 'non-system' or 'free for all' in terms of the erosion of a regime formerly maintained by American hegemonic leadership. Many orthodox commentators would find themselves in agreement with Wallerstein, who holds that America 'is no longer so strong that it can be called hegemonic, and therefore it can no longer call the tune politically: it must now negotiate and/or compete with its erstwhile client "partners"'.[2] Another concern is that not only is the collective macroeconomic management of the world economy difficult in present circumstances, but that in the absence of a dominant state, there is no understanding as to who will provide international public goods such as open markets, countercyclical capital flows and emergency liquidity.[3]

The previous chapter argued that the international monetary system since the late 1950s has been marked by considerable continuity, both in the evolution of the system away from a link with gold towards one based upon key currencies and in the rapid growth in importance of private capital markets. While this has indisputably coincided with some decline in the weight of the US in the world economy, the theory of hegemonic stability encounters an immediate difficulty. Although it suggests that American decline has resulted in increasing mercantilism and the erosion of the postwar 'liberal regimes', in fact the recent evolution of international money and finance has been decidedly in the direction of *liberalisation*: increasing freedom of capital flows, financial deregulation in the major countries and an unprecedented degree of financial market integration between them. The international trading system, though under some degree of stress, has not collapsed into the widespread protectionism that such theories would predict. It would therefore seem difficult to argue that greater instability in the international monetary system is due to an erosion of the ground rules of a liberal world economy. Indeed, new rules, particularly related to the regulation and prudential supervision of financial institutions, have had to be created.

More attention has been focused upon the failure of the major countries to achieve policy consistency or to undertake the joint management of the world economy. This chapter will consider the extent to which this as well as efforts to regulate international financial markets can be seen as the result of increasing plurality in the international balance of power. As a first step, we need to understand the nature of the dynamic changes occurring in the structure of the world financial system, and how these relate to the relationship between the US and its major allies, Japan and Europe.

7.2 The nature of the international financial revolution

The growth of international capital markets in recent years has greatly increased their impact upon the stability of the world economy. The value of world trade in 1990 amounted to more than $5.2 trillion, compared with US GDP in that year of $5.5 trillion. Though accurate figures are difficult to obtain, in 1986 the London Eurodollar market, virtually unregulated by public authorities, was reckoned to turn over the equivalent of $300 billion *per day*, or about $75 trillion per year. Yearly transactions in this market represented six times the value of world trade in 1979, but by 1986 were about 25 times the value of world trade and about 18 times the value of the annual output of the world's largest economy.[4] Throughout the 1980s, global financial transactions continued to grow very rapidly, as did cross-border direct investment, and both considerably outpaced the growth of international trade and output during the decade.[5]

Another indication of the extent to which capital flows have come to dominate and become increasingly separated from trade-related payments is the size of foreign exchange market transactions. An April 1989 study estimated that *daily* turnover in London, New York and Tokyo was $187 billion, $129 billion and $115 billion respectively. By April 1992, the equivalent figures had grown to $300 billion, $192 billion and $128 billion, while daily world foreign exchange turnover averaged about $1 trillion.[6] The great majority of these transactions, perhaps 90 per cent or more, are unrelated to current account flows. This is also indicative of the extent to which both the state of the balance of payments and the exchange rates of key currency countries have become detached from the state of the country's current account. Above all, this is the case for the US, which helps explain how in the first half of the 1980s a very strong dollar could coincide with an unprecedented deterioration in the US current and trade balances.

The extent to which the world's financial system has developed outside of a publicly regulated framework is indicated by the growth of the private 'offshore' capital markets. The Euromarkets (and International Banking Facilities (IBFs) in the US since 1981) provide an enormous pool of capital for corporate, sovereign and 'supranational' borrowers, yet are not subject to the regulations which apply to transactions in domestic markets. An indication of the phenomenal growth of the international loan and bond markets in recent years is given in table 7.1.

Access to this global capital market is determined simply by the creditworthiness of the borrower. Blue-chip borrowers such as GE, France, or the World Bank obtain the most favourable terms by issuing bonds in any major currency and swapping the proceeds (and probably the interest payments) into whichever form most suits their needs. Large institutional investors from the major countries (pension and life insurance funds and central banks) are the largest buyers of such bond issues. Globalisation has also occurred in equity markets, as the same investors and large corporations are able to switch rapidly between shares in different markets and as a growing number of firms list their

Table 7.1 Estimated net international lending, 1975–91 ($ billion).

Year	Net bank lending	Net bond financing	Double-counting	Net new bond & bank lending
1975	40	19	2	57
1976	70	30	4	96
1977	75	31	4	102
1978	90	29	6	113
1979	125	28	8	145
1980	160	28	8	180
1981	165	32	7	190
1982	95	58	8	145
1983	85	58	13	130
1984	90	83	28	145
1985	105	123	58	180
1986	205	158	81	295
1987	320	108	51	400
1988	260	139	68	350
1989	410	175	77	515
1990	465	132	79	550
1991	85	171	35	255
Outstanding end 1991	3,610	1,651	606	4,800

Source: BIS, *Annual Reports*.

stock on several different national exchanges. Cross-border equity trading grew on average by 35 per cent over 1979–89, with London the major centre for activity in foreign stocks. International portfolio capital flows have grown faster than direct capital flows, at 25 per cent per annum since the late 1970s; of total capital outflows of $443 from OECD countries in 1991, 63 per cent was portfolio investment related.[7]

Commercial banks, disintermediated by the 'securitisation' of capital markets, have increasingly turned towards off-balance-sheet business such as management of and participation in bond issues, the various forms of 'swaps' which accompany them and a wide range of equity-related activities. Recent years have witnessed an unprecedented spate of financial innovations, both in national markets and in the international markets. The 'unbundling' of financial products has (most notably in the US) reduced the value of the banking franchise, leading commercial banks to move into businesses that were traditionally the preserve of merchant/investment banks.[8] Partly as a result of this, the lines between international banking and bond markets have become increasingly blurred (as the growth of 'double-counting' in table 7.1

Table 7.2 Currency distributions: New international bank loans and bond issues.

Currency	International bank loans (%)					International bond issues (%)				
	1985	1988	1989	1990	1991	1985	1988	1989	1990	1991
$US	62.5	64.2	70.0	58.9	84.5	70.9	35.4	45.9	33.3	28.5
Pound	3.4	17.4	11.3	17.5	4.2	4.5	10.8	8.4	9.5	9.1
Yen	18.5	6.1	5.3	1.7	1.1	4.8	8.7	8.7	13.5	12.1
ECU	7.1	3.3	4.9	8.7	3.9	5.1	5.4	5.6	8.1	11.1
DM	2.1	2.8	3.5	6.7	2.1	7.0	11.6	7.5	8.3	7.1
Other	0.2	6.2	5.0	6.5	4.2	7.7	28.1	23.9	27.3	32.1

Note: Currencies are converted at end-1990 exchange rates for years 1988–91 and end-1986 exchange rates for 1985.
Source: OECD, *Financial Market Trends*.

indicates). At the end of 1989, stocks of international bonds outstanding were $1.25 trillion, while international interbank deposits (net of redepositing) were $3.5 trillion.[9]

Since the total foreign exchange reserves of central banks were almost $800 billion by mid-1990, it was clear by then that the international interbank market easily dominated the official sector. Central bank reserves are less than the equivalent of *two days*' turnover in the world's foreign exchange markets, which indicates that one central bank or even a number of central banks intervening together in exchange markets cannot hope to oppose a concerted onslaught on a particular currency or currencies by the exchange markets. The lack of quantitative power on the part of central banks means that timing in central bank intervention is of the essence, since to be effective it must act upon the exchange rate expectations which are held in the markets.

If the global financial revolution has been characterised by a dramatic shift in the balance of power away from national and international public authorities towards the private markets, how has it affected the roles of particular national currencies? As table 7.2 indicates, the dollar was still by far the most important vehicle currency in the international financial markets in the 1980s. The majority of international bank credits are still made in dollars, and although the proportion of international bonds issued in dollars has fallen significantly in recent years, this reflects in part the growth of currency swaps, with bonds issued in a variety of currencies often being swapped into dollars. In April 1992, half of total foreign exchange turnover was in *forward* (as opposed to spot) business, which is predominantly swaps-related.

Table 7.3 Shares of national currencies in foreign exchange reserves, 1978–90 (%).

Currency	1978	1979	1980	1981	1982	1983	1984	1985	1986	1987	1988	1989	1990
$US	76.0	73.2	68.6	71.4	70.5	71.4	70.1	65.0	67.1	67.9	64.7	60.3	56.4
Sterling	1.7	2.0	2.9	2.1	2.3	2.5	2.9	3.0	2.6	2.4	2.8	2.7	3.2
Yen	3.3	3.6	4.3	4.2	4.7	5.0	5.8	8.0	7.9	7.5	7.7	7.8	9.1
DM	10.9	12.5	14.9	12.7	12.3	11.8	12.6	15.2	14.6	14.5	15.7	19.1	19.7
SFR	2.1	2.5	3.2	2.7	2.7	2.4	2.0	2.3	2.0	2.0	1.9	1.5	1.5
FFR	1.2	1.3	1.7	1.3	1.0	0.8	0.8	0.9	0.8	0.8	1.0	1.4	2.1
Other	4.8	4.8	4.4	5.6	6.5	6.1	5.8	5.6	5.0	4.9	6.2	7.2	8.0

Note: ECUs have not been treated separately.
Source: IMF, *Annual Reports*.

Furthermore, 78 per cent of foreign exchange turnover was dollar-related, and the proportions are higher in New York and Tokyo.[10] Though volatility has increased the exchange risk of holding dollar assets as a store of value, the high liquidity of dollar markets, the broad range of dollar instruments and the low transactions costs in dollar markets ensure that it remains the main transactions and denominations currency in international financial markets.[11]

The great bulk of deposits in the international banking market are in dollars, though this has undergone some decline from 77 per cent in 1982, to 72 per cent in 1985 and 53 per cent at the end of 1989.[12] As table 7.3 shows, central banks have largely fallen in line with the private markets in maintaining the bulk of their foreign exchange reserves in dollars, though undertaking some diversification in recent years.[13] This is in part because central banks are an important source of international bank deposits, as well as the fact that considerations of liquidity, instruments and transactions costs operate for central banks as for private agents. The dollar remains the main denomination and invoicing currency in international trade (especially in commodities). For Japan, one of the world's major trading nations, only 10 per cent of imports and 33 per cent of exports were invoiced in Yen in 1987, the rest being largely invoiced in dollars (though this compares with 80 per cent DM-invoicing for German exports).[14] All in all, over the last decade the role of other currencies in the international financial and monetary systems has increased considerably, in particular that of the DM and Yen. But the dollar remains indisputably the principal reserve, transactions, denomination, and intervention currency for private and official actors. This has remained true despite a dramatic shift in the net asset positions of the three major countries over the past decade.

In summary, what is most striking about the last few decades is the liberalisation of capital flows between the major countries and the incredible growth of the Euromarkets, which has averaged about 30 per cent per year since the 1960s. This has so far outstripped the growth of global trade and output that financial flows now utterly dominate real flows between countries in quantitative terms. Before turning to examine the consequences of these changes, however, we must initially give a broad overview of their causes.

7.3 The causes of the international financial revolution

As with all revolutions, while there is a possibility that the present one in the international financial system could suffer some unexpected reversal, some permanent changes have undoubtedly been wrought. This issue is best approached by focusing on which of the causes themselves are more or less irreversible, and which constitute relatively reversible sources of change. It will become apparent that it is difficult directly to relate the changes in question to the declining weight of the US in the world economy.

One of the basic forces behind recent global financial evolution is technological change. Underlying the revolution in global finance is a revolution in communications and information processing which if anything may accelerate over time. Easy and virtually instantaneous access to knowledge characterises all business related to contemporary finance, which itself feeds through into an unprecedented degree of spontaneity and potential volatility in exchange and capital markets. In conjunction with increasing competition in global financial markets, this has served to heighten the sensitivity of actors to differentials in yields on similar assets in different markets. Reactions to news about policy shifts, interpreted policy shifts, weekly arrays of economic and financial data on all major economies, and even news of apparently unrelated events ('sunspots') can cause massive movements of funds between instruments and/or currencies. These developments mean that whatever the efforts of governments to cooperate, the political process will always be painfully slow in comparison to the reactions of financial markets, which implies limits to the stabilising impact of even fully coordinated economic policies.

Connected with the greater competitiveness and volatility of exchange and financial markets, the operating techniques of both banks and non-banks have become considerably more sophisticated. The rise of asset and liability management, as with financial innovation, has in part been a defensive response to a more volatile environment and partly the result of a recognition of opportunities which this presents. Exchange rate volatility creates both a need to hedge securities portfolios across markets and an incentive to speculate on exchange movements. The historically high levels of real interest rates which accompanied the process of disinflation in the early 1980s encouraged non-financial corporations to place increased importance upon financial profits in their operations. This has received considerable prominence in the case of the 'Zaitech' activities of Japanese companies, which have found themselves particularly flush with liquidity.[15] The long bull market in Japanese and other equity markets in the 1980s, probably not unrelated to increasing liquidity, gave further impetus to the diversification of asset portfolios, though this suggests that such diversification may have been in part a fair-weather phenomenon. What does appear to be a permanent change is the blurring of the distinction between banks and non-banks, as the latter have adopted more sophisticated financial management techniques and as some among them have established financial subsidiaries which compete with many banks (such as Ford, GM, Toyota, General Electric, Westinghouse, Sears, etc.).

High real interest rates have also been a major factor behind the process of securitisation of financial markets: they were an important cause (with the collapse of commodity prices) of the precipitation of the debt crisis in 1982 and the weakening of commercial banks' balance sheets, and they have increased the demand for high-yielding securities or 'junk bonds' and equities. While lower levels of real interest rates might favour real rather than financial investments on the part of firms, it is unlikely that either they or banks will return to the more staid practices and low levels of innovation of the 1950s and 1960s.

A third factor which has played an important role in the global financial revolution has been the generalised slowdown in productivity growth for the industrial economies from the 1970s. As noted in the previous chapter, this marked lowering of the potential rate of growth as compared with the previous two decades meant that in all major countries, the wealth that had been accumulated in the postwar boom was no longer reinvested at the same rate. Firms often found themselves with considerable liquidity and declining investment opportunities that could provide returns to match yields on securities. Pension funds and other institutions found themselves in possession of the vast assets of the increasingly wealthy postwar generation, itself more aware of differential returns. The long-term trend towards the institutionalisation of savings has concentrated decisions in fewer and more sophisticated hands, and the gradual move of the institutions towards more active portfolio management has placed further pressure upon existing market practices and arrangements within and across a range of countries.[16]

High private sector liquidity was paralleled on the international level by the emergence of major imbalances in the pattern of international trade and payments from the 1970s. The OPEC oil price increases and the initial 'low absorption' of foreign imports by OPEC countries led to very large current account surpluses with the rest of the world. The aggregate OPEC current account surplus over the period 1973–82 was in the region of $465 billion, much of which was redeposited in wholesale international deposit markets. As slow growth in the industrial countries led to a diminution of their collective current account deficit, the deficits run by the non-oil developing countries were increasingly financed by the 'recycling' of OPEC deposits in the form of syndicated bank lending.[17]

With the collapse of the oil price in the recession of the early 1980s, the shrinking OPEC surplus was replaced by one closer to the core of

Table 7.4 Financing the US current account deficit, 1980–91 ($ billion).

Year	Current account deficit	Net portfolio investment	Net official finance	Net direct investment
1980	−1.8	−8.6	9.1	−2.3
1981	−6.2	−23.0	1.2	15.6
1982	7.0	−7.2	−2.0	16.2
1983	44.3	28.7	4.0	11.6
1984	104.2	82.3	−0.7	22.6
1985	122.2	122.1	−5.8	5.9
1986	145.4	96.2	33.8	15.4
1987	160.2	76.2	56.9	27.1
1988	126.4	48.6	36.3	41.5
1989	101.2	79.2	−16.9	38.9
1990	90.5	48.3	29.8	12.4
1991	3.7	−3.3	22.6	−15.6

Note: Net errors and omissions and other short- and long-term capital are included in portfolio investment.
Source: IMF, *International Financial Statistics*.

the international economy: the large current surpluses accumulated above all by Japan and West Germany. These averaged $52 billion and $27 billion per annum over 1982–9 for Japan and West Germany respectively, together representing a cumulative total of about $630 billion over these eight years. The gradual removal of most restrictions on capital exports in these countries in the 1980s facilitated the recycling of these surpluses in the form of purchases of credit instruments (such as US Treasury bonds and Euro-bonds), equities and foreign direct investment. In contrast to the 1970s, the major recipient of capital flows from the major creditor nations during recent years has been the US, which has experienced extraordinarily large internal and external deficits in combination with low rates of domestic consumer saving.

The net inflow of private and official capital into the US over 1982–91 has been in the region of $900 billion, the counterpart of the cumulative current account deficit (table 7.4). The relationship between the current deficit and the federal budget deficit, which itself has amounted to about $1.9 trillion over the same period, might be expressed in the following terms. Since by definition, gross private investment equals the sum of government savings, gross private savings and the net capital inflow, it is clear that US domestic private savings have been insufficient to finance both the post-1982 recovery in growth and investment as well as a large government deficit. This has necessitated the considerable inflow of capital from abroad (or the current account deficit) noted above. High real interest rates helped to attract capital to the US, as well as helping to contain the inflationary potential of the large budget deficit.

Until 1986, private portfolio and direct capital inflows more than accounted for the total external financing of this deficit. The reasons are numerous: the disengagement of US banks from international lending, capital flight from Latin America, the removal of capital controls in other countries, an absence of attractive investment opportunities elsewhere, high US real interest rates and perhaps a speculative bubble in favour of the dollar from 1984, which saw the dollar rise to a peak of DM 3.31 and Yen 260 in early 1985. Over 1986–7, official inflows of capital, representing in part official intervention to brake the rapidly declining dollar, financed at least 30 per cent of the total US current deficit. Again, Japan, West Germany and other large surplus states (including those in East Asia) were the major participants in such intervention.[18] As yet, however, there has been no recurrence of the 1977–8 flight from the dollar, with portfolio and more recently direct private capital inflows remaining strong. This is testimony to the attractiveness of dollar assets in a period in which confidence in Federal Reserve policy has been high.

As the US moved into recession in 1990, the current account deficit began to decline, though the substantial improvement in 1991 was largely related to contributions from allies in the wake of the Gulf War. The persistence of the US budget deficit (and indeed its ballooning due to recession), not least because of increasingly large interest payments on outstanding debt, and the continuing low levels of private sector saving, do not signal an imminent return to current surpluses for the US. As a result, the main issue is likely to remain for a considerable time one of whether private financial markets can be induced to finance continuing deficits over the medium term without excessive cost to the US and world economies. As long as large fiscal deficits remain a fact in the US and other important countries (including, for example, Germany) at the same time as the demand for capital in other parts of the world has increased, high real interest rates and the impetus they have given to financial activity and innovation are likely to remain.

The generalised trend towards deregulation of domestic financial sectors and the liberalisation of capital flows has also played a major role in the financial boom, Connected to a neo-liberal revival led by the Anglo-Saxon countries, the political momentum in favour of deregulation has steadily spread to countries which have traditionally been more strongly committed to state interventionism. Countries formerly noted for their dirigiste attitudes, from Britain to France and even in Latin

America, have already privatised or intend to privatise large chunks of state assets nationalised after World War II. As the BIS noted recently:

> By the early 1990s none of the larger industrialised countries retained ceilings or other major constraints on lending. Compulsory portfolio investment requirements for banks were rare and, where they existed, of little significance; portfolio restrictions on institutional investors such as pension funds and insurance companies had been relaxed in several countries. Compulsory reserve requirements had been generally reduced. Controls on foreign exchange transactions and international capital flows had largely been lifted. Restrictions on lending rates were a thing of the past and only a few countries, notably Japan, retained significant controls on retail deposit rates or fixed brokerage commissions.[19]

As noted in Chapter 2, it has been increasingly difficult to maintain old regulations in the context of structural change and financial innovation. The pressure of growing international competition for financial business has added to this. This is not simply a phenomenon of a 'post-hegemonic era'; a competitive element has long been present, as when London sought from the late 1950s to re-establish its position as an international financial centre by offering offshore banking facilities in dollars. As we saw, by the early 1970s, the US itself was adopting a more aggressive stance aimed at recapturing much of the business which had long since moved offshore, ending the gold convertibility of the dollar and (in 1974) removing all existing controls on capital exports. From December 1981, US banks were permitted to offer International Banking Facilities (IBFs) from the US itself, on the same unregulated basis as their foreign subsidiaries operating in offshore markets.[20]

In the other major financial centre, London, capital controls imposed during the 1970s were fully removed by the Thatcher government in 1979. Germany, though ideologically committed to freedom of capital movement, had periodically imposed capital controls in periods when heavy inflows threatened to undermine domestic monetary stability, but otherwise maintained a fairly liberal policy.[21] The German banking system, like that of Japan, remained fairly heavily regulated until the 1980s, but both have fallen in line with the recent trend in an effort to achieve the perceived benefits of liberalisation and to prevent an erosion of the competitiveness of their domestic financial sectors. Both Japan and Germany were also until recently reluctant to allow their currencies to play an international role because of the loss of monetary control it was feared that this would entail. In spite of this reluctance, the DM had by the late 1970s come to play a significant reserve role, largely related to the workings of the 'Snake' and then the EMS, and the role of the Yen has also been steadily increasing (table 7.3).

The global financial revolution: Causes and consequences 207

Table 7.5 Net capital outflows, 1980–91, Japan and Germany ($ billion).

	Japan			Germany		
	Net portfolio investment	Net direct investment	Net official flows	Net portfolio investment	Net direct investment	Net official flows
1980	17.9	−2.1	−5.0	1.9	−3.6	15.6
1981	3.5	−4.7	−3.6	8.5	−3.6	−1.6
1982	−7.4	−4.1	4.7	−0.4	−1.7	−2.9
1983	−16.0	−3.2	−1.6	−5.0	−1.6	1.2
1984	−26.9	−6.0	−2.1	−7.1	−3.8	1.1
1985	−44.0	−5.8	0.6	−12.9	−3.2	−0.9
1986	−56.8	−14.2	−14.8	−28.8	−9.8	−1.5
1987	−30.7	−18.4	−37.9	−18.2	−7.7	−20.4
1988	−28.4	−34.7	−16.5	−57.2	−11.8	18.4
1989	−24.6	−45.2	12.8	−60.5	−7.7	10.6
1990	3.8	−46.3	6.6	−20.8	−20.0	−5.5
1991	−50.1	−29.4	6.6	36.5	−14.9	−2.1

Note: Net errors and omissions and other short- and long-term capital are included in portfolio investment.
Source: IMF, *International Financial Statistics*.

In the case of Japan, another factor working for liberalisation has been American pressure. The first Reagan administration believed that restrictions on the international use of the Yen were contributing to that currency's undervaluation, and hoped that liberalisation of Japanese capital exports would facilitate the recycling of its current surpluses. While such pressure, culminating in the Yen–Dollar Agreement of May 1984, made a significant contribution to Japanese moves in this direction, it is also apparent that the Japanese have become less reluctant to contemplate such liberalisation in recent years.[22] The very high level of Japanese savings, encouraged until 1988 by tax exemptions on interest on deposits and the complicated Post Office savings system, was greatly in excess of domestic requirements as investment rates and the budget deficit fell and then moved into substantial surplus (figure 7.5). The 1980 Revised Foreign Exchange and Foreign Trade Law suspended most foreign exchange controls and Japanese Life Insurance companies and Pension Funds can now invest up to 30 per cent of their assets overseas. The relaxation of capital controls, given the surplus savings available, promoted the development of a Euro-Yen market in commercial paper, CDs and Eurobonds, as well as assisting in the financing of the US deficit.

For Germany, allowing the accumulation of DM liabilities by foreigners eased the financing of its current account deficits over 1980–1. Since that time, there has been an understandable concern in both Germany and Japan that in the absence of capital exports, especially to the US, their large current account surpluses would become economically and politically intolerable for other countries. From the early 1980s, both countries have relied upon large net portfolio and direct investment outflows to finance their surpluses, with substantial official intervention occurring only rarely (see table 7.5).

Finally, as the success of Japanese banks and securities firms in the 1980s showed, financial liberalisation had its benefits. The foreign assets of Japan's banks grew faster than those of any other major country in the 1980s, even excluding the impact of the appreciation of the Yen. This raised the hopes of some Japanese that Japan might eventually come to play a role of a traditional financial centre.[23] Japan would lend abroad in Yen, rather than largely in dollars as has been the case. To some extent this is happening already: Malaysia, the Philippines, Indonesia and Thailand all have one third or more of their foreign debt denominated in Yen and hold significant Yen foreign exchange reserves, a trend which is likely to continue as intra-regional trade and investment grows more rapidly than trade with other countries.[24]

While there is no necessary reason to suppose that the trend towards deregulation might not suffer a reversal (especially in the event of a major financial crisis), the increasingly competitive nature of financial deregulation constitutes a powerful factor encouraging its continuation. Since the only way that national monetary authorities can regulate financial activity is by placing controls on the activities of financial actors operating in their 'national' jurisdictions (including foreign branches of domestic banks), the effect of one country adopting onerous regulations has usually been to push financial business to other centres. Even if one actor, say the US, were to regulate all dollar transactions (which need to be cleared in New York) irrespective of the nationality of banks, the effect could be to raise the transactions costs of conducting business in dollars, which in the longer term might encourage the evolution towards a more symmetrical multi-currency system. Strange has argued that this problem would not exist if the US were to invite foreign banks dealing in dollars into the Federal Reserve system on a *voluntary* basis, offering lender of last resort facilities in return for their agreement to observe system-wide rules.[25] This suggestion encounters the difficulty arising from the highly political nature of the lender of last resort role: would Congress allow the extension of the Federal Reserve system on a global scale when it has always been strongly opposed to the 'bailing out' of the big American banks, let alone (for example) large Japanese banks which for one reason or another found themselves short of dollars?

The suggestion that central banks in principle ought to supervise transactions in their *currencies* rather than banks of their own nationality (as under the 1975 Basle Concordat) implies that as the embryonic multi-currency system develops more fully all the major countries would need to cooperate to this end. The first steps towards such a cooperative approach to regulation were taken in the agreement between the UK and US on banks' minimum capital adequacy ratios in early 1987, followed by the Basle agreement on capital adequacy, which established a goal of capital requirements for all banks of 8 per cent of 'risk adjusted assets'. More difficult will be obtaining agreement on issues of taxation, prudential supervision and lender of last resort responsibility in a crisis.[26] The impetus towards deregulatory competition is likely to remain strong. It is a major issue, for example, in the ongoing American debate over the proposed repeal of the Glass-Steagall Act, and a key element of the 'competition between rules' which underlies the EC's Single Market Programme.

Finally, the shift to a system of floating exchange rates between the world's major currencies has also provided impetus to global financial change, though as noted above, this shift was itself in part the consequence of the rising importance of private capital and exchange markets. The volatility of exchange rates has fostered innovations such as forward and futures markets, currency options and swaps.[27] Again, though the shortcomings of floating exchange rates have become increasingly apparent in recent years, the size of short-term capital movements suggests that there is little likelihood of a return in the near future to a system of pegged exchange rates between the major currencies.

In summary, there are a number of processes underlying the international financial revolution of recent years which are unlikely to disappear rapidly. Even those factors which are apparently more related to cyclical factors, such as the conjunction of high real interest rates, large budget deficits and international payments imbalances, have structural aspects and are likely to persist for the time being. The diversity of these causes also implies that it is implausible to attribute it in any direct sense to the decline in the weight of the US in the world economy. The US twin deficits might be seen as symptomatic of American global over-commitment and declining national competitiveness, but the US itself has been a driving force behind the process of domestic and international financial deregulation. As we shall see, however, the consequences of these changes for the balance of power between states may be of considerable importance.

7.4 The economic consequences of financial integration

Most economists tend to focus upon the 'efficiency' gains of international financial liberalisation, arguing in particular that it improves the global efficiency of the allocation of capital.[28] This derives from the neoclassical ideal of a world free of mercantilist restrictions on the flow of capital, enabling greater competition and the matching of global savings and investment irrespective of national boundaries. In addition, it is commonly argued that new instruments such as financial futures and options unbundle and redistribute risk to those more willing to bear it, thereby lending greater stability to the system.[29]

In practice, however, the allocation of global capital is highly sensitive to shifts in expectations, which may result in considerable volatility in capital flows. Perceptions of risk can undergo rapid change, as with commercial bank lending to Latin America in 1982. With respect to securities markets, expectations regarding exchange rates and interest rates can play a vital role in determining capital flows, the most obvious case being that of the shifting attractiveness of dollar securities for foreigners over the last few years. Furthermore, it is not yet clear that the various innovations which have allowed the redistribution of market risks solve the problem of *systemic* interest and exchange risk – indeed, to the extent that they modify collective behaviour, they may worsen it.

It is also possible that the size and volatility of capital flows and asset prices (including exchange rates) in recent years has hampered adjustment to domestic and international imbalances. It is plausible, for example, to view the coincidence of a strong dollar and a massive deterioration in the US current account in the early 1980s as an efficient outcome, other than in a purely technical sense? Financial deregulation has led to a growing dissociation between current accounts and real exchange rates, especially for the US (see figure 7.1). Although there are many factors that may plausibly result in changes in the 'equilibrium' current account balance for a country, all other things being equal, one might expect that stability would be enhanced if a higher (lower) current surplus resulted in a higher (lower) real exchange rate for a particular country. From the mid-1970s to the mid-1980s, when the DM came to play a much greater international role, such a relationship was not in evidence for West Germany. For both the US and West Germany, there was a particularly severe dissociation in the first half of the 1980s, a period during which the dollar became highly overvalued relative to the DM and Yen.

The overvaluation of the dollar, the related shift in the global division of labour and the rise in US protectionism that it fostered placed undoubted strains upon the global trading system.[30] By facilitating the financing of domestic and external deficits, countries have been able to delay adjustment to imbalances for long periods of time, as was equally the case for Latin America in the late 1970s and early 1980s as for the US for the best part of the last decade.

Rising levels of international financial interdependence have come into increasing conflict with the system of policy-formulation based upon the nation-state. Financial market integration ensures the rapid transmission of economic impulses between the major countries. However, growing capital mobility has not rendered national borders and national policies irrelevant.[31] The persistence of substantial currency and country risks is shown by the continuation of large short-term interest rate differentials between countries, and the lack of convergence of long-term real interest rates even within highly integrated areas such as the EMS. Similar differentials arise in equity prices, even for the same company listed on different national exchanges. As most exchanges are dominated by domestic stock activity, substantial equity price differentials occur across borders. In November 1992, average price–earnings ratios in Tokyo, New York and London were 50, 16 and 14 respectively, reflecting an enormous divergence of perceived risk and return, as well as the advantages that accrue to 'insiders' in

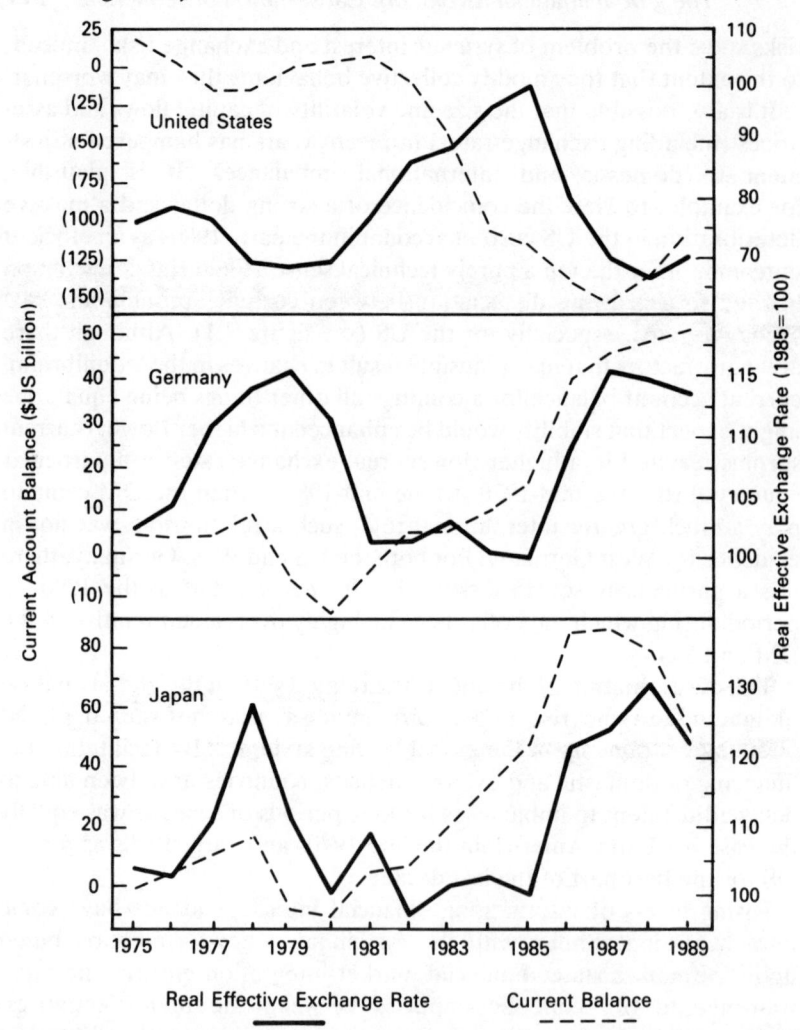

212 *Hegemony and the evolution of the international monetary system*

Note: Current account figures are for the end of periods, REERs are period averages.
Source: IMF, *International Financial Statistics*.

Figure 7.1 Current accounts and real exchange rates, US, Germany and Japan, 1975–89.

these markets. Finally, the mobility of physical capital remains substantially less than financial flows, though greater than that of labour.

The consequence of this is that capital mobility constrains some forms of national economic policy more than others. It affects the ability of governments to pursue autonomous trade, industrial and regional policies much less than macroeconomic policies.[32] Increasing capital mobility in the EMS, for example, has in the context of stable exchange rates severely limited the scope for autonomous monetary policy in particular. The more indirect and limited effects of fiscal policies upon interest rates mean that there is more autonomy here than for monetary policy. Even for countries which have been less concerned to maintain exchange rate stability, macroeconomic policies can have effects upon the exchange rate which are difficult to ignore.

It is important to recognise that increasing capital mobility has had important distributional consequences within and between states. For countries like the US, UK, and Japan, which have tended to place greater emphasis upon macroeconomic autonomy than exchange rate stability, this has favoured 'non-tradable' goods and service sectors, such as finance, defence, construction and real estate, over tradable goods (or relatively exchange rate sensitive) sectors such as manufacturing. These countries have also tended to be those which have suffered most from the excessive indebtedness of corporate and consumer sectors in the 1980s, which has led them to avoid large fluctuations in domestic interest rates. Other countries which have favoured exchange rate stability have tended to favour tradable goods sectors over non-tradable and interest sensitive sectors. More generally, mobile financial capital is more easily able to profit from interest and exchange rate volatility than immobile domestic firms or labour. Similarly, MNCs have through geographical diversification reduced their vulnerability to exchange rate fluctuations. On the other hand, governments have been generally weakened *vis-à-vis* mobile financial capital by the competitive downward pressure on tax rates on capital and highly paid labour across countries in recent years.[33]

As between states, major asymmetries continue to exist in the pattern of international financial linkages. First, that which has always favoured surplus states persists. In Europe, the strong currency economies (Germany, Switzerland and the Low Countries) have largely been able to avoid capital controls aimed at restricting the *outflow* of capital, although like Japan, they have on occasion attempted to discourage capital inflows through additional reserve requirements on non-resident deposits. The weaker currency economies for most of the 1970s and 1980s, such as France, Italy and the other Mediterranean countries, continued until recently to rely heavily upon capital controls, short-term interest rate differentials and periodic devaluations *vis-à-vis* Germany to the extent that their inflation performance has been inferior to their major trading partner.[34] Policies aimed at lowering inflation to German levels have enabled France, Italy and Spain more recently to discard most of these controls, but this and the case of the UK in the late 1980s and early 1990s underlines the point that pressure is concentrated upon deficit rather than surplus states to adjust.

Growing financial interdependence has also meant that the already strong linkages between the domestic US and Eurodollar markets have had an increasingly important effect upon financial conditions in other countries. Alexandre Lamfalussy, Director of the BIS, has remarked that '[in] general, financial impulses emanating from the US are transmitted remarkably quickly to other financial centres, despite fairly generalized floating.'[35] The volatility of interest rates was exacerbated by the Federal Reserve's change of operating procedure to one based upon monetary targeting in October 1979, as well as the process of deregulation of interest rates in the US and elsewhere since then.[36]

The continuing attraction of dollar assets to international investors because of the size and depth of US financial markets has already been noted. This asymmetry due to the international role of the dollar helps to explain why the US economy remained in a cyclical upswing from 1982–90 while sustaining such large current account deficits. In contrast, the reflationary experiment of France over 1981–2 was much more rapidly reversed due to a collapse in confidence in the franc.

The asymmetry in favour of the dollar can also be seen in the pattern of exchange rate intervention within the OECD. With the DM and the Yen as the main two alternative reserve currencies to the dollar for private and official agents, the Bundesbank and the Bank of Japan, both of whose foreign exchange reserves still consist largely of dollars, act as the main residual managers of the exchange rate of the dollar.[37] While the Bundesbank's exchange market intervention and (to some extent) short-term interest rate policies have at times been directed to the DM–dollar relationship, other EMS countries have concentrated upon maintaining appropriate exchange and interest rates *vis-à-vis* the DM.[38] The pre-eminent position of Germany in the European economy and monetary system has therefore served as a conduit of financial impulses originating from the US.

Impulses from the US tend to have a much greater effect on the rest of the world than vice versa. As in the interwar period, problems of US domestic economic management are likely to have important effects upon the rest of the world. The rapid changes which the US financial system has been undergoing and the growing levels of indebtedness on the part of both the US government and private sector has probably increased the degree of financial fragility in the economy and made its management increasingly difficult. Between 1976 and mid-1987, aggregate US debt rose from $2.5 trillion to nearly $8 trillion, and the ratio of total debt to GNP rose from 136 per cent to 178 per cent.[39] The leveraged buyout boom and bust, the thrift crisis and continuing problems with developing country loans for large commercial banks have been a cause for concern not only in the US but also for the world economy.

Similar concerns exist for the Japanese economy, given its role as the major international supplier of surplus funds in the 1980s. Some have argued, for example, that Japanese institutions precipitated the October 1987 world stock market crash by selling US Treasury bills and driving up yields.[40] Although horror-stories of Japanese financial dominance are often exaggerated, there can be little doubt as to the impact of shifts in flows of funds from Japanese institutions. What seems to have been a classic speculative bubble leading to excessive asset price inflation in Japan in the 1980s, particularly in shares and property, elicited theories of the uniqueness of Japanese stock markets (to the effect that prices could only ever go up). These were based upon psychological or institutional factors such as cultural 'solidarity' and large cross-shareholdings by Japanese corporations. Large falls eventually did come in 1989, 1990 and since, but the ineffectual policies forthcoming from Japanese authorities during the bull market was more reminiscent of US policy in the 1920s than policy in the other major surplus state, Germany. The imprudence of heavy lending by Japanese banks to the highly speculative property sector and their ability to count as capital unrealised securities gains has also been exposed after recent weakness in stock and property markets.[41] The indebtedness of the private sector in Japan has risen substantially in recent years: the indebtedness of non-financial companies increased from 94 per cent of GDP in 1975 to 135 per cent of GDP in 1990, while that of households increased from 45 per cent to 96 per cent of disposable income over the same period.[42]

The pattern of trade interdependence reinforces these financial asymmetries, especially for the US and Germany (see table 7.6). High trade interdependence means that expansions in domestic demand (such as through fiscal policy) will have a weakened impact upon domestic production due to 'spillovers' into imports.[43] Since Germany is the main export market for almost all other continental West European economies, there are further limits upon the extent to which these countries can deviate from German economic policy. The US, despite the growing proportion of trade in its national product in recent years, remains much less open than the other major economies, which provides it with a greater degree of policy autonomy. At the same time, the US is the main export market for the industrial countries as a whole. While the Japanese economy is also relatively less open than the

Table 7.6 Trade patterns of OECD countries.

	Exports as % of GDP:		Export market (% of total merchandise exports in 1987 sent to:)			
	1987	(1960)	OECD total	OECD North America	EEC	Major market
US	7	(5)	70	23	27	Canada 23
Japan	13	(11)	65	39	18	US 37
Germany	32	(20)	78	10	50	France 12
France	21	(14)	76	8	60	Germany 16
Britain	26	(20)	74	16	46	US 14
OECD		N.A.	75	19	44	US 15
EEC		N.A.	79	10	58	Germany 12

Source: IMF, *International Financial Statistics*; IMF, *Direction of Trade Statistics Yearbook*, 1988.

European economies, the importance of the US as its major export market makes this country very sensitive to variations in the Yen–dollar exchange rate.

The still central role of the US economy and its much greater degree of policy freedom due to the asymmetries mentioned above can also be seen in the relationships between national business cycles over the past decade or so. In an OECD study of these relationships, it was found that the US business cycle consistently led the OECD cycle by one month, while that of Japan, Germany and OECD Europe tended to lag by one month.[44] This confirms the general impression held by many that economic fluctuations in the US economy affect those of the rest of the world to a much greater extent than vice versa.[45]

The synchronisation of business cycles since the late 1960s is in contrast to the pattern of relative autonomy of the European, Japanese and North American economies that characterised the preceding postwar years.[46] There has also been a general increase in the amplitude of fluctuations in activity since that time, consistent with the hypothesis of increased synchronisation (table 7.7).

As with any explanation of business cycle fluctuations, one needs to exercise extreme caution in interpreting such evidence. However, it seems unlikely that both increasing synchronisation and volatility of cycles do not owe at least something to rising levels of interdependence and are not simply the result of conjunctural coincidence. As the OECD report concluded, 'the single most important continuing and generalised external influence (as distinct from specific 'shocks' such as the oil crisis)

Table 7.7 Peak to trough amplitudes in recessions, industrial output, major groupings, 1960–82.

Grouping	1960–3	1966–7	1969–71	1974–5	1980–2
North America	11.0	5.4	12.2	19.2	20.9
Japan	12.2	15.5[a]	10.7	26.1	15.4
OECD Europe	8.0	10.7	10.3	17.1	15.2
OECD Total	9.8	9.4	11.1	19.2	17.4

[a] 1964–5.
Source: OECD, 1987a, p. 65.

as regards cyclical activity on any OECD country will be the rest of the OECD bloc.'[47] When policy stances coincide, as in the 1972–3 synchronised expansion and the all-round deflation which followed the second oil crisis, the effects on OECD and world output tend to be magnified. Even for supposed 'exogenous' shocks such as the oil crises, the level of OECD activity as a whole is a significant determinant of commodity and oil prices, and the fact that commodities are denominated in dollars made OPEC very sensitive to the dollar devaluations which preceded the two oil crises.[48]

The debt crisis of the developing countries and the questions this raised as to the stability of the US and international banking system was a related consequence of the international financial revolution. The roots of the crisis lay in the two oil crises in the 1970s and the ability of the Latin American countries in particular to postpone adjustment to higher oil costs by borrowing through international financial markets. The role of the international commercial banks in the recycling process received encouragement from Western governments and perhaps from the existence of dependable lenders of last resort in the national jurisdictions.[49]

Expectations also played their part: the lending and borrowing undertaken until 1982 not only in Latin America but also in Texas was based upon expectations regarding interest rates and commodity prices formed in the wake of the first oil crisis. Real interest rates were negative throughout much of the 1970s, especially for developing countries whose terms of trade were constantly improving.[50] This suggested to borrowers that indebtedness would continue to pay benefits without the political sacrifices that foreign direct investment entailed, and to lenders that it would provide a steady source of interest income at a time when large companies in the OECD were turning increasingly towards securities markets for funds. The spectre of ever greater resource scarcity hung over this period, with most commentators expecting a continuing steady shift in the terms of trade in favour of commodity-exporters.

No one at that stage could have predicted the dramatic shift in US monetary policy in 1979, which instigated a rapid process of disinflation and sent real interest rates to record highs. Since most debt was contracted at spreads over market rates, the real burden of interest payments rapidly became unmanageable for many Third World and developed country debtors.[51] The real interest burden was exacerbated by the collapse of commodity prices, comparable in real terms to those that occurred in the Great Depression. This resulted in a severe drop in Third World export earnings, which until 1980 had kept pace with the growth of debt.[52]

The debt crisis highlights another consequence of the financial revolution: the increased difficulty of prudential supervision and regulation of financial markets. The globalisation and securitisation of financial markets impaired the transparency of balance sheets of financial institutions. The erosion of traditional relationships between borrowers and lenders may mean that in a downturn, access to bank credit facilities may be less readily available. In addition, the depth of secondary markets in many of the instruments which have recently appeared has yet to be tested, while the experience of the floating rate note and junk bond markets is not encouraging in this respect.[53] Though it would seem too early to decide whether these developments have considerably increased the fragility of the world's financial system, there is a clear danger in the present phase of transition that old regulatory approaches could easily become completely outmoded.

In summary, the economic consequence of the global financial revolution has been an increasing volatility of world interest rates, exchange rates and business cycles, with important distributional effects within and between countries, while the innovation and rising indebtedness associated with it raises questions about world financial fragility. The minimal policy coordination that has been forthcoming in recent years has been overwhelmed by the demands of increasingly integrated financial markets, suggesting that such macroeconomic coordination is unlikely to provide a solution to the problem of growing instability. As in the interwar period, major structural problems have re-emerged, such as the increasing difficulties in managing the US and other major economies, increasing financial fragility, and problems of slow growth and indebtedness in much of the developing world. All these factors raise considerable doubts that growing monetary and financial instability, such as it is, bears any simple relationship to the declining weight of the US in the world economy.

7.5 The political consequences of financial integration

International policy coordination

Interdependence and the failure of insulation through floating exchange rates have, not surprisingly, led to calls for a greater degree of policy coordination, while the major countries have had increasingly acrimonious disputes over responsibilities for adjustment to emergent disequilibria. The so-called 'locomotive dispute' between the major three countries over 1977–8 and continuing disagreements in the 1980s have often been seen as examples of the difficulties of post-hegemonic cooperation.[54]

Official rhetoric concerning the need for collective management of economic interdependence reached its heights under the Carter administration, many of whose appointees, most notably Fred Bergsten, Richard Cooper and Joseph Nye, were leading lights in the academic field of interdependence theory. As Bergsten, then Under-Secretary at the Treasury for International Monetary Affairs, argued in early 1979, 'in today's multipolar world, with the US no longer able to call the shots itself on most economic issues', all countries had a shared responsibility for the collective management of the world economy.[55] Economic summitry as a means of fostering such cooperation received special attention in these years.

Although the first Reagan administration with its pro-market philosophy shunned economic diplomacy of this kind, eventually it too came to promote policy coordination, primarily as a means of forcing Japan and West Germany to adopt reflationary measures. American and often European pressure on Japan and Germany has usually been particularly strong in periods when their current account surpluses have been large, such as in 1977–8 and since 1983, though this is no longer true for Germany (see figure 7.2).

The continued reluctance of these countries fully to accede to such pressure led Kindleberger to assert in the mid-1980s that largely 'because of the diffusion of economic power in the world, coordination of economic policy becomes more and more difficult, despite the fact that it is sought at the highest level.'[56]

It is doubtful whether an inability to force these countries to adopt macroeconomic policy measures which they strongly resist is in itself indicative of a decline of US power. There was never a golden age in which America could enforce such changes in other countries' economic policies. Rather, the contradiction between increasing levels of trade and financial interdependence and the primacy of national economic

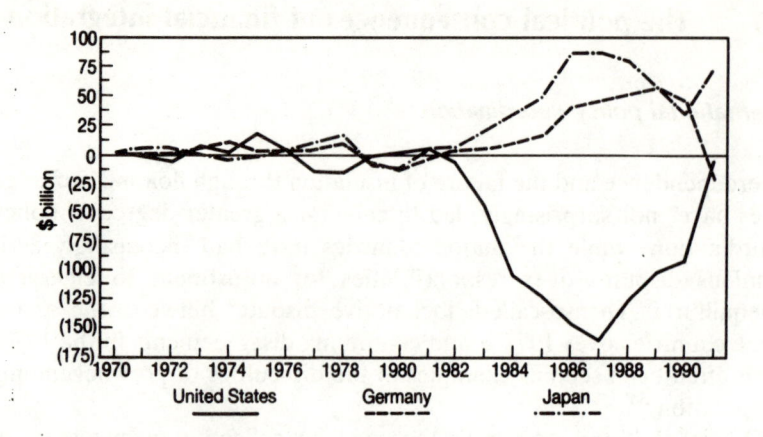

Source: IMF, *International Financial Statistics*.

Figure 7.2 Current account balances, major countries, 1970–91.

policy has become increasingly acute, and this (coupled with the fact that the major countries have never agreed upon the distribution of adjustment responsibilities) increases both the likelihood and the visibility of disagreement. What has changed is not so much America's ability to obtain economic policy concessions from other major countries, but that before the 1970s much lower levels of interdependence and the system of pegged exchange rates made explicit coordination less crucial.

At the same time, it is undoubtedly true that Germany and Japan, by consistently following an anti-inflation, export-oriented growth strategy in the 1970s and 1980s, have passed many of the costs of less favourable growth conditions onto other states. Flexible exchange rates failed to correct the traditional bias in favour of strong surplus states, while slower growth made the costs of such asymmetries more difficult for others to absorb. 'Policy coordination' has in many ways been the latest in a long litany of attempts to force surplus countries to accept a greater responsibility for adjustment.[57]

The problem with the locomotive approach and more recent macroeconomic policy disputes is that they often overlooked the fact that this was not the only asymmetry which persisted. The central role of the dollar in the international monetary and financial system means that such disputes cannot be understood simply in terms of the adjustment responsibilities of *surplus and deficit* states. From the point of view of the Germans and Japanese, the key problem with periodic US demands for reflation has been the absence of a firm American commitment to stabilise the internal and external value of the dollar. The importance of trade and raw materials imports to the Europeans and Japanese has made them especially concerned about the impact of dollar instability upon oil and commodity prices.[58]

The crisis of the dollar over 1977–8 was heightened by the impression given by the Carter administration that it was unconcerned about the external value of the dollar, and in fact that it welcomed dollar depreciation. In January 1978, at a time of severe dollar weakness and large external deficits, the US Council of Economic Advisors argued that:

> Especially for large countries like the US, where the economic cost of changing domestic growth is large relative to the improvement in the current account that would result, it is not appropriate to modify domestic objectives for economic growth in order to reduce the current account deficit.[59]

In mid-1977, the American Treasury Secretary Michael Blumenthal attempted to place pressure on the Germans and Japanese by publicly arguing that they should either reflate or accept further appreciation of their currencies. This was the beginning of the unofficial US policy of 'talking down the dollar', which has had echoes into the 1980s with the attempt by the US from 1985 to get Germany and Japan to accept a similar choice.[60] The general perception on the part of markets was that the US was unwilling to make policy adjustments in order to correct the misalignment of the dollar in exchange markets. As the BIS remarked in 1979, 'what was lacking was conclusive evidence that the US authorities really did care about the internal and external value of the dollar.'[61]

It was only with the turning-point of the dollar rescue package of November 1978 (including a $15 billion dollar swap agreement with other central banks, provisions for the issue of up to $10 billion of foreign currency ('Carter') bonds, a $3 billion IMF drawing and a further tightening of monetary policy), that some degree of market confidence in the dollar was restored.[62] The difference between the 1977–8 dispute and that in the first half of the 1980s can be seen in figures 7.2 and 7.3, which show how the US current deficits in the earlier period coincided with a major deterioration in the overall balance, much of which was due to short-term capital outflows. It was not so much US *current* deficits to which other countries objected – after all, these provided a stimulus to their own economies and exports – but that in 1977–8 these were accompanied by a collapse of confidence in the dollar and large capital inflows into the strong currency countries.

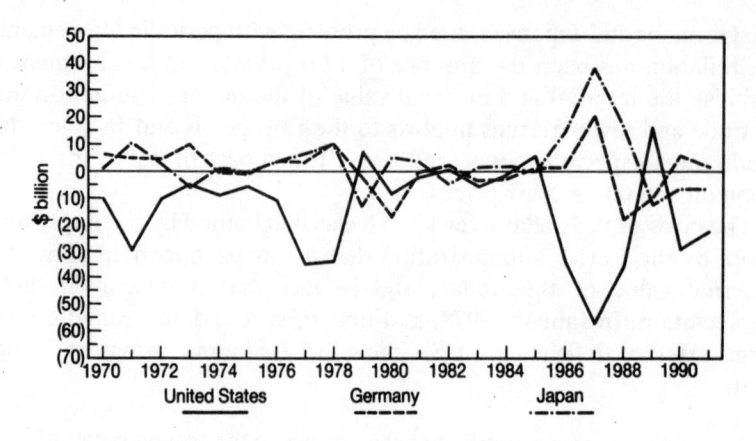

222 *Hegemony and the evolution of the international monetary system*

Source: IMF, *International Financial Statistics.*

Figure 7.3 Balances on official settlements, major countries, 1970–91.

By way of contrast, until 1985 the deterioration of the US current account was not accompanied by a loss of private market confidence in the dollar, reflected in the very low overall deficits run by the US in these years. Other countries, while benefiting considerably from the American-led expansion, objected to the high level of real interest rates which a loose fiscal policy and a tight monetary policy brought.[63] The depreciation of their own currencies in the early 1980s led them to concentrate upon containing domestic demand and relying upon export-led growth. The Reagan administration was eventually brought to the realisation that the negative effects of the strong dollar on US exports and manufacturing jobs made necessary a reversal of its policy of leaving the determination of the exchange rate of the dollar entirely to the market.[64] The Plaza Agreement of September 1985 was a belated recognition of the need to take a concerted stand to push the dollar to encourage a depreciation of the dollar to levels compatible with long-term balance (see figure 7.4).

In retrospect, such agreements look very much like exchange rate policy on the cheap. It would be perverse, after all, to blame the currency misalignments of the 1980s entirely upon the markets. Net US dissaving has necessitated large capital inflows; when these have not been entirely forthcoming from private foreign investors, central banks have been obliged to intervene heavily to support the dollar, as in the wake of the Louvre Accord of February 1987. In the first half of 1987

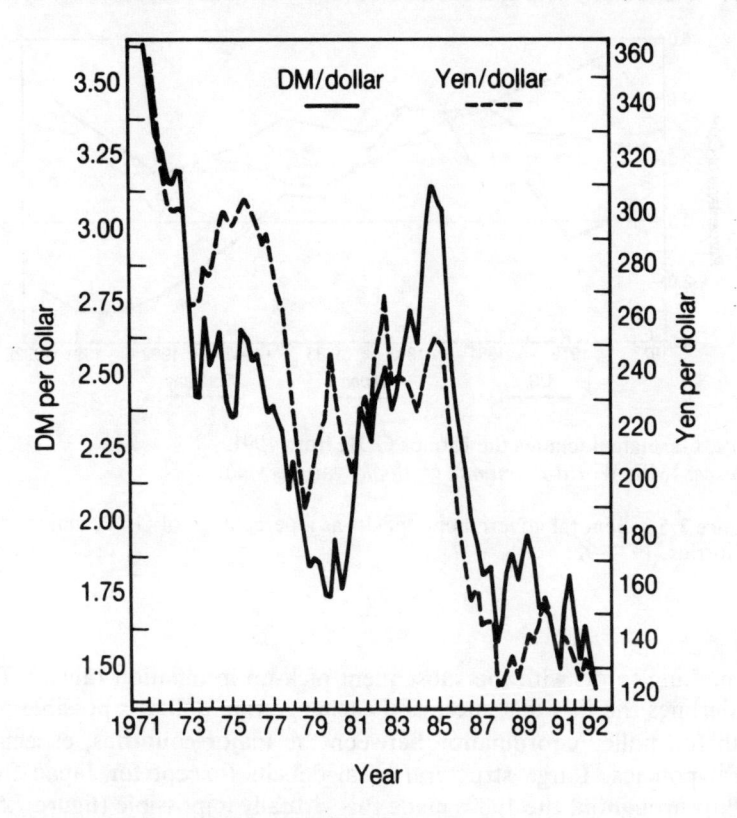

Note: Figures are end of quarter spot rates.
Sources: OECD, 1990a; IMF, *International Financial Statistics*.

Figure 7.4 Mark/dollar and Yen/dollar exchange rates, 1971–92.

alone, Japan, Germany, and the UK accumulated $48 billion in foreign exchange reserves (though not all of this reflected intervention to support the dollar). The argument that the irresponsibility has been entirely on the part of the surplus states ignores the fact that the US has for much of the recent past pursued policies inconsistent with exchange rate stability, and that much of the burden of exchange rate management has rested upon other states. For Germany and Japan in particular, fluctuations in the size and composition of their foreign exchange reserves increasingly reflected their periodic attempts to manage their exchange rates against the dollar. Over 1977–8 and after 1985 they and other monetary authorities accepted considerable overshooting of domestic monetary targets, which may have had

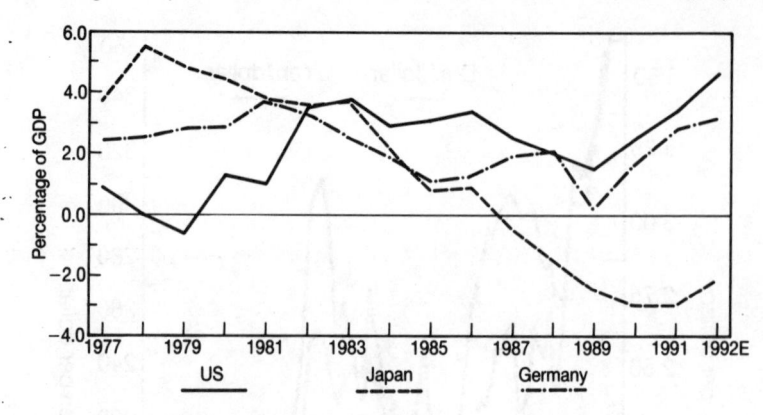

Note: Germany includes the former GDR from 1991.
Source: IMF, *World Economic Outlook*, various years.

Figure 7.5 General government deficits as a percentage of GDP, major countries, 1977–92.

something to do with the subsequent pick-up in inflation rates.[65] This underlines the fact that successful exchange rate policy is possible only with full policy coordination between the major countries, especially fiscal policies. Large structural fiscal deficits (except for Japan from 1986) throughout the 1980s made this virtually impossible (figure 7.5).

Gilpin has argued that the unwillingness of Germany to continue to support the dollar in 1979 was a major reason for the shift in US monetary policy under Volcker, and that 'this policy reversal was the end of American hegemony'.[66] This view underplays the domestic roots of the crisis and exaggerates the extent to which Germany, or even all of the other countries together, could hold the dollar once financial markets lost confidence in the US's ability or willingness to adopt an appropriate policy mix and to stabilise the exchange rate. This misunderstanding stems from a tendency to see US 'weakness' as the consequence of an inability to control other countries' policies, rather than as due to the fundamental changes which have taken place in the international monetary and financial system.

What is perhaps most surprising about the episodes of 1977–8 and the mid-1980s is the extent to which Japan and at times Germany *have* been willing to adopt expansionary measures under pressure. In the locomotive dispute, by the end of 1977 the Japanese had pledged to undertake further public works expenditure, to achieve a growth rate of 7 per cent for 1978 and even to remove its current surplus. The increasingly isolated German government finally agreed at the July 1978 Bonn Summit to take expansionary fiscal measures of DM31 billion, although this came to be seen in Germany as a major cause of the current deficits and weak mark at the end of the decade.[67] The Japanese have been much more willing than the Germans in recent years to accede to international pressure to change their policies, in part because of their more favourable fiscal position. In the recent Structural Impediments Initiative (SII) talks, they agreed to increase public works expenditure as well as a wide range of microeconomic reforms designed to increase the penetration of Japanese markets by foreign goods.

One of the reasons for Japanese receptivity to American pressure has been the existence of powerful pressure groups which have consistently favoured reflation to appreciation.[68] It also owes much to the considerably greater export dependence of the Japanese upon the American market. For Chancellor Schmidt, the concessions made at the London and Bonn Summits in 1977 and 1978 were part of a strategy to convince the Carter administration of the need for a strong response to the developing 'Euromissile gap' with the Soviet Union and for American commitment to domestic oil price de-control. It was also part of the broad German aim to encourage the adoption of more responsible policies by the US in order that a chronically weak dollar not exert too great a centrifugal force on the newly emerging EMS.[69] These factors were not present in the 1980s, while the German reluctance to undertake domestic expansionism despite growing American and European disapproval in the early 1980s was in part a product of the conventional wisdom that the reflation agreed to in 1978 was an unmitigated disaster. Since German reunification in 1990, complaints about German policy have been reminiscent of the criticisms of US policy in the early 1980s, as a fiscal policy seemingly out of control has combined with a tight monetary policy to place enormous strain on those countries pegged to the DM through the EMS.

Even if such disagreements were not present, international financial integration may have proceeded too far for the cumbersome process of macroeconomic consultation to have a major effect in terms of exchange rate stabilisation. Is it realistic to expect, as does McKinnon, that policy coordination could be so precise, fluent and convincing to markets that we could return to a world of fixed exchange rates? Even under the much less ambitious Williamson proposal for wide target zones for exchange rates, the degree of policy coordination envisaged remains well beyond that of recent experience.[70] Part of the unrealism of McKinnon's proposal is that it sees monetary policy coordination as central, when fiscal imbalances have been at the root of many of the problems of the 1980s.

This is not to deny that policy coordination is a worthwhile aim, but to argue that it is unreasonable to expect that it alone can provide the answer to the world's monetary problems. As long as it is unlikely that the US, Germany, or Japan would be willing to change course in macroeconomic policy when a clear dilemma arose between domestic and exchange rate objectives, the prospects for managed exchange rates in present circumstances would seem to be bleak. It seems unlikely, for example, that the US would have been willing to cut the fiscal deficit in the years 1981–5 so as to limit upward pressure on the dollar under a McKinnon or Williamson-style system, just as Germany has ignored calls to reduce its fiscal deficit and the Bundesbank's key interest rates despite their devastating impact on the EMS in late 1992. The main reason why a pegged exchange rate system became unacceptable to the US in the early 1970s was because there were powerful domestic interests who saw a strong external constraint as inappropriate for such a relatively closed economy. Likewise, the Germans and other countries remain extremely sceptical of any attempt to fix target zones for exchange rates between the key currencies (let alone fixed rates), because of their belief that such a system would be just another 'inflation-machine'.[71] Finally, the difficulties of deciding upon appropriate exchange rates have been enormously complicated by the rising net external indebtedness of the US, and this will be likely to militate against the likelihood of such proposals being accepted or workable in a context of financial integration.[72]

In contrast, the EMS has probably provided the most successful example of a system in which a high degree of financial integration has been compatible with stable exchange rates because of close policy coordination.[73] High levels of trade and capital integration in the EC have created powerful domestic constituencies in favour of exchange rate stability, leading countries like France and Italy to pursue long-term inflation convergence with Germany by pegging to the DM. Periodically, higher inflation in the Mediterranean countries has necessitated realignment *vis-à-vis* the DM, the latest round being in 1992. Even so, the EMS was widely seen as a success story at the beginning of the 1990s, with countries like the UK, Spain and Portugal becoming full members, the EFTA countries becoming proxy members by 'shadowing' the Ecu, and the removal of capital controls accelerating throughout the EC in conjunction with the Single Market programme. In the lead-up to the Maastricht agreement on Economic and Monetary Union, and with the last realignment having occurred in 1987, the EMS was increasingly seen as evolving towards a system of fixed exchange rates and eventual EMU.[74]

However, two shocks had by the end of 1992 brought the system to the brink of collapse: the unexpected weakness of economic recovery in the US, and the financial pressures stemming from German re-unification. The first brought the lowest US interest rates since the 1960s and compounded the economic downturn in Europe, driving the dollar to record lows against the other major currencies in summer 1992. The second produced ballooning budget deficits in Germany as economic collapse in the east accelerated, while the resulting inflationary pressures led the Bundesbank to raise interest rates as M3 targets were continuously overshot. As Europe headed into recession over 1991–2, interest rates remained unusually high, placing enormous pressure on countries with overvalued exchange rates (such as Italy and Spain) and on interest-sensitive countries (such as the UK, Sweden and Finland). In the most serious exchange crisis since those of the dollar in the 1970s, massive central bank intervention in September was unable to prevent capital flight out of sterling and the lira from forcing these two currencies out of the system altogether. Nor could punitive Swedish interest rates in the end salvage that country's policy of pegging to the DM. Others, such as Spain, Portugal and Ireland, only remained within the EMS through the imposition of capital controls and/or devaluation, or in the case of France, through massive concerted intervention by the Bundesbank and the Bank of France.

As under the dollar standard in the early 1970s, the relative absence of control upon the key currency country of the system, Germany, had increasingly become a problem for, rather than a solution to, Europe's macroeconomic dilemmas. By the end of 1992, the broad EMS of the beginning of the 1990s was in tatters as the difficulty of pursuing policy convergence in circumstances of high financial integration had once again become clear. The vision of Europe gradually moving forward to a common exchange rate and monetary policy had disappeared, making the prospects of coordination at the broader international level all but impossible.

International prudential supervision

The dramatic expansion of cross-border financial transactions in recent years has also increased pressures upon countries to agree common rules to regulate and supervise financial markets. The main forum in which such issues are discussed is the Basle Committee of the G-10 countries, operating under the auspices of the BIS. Set up after the failure of the Herstatt Bank in Germany in 1974, its first main concern was to ensure that there was agreement on the lines of responsibility of bank supervision, particularly in the Euromarkets, the absence of which had been exposed by the Herstatt collapse. The so-called 'Basle

Concordat', which became public in 1975, held that the primary responsibility for supervision lay with the 'home' authorities of the country in which a bank's parent office was located, although host country authorities were also to play a role in the supervision of foreign-owned subsidiaries operating in their jurisdiction. The practical difficulties involved in such overlapping responsibilities were clarified in 1981, when it was agreed that home authorities should supervise banks on a consolidated basis.[75]

However, when Italian authorities refused to protect the depositors of the Luxembourg subsidiary of Italy's largest bank, Banco Ambrosiano, when it failed in July 1982, it exposed a major gap in the Basle Concordat. Though the principle of parent authority responsibility was reinforced in 1983, the Bank of Credit and Commerce International (BCCI) scandal in 1991 further underlined its shortcomings. Though based in Luxembourg, the bank operated in a number of countries and its largest shareholder was the government of Abu Dhabi. The complete absence of any clear lines of responsibility had permitted a fraud of unprecedented proportions to go undetected for years, raising allegations of negligence on the part of the Bank of England and other supervisory authorities. This has left the Basle Concordat looking inadequate for circumstances in which there is not a strong centralised and transparent structure of ownership and control. Consistent with the principle of 'mutual recognition' underlying the EC's Single Market Programme, the EC also adopted the principle of home country control as the basis of its Single Banking Directive of 1989. However, the BCCI scandal makes it even more likely that in practice, the Bank of England will be unlikely to leave the supervision of foreign bank subsidiaries in London entirely up to the home authorities in Greece (or indeed Luxembourg).

The second major area of concern has been the divergence of capital adequacy requirements between national monetary authorities. This culminated in the Basle Capital Adequacy Accord of July 1988, aimed at the establishment of minimum capital adequacy standards across the major countries. The EC, in the Own Funds and Solvency Ratios Directives of 1989, largely adopted the Basle Accord standards.[76] The major impetus here came from the US regulatory authorities, which were concerned both about the undercapitalisation of American commercial banks in the wake of the debt crisis, as well as the competitive disadvantage which they suffered *vis-à-vis* their US rivals who were subject to less onerous constraints upon their international lending activities. In order to strengthen the capital base of US banks without further endangering their competitiveness, US authorities pursued an international accord which would create a 'level playing field'. This was achieved by first signing a bilateral accord with the Bank of England in 1987, ensuring that the other major countries (and particularly Japan) had little choice but to go along with the Accord of 1988. As Kapstein has suggested, this represented 'a landmark financial agreement . . . [and] illustrates the enduring strength of the United States in shaping and advancing policies in international economic relations'.[77] The Basle Accord set a minimum capital standard of 8 per cent of risk-weighted assets, of which at least 4 per cent must consist of 'Tier 1' or core capital, to be achieved by the end of 1992.[78]

Nevertheless, there are a number of shortcomings which may be noted.[79] First, the Accord allowed for a significant degree of national discretion in terms of how countries might achieve the minimum requirements by end-1992. The most publicised example was the discretion allowed with respect to Tier 2 capital, such as the way in which the Japanese succeeded in being able to count up to 45 per cent of revaluation reserves (such as unrealised securities and real estate asset gains) as Tier 2 capital, despite the vigorous opposition of the well-capitalised German banks. Another area of discretion is the weightings that are assigned to different counterparty credit risks, whereby for example countries can decide whether to assign a zero or 'low' (10–20 per cent) risk weighting on fixed rate domestic and foreign OECD government securities.

Second, innovations in international banking since the 1970s have vastly increased the difficulty of assessing risk. Although the Basle Committee was concerned to capture off-balance sheet risk in the Accord because of the increasing importance of non-traditional banking business, there is only limited agreement on how to assess such risks. The rapid pace of financial innovation in many derivative products in swaps, options and futures markets has left bank regulators, as the Director of the BIS admitted recently, 'in a total and absolute mess'.[80] Risks related to obligations in such markets are partly credit (that is, counterparty) related, though this in itself can be quite complicated. Even more important, yet less well understood by both market participants and regulators, is 'market risk', above all yield curve (interest rate) risk and foreign exchange risk. Negotiations are continuing about how to measure and allow for such risk.

A final area of difficulty concerns which institutions should be subject to the Accord. After having reduced the 'uneven' playing fields between banks of different countries, the Accord threatens to increase regulatory divergencies between different types of financial institution. For example, the Accord potentially disadvantages universal banks of the European kind which are subject to the capital requirements relative to specialist firms in the securities, insurance and consumer finance industries which are not. The EC and a Basle sub-committee chaired by Gerald Corrigan of the Federal Reserve Bank of New York have been negotiating a similar capital accord for securities firms, but large differences in regulatory structures between countries, the complexity of the risks referred to above, and disagreement over other technical issues such as the 'netting' of counterparty risks in securities markets have prevented an international agreement emerging thus far. At the same time, whether insurance firms and the growing number of non-banks such as large industrial and retail firms with financial operations, not to mention large financial services companies such as American Express, ought to be brought under a general capital adequacy agreement is as yet unclear. All this is apart from the problem of how to ensure that small offshore financial centres in particular are willing and able to abide by such agreements.

Therefore, though the achievements of the Basle Committee in recent years should not be underestimated (indeed, they indicate the extent to which international agreements on technical but still highly political issues are possible in present circumstances), there is a danger that they can create new opportunities for regulatory arbitrage by private actors. It is not yet clear as to whether the Accord has pushed banks towards less capital intensive activities, though it seems that it is a major explanation of the virtual withdrawal of Japanese banks from the international lending market over the past year.[81] There is also a large question mark over whether regulators can ever keep up with the pace of innovation in financial markets; at the very least, regulations need to be constantly revised in the light of changing market practices. Finally, one of the consequences of the globalisation of the financial services industry is that ambiguities in the jurisdictions of regulators and their subjects are likely if anything to multiply over time.

A changing balance of financial power?

The paradox of the present era may well be that while stabilising US policies are more than ever a necessary ingredient of international monetary order in spite of US decline, the long-term consequences may be such as to produce a more symmetrical multi-currency system.[82] The encouragement given by successive administrations in the 1970s to US bank lending to Latin America has exacerbated the pressing domestic problems of asset quality facing the US financial system, and made its stability more dependent upon events in politically volatile countries. The long overvaluation of the dollar in the first half of the 1980s accelerated the process of the increasing trade integration of the US into the world economy, thereby contributing towards the erosion of a long-standing asymmetry in international interdependence. The rapid growth of US exports in the last few years and the increasing levels of import penetration and foreign investment in many US industrial sectors suggest that the importance of the traded goods sector in the US economy may have undergone a structural shift in the 1980s (table 7.8). Third, while the pre-eminent international role of the dollar is indisputable, the deregulatory process has been accompanied by some degree of portfolio diversification by private and official actors towards non-dollar assets. The growing competition between the major financial centres for international financial business may ultimately accelerate the transition from a dollar-centred system to a more symmetrical multi-currency system.

Finally, the twin deficits run by the US through the 1980s have led to the US changing from being the world's largest net creditor to its largest net debtor in book-value and current cost terms, which may have implications for the political balance of power between the major countries. There has been an increasing concern in much of the literature that the consequence of the Reagan years has been to reduce American autonomy by ensuring reliance upon European and especially Japanese finance well into the next decade.[83] Ironically, while it might be said that US policy since the Nixon years has been driven by a desire to maximise US autonomy *vis-à-vis* the rest of the world, the result may have been to increase the constraints upon US freedom of manoeuvre relative both to its major allies and to international financial markets. Similarly, it is sometimes argued that the increasing role of private international financial markets has eroded the market power which accrued to reserve currency countries under the gold exchange standard by enabling access to liquidity for all states which remain creditworthy.[84]

It would be foolish to attempt to predict how long these trends will take to work themselves through the structure of international relations. At present, the international monetary and financial system remains highly asymmetrical, biased in favour of the US economy and the dollar, and it is likely that this asymmetry will persist for a considerable time yet. The US economy remains the single largest in the world, and as it has become more integrated into the international trading system, its relative importance as the major importer has increased over time (table 6.2, p.153). Most striking has been the increasing import penetration of the US manufacturing sector since the 1960s, to levels significantly higher than for the economy as a whole and more in line with other industrial countries, excepting Japan (see table 7.8). This development has been especially important for Japan and the Pacific Rim states, making Japan and these countries more receptive to American pressures to reflate their economies, liberalise their financial systems

Table 7.8 Import and export penetration for major economies 1960–87.

	Import penetration of manufacturing industry (percentage of manufacturing value-added at current prices)				Exports of manufactures as a percentage of world exports of manufactures[1] at current prices				
	1960	73	80	85	87[2]	1960	73	80	85	87[2]
US	4.6	13.8	21.5	31.0	35.1	22.3	14.8	15.6	15.2	12.7
Japan	7.5[3]	8.0	10.4	10.2	9.6	6.2	11.5	13.5	17.9	16.3
Germany	24.6[4]	25.1	39.0	47.1	43.0	17.4	19.9	18.1	16.9	19.5
UK	16.3	39.1	51.1	69.5	72.2	15.0	8.5	8.8	7.1	7.2

Notes: [1] Excluding exports from LDCs and Eastern Europe.
[2] Partly estimated.
[3] 1967.
[4] 1970.

Source: BIS, *Annual Report*, 53, 1987–8.

and to accept currency appreciation. Similarly, the dependence of Latin American exports on the US market (and the desire to maintain a working relationship with the country which is the major source of new capital exports) probably played an important role in preventing the emergence of a debtor's cartel and in leading these countries to adopt bold liberalising policies in recent years.

What is striking is the extent to which the decline in the weight of the US in the world economy has not been accompanied by a comparable shift in the asymmetries which characterise the international financial system. Continuous net dissaving on the part of the US may have actually slowed the emergence of a more symmetrical multi-currency system in the 1980s. There is little indication that international financial markets will be unwilling to finance US current deficits in the region of $100 billion or more per annum, in the absence of a collapse of confidence in policy. Financial deregulation and asset portfolio growth in other countries will produce a net demand for new dollar assets over time. This may be due in part to the tendency in financial markets to economise on transactions costs by using a single currency as the main vehicle currency of international transactions, as well as the size and depth of US financial markets. While instability in the value of the dollar has led to some diversification on the part of private and official actors into non-dollar assets, it has retained its pre-eminent role as the international unit of account, medium of exchange and store of value for private and official actors.

Some have suggested that the US actively promote the emergence of a more symmetrical system by issuing non-dollar denominated Treasury bonds (as did the Carter administration in 1978).[85] The association of foreign currency denominated Treasury bonds with the Carter administration would in itself be likely to preclude future administrations from opting for a similar solution. More fundamentally, the US is understandably reluctant to guarantee the foreign currency value of future and existing liabilities, especially when access to dollar reserves via capital markets is relatively easy for many central banks. This is also the key obstacle to the proposal for a substitution account (whereby existing dollar reserves could be swapped into primary reserve assets such as the SDR). The US, in other words, retains the ability to determine (at least in a negative sense) the pace of international monetary reform, in particular concerning any future role for the SDR or a reform of the exchange rate system.

While it should not be surprising that the US cannot have its own way on such matters of reform, some authors exaggerate the extent to which this is indicative of declining US power. Joanne Gowa, for example, in documenting the failure of the major countries to agree to a substitution account for dollar reserves in the late 1970s, concluded that a major reason for the lack of progress was the inability of the US to force the others to accept its position.[86] As she points out, Congress would have been unwilling to accept a substitution account for the dollar if the US would (as other states wanted) have to guarantee the value of existing dollar holdings. American power consists not in an ability to force adoption of its preferred solutions, but to prevent collective reform if the costs are perceived as being too high for itself.

Even in the EMS, the unwillingness of the European countries to extend the reserve role of the Ecu meant that the dollar remained for some time the main intervention currency and reserve asset for EMS members.[87] Though the EMS has provided its members with a low inflation, DM-centred monetary anchor, it has been unable to insulate them from fluctuations in the DM–dollar exchange rate. As such, it has not provided the EC with a bargaining weapon in monetary negotiations in the same way that the Common External Tariff has in trade matters. Ludlow's judgement as to the prerequisite for the initial success of the EMS has remained substantially true: '[in] the final analysis a durable EMS required a healthy dollar: it could only in the short run be a substitute for a weak one.'[88] Though it is sometimes claimed that fully-fledged European Monetary Union (EMU) could provide such autonomy, is this realistic given the high levels of financial interdependence within the OECD area? Substituting a revamped Ecu for the DM and an independent 'EuroFed' for the Bundesbank may actually make little difference on the international level, though within the EC it would decrease German dominance and make monetary management more symmetrical and more inward-oriented (in the manner of US monetary policy) than at present. Until markets became comfortable with an enhanced Ecu and EuroFed policy, the Europeans might suffer a loss of influence in international money and finance relative to that which they indirectly enjoy at present through the DM.

Of course, for countries other than Germany that have pegged to the DM, it might be said that only through EMU would they be able to regain the influence that they have lost through the EMS. This seems particularly true for the French, who have managed to remain within the EMS at such cost. However, it took some time for governments, market participants and commentators to realise that in spite of the integration hubris of the late 1980s, the EMS was facing its most serious crisis ever at the very same time that it became seen as the first stage on the path towards EMU. After all, the EMS had survived franc, lira and even dollar crises before, but the pressures of German reunification struck the EMS at its core. Along with the doubts over the future of the Maastricht Treaty, there seems little doubt that the prospects for EMU have been set back considerably. On the economic side, the growing divergence in macroeconomic and exchange rate policy in Europe over 1992 suggests that the strict convergence criteria for EMU are unlikely in any case to be met by more than a few countries. But perhaps more fundamentally, the policy stalemate in Germany itself probably makes it less likely that this key country would wish to reduce its own monetary autonomy through EMU, whether of a 'narrow' or a 'broad' form.

Much recent literature notwithstanding, neither can Japan yet be seen as an independent financial centre in the traditional sense. The Yen remains relatively insignificant as a global reserve currency despite recent deregulatory moves, and although Japan acted as the major financier of American indebtedness in the 1980s, that it did so *in dollars* has entailed enormous losses for Japanese institutions since 1985. The Japanese are aware that in one form or another they will have to continue to finance America's current account deficits because of their economic and political dependence upon America. Japanese Ministry of Finance figures show that in the late 1980s, US securities trading represented well over 80 per cent of total foreign securities trading by Japanese institutions, who routinely took 30–40 per cent of issues at the US Treasury's quarterly refunding auctions.[89]

This has entailed significant costs for the US, though not as much as would be the case if foreign borrowing had been denominated in Yen or had been largely achieved through foreign direct investment in American industry (though levels of foreign owned firm participation in US industries increased substantially during the 1980s[90]). The postponement of fiscal adjustment in the US created a dependence on Japanese finance in particular, with the US unable to determine the price at which foreigners were willing to provide funds. Nevertheless, events over 1990–2 demonstrated that those who feared that a continuing US need for foreign finance would place a severe constraint upon US monetary policy were mistaken. In an effort to lift the US economy from recession, the US Federal Reserve reduced short-term interest rates to their lowest level for decades. Although the dollar fell to all-time lows in summer 1992, there was no dollar crisis as in the 1970s and the currency recovered substantially in the autumn. To the extent that large US current deficits re-emerge in the 1990s, however, this may hamper at least to some extent Japan's evident desire to utilise its large current surpluses in the manner of traditional financial centres, that is, lending to its own region in Yen.

All this presumes, of course, that large Japanese current surpluses (and corresponding American deficits) are here to stay. There are two main schools of thought on this issue. The first sees Japanese manufacturing industry as invincible, flexible enough to adjust to shocks such as a series of oil price hikes and the appreciation of the Yen in the second half of the 1980s. This school also sees Japan as an inherently closed economy, due to cultural and institutional factors which create immovable non-tariff barriers to Western products. Most importantly, Japan's financial wealth will eventually launch it into the truly great power or hegemonic league.[91] Another school maintains that Japan's rapid Westernisation and demographic changes, as well as foreign pressure (especially from the US), will eventually erode the high Japanese propensity to save, as the low Japanese propensity to travel abroad is already eroding. The strong Yen will in this view continue to encourage Japanese firms to shift production offshore and consumers to buy increasing amounts of foreign products. Japan will become a wealthy but relatively normal country, unlikely to challenge seriously the US as the dominant great power over coming decades.[92]

It is worth pointing out that in the 1950s and 1960s, foreigners tended to see US current surpluses and the seeming invincibility of American multinationals in similar terms to those of contemporary Japan. Much of the political economy literature on the rise of Japan's banks and securities firms in the 1980s exaggerates their dominance in these industries.[93] While it is true that Japanese banks and securities firms in the 1980s came to dominate 'league tables' using measures such as assets, market capitalisation and Eurobond underwriting, such analyses overlook the fact that Japanese institutions are much weaker in the high growth, innovation-intensive, 'non-commodity' areas of international banking and securities businesses. After all, the most profitable areas of banking in the 1980s and 1990s were more often in off-balance sheet and fee-related activities, and this is even more the case after the Basle Accord. Some Japanese banks have begun to make their presence felt in 'plain vanilla' international interest and currency swaps markets, but with bid-offer spreads having fallen to about 3 basis points in the dollar swaps market, these are increasingly low-margin activities too. In the highly lucrative derivatives markets, as in advisory services, American, Swiss and sometimes German banks dominate and Japanese banks are not major players.

The structure of Japan's economy may also alter considerably over the next decade, as its industrial firms shift production offshore in order to retain competitive advantage and market share. The low proportion of Japanese GNP produced abroad (compared to other major economies) is likely to rise, as did America's after the war, possibly reducing the current surplus. This, and the likelihood that the ageing of the Japanese population along with the social changes occurring in the country will reduce the high levels of saving, point to a long-term decline in the Japanese current surplus. No one can be sure, however, as to how long this will take, and whether recent trends in this direction will prove to be lasting.

In the meantime, the Japanese authorities have had some difficulty in managing the country's wealth. The difficulty of penetrating Japanese markets has at times risked the relationship with its major ally, the US, even though the continued openness of foreign markets to Japanese goods will depend increasingly upon Japanese concessions on import barriers. The inability or unwillingness of Japanese authorities to manage with much degree of surety the speculative boom in stocks and property has, as noted above, raised doubts about the stability of the Japanese financial system. Deregulation in the 1980s has reduced the direct control of the authorities over the financial system, but the tools of open market policy are relatively underdeveloped in Japan. The Ministry of Finance, due to its desire for cheap funds, has been a major counterweight against the desire of the Bank of Japan (and the Americans) to see the development of a genuine Treasury bill market in Japan.[94] Nevertheless, there has been a powerful coalition of forces between internationalists in the bureaucracy and government, the domestic financial community, and foreign governments and banking interests which has pushed Japan firmly down the road of financial liberalisation.[95]

An important factor behind the continuing dominance of the US in the field of international money and finance has been the extent to which this dominance has been paralleled by the dependence of Western Europe and Japan upon US military protection. To discern a direct link between the security relationship and that in the financial arena is difficult, but it would be wrong to underestimate its importance. As we saw in Chapter 1, the concentration of much recent work in international relations upon specific 'issues' or regimes has often encouraged a compartmentalisation of the concept of power. The view put forward here is that US power in international monetary relations has never consisted of an ability to 'control outcomes' by enforcing rules or policy-changes on the part of other sovereign states. Rather, it has consisted primarily in terms of its continuing ability to constrain *the set of possible outcomes* in the international monetary and financial arena and to make certain outcomes which have reflected the interests of powerful US groups much more likely than others. This is what is referred to in the literature as *structural* power, as opposed to *relational* power, which is the ability of one actor to get another to act against the latter's will.[96]

The US promoted a deregulated international monetary system largely through its ability to forestall collective efforts aimed at instituting a greater degree of international public management and through its ability to use the structural asymmetries in the global trade and financial system in its favour. Although Germany and Japan have not accepted full responsibility for adjustment to imbalances within the OECD area, neither have they supported the French on the fundamental issues of monetary reform. In other words, the major non-American financial powers have acquiesced to a considerable degree in the process of international monetary deregulation since the 1960s, because they have been able to pass a substantial proportion of the costs of this system onto other states and because the benefits for themselves have been considerable.

It seems difficult not to conclude that one of the ultimate reasons for France's own consistent failure in the field of international monetary diplomacy was its inability to convince Germany and the rest of Western Europe that it provided a viable security alternative to the American alliance.[97] For the Japanese, despite their success first in the trade and subsequently in the financial arenas, their dependence upon American markets and military protection has been reflected in their greater deference to American pressure and has contributed to their postwar reluctance to tread a more autonomous regional path, both in finance and on defence matters. In many ways, therefore, the notion that the 'implicit bargain' of the postwar period between America and its allies collapsed with the Bretton Woods system in the early 1970s has been exaggerated. Cohen described this bargain thus:

> America's allies acquiesced in a hegemonic system that accorded the United States special privileges to act abroad unilaterally to promote US interests. The United States, in turn, condoned its allies' use of the system to promote their own economic prosperity, even if this happened to come largely at the expense of the United States . . . The breakdown of the system in 1971 may be read as the bargain's final collapse.[98]

Such a view obscures the degree of continuity in the evolution of the international monetary system since the late 1950s and exaggerates the extent to which any 'breakdown' that did occur was due to a decline of American power in the system. The notion of the breakdown in the implicit bargain also underestimates the extent to which the structure of the world monetary and financial system continued to reflect patterns of security dependence, ultimately because Japan and West Germany were unable to afford to provoke a change in US security commitments. President Reagan remarked in his opening address to the 1983 Annual Meeting of the IMF (after ruling out an increase in American taxes to finance the budget deficit): 'let me make clear that [the federal deficit] is caused in part by our determination to provide the military strength and political security to ensure peace in the world'.[99] This is not to argue that US military protection has necessarily been the decisive element of US structural power in the politics of international money and finance, but that it created a powerful coalition within the other major states between foreign policy internationalists and domestic financial and export interests.

On the security side, the world has come a long way since 1983. Then, Reagan could almost challenge his major allies to choose between financing the American deficit and altering the security arrangements that have largely prevailed since the late 1940s. Whether the implicit bargain, increasingly strained since Nixon's challenge to US allies in 1971, will survive the 1990s and a new Democratic Presidency in the US is perhaps doubtful. Does this mean that the end of the Cold War will remove the cornerstone of postwar cooperation in international money and finance?

There are already signs that a united Germany will play a less submissive foreign policy role than in the past and one less congruent with US interests. The same might be said about Europe as a whole, though the absence of a coherent European 'interest' on many important issues, such as on the Uruguay Round negotiations, or on the issue of the openness of the EC's Single Market to foreign banks, has often worked to the advantage of the US.[100] As for Japan, the enormous pressure for liberalisation placed upon it by the US through the SII talks and other bilateral initiatives during the 1980s and 1990s has created considerable resentment and resistance in certain quarters, though it is difficult to see such resistance becoming significant.[101]

However, even if the 'security glue' of the postwar international political economy is in the process of dissolving, it does not follow that the breakdown of the market-based system of international trade and finance is inevitable or even likely. Above all, powerful trade and financial interests in Japan and Germany have a major stake in the continuation of the system.[102] Although the existence of the EC and the conclusion of the European Economic Area agreement with the EFTA states in 1992 might be said to provide Germany with a regional alternative that Japan does not have, this too can be exaggerated. Important German exporters and MNCs have a major interest in the continued openness of the US market, as does the German financial sector.[103]

In spite of the North American Free Trade Area agreement, America too has a much greater economic stake in an open world economy than in the interwar period, and this stake has increased considerably in recent years, despite the disappearance of its formerly large trade and current account surpluses. Of the major economies, American business remains the most multinational; indeed, the extent of its globalisation may have been a major cause of the disappearance of these surpluses. It also has a major interest in attracting foreign capital, both portfolio and direct, to finance its deficits and to provide a much-needed infusion of competition, new management techniques and technologies, despite the disadvantages to some domestic groups.

All this is to say that the economic interdependence that has developed since the war has reached a point where the three major economic powers would have much to lose from any disintegration of this interdependence. In contrast to the 1930s, when the US, Japan and Germany were all committed to achieving economic autarky, they have continued to move in the direction of further integration, albeit at times slowly and unsurely.

Finally, there is some hope that recent developments in security arrangements may help to break the impasse in which international economic relations seem to be stuck. If, as has been argued here, an important reason why US policies have often been destabilising for the world economy has been because of the lack of external constraints upon them, some degree of erosion of the asymmetries that presently favour America may be a good thing. If its major allies feel less dependent upon US military protection than in the past, they may feel able to strike a harder bargain on a range of issues, such as stronger US commitments to address its fiscal and savings deficits. On the US side, the 'peace dividend' may help it to tackle these problems, while it is unlikely to lose much of its bargaining power in international financial and trade negotiations. Although speculation about the future in this subject is usually made rapidly redundant by events, the above does suggest that there is no *necessary* reason why the development of a more symmetrical relationship in trade and finance between the three major blocs should be the unmitigated disaster for the world economy that much recent literature has implied.

7.6 Conclusion

We have seen that the international financial revolution of recent years, with the encouragement of the US and the increasingly explicit cooperation of its major allies, has transformed the nature of the international monetary system into one quite antithetical to that envisaged at Bretton Woods. This transformation is not simply a product of cooperation between states to foster a system based upon market principles, since there is a competitive aspect to the deregulatory process. Given the tendency of financial markets to innovate and to erode the regulatory constraints imposed by public authorities over time, in a world of separate states there may be a natural long run tendency for a Bretton Woods-style international monetary system to be undermined. This is partly due to the natural temptation in international relations for individual states to encourage change that they perceive to be in their favour, and in part due to the inertia of international political arrangements relative to the dynamism of market forces.

This view of the recent evolution of the world's monetary and financial structure places no particular emphasis upon the 'decline of American power' in the process, though there is no doubt that on a range of measures, US power has declined relative to other major states. However, because asymmetries that favour the US in finance and trade have been reinforced by others in the security field, it is very difficult to say how significant this decline in American power is. Growing levels of financial integration have made these asymmetries more pressing for the other states in the system, which feel as never before financial impulses emanating from the US economy.

For all states taken together, however, it is true to say that they have suffered a loss of power *vis-à-vis* the market, or more specifically financial capital and footloose industrial firms of all kinds. This quantitative dominance of the market is attenuated by its inability to find its own endogenous equilibria for exchange rates and international lending. The public sector has considerable potential for guidance, and could be said to possess a kind of *qualitative* dominance. However, financial deregulation has meant that state guidance is increasingly less frequent than in the past.

In addition, public authorities have failed to provide clearer guidance to the private markets because of the inevitable difficulties of policy coordination, and because the most important state, the US, has frequently adopted a hands-off policy with respect to the management of the system. The Bank of Japan, the Bundesbank and a few other central banks have often become by default the residual managers of the system. Recent years have shown that exchange rate policies without attention to continuing imbalances in savings and investment between countries lack credibility and may even destabilise financial markets, as the October 1987 crash suggests.

The exigencies of financial integration have led some economists to argue for the partial disintegration of the global financial system to enable governments to regain an adequate degree of national policy autonomy, usually by means of an interest equalisation tax on capital transfers.[104] There are major difficulties with this argument. First, the advanced stage of the blurring between domestic and international financial markets which has been reached suggests that it is by no means clear how capital controls would be successfully implemented. Even in the international monetary system of the late 1940s to the late 1950s, when controls on capital flows were abundant and the sophistication of the markets much inferior to that at present, speculative flights from currencies were by no means unknown (especially for sterling). The problem that has always existed and which, given the increasingly important role of MNCs in world trade, is much more acute today, is how to distinguish in practice between current and capital account transactions.[105]

Second, and perhaps more fundamentally, the degree of political cooperation necessary to achieve controlled disintegration would probably be at least as great as that required for the cooperative regulation of the system. The international success of Japanese banks and securities companies in the 1980s highlighted the fact that increasingly a number of countries which formerly strongly resisted financial liberalisation now see much to gain from it. Countries which already possess important international financial centres, such as London, New York and Tokyo, have become ever more concerned that attempts at regulation of the activities of onshore financial markets will only drive such business to other centres with less regulatory zeal. Second- and third-tier financial centres such as Frankfurt, Paris, Singapore and Sydney have sought to modernise and liberalise their regulatory and settlement systems so as to attract the international business which has tended to migrate to the larger centres.

Finally, there is the objection made by most economists and bankers that 'throwing sand into the works' of the world financial system would decrease efficiency and threaten world economic prosperity. It can be argued that this objection carries less force because exchange rate volatility and misalignment pose a considerable threat to the openness of the international trading system. On the other hand, there is a great need for capital to flow from surplus countries to those with higher rates of return on investment and capital shortages. That the US in the 1980s attracted much of the world's surplus funds (and often for consumption rather than investment) reflects on the inadequacy of policies, past and present, in the US and in the developing countries, as much as upon a regime of freer capital flows.

The argument that what requires restriction is short-term 'speculative' capital flows, while allowing free movement for long-term investment capital, runs into the practical problem of distinguishing between these categories. Attempting to regulate away 'short-termism', especially given strong tendencies towards competitive deregulation and financial innovation, would most likely be bound to fail. It also supposes naively that short-term flows are bad and long-term flows are always good. The experience of publicly channelled investments through the World Bank and other international organisations does not present an unblemished record either, though this is certainly one channel which in general can probably serve the needs of some sovereign borrowers more efficiently than can private capital markets.

The likely unworkability and undesirability of controls on capital flows makes even more pressing the need for a global regulatory framework for financial markets. The existence of lenders of last resort in the major countries prevents the collapse of important national banks, but this creates a problem of moral hazard which may be especially important on an international level. The Basle Capital Adequacy Accord is only a first step towards the creation of such a framework, which by its very nature must be the product of agreement between all major countries (in the first instance, the G-10), given the inevitability of regulatory arbitrage by financial actors. In addition to consistent risk-based capital requirements, effective regulation requires specific agreement upon who regulates whom, reporting and accounting standards, as well as required disclosure and business practice, all of which can vary significantly between countries. Although this requires a joint effort from the Americans, Japanese and Europeans, it goes without saying that the key role of the US and its banks in the international financial system necessitates that it lead the way in creating such a framework. This in turn may require that the US first embark upon a restructuring of its domestic regulatory structure, in which a wide range of state and federal institutions with considerable functional overlap attempt to regulate a financial system that has long since made this structure outmoded.

In the absence of widespread distress in international financial markets, piecemeal agreements are more likely to characterise attempts at international monetary reform than the Bretton Woods-style 'blueprints' sometimes offered by economists. Bretton Woods aimed at *creating* a monetary system out of the ashes of the 1930s and wartime period, whereas present reformers must concentrate on largely working within the bounds of a highly developed system in which major countries have substantial vested interests. If, as is not unlikely, such cooperation is not forthcoming, the direction of future change to a large extent will be determined by the markets. This may be likely to bring further evolution towards a multi-currency system, which may bring a greater degree of balance to the present system. On the other hand, the continuing dependence of the Japanese upon the US, and the divisions that are all too visible in Europe, are brakes upon the continued erosion of the present asymmetries.

As in the interwar period, the contribution that macroeconomic policy coordination can make will be limited as long as such structural problems remain unsolved. The US deficits and high real interest rates, the still unresolved issue of the distribution of the burden of Western defence, Third World indebtedness and the erosion of monetary control through financial innovation and fiscal profligacy, will all place severe constraints upon monetary management. For the US, the costs of financing deficits in excess of the net demand for new dollar assets may increase considerably in the 1990s. In the last decade, the absence of profitable opportunities outside the US made less costly the financing of its deficit, but demands for capital from Eastern Europe, the ex-Soviet Union and a newly market-oriented Latin America, not to mention the projected costs of an environmental clean-up and the relief of pressing problems in Sub-Saharan Africa, are likely to increase considerably the demand for capital in the next decade. The US, Europe and Japan all need to play a central part in the resolution of these global problems, and it will be to their own cost and that of the rest of the world if they fail in the attempt to 'put their own house in order' before tackling these pressing issues.

Notes

1. Gilpin, 1987, p.88.
2. Wallerstein, 1982, p.40. See also Krasner, 1982, p.30; Spero, 1981, p.65; Keohane, 1979, pp.103–9; Shonfield, 1982, pp.81; Mandel, 1980, pp.30–6.
3. Kindleberger, 1986, p.9.
4. These figures are taken from IMF, *International Financial Statistics*; Haberer, 1988; Drucker, 1986.
5. O'Brien (1992); Julius (1990).
6. Bank of England, *Quarterly Bulletin*, November 1989, pp.531–5, November 1992, p.409.
7. BIS, *Annual Report 91–92*, pp.93–4; O'Brien, 1992, pp.44–6.
8. As usual, US financial institutions and markets have set the pace in innovation. For an overview, see BIS, 1986; US Federal Reserve, *Bulletin*, January 1988, pp.1ff; Goodhart, 1986b; Bank of England, *Quarterly Bulletin*, September 1986, pp.367ff; Chairman of the Federal Reserve Board Greenspan's April 4, 1990 statement to the Congressional Task Force on the International Competitiveness of US Financial Institutions, in US Federal Reserve, *Bulletin*, June 1990, pp.439–43.
9. BIS, *International Banking and Financial Market Developments*, August 1990, p.1.
10. *ibid.*, pp. 1–5; Bank of England, *Quarterly Bulletin*, November 1992, pp.408–11.
11. Horii, 1986, pp.41–4.
12. Morgan Guaranty, *World Financial Markets*, November/December 1987,

p.17; BIS, *International Banking and Financial Market Developments*, August 1990, p.5.
13. As Horii (1986, p.8) points out, these official figures considerably overestimate the extent of the diversification away from the dollar which has occurred in recent years. Much of the apparent reduction in the dollar's role reflects inadequate data, changes in measurement and exchange rate changes ('passive' diversification).
14. Osugi, 1990, p.46.
15. See *Euromoney*, November 1986, pp.36–55.
16. Kaufman, 1988, p.115; BIS, *Annual Report 91–92*, p.194.
17. For a discussion, see Llewellyn, 1985. The figures, and those to follow, are taken from IMF, *International Financial Statistics*.
18. Brender, Gaye and Kessler, 1986, pp.70–2, 148–62; Morgan Guaranty, *World Financial Markets*, November/December 1987, p.9.
19. BIS, *Annual Report 91–92*, p.192.
20. The Depository Institutions Deregulation and Monetary Control Act of 1980 also mandated the removal of all remaining interest rate ceilings by April 1986 (US Federal Reserve, *Bulletin*, January 1988, p.5).
21. Fukao and Hanazaki, 1987, p.44; Bundesbank, *Monthly Report*, 37(7), July 1985, pp.13–23, and 39(5), May 1987, pp.34–42.
22. See Osugi, 1990; Economic Planning Agency of Japan, 1984, pp.153–4; Frankel, 1984; *Far Eastern Economic Review*, November 19, 1987, pp.68–9; BIS, *Annual Report*, 1984/85, p.123.
23. See *Euromoney*, 'Pacific Basin Financing', May 1987, pp.24–38.
24. Emmott, 1989, pp.180–6; Frankel, 1991.
25. Strange, 1986, pp.165–81.
26. See Bank of England, *Quarterly Bulletin*, 27(1), February 1987, pp.85–93; *Euromoney*, June 1987, pp.70–9; Guttentag and Herring, 1983; the various statements on this subject by Gerald Corrigan, President of the FRBNY, in FRBNY, *Quarterly Review*, 11(4), Winter 1986–7, and volume 12, issues 1–4.
27. de Lattre, 1985, pp.85–97.
28. For example, Fukao and Hanazaki, 1987, p.37; de Vries, 1990, pp.3–4.
29. See Lamfalussy, 1986, p.20.
30. McKinnon, 1988, pp.83–91.
31. Frieden, 1991.
32. *Ibid.*, p.430.
33. *Ibid.*, p.435.
34. See Tsoukalis, 1987, pp.14ff.
35. Lamfalussy, 1985, p.410. See also King, 1982; Micossi and Padoa-Schioppa, 1984.
36. *Federal Reserve Bulletin*, January 1988, pp.4–5.
37. At least until 1987, intervention by the American authorities tended to be very infrequent. See Horii, 1986, p.8.
38. Tsoukalis, 1987, pp.14–21.
39. *Federal Reserve Bulletin*, January 1988, p.1. For a review of these difficulties, see Carron, 1982; Wojnilower, 1985; Minsky, 1986; Simpson, 1984; Pollin, 1985; FRBNY, 'Financial Innovation: A Complex Problem Even in a Simple Framework', *Quarterly Review*, 9(2), Summer 1984, pp.1–8; 'Major Borrowing and Lending Trends in the US Economy, 1981–5', *Federal Reserve Bulletin*, 72(8), August 1986, pp.511–24, and Paul

Volcker's statement to Congress on rising indebtedness in the US economy, printed in *ibid.*, 72(6), June 1986, pp.398–403.
40. Murphy, 1989, pp.73–4. Murphy argues that the collapse of the Continental Bank of Illinois in 1984 was also due to a withdrawal of Japanese funds.
41. See Emmott, 1989, pp.166–71.
42. BIS, *Annual Report 91–92*, p.195.
43. Larsen, Llewellyn and Potter, 1983, pp.49–50.
44. OECD, 1987a, p.57.
45. For comprehensive surveys of the empirical evidence and trends, see OECD, 1987a; Moore, 1983, ch.6; Zarnowitz, 1985.
46. A crude visual indication of increasing business cycle synchronisation since the 1960s can be obtained from OECD, 1990b, part III, especially pp.166–70.
47. OECD, 1987a, p.19.
48. See Larsen, Llewellyn and Potter, 1983, pp.49–62.
49. See Allsopp and Joshi, 1985; Guttentag and Herring, 1985; Frieden, 1987.
50. de Vries, 1990, p.7.
51. See Congdon, 1988, and Figure 7.6. As Congdon points out, until real interest rates return to more normal levels, the real burden of indebtedness is likely to continue to grow for those who borrowed heavily in the 1970s.
52. Drucker, 1986, pp.771–4; Commonwealth Group of Experts, 1984, pp.19–20.
53. For a discussion, see BIS, 1986; Lamfalussy, 1986.
54. For official and academic literature which emerged largely in response to the locomotive dispute, see OECD, *Economic Outlook*, December 1976, p.5, and December 1977, pp.3–8; OECD Secretary General, 1979, pp.7ff; *ERP*, 1977, pp.4–5,124–5; Whitman, 1977; Keohane, 1979; Destler and Mitsuyu, 1982; Cooper, 1986, ch.3; Bergsten, 1980, pp.21–3.
55. Bergsten, 1980, p.21.
56. Kindleberger, 1985a, p.14.
57. See Corden, 1978, and Williamson, 1978, for two opposing views on this responsibility.
58. Bundesbank, *Annual Report*, 1987, pp.35–43; Ozaki and Arnold, 1983, pp.2–25; Akao, 1983, pp.1–9, 52–66.
59. *ERP*, 1978, p.125. For similar views in the 1980s, see *ERP*, 1985, ch.3.
60. See *The Economist*, August 6, 1977, p.9; *Financial Times*, January 22 and 23, 1987.
61. BIS, *Annual Report*, 1978–9, p.4. The belief in the Carter administration was that as recovery proceeded (real GDP growth averaged 5.2 per cent 1976–8) and tax receipts grew, the economy would need *further* fiscal stimulus to counteract the automatic stabilisers and keep growth and employment high (see *ERP*, 1978, pp.73–5). Such 'ultra-Keynesian' conceptions of fiscal policy could only have contributed to the general impression of US policy as 'growth regardless of the external costs'. For a critical view of benign neglect, see Burns, 1987.
62. *Ibid.*, pp.135–7.
63. Shafer, 1988, p.179.
64. See FRBNY, *Quarterly Review*, 10(4), Winter 1985–6, pp.45–8.
65. Bundesbank, *Annual Report*, 1978, pp.1–18, and 1987, pp.31–42; Morgan Guaranty, *World Financial Markets*, November–December 1987, pp.6–10; Emminger, 1979.

66. Gilpin, 1987, p.332.
67. *The Economist*, November 29, 1977, pp.92–3; Garavoglia, 1984, p.17; Bundesbank, *Annual Report*, 1978, pp.15–18; OECD, *Economic Outlook*, 42, December 1987, pp.63–71, 86–91.
68. Destler and Mitsuyu, 1982, pp.247–55; Ludlow, 1982, p.76; Putnam, 1984, p.82; *Far Eastern Economic Review*, 14 May, 30 April, and 11 June, 1987.
69. Carr, 1985, pp.125–37; Ludlow, 1982, pp.127–32.
70. See the elaborate proposals in Williamson and Miller, 1987, ch.2,3.
71. Williamson and Miller, 1987, p.53.
72. McKinnon (1988, p.96), for example, argued that PPP exchange rates between the three major countries (for the beginning of 1988) would be achieved at 199 Yen and 2.16 DM per dollar, when actual exchange rates at the beginning of 1988 were around 130 Yen and 1.70 DM per dollar. Even then, many market participants were of the opinion that in order to achieve the orderly financing of the US external deficit over the next few years, the dollar would still need to go substantially lower. Many Japanese banks foresaw a rate of 100 Yen per dollar or less as likely by the end of 1988, though this failed to materialise (*Financial Times*, May 23, 1988; Morgan Guaranty, *World Financial Markets*, November/December 1987, pp.14–16). In May 1990, one City firm estimated PPPs at 170 Yen and 1.97 DM per dollar, but argued that exchange rates consistent with long-term 'basic balance' were closer to 115 Yen and 1.60 DM per dollar (UBS Phillips and Drew, *Economic Briefing*, 220, 14 May 1990).
73. See Giavazzi and Giovannini, 1989; Gros and Thygesen, 1992.
74. See Tsoukalis, 1991, ch. 7.
75. Kapstein, 1991, pp.6–7.
76. Golembe and Holland, 1990.
77. Kapstein, 1991, pp.1–2.
78. See Basle Committee, 1988.
79. For a good discussion, see Price Waterhouse, 1991.
80. Remarks of Dr Alexandre Lamfalussy to the Oxford International Political Economy Society, 3 February 1992.
81. BIS, *Annual Report 91–92*, p.161.
82. Here I part with the 'revivalist' school in the debate on US power.
83. For example, Gilpin, 1987, pp.334–40, 348–51; Murphy, 1989, pp.78–83.
84. For example, Corden, 1985, pp.90–1. Robert Aliber has argued that the 'privatisation' of the international monetary system means that it 'more nearly resembles a perfectly competitive model [where] there are fewer monopoly centres of power [and in] a perfectly competitive market, no one has power.' Robert Aliber, 'Comments on Strange', 1982, p.98.
85. For private and official Japanese suggestions that the US issue such 'Reagan bonds', see *International Financial Review*, 668, April 11, 1987, p.1188; *Financial Times*, May 20, 1988.
86. See Gowa, 1984.
87. Tsoukalis, 1987, p.16.
88. Ludlow, 1982, p.129.
89. *Financial Times*, September 12, 1990, p.32. The illiquidity of the Japanese government bond market to been a major factor behind the attractiveness of the US Treasury market to Japanese investors.
90. See Graham and Krugman, 1991.
91. For example, Burstein, 1988.

92. See Emmott, 1989, pp.230–41. Helleiner (1992) provides a general discussion.
93. See for example, Helleiner, 1992, p.41; Gilpin, 1987, p.329.
94. See Osugi, 1990, pp.36–40. The Bank of Japan has tended to underwrite almost exclusively the majority of Treasury bill auctions at low interest rates, making open market operations difficult.
95. See Federal Reserve *Bulletin*, August 1992; Funabashi, 1988, p.89 and *passim*.
96. Strange, 1988, ch. 2.
97. See Treverton, 1978.
98. Cohen, 1977, p.97. See also Gilpin, 1987, p.136.
99. IMF, *Summary Proceedings*, 1983, p.3.
100. For a good discussion, see Woolcock, 1991.
101. For an example, see Morita and Ishihara, 1990.
102. For a general discussion, see Frieden, 1989.
103. See Walter, 1993.
104. For example, Tobin, 1982b, p.116; Dornbusch, 1986, pp.223–5.
105. See Cooper, 1965.

Conclusion

Hegemony and international monetary order

A constant theme which has run through this book is the danger of assuming too simple a relationship between politics and economics in international relations. The theory of hegemonic stability has been offered as a clarification of this relationship, positing that the international balance of power is a fundamental determinant of the evolution and stability of the world economy. With respect to international monetary relations, we have found that this theory is often seriously misleading in its predictions and analyses.

The ambiguity of the term 'hegemony' often impairs rather than improves understanding in this field, and for this reason we have attempted to refine the roles that a hegemon or dominant state might play in the production of international monetary order. The distinction between roles of rule enforcement, the encouragement of policy coordination between states, and the management and prudential supervision of the international monetary and financial system enabled us better to understand the different claims that have been made for hegemony.

Our analysis of the evolution of the international monetary system since the late nineteenth century suggests that despite the claims made by a number of authors, practice diverged considerably from the theory. The hegemonic function of rule provision and maintenance was seen to be of limited descriptive value. Britain played at most a very indirect role in the establishment of the economic and monetary ground rules in the second half of the nineteenth century and had little influence over policies in other major states. The Bretton Woods system was not the coherent set of rules that it is often made out to be, nor entirely a case of America successfully imposing its vision of a postwar world on the other states.

If the basis of British and American power did not lie in an ability to enforce rules or regimes, what then constituted their power and their unique positions? For much recent international relations literature, power has been seen as issue-specific in circumstances of economic interdependence. This risks making the same mistake that pluralist theories of power made in the 1950s in the debates on power in domestic society. It was easy to conclude that the lack of any obvious dominance by one actor or group over a whole range of outcomes of bargaining situations implied that the distribution of power in the system was pluralistic. Similarly, by focusing upon issues and outcomes in monetary and trade affairs in recent decades, international relations writers concluded that America was 'no longer' a hegemonic power and that the pluralistic distribution of power in the international system was the fundamental cause of the breakdown of international regimes and economic order.

Rather than resting upon an ability to 'control outcomes' by enforcing rules or policy-changes on the part of other sovereign states, US power after 1945 consisted primarily in terms of its ability to constrain the set of possible outcomes in the international monetary arena and to use the asymmetries in its favour to encourage the evolution of a quite different system to that outlined at Bretton Woods in 1944.[1] Once the sphere of power is broadened to include not just agenda issues, but this wider context within which particular issues (but not all possible issues) arise,[2] it is clear that overall relationships between states do not need *overtly* to intrude upon bargaining situations in order to exercise an important influence over outcomes. Besides constituting a better foundation for political economy, this broader concept of power makes clearer the difference between British and American dominance in their respective periods.

Security relations after 1945 have reinforced financial and trade asymmetries in favour of the US, but this was much less the case for the pre-1914 system. While Britain's position in the Empire was crucial in its global pattern of trade and payments, the other major powers were not dependent upon British military protection in the way that they were later dependent upon America's. To a large extent, Britain had to rely upon the self-interest of other important powers in maintaining an orderly system, which for a good deal of the time was sufficient. The limited role of the state in monetary affairs, the hold that gold possessed upon the imagination and the willingness of the ruling élites to accept a significant degree of real economic instability were probably most important in fostering broad adherence to the 'passive' rules of the game. Such perceptions of mutual self-interest, especially for the French, even extended as far as providing emergency assistance to the Bank of England during crises. For the most part, however, Britain's financial pre-eminence allowed it to rely upon the attractiveness of sterling assets for foreigners to finance deteriorations in its payments position.

This quite clearly did not apply to the interwar period. The prewar structure of limited cooperation was shattered by World War I and its aftermath. Above all, the breakdown of the Concert of Europe removed the political framework within which such cooperation could proceed, and within which self-interest could be limited. In any case, it is doubtful whether the very loose framework of the Concert could have dealt with the changes which were under way and which the war accelerated.

The much greater economic role for the state after the war effectively doomed the gold standard, as a regime in which a tight external constraint on the monetary affairs of nations operated. A number of factors symptomatic of a more fundamental breakdown than just of international monetary relations militated against a new solution: intellectual limitations, inadequate institutions, American protectionism, and the German problem, to name a few. On the domestic level, the inability of the major powers to solve the pressing political and social problems of the time meant that the restored gold standard was built on very unstable foundations. While the literature has often presented the period as one of hegemonic transition, a deeper 'great transformation', to use Polanyi's phrase, was occurring in the relationship between state and civil society that made the restoration of the gold standard unviable. This shift ultimately broke the power of *haute finance* over British policy for a generation.[3]

The stability of the three decades after 1945 was in part due to the US using its dominance to promote international adjustment and the resolution of some of these international problems. It was also due, however, to the emergence of an international monetary system more in keeping with the heightened economic and social role of the state. Not even America's dominant position could have enforced a solution if the other powers, especially Britain, had not recognised the need for a compromise between an orderly international monetary system and the role of the national welfare state at home. The compromise which gradually emerged, and in which Bretton Woods played only a very limited role, provided sufficient room for manoeuvre for most major countries whilst preventing the collapse into chaos that all feared. It enabled the major countries to climb out of the trade autarky of the 1930s and to find better solutions to the domestic problems of the post World War I era.

In many ways it was the very success of this compromise that subsequently placed the most strain upon the system. The rise of trade and financial interdependence came into increasing conflict with a system of economic policy-making founded upon state sovereignty. This was felt most acutely in the US itself, a country that had been used to a high degree of autonomy and which had seen that autonomy partially eroded under the gold-dollar standard. Already in the mid-1960s, the US had decided to rid itself of one of the major thorns in its side, that of gold. Subsequently, it lost interest in a fixed exchange rate system which placed little pressure upon surplus countries to adjust, and promoted one in which (it believed) the market would perform this task. The US's ability to encourage financial deregulation and forestall efforts at reviving collective management represented a considerable display of power, whatever one's view of the outcome.

If hegemonic rule-enforcement played little part in either period, the argument that the financial dominance of both countries enabled them to act as world monetary managers was also found to be flawed. For the pre-1914 era, it was difficult to find much evidence pertaining to this question, and no good reason to believe that Britain's short-term liabilities to the rest of the world did fluctuate in a stabilising manner. Considerably more evidence exists as to the role of the US after 1945, though again it is difficult to draw conclusive results. We found no clear trend towards a countercyclical movement of the US liquidity position *vis-à-vis* the rest of the world, or of its long-term capital exports, either during the Bretton Woods era or afterwards. As with London's financial system before 1914, the main concern of US banks and their foreign subsidiaries was with their solvency and with the profitability of their operations, which at times conflicted with systemic stability. That is, while Britain and the US may have provided services of financial intermediation for the rest of the world, there is little reason to suppose that in doing so they also acted as *central* banks for the international monetary system as a whole.

The relatively good performance and stability of the world economy before 1914 and especially in the 1950s and 1960s no doubt owed something to these liquidity services, and also to the pattern of fixed exchange rates which prevailed. There was a host of other non-monetary factors which may have been at least as important in facilitating the maintenance of an orderly international monetary system. The relative openness of the international trading system and the absence of chronic creditor positions (such as that of the US in the interwar period), stable foundations for German growth, and the effect of productivity catch-up all provided a much more favourable environment for growth than in the interwar period. In addition, after 1945 the readiness of national authorities to step in to prevent the spread of financial crises or to maintain the level of demand was a fundamental stabilising factor.

In the interwar period and since the 1970s, high levels of financial and trade interdependence led to increasingly synchronised business cycles for the major economies, tending to produce greater volatility in international business cycles.[4] The 1920s saw increasing financial linkages in particular between the US, Britain, and Germany, and the important role of short-term capital constituted, in the circumstances, an especially weak link in the chain. Similarly, since the 1970s, the growing financial linkages between the US, Germany, Japan, and Britain have worked for growing exchange rate and macroeconomic instability. Financial interdependence in the two periods proved especially disruptive when it internationalised problems of economic management in the major economies.

The two basic factors behind the rise in international monetary instability in the twentieth century have been the rise of the national welfare state and of high levels of financial interdependence, factors which have borne no clear or simple relation to the shifting balance of power in the international states-system, although two world wars did much to promote one and temporarily to retard the other. Increasing wealth, technological change and the dynamic relationship between financial innovation and competitive deregulation are all likely to undermine regulatory structures aimed at the constraint of international financial flows. The trend towards greater financial integration over the past century suggests further that any international trade or monetary system which is unable to cope with relative freedom of capital movement will have a limited chance of long-run survival, as the recent experience of the EMS has shown. Both international monetary and trading systems need to be flexible enough to cope with change, as do the regulatory structures which assist in their stable operation. The inertia which such regulatory structures exhibit on the international level, as on the domestic, is unlikely to be reducible to hegemonic decline, but more often is due to the shallowness of cooperation between states and to reigning prejudices.

The question that needs to be posed today is whether we have come full circle since the 1920s. The gradual restoration of international capital flows in the 1950s and 1960s eventually rendered the fixed exchange rate system between the US, Europe, and Japan unworkable in the context of macroeconomic policy autonomy. Yet the international financial revolution went further than this, as it became increasingly apparent in the 1970s that flexible exchange rates could not provide effective insulation from growing financial integration. Macroeconomic policy came under particular pressure in those countries that had typically sought to solve distributional problems through higher inflation, such as Britain, France and Italy. Even the US came under pressure to shift course over 1978–9, and the deflation undertaken there under Paul Volcker was mirrored in the early 1980s in France after the U-turn of the Mitterrand government. Has the power of *haute finance* returned us to a world in which it is 'market discipline' which is the fundamental characteristic of the contemporary system, as under the international gold standard?[5]

Certainly, there is a plausible connection between the retreat of the welfare and regulatory state in Europe and many other countries over the past decade or more and the growing mobility of financial capital and multinational firms. The example of Sweden in the past few years, until quite recently seen as the outstanding model of social democracy and economic openness, is instructive in this regard. As financial capital and large Swedish corporations increasingly migrated offshore in the 1980s to avoid the country's regulatory and tax system, the welfare state in Sweden was thrust into a crisis from which it may never fully recover. As in other countries in the 1980s, Sweden has been forced to adopt more 'favourable' tax and regulatory structures by this flight of capital, and in the process it has begun to dismantle some of the key aspects of social welfarism that have prevailed since 1945. One may wonder how other apparently more resilient models such as that of German or Austrian social democracy will fare in coming years.

In the 1980s, it appeared that the shift towards a market oriented international financial system enhanced the asymmetry in favour of 'disciplined' surplus countries. Market discipline has tended to fall most heavily upon countries with a tendency towards chronic basic deficits in their balance of payments; the surplus countries of Germany, Japan, Switzerland and Benelux have benefited most from this shift, since other countries (other than the US) have had to adjust their policies in an effort to eliminate such tendencies. For a country like France since 1983, which has been relatively successful in doing so, the economic and social costs of financial orthodoxy have been considerable.

In another sense, however, 'market discipline' has often failed miserably to produce sustainable or responsible policies. The best examples are the US during the 1980s, Latin America during the 1970s, Scandinavia and some of the other 'Anglo-Saxon' economies such as Canada, Australia and the UK, where levels of indebtedness rose to unprecedented levels in the 1980s. Perhaps most ironic, if not surprising, is that market discipline has failed to prevent irresponsible economic behaviour in the two key surplus states, Japan and Germany. In Japan and the other highly indebted economies, excessive asset price inflation during the 1980s has left them struggling beneath substantial debt burdens which appear to be a major constraint upon economic recovery. The nationalisation of debts has been a common response, from the US treatment of the Savings and Loans problem to the nationalisation of failed banks in Scandinavia (and possibly, before long, in Japan).[6] The inherent inability of markets to provide objective standards of good and poor financial behaviour means that market discipline tends to be greatest only after situations have become 'unsustainable' (another subjective term).

Germany's problem has been different, in that despite the massive deterioration in the country's current account and its fiscal position since 1990, the credibility of the Bundesbank has prevented market discipline from playing any substantial constraining role until now. As mentioned earlier, this produced a full-blown crisis of the EMS which had not been resolved at the time of writing in November 1992, and which only the onset of recession in Germany itself might ameliorate.

This fundamental weakness of market discipline points to a short-coming in some of the recent Gramscian literature which talks of the 'social hegemony' or structural power of capital.[7] The value of this perspective is that it suggests how an explanation of recent changes in terms of a shift in power from 'states to markets' is inadequate, since it loses sight of which social groups win or lose. The financial revolution outlined in the previous chapter was in the interests of certain groups in domestic society rather than others: sophisticated financial capital as opposed to small savers, securities firms as opposed to most commercial banks in the US, footloose industrial firms as opposed to immobile domestic firms, and skilled white collar labour as opposed to relatively immobile labour in manufacturing industries. A fuller analysis would need to take into account these social cleavages and the way in which advantaged groups may have favoured policies consistent with financial liberalisation.

However, it is immobile groups of any kind which have been disadvantaged by the financial revolution.[8] In this sense, one of the major disadvantaged actors has been the territorial state itself, perhaps the least geographically mobile of all social institutions (as Sweden and others have found). This allows us to talk (in a very qualified manner) of the way in which a shift towards a market oriented system has favoured some states rather than others and has weakened the collective power of states in the system. On the other hand, analysts should also beware of assigning structural power to 'the market', since as we have seen, there is no collective market 'intent' and no objective market discipline.

Foreign exchange traders have become increasingly unconcerned about 'economic fundamentals' in the last two decades and more focused on short-term factors; the crisis of the EMS in recent months, particularly the attack on the franc, demonstrates this clearly enough.

As an explanation of the causes of international monetary stability, or instability, the theory of hegemony places too great an explanatory burden upon a quantitative conception of the shifting balance of international power. As in all social science, the possibilities for disagreement over causality are potentially infinite, because we always have an overdetermined system. The presence of a dominant state says little about whether the policies of major countries are farsighted, whether domestic institutions and policy tools are adequate, or whether the intangible quality of leadership is likely to be present. The tendency in much recent thinking to conflate 'hegemony' with such leadership is surely mistaken. Given the array of other variables which might be crucial for monetary stability, to suggest that one variable (hegemony) is necessary is both methodologically and historically implausible. Financial stability in major economies has been much more crucial for the stability of the world economy than the shape of the international balance of power.

If this is so, then the tendency to place the blame for disorder upon states which 'free-ride' on the back of the hegemon is also often overdone. While France in the 1920s and 1960s and Germany and Japan more recently have received much implicit and explicit condemnation for their policies, what is often played down is the way in which Britain in the 1920s and America since the late 1950s were able, partly because of their dominant positions, to avoid adjustment to fundamental imbalances. Which of these kinds of behaviour ought we to describe as 'mercantilistic'? The moral opprobrium that attaches to the term 'mercantilism' becomes less appropriate when it is recognised that all economic and monetary orders contain asymmetries which result in a skewed distribution of costs and benefits.

The forces tending to create hierarchy in financial structures are particularly strong and have continued to work in favour of the US and the dollar through the 1980s. The economic benefits for financial markets of using the dollar as the main key currency have been in no small part due to the relative attractions of US financial markets and the leading role of American banks in the development of new products and techniques in international finance. This has been in spite of other strong forces pushing in the other direction: the rise of a DM-centred European currency bloc, the rise of Japanese financial strength, short-sighted American policies and the continued relatively poor performance of the US economy.

These forces have had a considerable impact, even so. The tendency of the market to reward stability has been amply demonstrated in the success of the German-centred EMS until 1992. The role of the Yen is likely to increase over coming decades, given the present large imbalance between Japan's economic importance and its dependence upon America. The role of the US as the hub of East Asia's international finance, trade and politics was a product of the post-1945 settlement and the Cold War, and is already in the process of being eroded. These trends point to the emergence of an even more pronounced three-bloc structure in international trade and finance, which is likely to produce a more symmetrical (though still oligopolistic) system than at present.

We have argued that this development may result in a healthier balance between the major countries. It would also be more in keeping with the 'collective management' of international economic interdependence by a small number of actors with a strong interest in such management. Cooperation on a self-interested basis is likely to be difficult to elicit from states when asymmetries are perceived as being too great. The lack of constraint upon dominant states in highly asymmetrical systems is likely in itself to constitute a destabilising factor. A system in which costs and benefits are more equally distributed may have a better chance of maintaining cooperation over the longer term between the major states. Given the rapid changes occurring in the military relationships between the major powers, less reliance upon existing security structures to produce such cooperation would be an added benefit.

Notes

1. For a similar point, see Susan Strange, 1986, ch.2, and 1987.
2. For a clear discussion, see Lukes, 1974.
3. Polanyi, 1957. I would like to thank Stephen Gill for this clarification.
4. Zarnowitz, 1985, pp.530, 532.
5. See Gill and Law, 1988, pp.185–8.
6. See IMF, *World Economic Outlook*, October 1992, 'Asset Price Deflation and Financial Fragility'.
7. See Gill and Law, 1988; Cox, 1987.
8. For an analysis, see Frieden, 1991, and Reich, 1991.

Bibliography

Aglietta, Michel (1985) 'The creation of international liquidity', in Tsoukalis, L. (ed.) (1985) *The Political Economy of International Money*, London: RIIA/Sage, pp.171–202.
Aglietta, Michel and André Orléan (1984) *La violence de la monnaie*, 2nd edn, Paris: Presses universitaires de France.
Akao, Nobutoshi (1983) *Japan's Economic Security*, Aldershot: Gower.
Aliber, Robert (1982), 'Comments on Strange', in Lombra and Witte, pp.95–8.
Allsopp, Christopher (1987) 'The rise and fall of the dollar: A comment', *Economic Journal*, 97 (March), pp.44–8.
Allsopp, Christopher and Vijay Joshi (1985) 'The assessment: The international debt crisis', *Oxford Review of Economic Policy*, 2(1), pp.i-xxxiii.
Amin, Samir, Giovanni Arrighi, Andre Gunder Frank and Immanuel Wallerstein. (1982) *Dynamics of Global Crisis*, London: Macmillan.
Arendt, Hannah (1958) *The Human Condition*, Chicago: University of Chicago Press.
Armstrong, Philip, Andrew Glyn and John Harrison (1984) *Capitalism Since World War II*, London: Fontana.
Arrighi, Giovanni (1982) 'A crisis of hegemony', in S. Amin *et al.*, *op. cit.*, pp.55–108.
Arrow, Kenneth J. (1978) 'The future and the present in economic life', *Economic Inquiry*, 16(2), pp.157–69.
Arrow, Kenneth J. (1983) 'General economic equilibrium: Purpose, analytic techniques, collective choice', in Arrow, K.J. *Collected Papers of Kenneth J. Arrow*, vol.2, Oxford: Blackwell, pp.199–226.
Artis, M.J. and M.K. Lewis (1976) 'The demand for money in the United Kingdom 1963–1973', *Manchester School*, 44(2), pp.147–81.
Avery, William P. and David P. Rapkin (eds.). (1982) *America in a Changing World Political Economy*, New York: Longman.
Bank for International Settlements. *International Banking and Financial Market Developments*, quarterly, Basle: BIS.
Bank for International Settlements. *Annual Reports*, Basle: BIS.

Bank for International Settlements (1986) *Recent Innovations in International Banking*, prepared by a Study Group established by the Central Banks of the Group of Ten Countries, Basle: BIS.
Bank of England. *Quarterly Bulletin*, London: Bank of England.
Basle Committee on Banking Regulations and Supervisory Practices (1988) 'International convergence of capital measurement and capital standards', Basle.
Becker, William H. and Wells Jr, Samuel F., (eds.) (1984) *Economics and World Power*, New York: Columbia University Press.
Begg, David K. (1982) *The Rational Expectations Revolution in Macroeconomics*, Oxford: Philip Allan.
Bergsten, C. Fred (1975) 'The US and Germany: The imperative of economic bigemony', in his *Toward a New International Economic Order*, Lexington: D.C. Heath, pp.333–44.
Bergsten, C. Fred (1980) *The International Economic Policy of the United States: Selected Papers of C.F. Bergsten, 1977–79*, Lexington: D.C. Heath.
Bergsten, C. Fred, Robert O. Keohane and Joseph S. Nye (1975) 'International economics and international politics: A framework for analysis', in C.F. Bergsten and L.B. Krause (eds.), *World Politics and International Economics*, Washington, DC: Brookings Institution, pp.3–36.
Bernanke, Ben S. (1983) 'Nonmonetary effects of the financial crisis in the propagation of the Great Depression', *American Economic Review*, 73(3), pp.257–76.
Blaug, Mark (1985) *Economic Theory in Retrospect*, 4th edn, Cambridge: Cambridge University Press.
Blinder, Alan S. and Joseph E. Stiglitz (1983) 'Money, credit constraints, and economic activity', *American Economic Review*, Papers and Proceedings, 73(2), pp.297–302.
Bliss, Christopher (1986) 'The rise and fall of the dollar', *Oxford Review of Economic Policy*, 2(1), pp.7–24.
Block, Fred L. (1977) *The Origins of the International Economic Disorder*, Berkeley: University of California Press.
Bloomfield, Arthur I. (1959) *Monetary Policy Under the Gold Standard, 1880–1914*, New York: Federal Reserve Bank of New York.
Bloomfield, Arthur I. (1963) 'Short term capital movements under the pre-1914 gold standard', *Princeton Studies in International Finance*, 11.
Bloomfield, Arthur I. (1968a). 'Patterns of fluctuation in international investment before 1914', *Princeton Studies in International Finance*, 21.
Bloomfield, Arthur I. (1968b) 'Rules of the game of international adjustment?', in C.R. Whittlesey and J.S.G. Wilson (eds) (1968) *Essays in Money and Banking: In honour of R.S. Sayers*, Oxford: Oxford University Press, pp. 26–46.
Board of Governors of the Federal Reserve System (Guy V.G. Stevens, R.B. Berner, P.B. Clark, F. Hernández-Catá, H.J. Howe, S.Y. Kwack) (1984) *The US Economy in an Interdependent World: A Multicurrency Model* Washington, D.C.: Federal Reserve Board.
Bordo, Michael D. and Anna J. Schwartz (eds.) (1984) *A Retrospective on the Classical Gold Standard*, Chicago: University of Chicago Press.
Braudel, Fernand (1981a) *Civilization and Capitalism, 15th–18th Century: vol. I: The Structures of Everyday Life*, trans. from the French, London: Collins.

Braudel, Fernand (1981b) *Civilization and Capitalism, 15th–18th Century: vol. II: The Wheels of Commerce*, trans. from the French, London: Collins.
Brender, Anton, Pierre Gaye and Véronique Kessler (1986) *L'après-dollar: Analyse et simulation du système multi-devises*, Paris: CEPII/Economica.
Brett, E.A. (1983) *International Money and Capitalist Crisis*, London: Heinemann.
Brown, William A. (1940) *The International Gold Standard Reinterpreted, 1914–1934*, 2 vols, New York: National Bureau of Economic Research.
de Brunhoff, Suzanne (1978) *The State, Capital and Economic Policy*, trans. from the French, London: Pluto.
Bull, Hedley (1977) *The Anarchical Society*, London: Macmillan.
Bullock, Alan (1983) *Ernest Bevin: Foreign Secretary*, Oxford: Oxford University Press.
Burns, Arthur (1987) 'The anguish of central banking', 1979 Per Jacobsson Lecture, reprinted in Federal Reserve, *Quarterly Bulletin*, 73(9), pp.687–98.
Burstein, Daniel (1988) *Yen! Japan's New Financial Empire and its Threat to America*, New York: Simon & Schuster.
Cairncross, Alec (1985) *Years of Recovery: British Economic Policy, 1945–51*, London: Methuen.
Cairncross, Alec K. (1953) *Home and Foreign Investment, 1870–1913*, Cambridge: Cambridge University Press.
Calleo, David P. (1970) *The Atlantic Fantasy*, Baltimore: Johns Hopkins University Press.
Calleo, David P. (ed.) (1976) *Money and the Coming World Order*, New York: New York University Press.
Calleo, David P. (1982) *The Imperious Economy*, Cambridge, Mass: Harvard University Press.
Calleo, David P. and Benjamin M. Rowland (1973) *America and the World Political Economy*, Bloomington: Indiana University Press.
Carli, Guido (1985) 'Eurodollars: Policy analysis', in P. Savona and G. Sutija (eds.), *Eurodollars and International Banking*, Basingstoke: Macmillan, pp.139–161.
Carr, E.H. (1951) *The Twenty Years' Crisis*, 2nd edn, London: Macmillan.
Carron, Andrew S. (1982) 'Financial crises: Recent experience in US and international markets', *Brookings Papers on Economic Activity*, 2, pp.395–418.
Carus-Wilson, E.M. (ed.) (1964) *Essays in Economic History*, vol.I, London: Arnold.
Cass, David and Karl Shell (1983) 'Do sunspots matter?', *Journal of Political Economy*, 91(2), pp.193–227.
Cassel, Gustav (1921) *The World's Monetary Problems*, London: Constable.
Cassel, Gustav (1928) *Post-War Monetary Stabilization*, Ithaca: Columbia University Press.
de Cecco, Marcello (1974) *Money and Empire: The International Gold Standard, 1890–1914*, Oxford: Blackwell.
de Cecco, Marcello (1984) 'Modes of financial development: American banking dynamics and world financial crises', *European University Institute Working Papers*, 84.
Checkland, S.G. (1964) *The Rise of Industrial Society in England, 1815–85*, London: Longman.

Cipolla, Carlo M. (1977) *The Fontana Economic History of Europe, Vol. 5: The Twentieth Century – Part II*, Glasgow: Fontana.
Clark, Colin (1957) *The Conditions of Economic Progress*, 2nd edn, London: Macmillan.
Clarke, Stephen V.O. (1967) *Central Bank Cooperation, 1924–31*, New York: Federal Reserve Bank of New York.
Clarke, Stephen V.O. (1973) 'The reconstruction of the international monetary system: The attempts of 1922 and 1933', *Princeton Studies in International Finance*, 33 (November).
Cline, William R. (1983) 'International debt and the stability of the world economy', *Policy Analyses in International Economics*, 4 (September), Washington, DC: Institute for International Economics.
Cohen, Benjamin J. (1971) *The Future of Sterling as an International Currency*, London: Macmillan.
Cohen, Benjamin J. (1977) *Organizing the World's Money*, New York: Basic Books.
Committee on Finance and Industry (1931) *Report*, (Macmillan Report), Cmd 3897, London: HMSO.
Commonwealth Group of Experts (1984) *The Debt Crisis and the World Economy*, London: Commonwealth Secretariat.
Congdon, Tim (1988) *The Debt Threat*, Oxford: Blackwell.
Coombs, Charles A. (1976) *The Arena of International Finance*, New York: Wiley.
Cooper, Richard N. (1965) 'The interest equalization tax: An experiment in the separation of financial markets', *Finanz Archiv N.F.*, 24 (December), pp.447–71.
Cooper, Richard N. (1968) *The Economics of Interdependence: Economic Policy in the Atlantic Community*, New York: Council on Foreign Relations/McGraw-Hill.
Cooper, Richard N. (1986) *Economic Policy in an Interdependent World*, Cambridge, Mass: MIT Press.
Cooper, Richard N. (1987) *The International Monetary System*, Cambridge, Mass: MIT Press.
Cooper, Richard N., Macedo, J. de, Kenen, P.B. and Van Ypersele, J. (eds.) (1982) *The International Monetary System Under Flexible Exchange Rates*, Cambridge, Mass: Ballinger.
Corden, W. Max (1985) *Inflation, Exchange Rates and the World Economy*, 3rd edn, Oxford: Oxford University Press.
Corden, W. Max (1978) 'Expansion of the world economy and the duties of surplus countries', *The World Economy*, 1(2), pp.121–34.
Council of Economic Advisers, *Economic Report of the President*, Washington, DC: US Government Printing Office, various issues.
Cox, Robert W. (1981) 'Social forces, states and world orders: Beyond international relations theory', *Journal of International Studies, Millennium*, 10(2), pp.126–55.
Dam, Kenneth W. (1982) *The Rules of the Game*, Chicago: University of Chicago Press.
Davidson, Paul (1978) *Money and the Real World*, 2nd edn, London: Macmillan.
Denison, Edward F. (1985) *Trends in American Economic Growth, 1929–82*, Washington, DC: Brookings Institution.

Desai, Meghnad (1981) *Testing Monetarism*, London: Pinter.
Despres, Emile, Charles P. Kindleberger and Walter S. Salant (1966) 'The dollar and world liquidity – A minority view', *The Economist*, 5 (February), pp.526–9.
Destler, Ian M. and H. Mitsuyu (1982) 'Locomotives on different tracks 1977–9', in Ian M. Destler and Hideo Sato (eds.), *Coping With US–Japanese Economic Conflicts*, Lexington: D.C. Heath, pp.243–69.
Deutsche Bundesbank, *Annual Reports*, Frankfurt am Main: Deutsche Bundesbank.
Deutsche Bundesbank, *Monthly Reports*, Frankfurt am Main: Deutsche Bundesbank.
Deutsche Bundesbank, *Auszüge aus Presseartikeln*, Frankfurt am Main: Deutsche Bundesbank.
Dickson, P.G.M. (1967) *The Financial Revolution in England: A Study in the Development of Public Credit, 1688–1756*, London: St Martin.
Dornbusch, Rudiger (1976) 'Expectations and exchange rate dynamics', *Journal of Political Economy*, 84(6), pp.1161–76.
Dornbusch, Rudiger (1983) 'Flexible exchange rates and interdependence', *IMF Staff Papers*, 30(1), pp.3–30.
Dornbusch, Rudiger (1986) 'Flexible exchange rates and excess capital mobility', *Brookings Papers on Economic Activity*, 1, pp.209–26.
Dornbusch, Rudiger (1987) 'Exchange rate economics: 1986', *Economic Journal*, 97 (March), pp.1–18.
Dornbusch, Rudiger (1988) 'Doubts about the McKinnon standard', *Journal of Economic Perspectives*, 2(1), pp.105–12.
Dornbusch, Rudiger and Frenkel, Jacob A. (1984) 'The gold standard and the Bank of England in the crisis of 1947', in M.D. Bordo and A.J. Schwartz (eds.), *op. cit.*, pp.233–64.
Drucker, Peter F. (1986) 'The changed world economy', *Foreign Affairs*, 64(4), pp.768–91.
Dutton, John (1984) 'The Bank of England and the rules of the game under the international gold standard: New evidence', in M.D. Bordo and A.J. Schwartz (eds.), *op. cit.*, pp.173–95.
Eaton, Jonathan, Mark Gersovitz and Joseph E. Stiglitz (1986) 'The pure theory of country risk', *European Economic Review*, 30(3), pp.481–513.
Economic Planning Agency of Japan (1984) *Economic Survey of Japan, 1983–4*, Tokyo: EPA.
Eichengreen, Barry (ed.) (1985) *The Gold Standard in Theory and History*, London: Methuen.
Eichengreen, Barry (1987a) 'Hegemonic stability theories of the international monetary system', *National Bureau of Economic Research Working Papers*, 2193 (March).
Eichengreen, Barry (1987b) 'The gold-exchange standard and the Great Depression', *National Bureau of Economic Research Working Paper*, 2198 (March).
Emminger, Otmar (1979) 'The exchange rate as an instrument of policy', *Lloyds Bank Review*, 133 (July), pp.1–22.
Emmott, Bill (1989) *The Sun Also Sets*, London: Simon & Schuster.
Ethier, W.J. and R.C. Marston (eds.) (1985) 'International financial markets and capital movements: A symposium in honour of Arthur I. Bloomfield', *Princeton Essays in International Finance*, 157 (September).

Federal Reserve Bank of New York, *Quarterly Review*, New York: FRBNY.
Feinstein, C.H. (1972) *National Income, Expenditure and Output of the United Kingdom, 1855-1965*, Cambridge: Cambridge University Press.
Fisher, Irving (1933) 'The debt-deflation theory of great depressions', *Econometrica*, 1, pp.337-57.
Flora, Peter (ed.) (1983) *State, Economy and Society in Western Europe, 1815-1975*, vol.I, Frankfurt: Campus Verlag.
Floud, Roderick and Donald McCloskey (eds.) (1981) *The Economic History of Britain, Volume 2: 1860 to the 1970s*, Cambridge: Cambridge University Press.
Floyd, John (1985) *World Monetary Equilibrium*, London: Philip Allan.
Foreign Relations of the United States (FRUS) (1974-7), Washington, DC: Department of State.
Frankel, Jeffrey A. (1984) 'The yen-dollar agreement: Liberalizing Japanese capital markets', *Policy Analyses in International Economics*, 9 (December), Institute for International Economics, Washington, DC.
Frankel, Jeffrey A. (1991) 'Is a Yen bloc forming in East Asia?', in Richard O'Brien (ed.), *Finance and the International Economy: 5*, Oxford: Oxford University Press/Amex Bank Review, pp.4-20.
Frenkel, Jacob A. and Harry G. Johnson (eds.) (1976a) *The Monetary Approach to the Balance of Payments*, London: Allen and Unwin.
Frenkel, Jacob A. and Harry G. Johnson (1976b) 'The monetary approach to the balance of payments: Essential concepts and historical origins', in J.A. Frenkel and H.G. Johnson (eds.), 1976a, pp.21-45.
Frenkel, Jacob A. and Michael L. Mussa (1980) 'The efficiency of foreign exchange markets and measures of turbulence', *American Economic Review*, Papers and Proceedings, 70(2), pp.374-81.
Frieden, Jeffry A. (1987) *Banking on the World: The Politics of American International Finance*, New York: Harper & Row.
Frieden, Jeffry A. (1989) 'Capital politics: creditors and the international political economy', *Journal of Public Policy*, 8, pp.265-86.
Frieden, Jeffry A. (1991) 'Invested interest: the politics of national economic policies in a world of global finance', *International Organization*, 45(4), Autumn, pp.425-51.
Friedman, Benjamin M. (1983) 'The roles of money and credit in macroeconomic analysis', in James Tobin (ed.), *Macroeconomics, Prices and Quantities*, Oxford: Blackwell, pp.161-99.
Friedman, Milton (1953) 'The case for flexible exchange rates', in Friedman, M., *Essays in Positive Economics*, Chicago: University of Chicago Press.
Friedman, Milton (1956) *Studies in the Quantity Theory of Money*, Chicago: University of Chicago Press.
Friedman, Milton (1960) *A Program for Monetary Stability*, New York: Fordham University Press.
Friedman, Milton (1969) *The Optimum Quantity of Money and Other Essays*, London: Macmillan.
Friedman, Milton (1982) 'Comments on the critics', *Journal of Political Economy*, 80(5), pp.906-50.
Friedman, Milton and Anna J. Schwartz (1963) *A Monetary History of the United States, 1867-1960*, Princeton: Princeton University Press.
Friedman, Milton and Anna J. Schwartz (1982) *Monetary Trends in the United States and the United Kingdom*, Chicago: University of Chicago Press.

Fukao, Mitsuhiro and Masahuru Hanazaki (1987) 'Internationalization of financial markets and the allocation of capital', *OECD Economic Studies*, 8 (Spring), pp.35–92.
Funabashi, Yoichi (1988) *Managing the Dollar: From the Plaza to the Louvre*, Washington, DC: Institute for International Economics.
Gaddis, John L. (1982) *Strategies of Containment*, New York: Oxford University Press.
Gale, Douglas W. (1982) *Money: In Equilibrium*, Cambridge: Cambridge University Press.
Gale, Douglas W. (1983) *Money: In Disequilibrium*, Cambridge: Cambridge University Press.
Gamble, Andrew (1981) *An Introduction to Modern Social and Political Thought*, London: Macmillan.
Garavoglia, Guido (1984) 'From Rambouillet to Williamsburg: An historical assessment', in C. Merlini (ed.) (1984), *Economic Summits and Western Decision Making*, London: Croom Helm, pp.1–42.
Gardner, Richard N. (1980) *Sterling–Dollar Diplomacy in Current Perspective*, New York: Columbia University Press.
Gardner, Richard N. (1985) 'Sterling–dollar diplomacy in current perspective', Paper presented to a conference on Finance, Trade and Development at Ditchley Park, April 12–14.
Giavazzi, Francesco and Alberto Giovannini (1989) *Limiting Exchange Rate Flexibility: The European Monetary System*, Cambridge, Mass: MIT Press.
Gilbert, Martin (1976) *Winston S. Churchill, 1874–1965, vol. 5: 1922–1939*, London: Heinemann.
Gilbert, Milton (1980) *Quest for World Monetary Order* (ed. P. Oppenheimer and M. Dealtry), New York: Wiley.
Gilpin, Robert (1972) 'The politics of transnational economic relations', in R.O. Keohane and J.S. Nye (eds.) (1972) *Transnational Relations and World Politics*, Cambridge, Mass: Harvard University Press, pp.48–69.
Gilpin, Robert (1975) *US Power and the Multinational Corporation*, New York: Basic Books.
Gilpin, Robert (1981) *War and Change in World Politics*, New York: Cambridge University Press.
Gilpin, Robert (1987) *The Political Economy of International Relations*, Princeton: Princeton University Press.
Gold, Joseph (1965) *Maintenance of the Gold Value of the Fund's Assets*, Washington, DC: IMF.
Golembe, Carter H. and David S. Holland (1990) 'Banking and securities', in Gary Clyde Hufbauer (ed.), *Europe 1992: An American Perspective*, Washington, DC: Brookings Institution.
Goodhart, Charles A.E. (1972) *The Business of Banking*, London: Weidenfeld and Nicolson.
Goodhart, Charles A.E. (1984) *Monetary Theory and Practice: The UK Experience*, London: Macmillan.
Goodhart, Charles A.E. (1986a) 'Why do we need a central bank?', Banca d'Italia, *Temi di discussione*, 57 (January).
Goodhart, Charles A.E. (1986b) 'Financial innovation and monetary control', *Oxford Review of Economic Policy*, 2(4), pp.79–102.
Goodhart, Charles A.E. (1987) 'Exchange rate economics 1986: A comment', *Economic Journal*, 97 (March), pp.19–22.

Gordon, R.J. (ed.) (1974) *Milton Friedman's Monetary Framework: A Debate with his Critics*, Chicago: University of Chicago Press.
Gowa, Joanne (1983) *Closing the Gold Window: Domestic Politics and the End of Bretton Woods*, Ithaca: Cornell University Press.
Gowa, Joanne (1984) 'Hegemons, IOs and markets: The case of the substitution account', *International Organization*, 38(4), pp.661–84.
Graham, Edward M. and Paul R. Krugman (1991) *Foreign Direct Investment in the United States*, Washington, DC: Institute for International Economics, 2nd edn.
Grandmont, Jean-Michel (1983) *Money and Value*, Cambridge: Cambridge University Press.
Grandmont, Jean-Michel and Pierre Malgrange (1986) 'Nonlinear economic dynamics: Introduction', *Journal of Economic Theory*, 40(1), pp. 3–12.
Gros, Daniel and Niels Thygesen (1992) *European Monetary Integration*, New York: St. Martin's Press.
Group of Ten Deputies (1985) *Report on the Functioning of the International Monetary System*, in *IMF Survey* (Supplement), Washington, DC: IMF.
Gunder Frank, André (1983) *The European Challenge*, Nottingham: Spokesman.
Gurley, J.G. and E.S. Shaw (1960) *Money in a Theory of Finance*, Washington: Brookings Institution.
Guth, Wilfried (1985) 'International liquidity reconsidered', *Kredit und Kapital*, 18(1), pp.1–26.
Guttentag, Jack M. and Richard J. Herring (1983) 'The lender of last resort function in an international context', *Princeton Essays in International Finance*, 151 (May).
Guttentag, Jack M. and Richard J. Herring (1985) *The Current Crisis in International Lending*, Washington, DC: Brookings Institution.
Haberer, Jean-Yves (1988) 'Le découplage de la finance et de l'economie: Contribution à l'evaluation des enjeux Européens dans la révolution du système financier international', Commission of the European Communities, Directorate-General for Economic and Financial Affairs, *Economic Papers*, 64 (May).
Haberler, Gottfried (1964) *Prosperity and Depression*, 5th edn, London: Allen and Unwin.
Hahn, Frank (1984) *Equilibrium and Macroeconomics*, Oxford: Blackwell.
Hahn, Frank (1977) 'Keynesian economics and general equilibrium theory: Reflections on some current debates', in G.C. Harcourt (ed.), *The Microeconomic Foundations of Macroeconomics*, London: Macmillan, pp.25–40.
Hamilton, James D. (1987) 'Monetary factors in the Great Depression', *Journal of Monetary Economics*, 19(2), pp.145–69.
Harris, Kenneth (1982) *Attlee*, London: Weidenfeld and Nicolson.
Harrod, Roy F. (1951) *The Life of John Maynard Keynes*, London: Macmillan.
Harvey, David (1982) *The Limits of Capital*, Oxford: Blackwell.
Hawtrey, Ralph G. (1962) [1932], *The Art of Central Banking*, London: Cass.
Hawtrey, Ralph G. (1938) *A Century of Bank Rate*, London: Longmans, Green.
Hawtrey, Ralph G. (1947) *The Gold Standard in Theory and Practice*, 5th edn, London: Longmans, Green.

von Hayek, Friedrich A. (1976) 'Denationalization of money', *Hobart Paper*, 70, London: Institute of International Affairs.
Hayes, Alfred (1974) 'The international monetary system: Retrospect and prospect', Federal Reserve Bank of New York, *Monthly Review*, 56(12).
Helding, Frederick (1979) 'The case for a world central bank', *Euromoney* (September), pp.60–3.
Helleiner, Eric (1992) 'States and the future of global finance', *Review of International Studies*, 18, pp.31–49.
Hendry, David F. (1985) 'Monetary economic myth and econometric reality', *Oxford Review of Economic Policy*, 1(1), pp.72–84.
Hicks, John (1937) 'Mr. Keynes and the "classics": A suggested interpretation', *Econometrica*, 5(2), pp.147–59.
Hicks, John (1967) *Critical Essays in Monetary Theory*, Oxford: Oxford University Press.
Hicks, John (1969) *A Theory of Economic History*, Oxford: Oxford University Press.
Hicks, John (1977) *Economic Perspectives*, Oxford: Oxford University Press.
Hicks, John (1982) *Money, Interest and Wages*, Oxford: Blackwell.
Hinshaw, Randall (ed.) (1967) *Monetary Reform and the Price of Gold*, Baltimore: Johns Hopkins University Press.
Hirsch, Fred and Michael W. Doyle (1977) 'Politicization in the world economy: Necessary conditions for an international economic order', in Fred Hirsch and E.L. Morse, *Alternatives to Monetary Disorder*, New York: Council on Foreign Relations/McGraw-Hill, pp.11–64.
Hirsch, Fred and Oppenheimer, Peter (1977) 'The trial of managed money: Currency, credit and prices, 1920–1970', in C.M. Cipolla, (1977) *op. cit.*, pp.603–97.
Hobbes, Thomas (ed.) (1651) *Leviathan* (ed. C.B. Macpherson, 1968), Harmondsworth: Penguin.
Hobsbawm, Eric J. (1979) *The Age of Capital 1848–1875*, New York: Mentor.
Hogan, Michael J. (1987) *The Marshall Plan: America, Britain and the Reconstruction of Western Europe, 1947–1952*, New York: Cambridge University Press.
Hoover, Kevin D. (1984) 'Two types of monetarism', *Journal of Economic Literature*, 19(2), pp.58–76.
Horii, Akinari (1986) 'The evolution of reserve currency diversification', *BIS Economic Papers*, 19 (December).
Horsefield, J. Keith (1969) *The International Monetary Fund, 1945–1965, vol.I*, Washington, DC: IMF.
Horvitz, Paul M. (1979) *Monetary Policy and the Financial System*, 4th edn, Englewood Cliffs: Prentice-Hall.
Howard, Michael (1972) *The Continental Commitment*, London: Temple Smith.
Howard, Michael (1981) *War and the Liberal Conscience*, Oxford: Oxford University Press.
Howson, Susan K. (1975) *Domestic Monetary Management in Britain, 1919–38*, Cambridge: Cambridge University Press.
International Monetary Fund (1982) *International Financial Statistics: Supplement No.4 on Trade Statistics*, Washington, DC: IMF.
International Monetary Fund (1983) *International Financial Statistics: Supplement No.6 on International Reserves*, Washington, DC: IMF.

International Monetary Fund (1984) *International Financial Statistics: Supplement No.8 on Output Statistics*, Washington, DC: IMF.
International Monetary Fund (various years) *Government Finance Statistics*, Washington, DC: IMF, yearbooks and monthly editions.
International Monetary Fund (1988) *International Financial Statistics: Supplement No.15 on Trade Statistics*, Washington, DC: IMF.
International Monetary Fund, *International Financial Statistics*, Washington, DC: IMF, yearbooks and monthly editions.
International Monetary Fund, *Annual Reports*, Washington, DC: IMF.
International Monetary Fund, *Summary Proceedings of the Annual General Meetings of the Board of Governors*, Washington, DC: IMF.
Julius, DeAnne (1990) *Global Companies and Public Policy*, London: Pinter/ RIIA.
Kapstein, Ethan B. (1991) 'Supervising international banks: origins and implications of the Basle Accord', *Princeton Essays in International Finance*, 185, December.
Katzenstein, Peter J. (ed.) (1978) *Between Power and Plenty: Foreign Economic Policies of Advanced Industrial States*, Madison: University of Wisconsin Press.
Kaufman, Henry (1988) 'The world needs a good cop, or a good panic', *Euromoney* (September), pp.115–20.
Kennan, George F. (1967) *Memoirs, 1925–50*, New York: Pantheon.
Kennedy, Paul (1981) *The Realities Behind Diplomacy*, Glasgow: Fontana.
Kennedy, Paul (1988) *The Rise and Fall of the Great Powers: Economic Change and Military Conflict from 1500 to 2000*, London: Unwin Hyman.
Kennedy, Paul (1990) 'Fin-de-Siècle America', *New York Review of Books*, 37(11), pp.31–40.
Keohane, Robert O. (1979) 'US foreign economic policy toward other advanced capitalist states', in K.A. Oye, R.J. Lieber and D. Rothchild (1979) *Eagle Entangled: US Foreign Policy in a Complex World*, New York: Longman, pp.91–122.
Keohane, Robert O. (1980) 'The theory of hegemonic stability and changes in international economic regimes, 1967–77', in Ole R. Holsti, R.M. Silverson and A.L. George, *Change in the International System*, Boulder: Westview Press.
Keohane, Robert O. (1982) 'Inflation and the decline of American power', in R.E. Lombra and W.E. Witte (eds.), *Political Economy of International and Domestic Monetary Relations*, Ames: Iowa State University Press.
Keohane, Robert O. (1984) *After Hegemony*, Princeton: Princeton University Press.
Keohane, Robert O. and Joseph S. Nye (eds.) (1972) *Transnational Relations and World Politices*, Cambridge, Mass: Harvard University Press.
Keohane, Robert O. and Joseph S. Nye (1973) 'World politics and the international economic system', in C. Fred Bergsten (ed.) (1973) *The Future of the International Economic Order: An Agenda for Research*, Lexington, Mass: DC Heath, pp.115–79.
Keohane, Robert O. and Joseph S. Nye (1977) *Power and Interdependence: World Politics in Transition*, Boston: Little, Brown.
Keynes, John Maynard (1919) *The Economic Consequences of the Peace*, London: Macmillan.
Keynes, John Maynard (1930) *A Treatise on Money*, 2 vols, London: Macmillan.

Keynes, John Maynard (1936) *The General Theory of Employment, Interest and Money*, London: Macmillan.
Keynes, John Maynard (1971–9) *The Collected Writings of John Maynard Keynes* [*CW*], London: Macmillan, for the Royal Economic Society.
Kindleberger, Charles P. (1956) *The Terms of Trade: A European Case Study*, New York: Wiley/MIT Press.
Kindleberger, Charles P. (1969) *American Business Abroad*, New Haven: Yale University Press.
Kindleberger, Charles P. (1970) *Power and Money*, London: Macmillan.
Kindleberger, Charles P. (1973) *The World in Depression, 1929–39*, Berkeley: University of California Press.
Kindleberger, Charles P. (1974) 'The formation of financial centers: A study in comparative economic history', *Princeton Studies in International Finance*, 3.
Kindleberger, Charles P. (1976) 'Systems of international economic organization', in D.P. Calleo (ed.) (1976) *op. cit.*, pp.15–40.
Kindleberger, Charles P. (1978a) *Manias, Panics and Crashes: A History of Financial Crises*, New York: Basic Books.
Kindleberger, Charles P. (1978b) 'The rise of free trade', in Kindleberger, C.P. (1978b), *Economic Response: Comparative Studies in Trade, Finance and Growth*, Cambridge, Mass.: Harvard University Press, pp.39–65.
Kindleberger, Charles P. (1981) *International Money: A Collection of Essays*, London: Allen and Unwin.
Kindleberger, Charles P. (1984) *A Financial History of Western Europe*, London: Allen and Unwin.
Kindleberger, Charles P. (1985a) 'The functioning of financial centers: Britain in the nineteenth century, the United States since 1945', in W.J. Ethier and R.C. Marston (eds.) (1985) *op. cit.*, pp.7–18.
Kindleberger, Charles P. (1985b) *Keynesianism vs. Monetarism and Other Essays in Financial History*, London: Allen and Unwin.
Kindleberger, Charles P. (1985c) 'The cyclical pattern of long-term lending', in C.P. Kindleberger (1985b) *op. cit.*, pp.141–54.
Kindleberger, Charles P. (1985d) 'The international causes and consequences of the great crash', in C.P. Kindleberger, (1985b) *op. cit.*, pp.267–73.
Kindleberger, Charles P. (1986) 'International public goods without international government', *American Economic Review*, 76(1), pp.1–13.
Kindleberger, Charles P. and Jean-Pierre Laffargue (eds.) (1982) *Financial Crises*, Cambridge: Cambridge University Press.
King, Kenneth (1982) 'US monetary policy and European responses in the 1980s', *Chatham House Papers*, 16.
Kitchin, Joseph (1931) 'Gold production', in *Royal Institute of International Afffairs* (1931), pp.58–68.
Klein, John J. (1978) *Money and the Economy*, 4th edn, New York: Harcourt Brace Jovanovich.
Knight, Frank H. (1921) *Risk, Uncertainty and Profit*, Boston: Houghton-Mifflin.
Kooker, Judith L. (1976) 'French financial diplomacy: The interwar years', in B.M. Rowland (ed.) (1976) *Balance of Power or Hegemony: The Interwar Monetary System*, New York: New York University Press, pp.83–145.
Koromzay, Val, John Llewellyn and Stephen Potter (1987) 'The rise and fall

of the dollar: Some explanations, consequences and lessons', *Economic Journal*, 97 (March), pp.23–43.
Krasner, Stephen D. (1976) 'State power and the structure of international trade', *World Politics*, 28(3), pp.317–43.
Krasner, Stephen D. (1982) 'American policy and global economic stability', in W.P. Avery and D.P. Rapkin (eds.) (1982) *op. cit.*, pp.29–48.
Kuznets, Simon (1966) *Modern Economic Growth*, New Haven: Yale University Press.
Laidler, David E.W. (1969) *The Demand for Money: Theories and Evidence*, Scranton: International Textbook Co.
Laidler, David E.W. (1982) *Monetarist Perspectives*, Oxford: Blackwell.
Lamfalussy, Alexandre (1981) 'Rules vs discretion: An essay on monetary policy in an inflationary Environment', *BIS Economic Papers*, 3 (April).
Lamfalussy, Alexandre (1985) 'The changing environment of central bank policy', *American Economic Review*, Papers and Proceedings, 75(2), pp.409–13.
Lamfalussy, Alexandre (1986) 'Is change our ally?', *The Banker* (September), pp.19–27.
Larsen, Flemming, John Llewellyn and Stephen Potter (1983) 'International economic linkages', *OECD Economic Studies*, 1 (Autumn), pp.43–92.
de Lattre, André (1985) 'Floating, uncertainty and the real sector', in L. Tsoukalis (ed.) (1985) *The Political Economy of International Money*, London: RIIA/Sage, pp.71–102.
League of Nations (Ragnar Nurkse) (1944) *International Currency Experience* Princeton, NJ: League of Nations.
Leffler, Melvyn P. (1979) *The Elusive Quest: America's Pursuit of European Stability and French Security, 1919–33*, Berkeley: University of North Carolina Press.
Leffler, Melvyn P. (1984) '1921–32 Expansionist impulses and domestic constraints', in W.H. Becker and S.F. Wells Jr. (eds.) (1984) *op. cit.*
Leontif, Wassily (1966) [1936] 'The fundamental assumption of Mr Keynes' monetary theory of unemployment', reprinted in Wassily Leontif, *Essays in Economics*, New York: Oxford University Press, vol. I, pp.87–92.
Lewis, W. Arthur (1978) *Growth and Fluctuations, 1870–1913*, London: Allen and Unwin.
Lindert, Peter (1969) 'Key currencies and gold, 1900–1913, *Princeton Essays in International Finance*, 24 (August).
Linklater, Andrew (1982) *Men and citizens in the theory of international relations*, London: Macmillan.
Lipietz, Alain (1985) *The Enchanted World*, trans. from the French, London: Verso.
Lipson, Charles (1985) *Standing Guard: Protecting Foreign Capital in the Nineteenth and Twentieth Centuries*, Berkeley: University of California Press.
Llewellyn, David T. (1985) 'The role of international banking', in L. Tsoukalis (ed.) (1985) *op. cit.*, pp.203–32.
Locke, John (1960) [1698] *op. cit., Two Treatises of Government*, Cambridge: Cambridge University Press.
Lombra, R.E. and W.E. Witte (ed.) (1982) *Political Economy of International and Domestic Monetary Relations*, Ames: Iowa State University Press.
Lucas, Robert E. (1977) 'Understanding business cycles', in Karl Brunner and

Allan H. Meltzer (eds.), *Stabilization of the Domestic and International Economy*, Carnegie-Rochester Conference Series on Public Policy, vol.5, Amsterdam: North Holland, pp.7–30.

Lucas, Robert E. (1981) 'Tobin and monetarism: A review article', *Journal of Economic Literature*, 19(2), pp.558–67.

Ludlow, Peter (1982) *The Making of the European Monetary System*, London: Butterworths.

Lukes, Steven (1974) *Power: A Radical View*, London: Macmillan.

Lundberg, Eric (1968) *Instability and Economic Growth*, New Haven: Yale University Press.

Maddison, Angus (1977) 'Economic policy and performance in Europe, 1913–1970', in C.M. Cipolla (ed.) (1977) *op. cit.*, pp.442–508.

Maddison, Angus (1982) *Phases of Capitalist Development*, Oxford: Oxford University Press.

Maddison, Angus (1987) 'Growth and slowdown in advanced capitalist economies: Techniques of quantitative assessment', *Journal of Economic Literature*, 25 (June), pp.649–98.

Maier, Charles S. (1975) *Recasting Bourgeois Europe*, Princeton: Princeton University Press.

Maizels, A. (1963) *Industrial Growth and World Trade*, Cambridge: Cambridge University Press.

Mandel, Ernest (1975) *Late Capitalism*, London: Verso.

Mandel, Ernest (1980) *Long Waves of Capitalist Development*, Cambridge: Cambridge University Press.

Mandel, Ernest (1985) *La Crise*, Paris: Flammarion.

Marks, Sally (1976) *The Illusion of Peace: International Relations in Europe, 1918–1933*, London: St Martins Press.

Marquardt, Jeffrey C. (1987) 'Financial market supervision: Some conceptual issues', *BIS Economic Papers*, 19 (May).

Marris, Steven (1984) 'Managing the world economy: Will we ever learn?', *Princeton Essays in International Finance*, 155 (October).

Marris, Stephen (1985) 'Deficits and the dollar: The world economy at risk', *Policy Analyses in International Economics*, 14 (December), Institute for International Economics, Washington, DC.

Marx, Karl (1976) [1867] *Capital*, vol.I, Harmondsworth: Penguin.

Marx, Karl and Friedrich Engels (1978) [1848] *The Manifesto of the Communist Party*, in Robert C. Tucker (ed.), *The Marx-Engels Reader*, 2nd edn, New York: W.W. Norton, pp.469–500.

Mathias, Peter (1969) *The First Industrial Nation*, London: Methuen.

McClam, Warren D. (1982) 'Financial fragility and instability: monetary authorities as borrowers and lenders of last resort', in C.P. Kindleberger and J.P. Laffargue (eds.) (1982) pp.256–91.

McCloskey, Donald N. and J. Richard Zecher. (1976) 'How the gold standard worked, 1880–1913', in J.A. Frenkel and H.G. Johnson (eds.) (1976a), pp.357–85.

McKinnon, Ronald I. (1979) *Money in International Exchange: The Convertible Currency System*, New York: Oxford University Press.

McKinnon, Ronald I. (1984) 'An international standard for monetary stabilization', *Policy Analyses in International Economics*, 8 (March), Institute for International Economics, Washington, DC.

McKinnon, Ronald I. (1988) 'Monetary and exchange rate policies for

international financial stability: A proposal', *Journal of Economic Perspectives*, 2(1), pp.83–103.
Meier, Gerald M. (1980) *International Economics: Theory of Policy*, New York: Oxford University Press.
Meier, Gerald M. (1982) *Problems of a World Monetary Order*, 2nd edn, New York: Oxford University Press.
de Menil, George and Anthony Solomon (1983) *Economic Summitry*, Washington, DC: Council on Foreign Relations.
Merlini, Cesare (ed.) (1984) *Economic Summits and Western Decision Making*, London: Croom Helm.
Micossi, S., and T. Padoa-Schioppa (1984) 'Short-term interest rate linkages between the US and Europe', Banca d'Italia, *Temi di Discussione*, 33 (August).
Mill, John Stuart (1940) [1848] *Principles of Political Economy*, 7th edn, London: Longmans.
Milward, Alan S. (1977) *War, Economy and Society, 1939–45*, London: Allen Lane.
Milward, Alan S. (1984) *The Reconstruction of Western Europe, 1945–51*, London: Methuen.
Minsky, Hyman P. (1979) 'Financial interrelations, the balance of payments and the dollar-crisis', in J.D. Aronson (ed.), *Debt and the Less Developed Countries*, Boulder: Westview Press, pp.103–22.
Minsky, Hyman P. (1982) *Inflation, Recession and Economic Policy*, Brighton: Wheatsheaf.
Minsky, Hyman P. (1986) *Stabilizing an Unstable Economy*, New Haven: Yale University Press.
Mishkin, Frederic S. (1982) 'Does anticipated monetary policy matter? An econometric investigation', *Journal of Political Economy*, 90(1), pp.22–51.
Mitchell, B.R. (1975) *European Historical Statistics*, London: Macmillan.
Mitchell, B.R. and P. Deane. (1962) *Abstract of British Historical Statistics*, Cambridge: Cambridge University Press.
Modelski, George (1978) 'The long cycle of global politics and the nation state', *Comparative Studies in Society and History*, 20(2), pp.214–38.
Modelski, George (1983) 'Long cycles of world leadership', in W.R. Thompson (ed.), *Contending Approaches to World System Analysis*, Beverley Hills: Sage, pp.115–39.
Modigliani, Franco (1944) 'Liquidity preference and the theory of interest and money', *Econometrica*, 12(1), pp.45–88.
Moggridge, D.E. (1969) *The Return to Gold, 1925*, Cambridge: Cambridge University Press.
Moggridge, D.E. (1972) *British Monetary Policy, 1924–31*, Cambridge: Cambridge University Press.
Moggridge, D.E. (1982) 'Policy in the crises of 1920 and 1929', in C.P. Kindleberger and J.-P. Laffargue (eds.) (1982), pp.171–87.
Moore, Basil (1983) 'Unpacking the post-Keynesian black box: Bank lending and the money supply', *Journal of Post-Keynesian Economics*, 5(4), pp.537–56.
Moore, Geoffrey H. (1983) *Business Cycles, Inflation and Forecasting*, 2nd edn, Cambridge, Mass: NBER/Ballinger.
Moreau, Emile (1954) *Souvenirs d'un Gouverneur de la Banque de France*, Paris: Génin.

Morgan Guaranty Trust Company, *World Financial Markets*, New York: MGT.
Morgenstern, Oskar (1959) *International Financial Transactions and Business Cycles*, Princeton: Princeton University Press.
Morita, Akio and Shintaro Ishihara (1990) *The Japan That Can Say 'No'*, Washington, DC: excerpted from the *Congressional Record*, Jefferson Educational Foundation.
Morse, Edward L. (1976) *Modernization and the Transformation of International Relations*, New York: Free Press.
Mundell, Robert A. (1968) *International Economics*, New York: Macmillan.
Mundell, Robert A. (1976) 'The international distribution of money', in J.A. Frenkel and H.G. Johnson (eds.) (1976a), pp.92–108.
Murphy, R. Taggart (1989) 'Power without purpose: The crisis of Japan's global financial dominance', *Harvard Business Review*, (March–April), pp.71–83.
Muth, John (1961) 'Rational expectations and the theory of price movements', *Econometrica*, 29(3), pp.315–35.
Myrdal, Gunnar (1960) *Beyond the Welfare State*, New Haven: Yale University Press.
National Advisory Council on International Monetary and Financial Policies, *Annual Reports*, Washington, D.C: US Government Printing Office.
National Industrial Conference Board (1929) *The International Financial Position of the United States*, New York: NICB.
Niehans, Jürg (1978) *The Theory of Money*, London: Johns Hopkins University Press.
Nomura Research Institute (1986) *The World Economy and Financial Markets in 1995: Japan's Role and Challenges*, Tokyo: NRI.
Nutter, G. Warren (1978) *Growth of Government in the West*, Washington, DC: American Enterprise Institute.
O'Brien, Richard (ed.) (1991) *Finance and the International Economy: 5*, Oxford: Oxford University Press/Amex Bank Review.
Odell, Peter R. (1983) *Oil and World Power*, 7th edn, Harmondsworth: Penguin.
OECD Secretary-General (1979) *Activities of the OECD in 1978*, Paris: OECD.
OECD (1985) *Exchange Rate Management and the Conduct of Monetary Policy*, Paris: OECD.
OECD (1987a) *OECD Leading Indicators and Business Cycles in Member Countries, 1960–85, Sources and Methods 39* (January), Paris: OECD.
OECD (1987b) 'Total factor productivity', OECD *Economic Outlook*, 42 (December), pp.39–48.
OECD (1990a) *Main Economic Indicators: Historical Statistics, 1969–88*, Paris: OECD.
OECD (1990b) *Historical Statistics, 1960–88*, Paris: OECD.
OECD *Financial Market Trends*, various issues, Paris: OECD.
OECD *Economic Outlook*, various issues, Paris: OECD.
OECD *Balances of Payments*, various years, Paris: OECD.
Oppenheimer, Peter M. (1987) 'The endogeneity of international liquidity', in Robert Z. Aliber (ed.), *The Reconstruction of International Monetary Arrangements*, London: Macmillan, pp.305–23.
Osugi, K. (1990) 'Japan's experience of financial deregulation since 1984 in an international perspective', *BIS Economic Papers*, 26 (January).
Oye, Kenneth A., Lieber, Robert J. and Rothchild, Donald (ed.) (1979) *Eagle Entangled: US Foreign Policy in a Complex World*, New York: Longman.

Ozaki, Robert and Walter Arnold (1985) *Japan's Foreign Relations*, Boulder: Westview Press.
Parboni, Riccardo (1981) *The Dollar and its Rivals*, trans. from the Italian, London: Verso.
Patinkin, Don (1965) [1954] *Money, Interest and Prices*, 2nd edn, New York: Harper and Row.
Pinder, John (1983) 'Interdependence: Problem or solution', in L. Freedman (ed.), *The Troubled Alliance*, London: Heinemann, pp.67–87.
Pippenger, John (1984) 'Bank of England Operations, 1893–1913', in M.D. Bordo and A.J. Schwartz (eds.) (1984), pp.203–27.
Polanyi, Karl (1957) [1944] *The Great Transformation: The Political and Economic Origins of our Time*, Boston: Beacon Press.
Pollin, Robert (1985) 'Stability and instability in the debt–income relationship', *American Economic Review*, Papers and Proceedings, 75(2), pp.344–50.
Postan, M.M. (1964a) 'The rise of a money economy', in E.M. Carus-Wilson (ed.) (1962) *op. cit.*, pp.1–12.
Postan, M.M. (1964b) 'Credit in medieval trade', in E.M. Carus-Wilson (ed.) (1962) *op. cit.*, pp.61–87.
Pressnell, L.S. (1982) 'The sterling system and financial crises before 1914', in C.P. Kindleberger and J.-P. Laffargue (eds.) (1982) *op. cit.*, pp.148–63.
Pressnell, L.S. (1968) 'Gold reserves, banking reserves, and the Baring crisis of 1890', in C.R. Whittlesey and J.S.G. Wilson (eds.) (1968), *Essays in Money and Banking: In Honour of R.S. Sayers*, Oxford: Oxford University Press, pp.167–228.
Price Waterhouse (1991) *Bank Capital Adequacy*, Price Waterhouse, August.
Putnam, Robert (1984) 'The western economic summits: A political interpretation', in C. Merlini (ed.) (1984) *op. cit.*, pp.43–88.
Putnam, Robert D. and Nicholas Bayne (1984) *Hanging Together*, Cambridge, Mass: Harvard University Press.
Reich, Robert B. (1991) *The Work of Nations*, New York: Simon & Schuster.
Ricardo, David (1951) [1811] 'The high price of bullion', reprinted in *The Works and Correspondence of David Ricardo, Volume III*, ed. P. Sraffa, Cambridge: Cambridge University Press.
Rosecrance, Richard (ed.) (1976) *America as an Ordinary Country*, Ithaca: Cornell University Press.
Rostow, Walt W. (1978) *The World Economy: History and Prospect*, London: Macmillan.
Rostow, Walt W. (1985) 'Is there a need for economic leadership? Japanese or US?', *American Economic Review*, Papers and Proceedings, 75(2), pp.285–91.
Rowland, Benjamin M. (1976) *Balance of Power or Hegemony: The Interwar Monetary System*, New York: New York University Press.
Royal Institute of International Affairs (1931) *The International Gold Problem: Collected Papers, 1929–31*, Oxford: Oxford University Press.
Ruggie, John Gerard (1982) 'International regimes, transactions, and change: Embedded liberalism in the postwar economic order', *International Organization*, 36(2), pp.379–415.
Russett, Bruce (1985) 'The mysterious case of vanishing hegemony; or, is Mark Twain really dead?', *International Organization*, 39(2), pp.207–31.
Sachs, Jeffrey D. (1984) 'Theoretical issues in international borrowing', *Princeton Studies in International Finance*, 54.

Salant, Walter S. (1972) 'Financial intermediation as an explanation of enduring "deficits" in the balance of payments', in Fritz Machlup et al. (eds.), *International Mobility and Movement of Capital*, New York: NBER/Columbia University Press, pp.607–59.

Samuelson, Paul A. (1972) [1967]. 'Money, interest rates and economic activity', reprinted in R.C. Merton (ed.), *The Collected Scientific Papers of Paul A. Samuelson*, vol.3, Cambridge, Mass: MIT Press, pp.550–70.

Samuelson, Paul A. (1980) 'A corrected version of Hume's equilibrating mechanism for international trade', in John S. Chipman and Charles P. Kindleberger (eds.), *Flexible Exchange Rates and the Balance of Payments*, Amsterdam: North-Holland, pp.141–58.

Sandretto, René (1983) *Le pouvoir et la monnaie: Réflexions sur la crise monétaire internationale contemporaine*, Paris: Economica.

Sargent, Thomas J. and Neil Wallace (1975) '"Rational" expectations, the optimal monetary instrument, and the optimal money supply rule', *Journal of Political Economy*, 83(2), pp.241–54.

Saul, S.B. (1960) *Studies in British Overseas Trade, 1870–1914*, Liverpool: Liverpool University Press.

Scammell, W.M. (1975) *International Monetary Policy: Bretton Woods and After*, London: Macmillan.

Scammell, W.M. (1983) *The International Economy Since 1945*, 2nd edn, London: Macmillan.

Scammell, W.M. (1987) *The Stability of the International Monetary System*, London: Macmillan.

Schuker, Stephen A. (1976) *The End of French Predominance in Europe: The Financial Crisis of 1924 and the Adoption of the Dawes Plan*, Chapel Hill: University of North Carolina Press.

Schwartz, Anna J. (1983) 'The postwar institutional evolution of the international monetary system', in Michael R. Darby, J.R. Lothian, A.E. Gandolfi, A.J. Schwartz and A.C. Stockman, *The International Transmission of Inflation*, Chicago: University of Chicago Press, pp.14–45.

Shackle, G.L.S. (1967) *The Years of High Theory: Invention and Tradition in Economic Thought 1926–39*, Cambridge: Cambridge University Press.

Shackle, G.L.S. (1972) *Epistemics and Economics*, Cambridge: Cambridge University Press.

Shafer, Jeffrey R. (1988) 'What the US current-account deficit of the 1980s has meant for other OECD countries', *OECD Economic Studies*, 10 (Spring), pp.149–84.

Shennan, J.H. (1974) *The Origins of the Modern European State*, London: Hutchinson.

Shonfield, Andrew (1965) *Modern Capitalism*, Oxford: Oxford University Press.

Shonfield, Andrew (1980) 'The politics of the mixed economy in the international system of the 1970s', *International Affairs*, 56(1), pp.1–4.

Shonfield, Andrew (1982) *The Use of Public Power*, Oxford: Oxford University Press.

Silk, Leonard (1987) '"Pax Americana" is flawed, but what could replace it?', *International Herald Tribune*, May 9–10, p.1.

Simpson, Thomas D. (1984) 'Changes in the financial system: Implications for monetary policy', *Brookings Papers on Economic Activity*, 1, pp.249–65.

Skidelsky, Robert J.A. (1976) 'Retreat from leadership: The evolution of

British economic foreign policy, 1870–1939', in B.M. Rowland (ed.) (1976) *op. cit.*, pp.147–92.
Smith, Adam (1910) [1776] *An Inquiry into the Nature and Causes of the Wealth of Nations*, 2 vols, London: Dent.
Snidal, Duncan (1985) 'The limits of hegemonic stability theory', *International Organization*, 39(4), pp.579–614.
Solomon, Robert (1982) *The International Monetary System, 1945–1981*, New York: Harper and Row.
Solow, Robert M. (1982) 'On the lender of last resort', in C.P. Kindleberger and J.-P. Laffargue (eds.) (1982) *op. cit.*, pp.237–47.
Spero, Joan E. (1977) *The Politics of International Economic Relations*, London: Allen and Unwin.
Spero, Joan E. (1981) *The Politics of International Economic Relations*, 2nd edition, London: Allen and Unwin.
Stein, Arthur A. (1984) 'The hegemon's dilemma: Great Britain, the United States and the international economic order', *International Organization*, 38(2), pp.355–86.
Stein, Jerome L. (ed.) (1976) *Monetarism*, Amsterdam: North-Holland.
Stern, Robert M., C.F. Schwartz, R. Triffin, E.M. Bernstein and W. Lederer (1977) 'The presentation of the US balance of payments: A symposium', *Princeton Essays in International Finance*, 123 (August).
Stern, Fritz (1987) [1977]. *Gold and Iron: Bismarck, Bleichröder, and the Building of the German Empire*, Harmondsworth: Penguin.
Stiglitz, Joseph E. and Andrew Weiss (1981) 'Credit rationing in markets with imperfect information', *American Economic Review*, 71(3), pp.393–410.
Stone, Norman (1983) *Europe Transformed, 1878–1919*, Glasgow: Fontana.
Strange, Susan (1970) 'International economics and international relations: A case of mutual neglect', *International Affairs*, 46(2), pp.304–15.
Strange, Susan (1976) 'International monetary relations', in Andrew Shonfield (ed.), *International Economic Relations of the Western World, 1959–71*, Oxford: Oxford University Press, vol.II, pp.18–359.
Strange, Susan (1982) 'Still an extraordinary power: America's role in a global monetary system', in R.E. Lombra and W.E. Witte (eds.) (1982) *op. cit.*, pp.73–93.
Strange, Susan (1986) *Casino Capitalism*, Oxford: Blackwell.
Strange, Susan (1987) 'The persistent myth of lost hegemony', *International Organization*, 41(1), pp.551–74.
Strange, Susan (1988) *States and Markets: An Introduction to International Political Economy*, London: Pinter.
Strange, Susan and David P. Calleo (1984) 'Money and world politics', in Susan Strange (ed.), *Paths to International Political Economy*, London: Allen and Unwin, pp.91–125.
Swoboda, Alexander K. (1980) 'Credit creation in the Euromarket: Alternative theories and implications for control', *Group of Thirty Occasional Paper*, 2.
Tawney, R.H. (1977) [1926] *Religion and the Rise of Capitalism*, Harmondsworth: Penguin.
Temin, Peter (1976) *Did Monetary Forces Cause the Great Depression?*, New York: Norton.
Thomas, Jean-Gabriel (1981) *Politique monétaire et auto-destruction du capital*, Paris: Economica.

Thornton, Henry (1962) [1802] *An Enquiry into the Nature and Effects of the Paper Credit of Great Britain*, ed. F. von Hayek, London: Cass.
Thurow, Lester C. (1980) *The Zero-Sum Society*, New York: Basic Books.
Thygesen, Niels (1985) 'Is the multiple currency standard a destabilizing factor?', in L. Tsoukalis (ed.) (1985) *op. cit.*, pp.137–69.
Tobin, James (1980) *Asset Accumulation and Economic Activity*, Oxford: Blackwell.
Tobin, James (1982a) 'Money and finance in the macroeconomic process', *Journal of Money, Credit and Banking*, 14(2), pp.171–204.
Tobin, James (1982b) 'The state of exchange rate theory: Some sceptical observations', in R.N. Cooper *et al.* (eds.) (1982) *op. cit.*, pp.115–28.
Treverton, Gregory (1978) *The Dollar Drain and American Forces in Germany*, Ohio: Ohio University Press.
Triffin, Robert (1961) *Gold and the Dollar Crisis*, 2nd edn, New Haven: Yale University Press.
Triffin, Robert (1968) *Our International Monetary System: Yesterday, Today, and Tomorrow*, New York: Random House.
Tsoukalis, Loukas (ed.) (1985) *The Political Economy of International Money*, London: RIIA/Sage.
Tsoukalis, Loukas (1987) 'The political economy of the European monetary system', Paper prepared for the Centro Europa Ricerche, Rome, September.
Tsoukalis, Loukas (1991) *The New European Economy: The Politics and Economics of Integration*, Oxford: Oxford University Press.
United Nations (1949) *International Capital Movements During the Interwar Period*, New York: UN.
United Nations (1954) *Statistical Yearbook*, New York: UN.
United Nations (1987) *World Economic Survey*, New York: UN.
United Nations (1989) *World Economic Survey*, New York: UN.
United Nations, *Economic Survey of Europe*, New York: UN, various years.
US Bureau of the Census (1956) *Statistical Abstract of the United States, 1956*, Washington, DC: US Government Printing Office.
US Bureau of the Census (1975) *Historical Statistics of the United States*, Washington, DC: US Government Printing Office.
US Commission on International Trade and Investment Policy (Williams Commission Report) (1971) *United States International Economic Policy in an Interdependent World*, Washington, DC: US Government Printing Office.
US Council on International Policy (Peter G. Peterson) (1971) *The United States in the Changing World Economy*, vol. I, Washington, DC: US Government Printing Office.
US Department of Commerce (1964) *Balance of Payments*, Washington, DC: US Government Printing Office.
US Federal Reserve Board, *Bulletin*, Washington, D.C.: Government Printing Office, various issues.
US Federal Reserve Board, *Annual Report*, Washington, DC: Government Printing Office.
US Treasury (1985) *Report on the Operation of the International Monetary and Financial System*, in *IMF Survey*, April 5.
Van Dormael, Armand (1978) *Bretton Woods: Birth of a Monetary System*, London: Macmillan.
van Buren Cleveland, Harold (1976) 'The international monetary system in the interwar period', in B.M. Rowland (ed.) (1976) *op. cit.*, pp.1–59.

Vaubel, Roland (1977) 'Free currency competition', *Weltwirtschaftliches Archiv*, 113, pp.435–59.
Vicarelli, Fausto (1985) 'From equilibrium to probability: A reinterpretation of the method of the *General Theory*', in Fausto Vicarelli (ed.), *Keynes's Relevance Today*, London: Macmillan.
Viner, Jacob (1945) 'Clapham on the Bank of England', *Economica*, 12 (May), pp.61–8.
Volcker, Paul (1978–9) 'The political economy of the dollar', Federal Reserve Bank of New York, *Quarterly Review*, 3(4), pp.1–12.
De Vries, Margaret and Horsefield, J. Keith (1969) *The IMF, 1945–1965*, vol. 2, Washington, DC: IMF.
de Vries, Rimmer (1990) 'Adam Smith: Managing the global wealth of nations', in J.P. Morgan, *World Financial Markets*, New York: J.P. Morgan, 1990(2).
Wallerstein, Immanuel (1982) 'Crisis as transition', in S. Amin *et al.* (1982) *op. cit.*, pp.11–54.
Walras, Léon (1954) [1926] *Elements of Pure Economics*, trans. from the French, London: Allen and Unwin.
Walter, Andrew (1993) 'The political economy of the new regionalism', in Louise Fawcett and Andrew Hurrell (eds), *Regionalism and International Order*, Oxford: Oxford University Press.
Waltz, Kenneth N. (1959) *Man, the State and War*, New York: Columbia University Press.
Waltz, Kenneth N. (1979) *Theory of International Politics*, Reading, Mass: Addison-Wesley.
Wegner, Manfred (1985) 'External adjustment in a world of floating: Different national experiences in Europe', in L. Tsoukalis (eds.) (1985) *op. cit.*, pp.103–35.
Whitman, Marina von N. (1977) 'Sustaining the international economic system: Issues for US policy', *Princeton Essays in International Finance*, 121 (June).
Whittlesey, C.R. and J.S.G. Wilson (eds.) (1968) *Essays in Money and Banking: In Honour of R.S. Sayers*, Oxford: Oxford University Press.
Wight, Martin (1979) *Power Politics*, (ed. H. Bull and C. Holbraad), Harmondsworth: Penguin.
Williams, David (1968) 'The evolution of the sterling system', in C.R. Whittlesey and J.S.G. Wilson (eds.) (1968) pp.266–97.
Williamson, John (1977) *The Failure of World Monetary Reform, 1971–74*, New York: New York University Press.
Williamson, John (1978) 'Don't surplus states have obligations?', *The World Economy*, 1(4), pp.419–26.
Williamson, John (1982) 'The failure of world monetary reform: A reassessment', in Richard N. Cooper *et al.*, (eds.) (1982) *op. cit.*, pp.297–306.
Williamson, John (1983) 'The exchange rate system', *Policy Analyses in International Economics*, 5 (September) Institute for International Economics, Washington, DC.
Williamson, John and Marcus H. Miller (1987) 'Targets and indicators: A blueprint for the international coordination of economic policy', *Policy Analyses in International Economics*, 22 (September) Institute for International Economics, Washington, DC.
Wojnilower, Albert M. (1980) 'The central role of credit crunches in recent financial history', *Brookings Papers on Economic Activity*, 2, pp.277–326.
Wojnilower, Albert M. (1985) 'Private credit demand, supply, and crunches

– How different are the 1980s?', *American Economic Review*, Papers and Proceedings, 75(2), pp.351–6.

Woodruff, William (1966) *The Impact of Western Man: A Study of Europe's Role in the World Economy, 1750–1960*, London: Macmillan.

Woodruff, William (1975) *America's Impact on the World*, London: Macmillan.

Woolcock, Stephen (1991) *Market Access Issues in EC–US Relations: Trading Partners or Trading Blows?* London: Pinter/RIIA.

Yeager, Leland B. (1975) *International Monetary Relations*, 2nd edn, New York: Harper and Row.

Yeager, Leland B. (1984) 'The image of the gold standard', in M.D. Bordo and A.J. Schwartz (eds.) (1984) pp.651–69.

Zacchia, Carlo (1977) 'International trade and capital movements 1920–70', in C.M. Cipolla (ed.) (1977) *op. cit.*, pp.509–602.

Zarnowitz, Victor (1985) 'Recent work on business cycles in historical perspective: A review of theories and evidence', *Journal of Economic Literature*, 23(2), pp.523–80.

Index

American banks, 41, 124, 182, 187, 206, 209, 228, 230, 236, 243, 256
asset market approach, 59–61
Australia, 95, 96, 105, 127
Austria, 94, 106, 132, 139, 179

balance of power, xiv, 16, 18, 87, 110, 111, 196, 198, 230–40
bank lending, 40, 42, 43, 46, 181, 201, 208, 210, 215, 217
Bank of England, 3, 31, 32, 34–6, 39, 40, 43, 46, 53, 66, 67, 73, 98–100, 102, 103–7, 110, 111, 120, 121, 126, 133–6, 138, 139, 228–9
Bank of France, 53, 89, 106, 107, 110, 130–2, 136, 139, 227
Bank of Japan, 214, 237, 248
Bank Rate, 96, 98, 102, 103, 110, 133, 136
banking, 3, 30, 32, 35–9, 44, 45, 52, 56, 65–7, 73, 74, 79, 86, 88, 98, 99, 102, 105, 109, 112, 137, 139, 144, 189, 197, 198, 199, 201, 203, 204, 206, 218, 227–30
barter, 28, 29
Basle capital adequacy accord, 209, 228–30, 243
Basle Committee, 227, 229–30
Basle Concordat, 209, 228

benign neglect, 70, 73, 178, 182, 183
Bergsten, C. Fred, 17, 23, 219
Berlin, 89, 92, 93, 102, 103, 107, 109, 110, 133
BIS (Bank for International Settlements), 46, 165, 168, 178, 197, 198, 206, 214, 221, 227
Bloomfield, Arthur I., 56, 67, 89, 95, 96, 98–100, 103–6, 108, 110
Blumenthal, Michael, 221
bond markets, 198–9, 203
Braudel, Fernand, 28–30
Bretton Woods system, xviii, 4, 15, 66, 151, 169, 177, 180, 183, 187, 188, 238, 240–1, 243, 250–2
Britain, xvi, 2–4, 16–18, 21, 28, 34, 85–93, 95–112, 116–19, 121–25, 128, 129, 130–4, 137, 139, 140, 142–5, 151, 152, 154, 156–63, 166, 177, 184, 186, 187, 205, 213, 214, 223, 226–7, 228–9, 249–56
British
  decline, 131
  empire, 88, 92
  hegemony, xvii, 85, 86, 111, 145, 249–52
Bundesbank, 75, 164, 171, 173, 178, 179, 214, 226–7, 234

Cairncross, Alec, xv, 95, 107, 108, 162

279

280 Index

Calleo, David, 18, 21, 22, 151, 170, 181
Canada, 95, 96, 127, 138, 144, 172, 178, 254
capital
  controls, 62, 186, 187, 189, 206, 208–9, 213, 232
  exports, 34, 97, 108, 119, 181, 206 208, 235–6, 252
  markets 19, 31, 32, 44, 52, 68, 77, 159, 176, 181, 189, 190, 196–201, 203, 208–16, 229, 236–7
capitalism, 11, 52, 125
Carter, Jimmy, 219, 221, 225
Cassel, Gustav, 128
central banks, 3, 34, 36–9, 42–7, 51, 52, 54, 56, 57, 63–7, 72, 73, 75, 93, 99, 105, 107, 111, 125, 127, 133, 134, 136, 139, 146, 151, 174, 177, 181, 183, 186, 198, 201, 209, 227, 241, 252
  cooperation, 125, 134, 146
Churchill, Winston, 123, 132, 151, 157
civilian powers, 14
Clarke, Stephen, 121, 125, 126, 128, 130, 132, 134–7, 139–41, 143, 146
classical economics, 134
Cohen, Benjamin, 47, 64, 65, 68, 72, 86, 96, 97, 100, 102, 106, 117, 133, 238
Cold War, 9, 11, 163, 238–9, 257
collective management, 177, 189, 219, 252, 257
commodity money, 28
competitive currencies, 52
competitive deregulation, 206, 209, 240
Concert of Europe, 109, 111, 251
Connally, John, 179
convertibility, 35, 43, 44, 54, 57, 68–72, 74, 100, 107, 126, 131, 139, 145, 155, 158, 159, 161, 162, 164, 167, 171, 173, 175, 179, 180, 186, 190, 206
Cooper, Richard, 4, 12, 13, 15, 63, 74, 219
crash (financial), 45, 52, 135, 137, 138, 215, 241

crawling peg system, 177
credit, 29, 32, 36, 37, 39–43, 45, 46, 54, 56, 64, 65, 67, 68, 76, 77, 99, 100, 101, 128, 130, 136, 140, 142, 144, 151, 184
crisis of 1931, 127, 140, 142
crisis of 1947, 159
currency convertibility, 43, 54, 126, 161, 164

Dawes loan, 124, 143
de Gaulle, General, 54, 172, 173
Debré Michel, 173
debt crisis, 200, 217–18
debt-deflation, 46
deflation, 46, 53, 55, 58, 76, 102–4, 128, 131, 133, 139–41, 143, 145, 146, 159, 217
developing countries, xiv, 46, 108, 201, 217–18
discount rates, iv, 56, 89, 93, 96, 102–4, 127, 135
disintermediation, 42
displacement of power, 15
DM (Deutschmark), 178–80, 187, 198, 199, 205–6, 208, 211, 214, 225–7, 234, 256
dollar, 19, 34, 61, 67, 69, 73, 117–19, 121, 128, 129, 131, 132, 139, 146, 156, 157, 159–65, 167–75, 177–83, 186–90, 197–9, 199–201, 205–9, 211, 214–15, 221–6, 233–5, 256
  deficits, 168, 174
  devaluation, 170, 187
  shortage, 121, 160, 170
  standard, 69, 73, 171, 173, 175, 179–83, 186, 189, 227
domestic monetary management, 136

ECA (Economic Cooperation Authority), 160–2
economic
  growth, 64, 188, 224, 227
  instability, 39, 98, 104, 112, 126, 127, 144
  uncertainty, 38, 57
Ecu, 52, 187, 198, 199, 226, 234
Edge Act, 124
EFTA (European Free Trade Association), 239

Index

Eichengreen, Barry, 54, 125, 133, 136
EMS (European Monetary System), xvi, xviii, 75, 211, 214, 225–7, 234, 253, 255–7
EMU (European Monetary Union), xvi, 226, 234–5
EPU (European Payments Union), 162, 163
equilibrium, 37, 39, 40, 55, 56, 58–61, 69, 71, 99, 128, 155, 157, 180, 182, 186
Equity markets, 197–8, 202, 203
Eurodollar market, 181, 196, 206, 214
'EuroFed', 234
Euromarkets, 12, 179, 190, 197, 199
Europe, xiv, 3, 9, 14, 21, 28–30, 36, 51, 87, 88, 91, 93, 95, 97, 101–4, 109, 111, 112, 117–19, 121, 123–6, 130–3, 135, 138–44, 151, 158, 159, 160, 162–6, 169–71, 176, 178, 179, 183–5, 188, 196, 213, 221, 226–8, 234–5, 239, 253–7
  Single Market Programme, 209, 228
European economy, 135, 143, 214
European integration, 160, 162, 225–7, 234–5, 253–7
exchange rate management, 172, 219–27, 241
exchange rate targeting, 77
exorbitant privilege, 172
expectations, 38, 39, 43, 44, 52, 53, 59–62, 102, 144, 180, 186, 190, 199, 210, 217
external deficits, 69, 122, 204, 205, 211

Federal Reserve System, 41–3, 45, 93, 120, 124, 135, 137, 139, 144, 156, 160, 173, 178, 205, 230, 235
Federal Reserve Bank of New York, 156, 230
financial
  centres, 33, 34, 89, 92, 101–3, 107, 109, 133, 135, 214, 230, 235, 242
  crisis, 46, 66, 110, 130, 139, 206, 253
  deregulation, 46, 196, 206–10, 225, 243
  fragility, 211, 215–16, 217–18, 227–30
  hierarchy, 3, 34, 36–8, 46, 47, 52, 72, 109, 133
  innovation, 40, 42, 198, 202–3, 206, 229, 236, 253
  instability, 37, 51, 86, 144, 190, 218
  integration, 62–4, 77, 78, 99, 121, 189, 190, 211–14, 214–18, 225–30, 240–4
  intermediation, 20, 69, 70, 183, 187
  revolution, 31, 195–244
Finland, xvii
fiscal policy, 38, 59, 134, 140, 168, 213, 222, 225, 227
fixed exchange rates, 43, 54, 62, 100, 189, 226–7
flexible exchange rates, xiii, 50, 58, 59, 62, 180, 181, 190, 209–10, 220
foreign investment, 89, 90, 107–9, 124, 137, 143, 170, 197, 198, 217
France, 30, 31, 53, 54, 87, 89, 90, 94–7, 100, 102, 106–8, 110, 119, 121, 122, 123, 124, 129–32, 134, 136–9, 141, 142, 144, 145, 151, 156, 159, 161–3, 166, 169, 173, 177, 178, 180, 189, 205, 213, 226–7, 238, 254, 256
Frankfurt, 33, 34
Franklin National Bank, 44
free trade, 9, 85, 90, 91, 124, 131
French policy, 134, 172, 173, 181
Frieden, Jeffry, xvii
Friedman, Milton, 37, 39, 61, 97, 127, 130, 135, 137, 138, 143
functions of hegemony, 3, 62
fundamental disequilibrium, 71, 129, 140, 154
futures markets, 41, 61, 210

GATT (General Agreement on Tariffs and Trade), 155
Germany, xvi, xvii, 106, 108, 122, 151, 204, 205, 206, 213–16, 219–27, 234–5, 239, 240, 253–7
Gilbert, Milton, 70, 71, 123, 132, 169, 171, 175

282 Index

Gilpin, Robert, xiv, 1, 16–22, 85, 86, 90, 106, 116, 117, 133, 150, 180, 195, 224
Glass-Steagall Act, 209
gold exchange standard, i, 67
gold standard, 53, 85, 90, 93, 99, 123
Goodhart, Charles, 39–41, 43, 45, 67, 77, 98, 99
Gowa, Joanne, 233–4
Gramscian theories, 255

Hawtrey, Ralph, 35, 36, 56, 120, 129, 130, 133, 134, 137
hegemony, vi, 1, 2, 18–22, 27, 47, 51, 58, 63, 66, 78, 85, 97, 98, 127, 134, 140, 145, 160, 162, 249–57
Hicks, John, 28, 30, 36

international lender of last resort, 138

Jamaica Agreement, 181
Japan, xvi, 4, 9, 14, 95, 127, 151, 171, 172, 178, 179, 183, 196, 199, 202, 204, 205, 206, 208, 209–13, 215–16, 219–26, 229, 231, 236–9, 253–7
Japanese banks, 206, 208, 215, 235–7
Japanese capital exports, 204, 208
Johnson administration, 173

Kellogg-Briand Pact, 125
Kennan, George, 160
Kennedy, Paul, 22, 23, 29, 31, 87, 109, 150, 151
Kennedy administration, 170, 177, 181
Keohane, Robert, xiv, 14, 15, 17–20, 22, 23, 66, 116, 150, 160, 180, 188, 195
key currencies, 66, 67, 76–8, 103, 129, 156, 157, 196
key currency, 66–77, 86, 103, 129, 157, 158, 169, 186, 187, 189, 197, 256
Keynes, John Maynard, 37–9, 57, 74, 123, 132, 141, 142, 152, 154, 156, 157, 174
Kindleberger, Charles, xiv, 2, 3, 12, 17, 19, 20, 27, 31–3, 35, 36, 52–4, 61, 64, 66, 69, 70–3, 86, 89, 91, 92, 99, 101, 102, 105, 106, 108, 116, 117, 128, 132, 134, 135, 138–42, 144, 158, 159, 162, 184, 196, 219

Lamfalussy, Alexandre, 40, 41, 214, 229
Latin America, 108, 158, 205–6, 210, 217, 233, 244, 254
law of uneven growth, 22
leadership, 3, 4, 16–21, 112, 116, 117, 123, 124, 129, 133, 144, 146, 173, 186, 188, 195, 256
Leffler, Melvyn, 121, 124, 125, 137, 143
lender of last resort, 3, 35–7, 45, 46, 52, 53, 64–6, 73, 86, 98, 103–6, 127, 135, 138–40, 145, 184, 209, 217, 252
liability management, 41, 43, 202
liberalism, 10, 11, 122, 155
Lindert, Peter, 88, 89, 95, 102, 103, 120
liquidity, 2, 32, 33, 38, 44, 45, 53, 64, 65, 67–9, 72, 76, 86, 98, 102, 104, 105, 135, 136, 140, 154, 155, 164, 168, 170, 171, 174, 180, 196, 198, 202, 203, 223, 243
locomotive dispute, 219
London, 16, 31–5, 86, 88, 89, 92, 96, 99–103, 105, 107, 109–11, 118, 119, 132, 133, 136, 164, 168, 181, 196, 197, 198, 206, 211, 228, 252
long-term capital, 72, 108, 184, 188, 252
long-distance trade, 29, 30
Louvre Accord (1987), 222
Ludlow, Peter, 234

Macmillan Committee, 88, 130, 132, 134
macroeconomic policy, 20, 58, 122, 218, 219–27, 234–5, 254–5
Maddison, Angus, 19, 22, 90, 93–6, 127, 137, 138, 144, 151, 153, 178
management, 2–4, 13, 19, 27, 33, 34,

Index 283

36, 39, 41, 43, 46, 47, 50, 51, 53, 64, 73, 78, 86, 89, 96, 97, 99, 102–5, 107, 111, 116, 119, 133, 136, 138, 144, 150, 172, 177, 189, 190, 196, 197, 219–30, 241–4, 249–57
Marshall Aid, 160, 161, 163
McKenna, Reginald, 132
McKinnon, Ronald, 61, 64, 66, 77, 182, 225–6
Medici, 30
mercantilism, 10, 68, 70, 155, 169, 196, 256
mercantilist policies, 131
Milward, Alan, 142, 145, 158, 161, 162
Moggridge, Dennis, 95, 100, 102, 103, 117, 118, 123, 132, 136, 139, 140, 142
monetarism, xiv, 64, 77
Monetary Approach, 55–7, 99
monetary instability, 112, 179, 184
monetary policy, xiv, 38, 43, 46, 59, 60, 64, 65, 75, 86, 97, 98, 107, 122, 130, 131, 132, 134–6, 143, 168, 170, 174, 178, 189, 190, 213, 221–2, 227, 234–5, 237, 252–4
monetary stability, xiv, 2, 24, 27, 35–7, 39, 46, 50, 63, 67, 77, 79, 111, 116, 123, 125, 133, 188, 256–7
monetary targeting, 40–2, 64
money, xiv, 3, 27–30, 32, 33, 35–40, 42–4, 47, 51–7, 64, 65, 67, 71–3, 77, 79, 86, 88, 89, 97, 99, 100, 102, 105–7, 110, 136, 139, 151, 156, 176, 196
Moreau, Emile, 130, 131
Morgan, J. P., xiii, 30
Morgenstern, Oskar, 89, 93, 99, 119, 127
Morgenthou, Henry, 156
multi-currency system, xiv, 67, 74, 75, 206, 208–9, 230, 231, 233, 257
multinational companies (MNCs), 236, 239–40, 241–2, 254–5
Myrdal, Gunnar, 122, 123, 146

NAC (National Advisory Council), 160, 161
NAFTA (North American Free Trade Area), 239
national welfare state, 12, 165, 169, 251–5
naval power, 87, 90
neo-realist synthesis, 21
New York, 16, 33, 34, 89, 93, 101, 109, 110, 118, 119, 121, 124, 130, 133, 135, 137, 139, 156, 173, 178, 187, 197, 201, 209, 211, 242
  stock market, 130, 135
Nixon, Richard, 173, 175, 176, 178, 179, 183, 186, 231
Norman, Governor of the Bank of England, 134, 135
Nurkse, Ragnar, 125, 129, 130
Nye, Joseph, 14, 15, 17, 19, 219

offshore centres, 164, 230
offshore markets, 187, 206
OPEC, 187, 203
open market operations, 43, 102, 136, 237
overvaluation of the dollar, 171, 211, 222

panic (financial), 2, 35, 52, 101
Paris, 33, 34, 89, 92, 101–3, 107, 109, 111, 118, 133, 139, 242
Pax Americana, 16, 17
Pax Britannica, 16, 17, 85
periphery, 90, 96, 104, 108, 109, 111, 112, 127, 142–4
Plaza Agreement (1985), 222
pluralist theories of power, 15, 250
policy consistency, 3, 85, 107, 195, 196
policy coordination, 13, 20, 62, 63, 77, 78, 133, 134, 138, 218–30, 234–5, 239–40, 241, 244, 254
political scientists, xiv, 2, 27, 50, 64, 78
post-hegemonic era, 20, 206
postwar boom, 145, 159, 163, 203, 252
power, xiv, 1, 4, 11, 13–23, 30–2, 34, 36, 37, 44, 47, 52, 58, 59, 61, 66, 68, 73, 86, 87, 90–2, 97, 99, 102, 107, 109–12, 116, 117, 123, 127, 130, 138, 143, 144, 146, 151, 152, 157, 160, 170, 171, 173, 174, 177, 180, 189, 190,

power (*continued*)
  195, 196, 199, 210, 219–20, 224–5, 230–44, 249–57
PPP (Purchasing Power Parity), 58–60, 77, 153
primary reserve assets, 175, 233
primitive money, 28
private banking, 30, 144
productivity, xiv, 17, 71, 151, 160, 169, 178, 189, 203, 253
protectionism, 91, 151, 163, 195, 196, 211
public goods, 20–2, 53, 66, 85, 86, 151, 196

Rambouillet Summit, 181
Reagan, Ronald, 208, 219, 222, 231, 238–9
real balance effect, 37
real interest rates, 202, 203, 205, 210, 217, 218, 222, 244
reconstruction, 123, 125, 126, 142, 143, 145, 152, 157, 159, 161, 164
recycling, 32, 33, 71, 187, 203–4, 217, 235, 242
regimes, 1–3, 10, 19, 20, 22, 23, 27, 63, 78, 116, 146, 195, 196, 237
regulation, 3, 46, 47, 72–4, 78, 196, 206–10, 218, 227–30, 237–9, 241–3, 252–4
reparation, 119, 124–6, 132, 141–3
reserves, iv, 35, 36, 40, 43, 44, 46, 54–8, 64–71, 73, 74, 76, 88, 89, 97, 98, 100, 102, 104, 106, 107, 110, 121, 124, 127–30, 132, 138, 139, 151, 161, 163–70, 172–5, 180, 187, 199, 200–1, 206, 208, 214, 223, 233–5
responsibilities for adjustment, 155, 219–27, 238–9, 244, 254–5
restoration of the international gold standard, 123, 124, 154
Rothschilds, 30
Ruggie, John, 1, 98, 145, 155
rule enforcement, 99, 249–50
rules of the game, 56–8, 86, 97–9, 130, 131, 145, 249–51

savings, 19, 31, 33, 44, 101, 108, 109, 202–5, 208, 210–11, 236, 240–1

Scandinavia, 254–5
scarce currency clause, 154
Schmidt, Helmut, 225
SDR (Special Drawing Right), 153, 174–6, 181, 233
SDR standard, 181
securitisation, 198, 203, 218, 229–30, 236
security factors, 225, 237–40, 250–1, 257
seignorage, 22, 68, 74, 172
Shaw, E.S., 104
short-term capital, 105, 112, 188
Shultz, George, 181, 186
Smithsonian Agreement (1971), 175, 179–81
Solomon, Robert, 20, 168, 169, 173, 174, 176–80, 184, 186
solvency, 35, 43, 53, 252
sovereignty, 12, 63, 72, 154, 155, 158, 174
specie-flow, 54, 55, 57
speculation, 61, 71, 129, 130, 135, 184, 242, 255–6
speculative bubble, 61, 205, 215
state theory of money, 29
sterilisation, 56, 57, 130, 131, 145
sterling, 19, 33, 34, 36, 40, 67, 86, 88, 92, 99, 100, 102, 105–7, 111, 121, 123, 124, 126–34, 137, 139–41, 146, 157, 158, 161–4, 184, 227, 251
  bloc, 162
  standard, 86
Strange, Susan, xiv, 18, 66, 164, 169, 184, 209
Structural Impediments Initiative (SII), 225
structural power, 237–9, 250, 255
substitution account, 233–4
supervision, 3, 47, 72, 78, 209, 227–30, 243, 249
swaps, 61, 197, 199, 229
Sweden, xvii, 254
Switzerland, 136, 179, 213

Thatcher Government, 206
theory of hegemonic stability, 1, 2, 7, 22, 23, 27, 76, 111, 133, 145, 150, 196, 219–25, 233–40, 249–57

Index **285**

thrifts, 44, 46, 215, 255
Tokyo, 197, 201, 211, 242
trade, xiv, 2, 9–15, 17, 19, 28–30, 33, 34, 54, 55, 57–60, 66, 69, 70, 75, 78, 85, 87, 88, 90, 91, 93, 95–7, 101, 103, 105, 108, 109, 112, 117, 118–20, 124–6, 131, 132, 137, 144, 151, 154, 155, 158, 159, 161, 162–6, 169, 175, 178, 188, 196, 197, 201, 211, 213, 216, 225, 226, 231–4, 236, 238, 241, 250, 252
tradable vs non-tradable sectors, 213
transparency, 33, 218
Triffin, Robert, 36, 56, 63, 68, 69, 71, 88, 95, 96, 98, 103, 126, 128, 129, 167, 168, 171, 172, 174, 187
Triffin Dilemma, 69, 71, 167
Tripartite Agreement, 156
Two Tier Arrangement, 171

US, xiv, 1–4, 14, 17–19, 23, 28, 39–42, 44–6, 54, 67, 86, 87, 90, 91, 93, 94–6, 100, 106, 117–32, 134–8, 141–5, 150–84, 186–90, 195–7, 200–44, 250–7
  business cycle, 137, 216–17
  Council of Economic Advisors, 221
  decline, 17, 23, 150, 151, 210, 219, 230–4, 239, 241
  hegemony, 23, 151, 219, 224, 230–44, 250–7
  power, 23, 219–44, 250–7

trade policy, 151

Vietnam, 14, 17, 173, 178
Viner, Jacob, 104, 107
volatile economies, 143, 144
Volcker, Paul, 42, 175, 224
von Hayek, Friedrich, 37, 39, 51–3

war, xiv, 3, 4, 9–11, 13, 16, 22, 23, 29, 30, 38, 39, 53, 63, 85, 87, 88, 93, 96, 101, 110–12, 116–26, 131–3, 136, 142, 143, 145, 146, 150–2, 154, 155, 157, 159, 160, 162, 163, 165, 169, 173, 174, 177, 178, 184, 187, 188, 205, 240, 251, 257
welfare state, 12, 123, 155, 165, 169, 251–5
White, Harry, 96, 152, 154, 156
Williamson, John, 60–2, 172, 175, 176, 225–6
world central bank, xiii, xiv, 63–5, 72, 75, 151, 174, 177, 181, 252
World War I, xiv, 3, 10, 53, 63, 85, 87, 88, 93, 96, 110, 117, 120, 121, 131, 142, 157, 160, 251–2
World War II, xiv, 4, 39, 95, 150, 151, 184

Yen, 75, 178, 180, 187, 201, 205, 206, 208, 211, 216, 235–7, 247, 257

Zaitech, 202
Zurich, 34, 103, 164